MDX with SSAS 2012 Cookbook

69 practical recipes to analyze multidimensional data stored in SSAS 2012 cubes, using high-performance MDX calculations and flexible MDX queries

Sherry Li

Tomislav Piasevoli

[PACKT] enterprise

PUBLISHING   professional expertise distilled

BIRMINGHAM - MUMBAI

MDX with SSAS 2012 Cookbook

First published: August 2011

Second edition: August 2013

Production Reference: 1200813

Published by Packt Publishing Ltd.
Livery Place
35 Livery Street
Birmingham B3 2PB, UK.

ISBN 978-1-84968-960-1

www.packtpub.com

Cover Image by Žarko Piljak (zpiljak@gmail.com)

Credits

Authors

Sherry Li

Tomislav Piasevoli

Reviewers

Prakash Chatla

Jeremy Kashel

Acquisition Editor

Akram Hussain

Lead Technical Editor

Arun Nadar

Technical Editors

Shashank Desai

Iram Malik

Project Coordinator

Anugya Khurana

Proofreaders

Judith Bill

Lesley Harrison

Indexer

Monica Ajmera Mehta

Production Coordinator

Nilesh R. Mohite

Cover Work

Nilesh R. Mohite

About the Authors

Sherry Li has worked with Microsoft SQL Server Business Intelligence stacks for many years. She lives in Phoenix, Arizona where she works for a major financial organization with responsibilities in implementing data warehousing and BI solutions. She specializes in ETL, dimensional modeling, cube design, and reporting in MDX and T-SQL. Sherry Li maintains her blog at bisherryli.com.

I owe tremendous thanks to Packt Publishing for giving me this opportunity to write this book. Readers who want to become proficient in MDX and have been asking for more.

I would like to thank Tomislav Piasevoli, for starting this book in SQL Server Analysis Servies 2008, and for his deep knowledge in MDX and cube design. I have learned so much from him.

In addition, I would like to thank Prakash Chatla and Jeremy Kashel, for their insight, helpful questioning ("I don't think the point you're trying to make comes across."), enthusiastic responses ("I think every BI consultant should read this book!").

I would also like to thank my friends, my past co-workers, for their earnest encouragement and my current co-workers for putting up with my late morning starts at the office.

Also I thank my father, for keeping me company late at night on Skype from the other side of the globe.

My daughter Shasha, for showing me funny videos on YouTube at night.

My husband, Jim, for loving me unconditionally.

My dog Atari, for always sitting by my feet, while I write late at night.

Tomislav Piasevoli (tomislav@piasevoli.com) is a Business Intelligence Specialist with years of experience in Microsoft SQL Server Analysis Services (SSAS). He lives in Croatia and works for SoftPro Tetral d.o.o., a company specializing in development of SSAS frontends and implementation of BI solutions.

His main interests are dimensional modeling, cube design, and MDX about which he blogs at http://tomislav.piasevoli.com. Tomislav also writes articles and speaks at regional conferences and user groups. For his contribution to the community, Microsoft awarded him with the Microsoft SQL Server MVP title.

I wish to thank everyone who contributed to this book, in one way or another. First and foremost, a big thank you goes to my wife Kristina and our three children—one of them was born while I was beginning to write this book—for having enormous patience throughout this period.

Secondly, I'd like to thank Chris Webb for vouching for me to the publisher and providing valuable information as one of the reviewers of this book. Greg Galloway, Marco Russo, Darren Gosbell, and Deepak Puri were the other precious reviewers of this book who corrected my mistakes and provided additional information relevant to the chapter topics.

Next, I'd like to thank all the people at Packt Publishing who worked on this book, to help make it better by assisting me during the book-writing process: Kerry George, Zainab Bagasrawala, Chris Rodrigues, and Merwine Machado.

There were also people who knowingly and unknowingly helped me with their ideas, articles, and helpful tips. My younger brother Hrvoje Piasevoli and Willfried Färber are representatives of the first group. The other group consists of bloggers and subject-matter experts whose articles I found useful for many recipes of this book. Here they are: Mosha Pasumansky, Teo Lachev, Jeffrey Wang, Jeremy Kashel, Vidas Matelis, Thomas Kejser (and other bloggers at SQLCAT site), Jeff Moden, Michael Coles, Itzik Ben-Gan, Irina Gorbach, Vincent Rainardi and in particular my reviewers again.

Additionally, I acknowledge countless contributors to MSDN SQL Server Analysis Services forum—whom I had the luck to meet—for the solutions they shared with the rest of us there.

Last but not least, a thank you goes to my current and former colleagues at SoftPro Tetral company who played a part by exchanging ideas with me during the time spent together all these years.

About the Reviewers

Prakash Chatla is a Business Intelligence Solution Architect and Software Developer who has over ten years of practical experience in building and implementing data warehousing and business intelligence solutions and products on the Microsoft platform in sectors, such as commercial distribution, financial services, online retailing, system integration services, software development, and the agricultural sector.

He used all his experience together with passion for programming in creating Microsoft BI client named PowerPanels available at `http://www.powerpanels.eu`. Currently, he and his team are building startup around PowerPanels.

> My sincere thanks to Tomislav Piasevoli, Anugya Khurana and my PowerPanels team.

Jeremy Kashel is a principal consultant with Adatis, a UK-based Microsoft Gold Partner, specializing in the Microsoft Business Intelligence stack.

Jeremy has over 10 years' experience in delivering SQL Server data warehouse and business intelligence projects for a variety of UK and international clients. When time permits, he blogs at blogs.`adatis.co.uk` and has also spoken at a number of Microsoft events. Jeremy is the lead author of the book *Microsoft SQL Server 2008 R2 Master Data Services, PacktPublishing*.

www.PacktPub.com

Support files, eBooks, discount offers and more

You might want to visit www.PacktPub.com for support files and downloads related to your book.

Did you know that Packt offers eBook versions of every book published, with PDF and ePub files available? You can upgrade to the eBook version at www.PacktPub.com and as a print book customer, you are entitled to a discount on the eBook copy. Get in touch with us at service@packtpub.com for more details.

At www.PacktPub.com, you can also read a collection of free technical articles, sign up for a range of free newsletters and receive exclusive discounts and offers on Packt books and eBooks.

http://PacktLib.PacktPub.com

Do you need instant solutions to your IT questions? PacktLib is Packt's online digital book library. Here, you can access, read and search across Packt's entire library of books.

Why Subscribe?

► Fully searchable across every book published by Packt
► Copy and paste, print and bookmark content
► On demand and accessible via web browser

Free Access for Packt account holders

If you have an account with Packt at www.PacktPub.com, you can use this to access PacktLib today and view nine entirely free books. Simply use your login credentials for immediate access.

Instant Updates on New Packt Books

Get notified! Find out when new books are published by following @PacktEnterprise on Twitter, or the *Packt Enterprise* Facebook page.

Table of Contents

Preface

Microsoft SQL Server Analysis is one of the keystones of Microsoft's Business Intelligence (BI) product strategy. It is the most widely deployed OLAP server around the world. Many organizations, both large and small, have adopted it to provide secure and high-performance access to complex analytics.

MDX (for Multi-Dimensional expressions) is the BI industry standard for multidimensional calculations and queries, and is the most widely accepted software language in multidimensional data warehouse. Proficiency with MDX is essential for any professional who works with multidimensional cubes. MDX is an elegant and powerful language, and also has a steep learning curve.

SQL Server 2012 Analysis Services has introduced a new BISM tabular model and a new formula language, Data Analysis Expressions (DAX). However, for the multi-dimensional model, MDX is still the only query and expression language. For many product developers and report developers, MDX still is and always will be the preferred language for both the tabular model and multi-dimensional model.

Despite its popularity, very few books are dedicated to MDX. MDX-related books often limit their content to explaining the concepts of multidimensional cubes, the MDX language concept and its functions, and other specifics related to working with Analysis Services.

This book presents MDX solutions for business requirements that can be found in the real world of business. You will find best practices, explanations on advanced subjects in full detail, and deep knowledge in every topic. Organized around practical MDX solutions, this book provides a full, in-depth treatment of each topic, sequenced in a logical progression from elementary to advanced techniques.

This book is written in a cookbook format. You can browse through the contents and look for solutions to a particular problem. Each recipe is relatively short and grouped by relevancy, so you can find solutions to related issues in one place. Related recipes are sequenced in a logical progression; you will be able to build up your understanding of the topic incrementally.

This book is designed for both beginners and experts in the MDX language. If you are a beginner, this book is a good place to start. Each recipe provides you with best practices and their underlying rationale, detailed sample scripts, and options you need to know to make good choices. If you are an expert, you will be able to use this book as a reference. Whenever you face a particular challenge, you will be able to find a chapter that is dedicated to the topic.

We hope that you will become confident not only in using the sample MDX queries, but also in creating your own solutions. The moment you start creating your own solutions by combining techniques presented in this book, our goal of teaching through examples is accomplished. We want to hear from you about your journey to MDX proficiency. Feel free to contact me.

What this book covers

Chapter 1, Elementary MDX Techniques, uses some simple examples to demonstrate the fundamental MDX concepts, features, and techniques that are the foundations for our further explorations of the MDX language.

Chapter 2, Working with Sets, focuses on the challenges and solutions of performing the logic operations, NOT, OR, and AND, on Sets.

Chapter 3, Working with Time, presents various time-related functions in MDX language that are designed to work with a special type of dimension called the **Time** and its typed attributes.

Chapter 4, Concise Reporting, focuses on techniques that you can employ in your project to make analytical reports more compact and concise, and therefore, more efficient.

Chapter 5, Navigation, shows common tasks and techniques related to navigation and data retrieval relative to the current context.

Chapter 6, Business Analytics, focuses on how to perform some of the typical business analysis, such as forecasting, allocating values, and calculating the number of days from last sale date.

Chapter 7, When MDX is Not Enough, discovers that MDX calculations are not always the place to look for solutions. It illustrates several techniques to optimize the query response times with a relatively simple change in cube structure.

Chapter 8, Advanced MDX Topics, contains more advanced MDX topics, such as dealing with parent-child hierarchies and unbalanced hierarchies, getting random samples from a random hierarchy, and complex sorting and iterations.

Chapter 9, On the Edge, presents topics that will expand your horizons, such as clearing cache for performance tuning, executing MDX queries in T-SQL environment, using SSAS Dynamic Management Views (DMVs), drillthrough, and capturing MDX queries using SQL Server Profiler.

What you need for this book

To run the examples in the book the following software will be required:

Database Installation

A full installation of Microsoft SQL Server 2012, or at least the following components are required:

- SQL Server 2012 engine
- Analysis Services 2012
- Microsoft SQL Server management Studio
- Microsoft SQL Server Data Tools (part of the Microsoft Visual Studio Shell 2010)

We recommend the Developer, Enterprise, or Trial Edition of Microsoft SQL Server. A few examples might not work using the Standard Edition.

To download Microsoft SQL Server 2012 Trial Edition, go to Microsoft SQL Server site `http://tinyurl.com/TrialSQLServer`.

You can find Microsoft SQL Server 2012 Developer Edition on `amazon.com`, using the link `http://tinyurl.com/DeveloperSQLServer2012`.

Sample Adventure Works 2012 Database

Both the relational database file and the multidimensional Adventure Works project files are required:

- `AdventureWorksDW2012_Data.mdf`: relational database
- Adventure Works Multidimensional Models SQL Server 2012—Enterprise Edition: SSAS project files

We recommend the Enterprise Edition of the Adventure Works cube project. To download the installation files, use the following link to go to CodePlex: `http://tinyurl.com/AdventureWorks2012`

For Creating PivotTable

Microsoft Excel 2007 (or newer) with PivotTable is required.

Most of the examples will work with older versions of Microsoft SQL Server (2005 or 2008 or 2008 R2). However, some of them will need adjustments because the Date dimension in the older versions of the Adventure Works database has a different set of years. To solve that problem simply shift the date-specific parts of the queries few years back in time, for example, turn the year 2006 into the year 2002 and Q3 of the year 2007 to Q3 of 2003.

Who this book is for

This book is for multidimensional cube developers or multidimensional database administrators. It is also for report developers who write MDX queries to access multidimensional cube. If you are a power cube user or an experienced business analyst, you will also find this book invaluable.

In other words, this book is for anyone who has been involved with multidimensional cube. This book is for you if you have found yourself in situations where it is difficult to deliver what your users want and you are interested in getting more information out of your multidimensional cubes.

Conventions

In this book, you will find a number of styles of text that distinguish between different kinds of information. Here are some examples of these styles and an explanation of their meaning.

Code words in text, database table names, folder names, filenames, file extensions, pathnames, dummy URLs, user input, and Twitter handles are shown as follows: "Alternatively, we could have used the `Aggregate()` function instead."

A block of code is set as follows:

```
SELECT
    { [Measures].[Reseller Order Quantity],
      [Measures].[Reseller Order Count] } ON 0,
    NON EMPTY
    { [Date].[Month of Year].MEMBERS } ON 1
FROM
    [Adventure Works]
WHERE
    ( [Promotion].[Promotion Type].&[New Product] )
```

When we wish to draw your attention to a particular part of a code block, the relevant lines or items are set in bold:

```
SELECT
    { [Measures].[Reseller Sales Amount] } ON 0,
    { ParallelPeriod( [Geography].[Geography].[Country],
                      2,
                      [Geography].[Geography].[State-Province]
                          .&[CA]&[US] ) } ON 1
FROM
    [Adventure Works]
```

New terms and **important words** are shown in bold. Words that you see on the screen, in menus or dialog boxes for example, appear in the text like this: "We can verify this by browsing the **Geography** user hierarchy in the **Geography** dimension in SQL Server Management Studio".

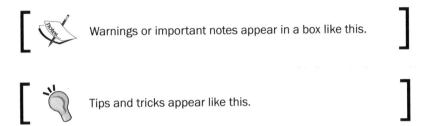

Warnings or important notes appear in a box like this.

Tips and tricks appear like this.

Reader feedback

Feedback from our readers is always welcome. Let us know what you think about this book—what you liked or may have disliked. Reader feedback is important for us to develop titles that you really get the most out of.

To send us general feedback, simply send an e-mail to feedback@packtpub.com, and mention the book title via the subject of your message.

If there is a topic that you have expertise in and you are interested in either writing or contributing to a book, see our author guide on www.packtpub.com/authors.

Customer support

Now that you are the proud owner of a Packt book, we have a number of things to help you to get the most from your purchase.

Downloading the example code

You can download the example code files for all Packt books you have purchased from your account at http://www.packtpub.com. If you purchased this book elsewhere, you can visit http://www.packtpub.com/support and register to have the files e-mailed directly to you.

Errata

Although we have taken every care to ensure the accuracy of our content, mistakes do happen. If you find a mistake in one of our books—maybe a mistake in the text or the code—we would be grateful if you would report this to us. By doing so, you can save other readers from frustration and help us improve subsequent versions of this book. If you find any errata, please report them by visiting `http://www.packtpub.com/submit-errata`, selecting your book, clicking on the **errata submission form** link, and entering the details of your errata. Once your errata are verified, your submission will be accepted and the errata will be uploaded on our website, or added to any list of existing errata, under the Errata section of that title. Any existing errata can be viewed by selecting your title from `http://www.packtpub.com/support`.

Piracy

Piracy of copyright material on the Internet is an ongoing problem across all media. At Packt, we take the protection of our copyright and licenses very seriously. If you come across any illegal copies of our works, in any form, on the Internet, please provide us with the location address or website name immediately so that we can pursue a remedy.

Please contact us at `copyright@packtpub.com` with a link to the suspected pirated material.

We appreciate your help in protecting our authors, and our ability to bring you valuable content.

Questions

You can contact us at `questions@packtpub.com` if you are having a problem with any aspect of the book, and we will do our best to address it.

1
Elementary MDX Techniques

In this chapter, we will cover:

- ▶ Putting data on x and y axes
- ▶ Skipping axes
- ▶ Using a WHERE clause to filter the data returned
- ▶ Optimizing MDX queries using the NONEMPTY() function
- ▶ Using the PROPERTIES() function to retrieve data from attribute relationships
- ▶ Basic sorting and ranking
- ▶ Handling division by zero errors
- ▶ Setting a default member of a hierarchy in the MDX script

Introduction

MDX is an elegant and powerful language, and also has a steep learning curve.

The goal of this chapter is to use some simple examples to demonstrate the fundamental MDX concepts, features and techniques that are the foundations for further explorations of the MDX language.

The chapter begins with several basic techniques: putting multi-dimensional data onto query axes, cube space restriction, empty cell removal, and the important concept of unique names for members, tuples, and sets. From there, we shall turn our attention to a few more advanced features, such as using the MDX functions, creating calculations in the cube space, manipulating strings, writing parameterized queries, and conditionally formatting cell properties. This will form the basis for the rest of the chapters in this book.

SSAS 2012 provides a sample **Analysis Services database**, the **Multidimensional Adventure Works DW**. All the MDX queries and scripts in this book have been updated for Analysis Services 2012, and verified against the 2012 Enterprise Edition of the Adventure Works DW Analysis Services database. Majority of the MDX queries and scripts should also run and have been tested in SSAS 2008 R2.

The **Query Editor** in **SQL Server Management Studio** (**SSMS**) is our choice of writing and testing MDX queries. The SQL Server 2012 comes with a free tool, **SQL Server Data Tools** (**SSDT**) for cube developers. Just as the **Business Intelligence Development Studio** (**BIDS**) was the tool that we used for cube design and MDX scripting in SSAS 2008, SSDT is the tool we will use in this cookbook for cube design and MDX scripting for SSAS 2012.

Putting data on x and y axes

Cube space in SSAS is multi-dimensional. MDX allows you to display results on axes from 0, 1, and 2 up to 128. The first five axes have aliases: **COLUMNS**, **ROWS**, **PAGES**, **SECTIONS**, and **CHAPTERS**. However, the frontend tools such as SQL Server Management Studio (SSMS) or other application that you can use for writing and executing MDX queries only have two axes, x and y axis, or **COLUMNS** and **ROWS**.

As a result, we have two tasks to do when trying to fit the multi-dimensional data onto the limited axes in our frontend tool:

▸ We must always explicitly specify a display axis for all elements in the **SELECT** list. We can use aliases for the first five axes: **COLUMNS**, **ROWS**, **PAGES**, **SECTIONS**, and **CHAPTERS**. We are also allowed to use integers, 0, 1, 2, 3, and so on. But we are not allowed to skip axes. For example, the first axis must be **COLUMNS** (or 0). **ROWS** (or 1) cannot be specified, unless **COLUMNS** (or 0) has been specified first.

▸ Since we only have two display axes to show our data, we must be able to "combine" multiple hierarchies into one query axis. In MDX and other query language terms, we call it "cross join".

It's fair to say that your job of writing the MDX queries is mostly trying to figure out how to project multi-dimensional data onto only two axes, namely, x and y. We will start by putting only one hierarchy on **COLUMNS**, and one on **ROWS**. Then we will use the **CROSSJOIN** function to "combine" more than one hierarchy into **COLUMNS** and **ROWS**.

Getting ready

Making a two by eight table below in a spreadsheet is quite simple. Writing a MDX query to do that can also be very simple. Putting data on the x and y axes is a matter of finding the right expressions for each axis.

	Internet Sales Amount
Australia	$9,061,000.58
Canada	$1,977,844.86
France	$2,644,017.71
Germany	$2,894,312.34
NA	(null)
United Kingdom	$3,391,712.21
United States	$9,389,789.51

All we need are three things from our cube:

▸ The name of the cube

▸ The correct expression for the Internet Sales Amount, so we can put it on the columns

▸ The correct expression of the sales territory, so we can put it on the rows

Once, we have the preceding three things, we are ready to plug them into the following MDX query, and the cube will give us back the two by eight table:

```
SELECT
    [The Sales Expression] ON COLUMNS,
    [The Territory Expression] ON ROWS
FROM
    [The Cube Name]
```

The MDX engine will understand it perfectly, if we replace columns by 0 and rows by 1. Throughout this book, we will use the number 0 for columns that is the x axis, and 1 for rows that is the y axis.

How to do it...

We are going to use the Adventure Works 2012 Multidimensional Analysis Service database enterprise edition in our cookbook. If you open the Adventure Works cube, and hover your cursor over the measure Internet Sales Amount, you will see the fully qualified expression, [Measures].[Internet Sales Amount]. This is a long expression. Drag-and-drop in SQL Server Management Studio works perfectly for us in this situation.

Long expression is a fact of life in MDX. Although the case does not matter, correct spelling is required and fully qualified and unique expressions are recommended for MDX queries to work properly.

Follow these two steps to open the Query Editor in SSMS:

1. Start **SQL Server Management Studio** (**SSMS**) and connect to your **SQL Server Analysis Services** (**SSAS**) 2012 instance (`localhost` or `servername\ instancename`).

2. Click on the target database **Adventure Works DW 2012**, and then right-click on the **New Query** button.

Follow these steps to save the time spent for typing the long expressions:

1. Put your cursor on measure Internet Sales Amount, and drag-and-drop it onto `AXIS(0)`.

2. To get the proper expression for the sales territory, put your cursor over the Sales Territory Country under the **Sales Territory | Sales Territory Country**. Again, this is a long expression. Drag-and-drop it onto `AXIS(1)`.

3. For the name of the cube, the drag-and-drop should work too. Just point your cursor to the cube name, and drag-and-drop it in your FROM clause.

This should be your final query:

```
SELECT
    [Measures].[Internet Sales Amount] ON 0,
    [Sales Territory].[Sales Territory Country].[Sales Territory
Country] ON 1
FROM
    [Adventure Works]
```

Downloading the example code

You can download the example code files for all Packt books you have purchased from your account at http://www.packtpub.com. If you purchased this book elsewhere, you can visit http://www.packtpub.com/support and register to have the files e-mailed directly to you.

When you execute the query, you should get a two by eight table, same as the following screenshot:

	Internet Sales Amount
Australia	$9,061,000.58
Canada	$1,977,844.86
France	$2,644,017.71
Germany	$2,894,312.34
NA	(null)
United Kingdom	$3,391,712.21
United States	$9,389,789.51

How it works...

We have chosen to put Internet Sales Amount on the Axis(0), and all members of Sales Territory Country on the Axis(1). We have fully qualified the measure with the special dimension [Measures], and the sales territory members with dimension [Sales Territory] and hierarchy [Sales Territory Country].

You might have expected an aggregate function such as SUM somewhere in the query. We do not need to have any aggregate function here because the cube understands that when we ask for the sales amount for Canada, we would expect the sales amount to come from all the provinces and territories in Canada.

There's more...

SSAS cubes are perfectly capable of storing data in more than two dimensions. In MDX, we can use the technique called "cross join" to "combine" multiple hierarchies into one query axis.

Putting more hierarchies on x and y axes with cross join

In MDX query, we can specify how multi-dimensions from our SSAS cube layout onto only two x and y axes. Cross joining allows us in both SQL and MDX to get every possible combination of two lists.

We wish to write an MDX query to produce the following table. On the columns axis, we want to see both Internet Sales Amount and Internet Gross Profit. On the rows axis, we want to see all the sales territory countries, and all the products sold in each country.

		Internet Sales Amount	Internet Gross Profit
Australia	Accessories	$138,690.63	$86,820.10
Australia	Bikes	$8,852,050.00	$3,572,267.29
Australia	Clothing	$70,259.95	$26,767.68
Australia	Components	(null)	(null)
Canada	Accessories	$103,377.85	$64,714.37
Canada	Bikes	$1,821,302.39	$741,451.22
Canada	Clothing	$53,164.62	$23,755.91
Canada	Components	(null)	(null)

This query lays two measures on columns (from the same dimension and hierarchy [Measures]), and two different hierarchies [Sales Territory Country] and [Product Categories] on rows.

```
SELECT
    { [Measures].[Internet Sales Amount],
      [Measures].[Internet Gross Profit]
    } ON 0,
    { [Sales Territory].[Sales Territory Country].[Sales Territory
      Country] *
      [Product].[Product Categories].[Category]
    } ON 1
FROM
    [Adventure Works]
```

To return the cross product of two sets, we can use either of the following two syntaxes:

```
Standard syntax: Crossjoin(Set_Expression1, Set_Expression2)
Alternate syntax: Set_Expression1 * Set_Expression2
```

We have chosen to use the alternate syntax for its convenience. The result from the previous query is shown as follows:

		Internet Sales Amount	Internet Gross Profit
Australia	Accessories	$138,690.63	$86,820.10
Australia	Bikes	$8,852,050.00	$3,572,267.29
Australia	Clothing	$70,259.95	$26,767.68
Australia	Components	(null)	(null)
Canada	Accessories	$103,377.85	$64,714.37
Canada	Bikes	$1,821,302.39	$741,451.22
Canada	Clothing	$53,164.62	$23,755.91
Canada	Components	(null)	(null)

Skipping axes

There are situations when we want to display just a list of members with no data associated with them. Naturally, we expect to get that list in rows, so that we can scroll through them vertically instead of horizontally. However, the rules of MDX say that we can't skip the axes. If we want something on rows (which is AXIS(1) by the way), we must use all previous axes as well (columns in this case, which is also known as AXIS(0)).

The reason why we want the list to appear on axis 1 and not axis 0 is because a horizontal list is not as easy to read as a vertical one.

Is there a way to display those members on rows and have nothing on columns? Sure! This recipe shows how.

Getting ready

Notation for empty set is this: { }. So for the axis 0, we would simply do this:

```
{ } ON 0
```

How to do it...

Follow these steps to open the Query Editor in SQL Server Management Studio (SSMS):

1. Start SQL Server Management Studio (SSMS) and connect to your SQL Server Analysis Services (SSAS) 2012 instance.

2. Click on the target database **Adventure Works DW 2012**, and then right-click on the **New Query** button.

Follow these steps to get a one-dimensional query result with members on rows:

1. Put an empty set on columns (AXIS(0)). Notation for the empty set is this: { }.

2. Put some hierarchy on rows (AXIS(1)). In this case we used the largest hierarchy available in this cube – customer hierarchy of the same dimension.

3. Run the following query:

```
SELECT
    { } ON 0,
    { [Customer].[Customer].[Customer].MEMBERS } ON 1
FROM
    [Adventure Works]
```

How it works...

Although we can't skip axes, we are allowed to provide an empty set on them. This trick allows us to get what we need – nothing on columns and a set of members on rows.

There's more...

Skipping the Axis(0) is a common technique to create a list for report parameters. If we want to create a list of customers whose name contains "John", we can modify the preceding base query to use two functions to get only those customers whose name contains the phrase John. These two functions are Filter() and InStr():

```
SELECT
    { } ON 0,
    { Filter(
            [Customer].[Customer].[Customer].MEMBERS,
            InStr(
                    [Customer].[Customer].CurrentMember.Name,
                'John'
            ) > 0
        )
    } ON 1
FROM
    [Adventure Works]
```

In the final result, you will notice the "John" phrase in various positions in member names:

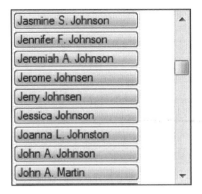

The idea behind it

Instead of skipping the `Axis(0)`, if you put a cube measure or a calculated measure with a non-constant expression on axis 0, you'll slow down the query. The slower query time can be noticeable, if there are a large number of members from the specified hierarchy. For example, if you put the `Sales Amount` measure on axis 0, the Sales Amount will have to be evaluated for each member in the rows. Do we need the Sales Amount? No, we don't. The only thing we need is a list of members; hence we've used an empty set {} on axis 0. That way, the SSAS engine doesn't have to go into cube space to evaluate the sales amount for every customer. The SSAS engine will only reside in dimension space, which is much smaller, and the query is therefore more efficient.

Possible workarounds – dummy column

Some client applications might have issues with the MDX statement skipping axes because they expect something on columns, and will not work with an empty set on axis 0. In this case, we can define a constant measure (a measure returning null, 0, 1 or any other constant) and place it on columns. In MDX's terms, this constant measure is a calculated measure. It will act as a dummy column. It might not be as efficient as an empty set, but it is a much better solution than the one with a regular (non-constant) cube measure like the `Sales Amount` measure.

This query creates a dummy value NULL on columns:

```
WITH
MEMBER [Measures].[Dummy] AS NULL

SELECT
    { [Measures].[Dummy] } ON 0,
    { [Customer].[Customer].[Customer].MEMBERS } ON 1
FROM
    [Adventure Works]
```

Using a WHERE clause to filter the data returned

A WHERE clause in MDX works in a similar way as the other query languages. It acts as a filter and restricts the data returned in the result set.

Not surprisingly, however, the WHERE clause in MDX does more than just restricting the result set. It also establishes the "query context".

Getting ready

The MDX WHERE clause points to a specific intersection of cube space. We use tuple expressions to represent cells in cube space. Each tuple is made of one member, and only one member, from each hierarchy.

The following tuple points to one year, 2008 and one measure, the [Internet Sales Amount]:

```
( [Measures].[Internet Sales Amount],
  [Date].[Calendar Year].&[2008]
)
```

Using a tuple in an MDX WHERE clause is called "slicing" the cube. This feature gives the WHERE clause another name, slicer. If we put the previous tuple in the WHERE clause, in MDX terms, we are saying, "show me some data from the cube sliced by sales and the year 2008".

That is what we are going to do next.

How to do it...

Open the Query Editor in SSMS, and then follow these steps to write a query with a slicer and test it:

1. Copy this initial query into the Query Editor and run the query. You will see the following result:

    ```
    SELECT
        { [Customer].[Customer Geography].[Country]
        } ON 0,
        { [Product].[Product Categories].[Category] } ON 1
    FROM
        [Adventure Works]
    ```

2. At this point, we should ask the question, "What are the cell values?" The cell values are actually the [Measures].[Reseller Sales Amount], which is the default member on the Measures dimension.

3. Add the previous tuple to the query as a slicer. Here is the final query:

```
SELECT
    { [Customer].[Customer Geography].[Country]
    } ON 0,
    { [Product].[Product Categories].[Category] } ON 1
FROM
    [Adventure Works]
WHERE
    ( [Measures].[Internet Sales Amount],
      [Date].[Calendar Year].&[2008]
    )
```

4. The result should be as shown in the following screenshot:

	Australia	Canada	France	Germany	United Kingdom	United States
Accessories	$81,309.16	$59,758.93	$37,421.30	$36,908.60	$43,481.35	$148,170.91
Bikes	$2,440,928.44	$581,424.73	$870,221.82	$1,025,888.91	$1,148,585.76	$3,095,275.19
Clothing	$41,646.69	$32,444.55	$14,535.92	$14,093.26	$18,219.16	$80,585.06
Components	(null)	(null)	(null)	(null)	(null)	(null)

5. Ask the question again, "What are the cell values?" The cell values are now the `[Measures].[Internet Sales Amount]`, and no longer the default measure.

How it works...

We can slice the data by pointing to a specific intersection of cube space. We can achieve this by putting a tuple in the WHERE clause.

In the preceding example, the cube space is sliced by sales and year 2008. The cell values are the Internet Sales Amount for each country and each product category, sliced by year 2008.

There's more...

Notice that the data returned on the query axes can be completely different from the tuple in the WHERE clause. The tuples in the slicer will only affect the cell values in the intersection of rows and columns, not what are on the columns or rows axes.

If you need to display sales and year 2008 on the query axes, you would need to move them to the query axes, and not in the WHERE clause.

This query has moved the sales to the columns axis, and the year 2008 to the rows axis. They both are "crossjoined" to the original hierarchies on the two query axes:

```
SELECT
    { [Measures].[Internet Sales Amount] *
      [Customer].[Customer Geography].[Country]
    } ON 0,
    { [Date].[Calendar Year].&[2008] *
      [Product].[Product Categories].[Category]
    } ON 1
FROM
    [Adventure Works]
```

Run the query and you will get the following result. The call values are the same as before, but now we have the year 2008 on the rows axis, and the **Internet Sales Amount** on the columns axis.

		Internet Sales Amount	Internet Sales Amount	Internet Sales Amount	Inter
		Australia	Canada	France	
CY 2008	Accessories	$81,309.16	$59,758.93	$37,421.30	
CY 2008	Bikes	$2,440,928.44	$581,424.73	$870,221.82	
CY 2008	Clothing	$41,646.69	$32,444.55	$14,535.92	
CY 2008	Components	(null)	(null)	(null)	

Optimizing MDX queries using the NonEmpty() function

The NonEmpty() function is a very powerful MDX function. It is primarily used to improve query performance by reducing sets before the result is returned.

Both **Customer** and **Date** dimensions are relatively large in the Adventure Works DW 2012 database. Putting the cross product of these two dimensions on the query axis can take a long time. In this recipe, we'll show how the NonEmpty() function can be used on the **Customer** and **Date** dimensions to improve the query performance.

Getting ready

Start a new query in SSMS and make sure that you're working on the Adventure Works DW 2012 database. Then write the following query and execute it:

```
SELECT
    { [Measures].[Internet Sales Amount] } ON 0,
    NON EMPTY
```

```
Filter(
            { [Customer].[Customer].[Customer].MEMBERS } *
            { [Date].[Date].[Date].MEMBERS },
            [Measures].[Internet Sales Amount] > 1000
        ) ON 1
FROM
    [Adventure Works]
```

The query shows the sales per customer and dates of their purchases, and isolates only those combinations where the purchase was over 1000 USD.

On a typical server, it will take more than a minute before the query will return the results.

Now let's see how to improve the execution time by using the NonEmpty() function.

How to do it...

Follow these steps to improve the query performance by adding the NonEmpty() function:

1. Wrap NonEmpty() around the cross join of customers and dates so that it becomes the first argument of that function.

2. Use the measure on columns as the second argument of that function.

3. This is what the MDX query should look like:

```
SELECT
    { [Measures].[Internet Sales Amount] } ON 0,
NON EMPTY
    Filter(
        NonEmpty(
                { [Customer].[Customer].[Customer].MEMBERS } *
                { [Date].[Date].[Date].MEMBERS },
                { [Measures].[Internet Sales Amount] }
            ),
        [Measures].[Internet Sales Amount] > 1000
        ) ON 1
FROM
    [Adventure Works]
```

4. Execute that query and observe the results as well as the time required for execution. The query returned the same results, only much faster, right?

How it works...

Both the **Customer** and **Date** dimensions are medium-sized dimensions. The cross product of these two dimensions contains several million combinations. We know that typically, the cube space is sparse; therefore, many of these combinations are indeed empty. The `Filter()` operation is not optimized to work in block mode, which means a lot of calculations will have to be performed by the engine to evaluate the set on rows, whether the combinations are empty or not.

Fortunately, the `NonEmpty()` function exists. This function can be used to reduce any set, especially multidimensional sets that are the result of a cross join operation. It removes the empty combinations of the two sets before the engine starts to evaluate the sets on rows. A reduced set has fewer cells to be calculated, and therefore the query runs much faster.

There's more...

Regardless of the benefits that were shown in this recipe, `NonEmpty()` should be used with caution. Here are some good practices regarding the `NonEmpty()` function:

> ▸ Use it with sets, such as named sets and axes.
> ▸ Use it in the functions which are not optimized to work in block mode, such as with the `Filter()` function.
> ▸ Avoid using it in aggregate functions such as `Sum()`.
> ▸ Avoid using it in other MDX set functions that are optimized to work in block mode. The use of `NonEmpty()` inside optimized functions will prevent them from evaluating the set in block mode. This is because the set will not be compact once it passes the `NonEmpty()` function. The function will break it into many small non-empty chunks, and each of these chunks will have to be evaluated separately. This will inevitably increase the duration of the query. In such cases, it is better to leave the original set intact, no matter its size. The engine will know how to run over it in optimized mode.

NonEmpty() versus NON EMPTY

Both the `NonEmpty()` function and the `NON EMPTY` keyword can reduce sets, but they do it in a different way.

The `NON EMPTY` keyword removes empty rows, columns, or both, depending on the axis on which that keyword is used in the query. Therefore, the `NON EMPTY` operator tries to push the evaluation of cells to an early stage whenever possible. This way the set on axis becomes already reduced and the final result is faster.

Take a look at the initial query in this recipe, remove the `Filter()` function, run the query, and notice how quickly the results come, although the multidimensional set again counts millions of tuples. The trick is that the `NON EMPTY` operator uses the set on the opposite axis, the columns, to reduce the set on rows. Therefore, it can be said that `NON EMPTY` is highly dependent on members on axes and their values in columns and rows.

Contrary to the `NON EMPTY` operator found only on axes, the `NonEmpty()` function can be used anywhere in the query.

The `NonEmpty()` function removes all the members from its first set, where the value of one or more measures in the second set is empty. If no measure is specified, the function is evaluated in the context of the current member.

In other words, the `NonEmpty()` function is highly dependent on members in the second set, the slicer, or the current coordinate, in general.

Common mistakes and useful tips

If a second set in the `NonEmpty()` function is not provided, the expression is evaluated in the context of the current measure in the moment of evaluation, and current members of attribute hierarchies, also in the time of evaluation. In other words, if you're defining a calculated measure and you forget to include a measure in the second set, the expression is evaluated for that same measure which leads to null, a default initial value of every measure. If you're simply evaluating the set on the axis, it will be evaluated in the context of the current measure, the default measure in the cube or the one provided in the slicer. Again, this is perhaps not something you expected. In order to prevent these problems, always include a measure in the second set.

`NonEmpty()` reduces sets, just like a few other functions, namely `Filter()` and `Existing()` do. But what's special about `NonEmpty()` is that it reduces sets extremely efficiently and quickly. Because of that, there are some rules about where to position `NonEmpty()` in calculations made by the composition of MDX functions (one function wrapping the other). If we're trying to detect multi-select, that is, multiple members in the slicer, `NonEmpty()` should go inside with the `EXISTING` function/keyword outside. The reason is that although they both shrink sets efficiently, `NonEmpty()` works great if the set is intact. `EXISTING` is not affected by the order of members or compactness of the set. Therefore, `NonEmpty()` should be applied earlier.

You may get **System.OutOfMemory** errors if you use the `CrossJoin()` operation on many large hierarchies because the cross join generates a Cartesian product of those hierarchies. In that case, consider using `NonEmpty()` to reduce the space to a smaller subcube. Also, don't forget to group the hierarchies by their dimension inside the cross join.

Using the PROPERTIES() function to retrieve data from attribute relationships

Attribute relationships define hierarchical dependencies between attributes. A good example is the relationship between attribute `City` and attribute `State`. If we know the current city is Phoenix, we know the state must be Arizona. This knowledge of the relationship, **City | State**, can be used by the Analysis Services engine to optimize performance.

Analysis Services provides the `Properties()` function to allow us to retrieve data based on attribute relationships.

Getting ready

We will start from a classic Top 10 query that shows the **Top 10 Customers**. Then we will use the `Properties()` function to retrieve each top 10 customer's yearly income.

This table shows what our query result should be like:

	Internet Sales Amount	Yearly Income
Nichole Nara	$13,295.38	100000 - 120000
Kaitlyn J. Henderson	$13,294.27	100000 - 120000
Margaret He	$13,269.27	100000 - 120000
Randall M. Dominguez	$13,265.99	80000 - 90000
Adriana L. Gonzalez	$13,242.70	80000 - 90000
Rosa K. Hu	$13,215.65	40000 - 70000
Brandi D. Gill	$13,195.64	100000 - 120000
Brad She	$13,173.19	80000 - 90000
Francisco A. Sara	$13,164.64	40000 - 70000
Maurice M. Shan	$12,909.67	80000 - 90000

Once we get only the top 10 customers, it's easy enough to place the customer on the rows, and the Internet sales amount on the columns. What about each customer's yearly income?

Customer geography is a user-defined hierarchy in the customer dimension. In the SSMS, if you start a new query against the Adventure Works DW 2012 database, and navigate to **Customer | Customer Geography | Customer | Member Properties**, you will see that the yearly income is one of the member properties for the attribute `Customer`. This is a good news, because now we can surely get the **Yearly Income** for each top 10 customer using the `PROPERTIES()` function:

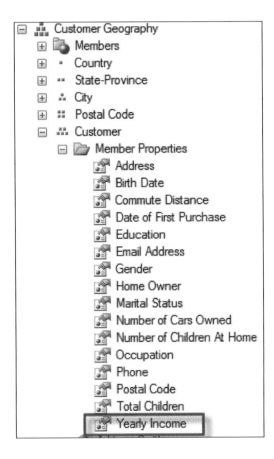

How to do it...

In SSMS, let us write the following query in a new Query Editor against the Adventure Works DW 2012 database:

1. This query uses the `TopCount()` function which takes three parameters. The first parameter `[Customer].[Customer Geography].[Customer].MEMBERS` provides the members that will be evaluated for the "top count", the second integer `10` tells it to return only 10 members and the third parameter `[Measures].[Internet Sales Amount]` provides a numeric measure as the evaluation criteria.

   ```
   -- Properties(): Initial
   SELECT
       [Measures].[Internet Sales Amount] on 0,
       TopCount(
           [Customer].[Customer Geography].[Customer].MEMBERS,
           10,
           [Measures].[Internet Sales Amount]
           ) ON 1
   FROM
       [Adventure Works]
   ```

2. Execute the preceding query, and we should get only 10 customers back with their Internet sales amount. Also notice that the result is sorted in the descending order of the numeric measure. Now let's add a calculated measure, like:

   ```
   [Customer].[Customer Geography].currentmember.Properties("Yearly Income")
   ```

3. To make the calculated measure "dynamic", we must use a member function `.CurrentMember`, so we do not need to hardcode any specific member name on the customer dimension. The `Properties()` function is also a member function, and it takes another attribute name as a parameter. We've provided "Yearly Income" as the name for the attribute we are interested in.

4. Now place the preceding expression in the `WITH` clause, and give it a name `[Measures].[Yearly Income]`. This new calculated measure is now ready to be placed on the columns axis, along with the Internet sales amount. Here is the final query:

   ```
   WITH
   MEMBER [Measures].[Yearly Income] AS
       [Customer].[Customer Geography].currentmember
         .Properties("Yearly Income")

   SELECT
       { [Measures].[Internet Sales Amount],
         [Measures].[Yearly Income]
   ```

```
    } on 0,
    TopCount (
        [Customer].[Customer Geography].[Customer].MEMBERS,
        10,
        [Measures].[Internet Sales Amount]
        ) ON 1
FROM
    [Adventure Works]
```

5. Executing the query, we should get the yearly income for each top 10 customer. The result should be exactly the same as the table shown at the beginning of our recipe.

How it works...

Attributes correspond to columns in the dimension tables in our data warehouse. Although we don't normally define the relationship between them, in the relationship database, we do so in the multidimensional space. This knowledge of attribute relationships can be used by the Analysis Services engine to optimize the performance. MDX has provided us the `Properties()` function to allow us to get from members of one attribute to members of another attribute.

In this recipe, we only focus on one type of member properties, that is, the user-defined member property. Member properties can also be the member properties that are defined by Analysis Services itself, such as `NAME`, `ID`, `KEY`, or `CAPTION`; they are the intrinsic member properties.

There's more...

The `Properties()` function can take another optional parameter, that is the `TYPED` flag. When the `TYPED` flag is used, the return value has the original type of the member.

The preceding example does not use the `TYPED` flag. Without the `TYPED` flag, the return value is always a string.

In many business analysis, we perform arithmetical operations numerically. In the next example, we will include the `TYPED` flag in the `Properties()` function to make sure that the `[Total Children]` for the top 10 customers are numeric.

```
WITH
MEMBER [Measures].[Yearly Income] AS
    [Customer].[Customer Geography].currentmember.Properties("Yearly
Income")
MEMBER [Measures].[Total Children] AS
    [Customer].[Customer Geography].currentmember.Properties("Total
Children", TYPED)
MEMBER [Measures].[Is Numeric] AS
    IIF(
```

```
        IsNumeric([Measures].[Total Children]),
        1,
        NULL
        )

SELECT
    { [Measures].[Internet Sales Amount],
      [Measures].[Yearly Income],
      [Measures].[Total Children],
      [Measures].[Is Numeric]
    } ON 0,
    TopCount(
     [Customer].[Customer Geography].[Customer].MEMBERS,
     10,
     [Measures].[Internet Sales Amount]
     ) ON 1
FROM
    [Adventure Works]
```

	Internet Sales Amount	Yearly Income	Total Children	Is Numeric
Nichole Nara	$13,295.38	100000 - 120000	2	1
Kaitlyn J. Henderson	$13,294.27	100000 - 120000	3	1
Margaret He	$13,269.27	100000 - 120000	3	1

Attributes can be simply referenced as an attribute hierarchy, that is, when the attribute is enabled as an Attribute Hierarchy.

In SSAS, there is one situation where the attribute relationship can be explored only by using the PROPERTIES() function, that is when its property AttributeHierarchyEnabled is set to False.

In the employee dimension in the Adventure Works cube, employees' SSN numbers are not enabled as an Attribute Hierarchy. Its property AttributeHierarchyEnabled is set to False. We can only reference the SSN number in the PROPERTIES() function of another attribute that has been enabled as Attribute Hierarchy, such as the Employee attribute.

Basic sorting and ranking

Sorting and ranking are very common requirements in most business analysis, and MDX provides several functions for this purpose. They are:

- ▶ TopCount and BottomCount
- ▶ TopPercent and BottomPercent
- ▶ TopSum and BottomSum

- ▶ Order
- ▶ Hierarchize
- ▶ Rank

All of these functions operate on sets of tuples, not just on one-dimensional sets of members. They all, in some way, involve a numeric expression, which is used to evaluate the sorting and the ranking.

Getting ready

We will start with the classic Top 5 (or Top-n) example using the `TopCount ()` function. We will then examine how the result is already pre-sorted, followed by using the `Order ()` function to sort the result explicitly. Finally, we will see how we can add a ranking number by using the `Rank ()` function.

Here is the classic Top 5 example using the `TopCount ()` function

```
TopCount (
          [Product].[Subcategory].children,
          5,
          [Measures].[Internet Sales Amount]
     )
```

It operates on a tuple (`[Product].[Subcategory].children, [Measures].[Internet Sales Amount]`).

The result is the five `[Subcategory]` that has the highest `[Internet Sales Amount]`.

The five subcategory members will be returned in order from the largest `[Internet Sales Amount]` to the smallest.

How to do it...

In SSMS, let us write the following query in a new Query Editor, against the Adventure Works DW 2012 database. Follow these steps to first get the top-n members:

1. We simply place the earlier `TopCount ()` expression on the rows axis.

2. On the columns axis, we are showing the actually sales amount for each product subcategory.

3. In the slicer, we use a tuple to slice the result for the year 2008 and the Southwest only.

4. The final query should look like the following query:

```
SELECT
          [Measures].[Internet Sales Amount] on 0,
          TopCount (
```

```
            [Product].[Subcategory].children,
            5,
            [Measures].[Internet Sales Amount]
       ) ON 1
   FROM
       [Adventure Works]
   WHERE
       ( [Date].[Calendar].[Calendar Quarter].&[2008]&[1],
         [Sales Territory].[Sales Territory Region].[Southwest]

       )
```

5. Run the query. The following screenshot shows the Top-n result:

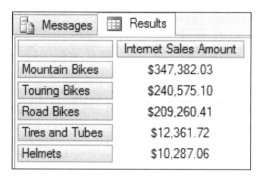

6. Notice that the returned members are in order from the largest numeric measure to the smallest.

Next, in SSMS, follow these steps to explicitly sort the result:

1. This time, we will put the TopCount() expression in the WITH clause, creating it as a Named Set. We will name it [Top 5 Subcategory].

2. On the rows axis, we will use the Order() function, which takes two parameters: which members we want to return and what value we want to evaluate on for sorting. The named set [Top 5 Subcategory] is what we want to return, so we will pass it to the Order() function as the first parameter. The .MemberValue function gives us the product subcategory name, so we will pass it to the Order() function as the second parameter. Here is the Order() function expression we would use:

```
ORDER (
        [Top 5 Subcategory],
        [Product].[Subcategory].MEMBERVALUE
    )
```

3. Here is the final query for sorting the result:

```
-- Order members with MemberValue
WITH
SET [Top 5 Subcategory] as
    TopCount (
        [Product].[Subcategory].CHILDREN,
        5,
        [Measures].[Internet Sales Amount]
    )

SELECT
    [Measures].[Internet Sales Amount] on 0,
    ORDER (
        [Top 5 Subcategory],
        [Product].[Subcategory].MEMBERVALUE
    ) ON 1
FROM
    [Adventure Works]
WHERE
    ( [Date].[Calendar].[Calendar Quarter].&[2008]&[1],
      [Sales Territory].[Sales Territory
        Region].[Southwest] )
```

4. Executing the preceding query, we get the sorted result as the screenshot shows:

	Internet Sales Amount
Helmets	$10,287.06
Mountain Bikes	$347,382.03
Road Bikes	$209,260.41
Tires and Tubes	$12,361.72
Touring Bikes	$240,575.10

Finally, in SSMS follow these steps to add ranking numbers to the Top-n result:

1. We will create a new calculated measure [Subcategory Rank] using the Rank() function, which is simply putting a one-based ordinal position of each tuple in the set [Top 5 Subcategory]. Since the set is already ordered, the ordinal position of the tuple will give us the correct ranking. Here is the expression for the Rank() function:

```
RANK (
    [Product].[Subcategory].CurrentMember,
    [Top 5 Subcategory]
)
```

2. The following query is the final query. It is built on top of the first query in this recipe. We've added the earlier `Rank()` function and created a calculated measure `[Measures].[Subcategory Rank]`, which is placed on the columns axis along with the Internet Sales Amount.

```
WITH
SET [Top 5 Subcategory] AS
    TopCount (
        [Product].[Subcategory].children,
        5,
        [Measures].[Internet Sales Amount]
    )
MEMBER [Measures].[Subcategory Rank] AS
    RANK (
        [Product].[Subcategory].CurrentMember,
        [Top 5 Subcategory]
    )

SELECT
    { [Measures].[Internet Sales Amount],
      [Measures].[Subcategory Rank]
    } ON 0,
    [Top 5 Subcategory] ON 1
FROM
    [Adventure Works]
WHERE
    ( [Date].[Calendar].[Calendar Quarter].&[2008]&[1],
      [Sales Territory].[Sales Territory Region].[Southwest] )
```

3. Run the preceding query. The ranking result is shown in the following screenshot:

	Internet Sales Amount	Subcategory Rank
Mountain Bikes	$347,382.03	1
Touring Bikes	$240,575.10	2
Road Bikes	$209,260.41	3
Tires and Tubes	$12,361.72	4
Helmets	$10,287.06	5

How it works...

Sorting functions, such as `TopCount()`, `TopPercent()`, and `TopSum()` operate on sets of tuples. These tuples are evaluated on a numeric expression and returned pre-sorted in the order of a numeric expression.

Using the `Order()` function, we can sort members from dimensions explicitly using the `.MemberValue` function.

When a numeric expression is not specified, the `Rank()` function can simply be used to display the one-based ordinal position of tuples in a set.

There's more...

Like the other MDX sorting functions, the `Rank()` function, however, can also operate on a numeric expression. If a numeric expression is specified, the `Rank()` function assigns the same rank to tuples with duplicate values in the set.

It is also important to understand that the `Rank()` function does not order the set. Because of this fact, we tend to do the ordering and ranking at the same time. However, in the last query of this recipe, we actually used the `Order()` function to first order the set of members of the subcategory. This way, the sorting is done only once and then followed by a linear scan, before being presented in sorted order.

As a good practice, we recommend using the `Order()` function to first order the set and then ranking the tuples that are already sorted.

Handling division by zero errors

Handling errors is a common task, especially the handling of division by zero type errors. This recipe offers a common practice to handle them.

Getting ready

Start a new query in SQL Server Management Studio and check that you're working on Adventure Works database. Then write and execute this query:

```
WITH
MEMBER [Date].[Calendar Year].[CY 2006 vs 2005 Bad] AS
    [Date].[Calendar Year].[Calendar Year].&[2006] /
    [Date].[Calendar Year].[Calendar Year].&[2005],
    FORMAT_STRING = 'Percent'
SELECT
    { [Date].[Calendar Year].[Calendar Year].&[2005],
      [Date].[Calendar Year].[Calendar Year].&[2006],
      [Date].[Calendar Year].[CY 2006 vs 2005 Bad] } *
      [Measures].[Reseller Sales Amount] ON 0,
    { [Sales Territory].[Sales Territory].[Country].MEMBERS }
    ON 1
FROM
    [Adventure Works]
```

This query returns six countries on the rows axis, and two years and a ratio on the column axis.

	CY 2005	CY 2006	CY 2006 vs 2005 Bad
	Reseller Sales Amount	Reseller Sales Amount	Reseller Sales Amount
France	(null)	$857,123.18	1.#INF
Germany	(null)	(null)	(null)
United Kingdom	(null)	$841,757.76	1.#INF
Canada	$1,513,359.46	$4,822,999.20	318.69%
United States	$6,552,075.85	$17,622,549.51	268.96%
Australia	(null)	(null)	(null)

The problem is that we get **1.#INF** on some ratio cells. **1.#INF** is the formatted value of infinity, and it appears whenever the denominator **CY 2005** is null and the nominator **CY 2006** is not null.

We will need help from the IIF() function, which takes three arguments: iif(<condition>, <then branch>, <else branch>). The IIF() function is a **Visual Basic for Applications (VBA)** function and has a native implementation in MDX. The IIF ( ) function will allow us to evaluate the condition of **CY 2005**, then decide what the ratio calculation formula should be.

How to do it...

Follow these steps to handle division by zero errors:

1. Copy the calculated member and paste it as another calculated member. During that, replace the term Bad with Good in its name, just to differentiate between those two members.
2. Copy the denominator.
3. Wrap the expression in an outer IIF() statement.
4. Paste the denominator in the condition part of the IIF() statement and compare it against 0.
5. Provide null value for the true part.
6. Your initial expression should be in the false part.
7. Don't forget to include the new member on columns and execute the query:

```
WITH
MEMBER [Date].[Calendar Year].[CY 2006 vs 2005 Bad] AS
    [Date].[Calendar Year].[Calendar Year].&[2006] /
    [Date].[Calendar Year].[Calendar Year].&[2005],
    FORMAT_STRING = 'Percent'
MEMBER [Date].[Calendar Year].[CY 2006 vs 2005 Good] AS
```

```
IIF([Date].[Calendar Year].[Calendar Year].&[2005] = 0,
    null,
      [Date].[Calendar Year].[Calendar Year].&[2006] /
      [Date].[Calendar Year].[Calendar Year].&[2005]
    ),
    FORMAT_STRING = 'Percent'
SELECT
    { [Date].[Calendar Year].[Calendar Year].&[2005],
      [Date].[Calendar Year].[Calendar Year].&[2006],
      [Date].[Calendar Year].[CY 2006 vs 2005 Bad],
      [Date].[Calendar Year].[CY 2006 vs 2005 Good] } *
    [Measures].[Reseller Sales Amount] ON 0,
    { [Sales Territory].[Sales Territory].[Country].MEMBERS }
    ON 1
FROM
    [Adventure Works]
```

The result shows that the new calculated measure has corrected the problem. The last column [**CY 2006 vs 2005 Good**] is now showing (null) correctly when the denominator **CY 2005** is null and the nominator **CY 2006** is not null.

	CY 2005	CY 2006	CY 2006 vs 2005 Bad	CY 2006 vs 2005 Good
	Reseller Sales Amount	Reseller Sales Amount	Reseller Sales Amount	Reseller Sales Amount
France	(null)	$857,123.18	1.#INF	(null)
Germany	(null)	(null)	(null)	(null)
United Kingdom	(null)	$841,757.76	1.#INF	(null)
Canada	$1,513,359.46	$4,822,999.20	318.69%	318.69%
United States	$6,552,075.85	$17,622,549.51	268.96%	268.96%
Australia	(null)	(null)	(null)	(null)

How it works...

A division by zero error occurs when the denominator is null or zero and the numerator is not null. In order to prevent this error, we must test the denominator before the division and handle the two scenarios in the two branches using the IIF() statement.

In the condition part of the IIF statement, we've used a simple scalar number zero to determine if [Measures].[Reseller Sales Amount] in the following slicer is zero or not. If it is zero, then it will be true and the calculated member will be NULL:

```
[Date].[Calendar Year].[Calendar Year].&[2005] = 0
```

What about the NULL condition? It turned out for a numerical value; we do not need to test the NULL condition specifically. It is enough to test just for zero because `null = 0` returns true. However, we could test for NULL condition if we want to, by using the `IsEmpty()` function.

For the calculated member `[CY 2006 vs 2005 Good]` we could wrap the member with the `IsEmpty()` function. The result will be the same:

```
MEMBER [Date].[Calendar Year].[CY 2006 vs 2005 Good] AS
    IIF(IsEmpty([Date].[Calendar Year].[Calendar Year].&[2005]),
        null,
        [Date].[Calendar Year].[Calendar Year].&[2006] /
        [Date].[Calendar Year].[Calendar Year].&[2005]
        ),
    FORMAT_STRING = 'Percent'
```

There's more...

SQLCAT's SQL Server 2008 Analysis Services Performance Guide has a lot of interesting details regarding the `IIF()` function, found at `http://tinyurl.com/PerfGuide2008R2`.

Additionally, you may find the blog article *MDX and DAX topics* by Jeffrey Wang explaining the details of the `IIF()` function, found at `http://tinyurl.com/IIFJeffrey`.

Earlier versions of SSAS

If you're using a version of SSAS prior to 2008 (that is, 2005), the performance of the `IIF()` function will not be as good. See Mosha Pasumansky's article for more information: `http://tinyurl.com/IIFMosha`.

Setting a default member of a hierarchy in the MDX script

Setting a default member is a tempting option which looks like it can be used on any dimension we would like to use it on. The truth is far from that. Default members should be used as exceptions and not as a general rule when designing dimensions.

The reason for that is not so obvious. The feature looks self-explanatory, and it's hard to anticipate what could go wrong. If we're not careful enough, our calculations can become unpredictable, especially on complex dimensions with many relationships among attributes.

Default members can be defined in three places. The easy-to-find option is the dimension itself, using the `DefaultMember` property found on every attribute. The second option is the role, on **Dimension Data** tab. Finally, default members can be defined in the MDX script. One of the main benefits of this place is easy maintenance of all default members in the cube because everything is in one place, and in the form of an easy-to-read text. That is also the only way to define the default member of a role-playing dimension.

In this recipe we'll show the most common option, that is, the last one, or how to set a default member of a hierarchy in the MDX script. More information on setting the `DefaultMember` is available at `http://tinyurl.com/DefaultMember2012`.

Getting ready

Follow these steps to set up the environment for this recipe:

1. Start SSMS and connect to your SSAS 2012 instance.

2. Click on the **New Query** button and check that the target database is **Adventure Works DW 2012**. Then execute the following query:

```
WITH
MEMBER [Measures].[Default account] AS
      [Account].[Accounts].DefaultMember.Name
SELECT
   { [Measures].[Amount],
     [Measures].[Default account] } ON 0
FROM
   [Adventure Works]
```

3. The results will show that the default member is **Net Income** account and its value in this context is a bit more than 12.6 million USD.

4. Next, open **Adventure Works DW 2012** solution in SSDT.

5. Double-click on the **Adventure Works** cube and go to the **Calculations** tab. Choose **Script View**.

6. Position the cursor at the beginning of the script, just beneath the **CALCULATE** command.

How to do it...

Follow these steps to set a new default member:

1. Enter the following expression to set a new default account:

```
ALTER CUBE CurrentCube
   UPDATE DIMENSION [Account].[Accounts],
     Default_Member = [Account].[Accounts].&[48];
                     //Operating Profit
```

2. Save and deploy (or just press the **Deploy MDX Script** icon if you're using **BIDS Helper 2012**).

3. Run the previous query again.

4. Notice that the result has changed. The new default account is **Operating Profit**, the one we specified in the MDX script using `ALTER CUBE` command. The value changed as well – now it's above 16.7 million USD.

How it works...

The `ALTER CUBE` statement changes the default member of a hierarchy specified in the `UPDATE DIMENSION` part of the statement. The third part is where we specify which member should be the default member of that hierarchy.

Don't mind that it says **UPDATE DIMENSION**. SSAS 2005 interprets that as a hierarchy.

There's more...

Setting the default member on a dimension with multiple hierarchies can lead to unexpected results. Due to attribute relations, related attributes are implicitly set to corresponding members, while the non-related attributes remain on their default members, that is, the *All* member (also known as the root member). Certain combinations of members from all available hierarchies can result in a nonexisting coordinate. In that case, the query will return no data. Other times, the intersection will only be partial. In that case, the query will return the data, but the values will not be correct, which might be even worse than no data at all.

Enter the following expression in the MDX script, deploy it, and then analyze the result in the **Cube Browser** tab:

```
ALTER CUBE CurrentCube
    UPDATE DIMENSION [Date].[Calendar],
        Default_Member = [Date].[Calendar]
                    .[Calendar Year].&[2007];
                    -- "current" year on the user hierarchy
```

The expression sets the year 2007 as the default member of the `[Date].[Calendar]` user-defined hierarchy.

The analysis of the **Sales Amount** measure in the **Cube Browser** shows good results in almost all cases except in a few. Fiscal hierarchies that have the fiscal year level in them return empty or incomplete results when used in a slicer. They are empty because the intersection between the fiscal year 2006 and the calendar year 2007 (the latter being the default member in the calendar hierarchy) is a nonexisting combination. Remember, the calendar year 2007 doesn't get overwritten by the fiscal year 2006. It gets combined (open the **Date** dimension in SSDT and observe the relationships in the corresponding tab). Moreover, when you put the fiscal year 2007 into the slicer, you only get a portion of data, the portion which matches the intersection of the calendar and the fiscal year. That's only one half of the fiscal year, right? In short, you have a potential problem with this approach.

Can we fix the result? Yes, we can. The correct results will be there when we explicitly select the *All* member from the **Date.Calendar** hierarchy in the slicer. Only then will we get good results using fiscal hierarchies. The question is – will the end users remember that every time?

The situation is similar when the default member is defined on an attribute hierarchy, for example, on the **Date.Calendar Year** hierarchy. By now, you should be able to modify the previous expression so that it sets the year 2007 as the default member on the [Date]. [Calendar Year]. Test this to see it for yourself.

Another scenario could be that you want to put the current date as the default member on the **Date.Date** hierarchy. Try that too, and see that when you use the year 2006 from the **Date. Calendar Year** hierarchy in the slicer, you get an empty result. Again, the intersection formed a nonexisting coordinate.

To conclude, you should avoid defining default members on complex dimensions. Define them where it is appropriate: on dimensions with a single non-aggregatable attribute (that is, when you set the IsAggregatable property of an attribute to False) or on dimensions with one or more user hierarchies where that non-aggregatable attribute is the top level on each user hierarchy, and where all relationships are well defined.

The **Account** dimension used in this example is not such a dimension. In order to correct it, two visible attributes should be hidden because they can cause empty results when used in a slicer. Experimenting with a scope might help too, but that adds to the complexity of the solution and hence the initial advice of keeping things simple when using default members should prevail.

Take a look at other dimensions in the **Adventure Works DW 2012** database. There you will find good examples of using default members.

Helpful tips

When you're defining the default members in an MDX script, do it at the beginning of the script. This way the calculations that follow can reference them.

In addition, provide a comment explaining which member was chosen to be the default member, and perhaps why. Look back at the code in this recipe to see how it was done.

2
Working with Sets

In this chapter, we will cover:

- ▸ Implementing the NOT IN set logic
- ▸ Implementing the logical OR on members from different hierarchies
- ▸ Implementing the logical AND on members from the same hierarchy
- ▸ Iterating on a set in order to reduce it
- ▸ Iterating on a set in order to create a new one
- ▸ Iterating on a set using recursion
- ▸ Dissecting and debugging MDX queries

Introduction

Sets are collections of tuples with the same dimensionality. Logical operations, **NOT**, **OR** and **AND**, are performed on sets in MDX. When putting the two tuples together to form a set, we ask for the results that contain a tuple. Therefore, the sets in MDX naturally implies logic **OR**.

The first part of the chapter focuses on the challenges and solutions of performing logic operations NOT, OR and AND, on sets.

Iterations and recursions can also be performed on sets. The second half of the chapter concentrates on iterations and recursions, and the different ways to perform them. Finally, we will cover how to apply the iteration technique to dissect and debug MDX queries and calculations.

Implementing the NOT IN set logic

There are times when we want to exclude some members from the result. We can perform this operation using a set of members on an axis or using a set of members in a slicer, that is, the WHERE part of an MDX query. This recipe shows how to do the latter, that is, how to exclude some members from a set in a slicer. The principle is the same for any part of an MDX query.

Getting ready

Start a new query in SSMS and check that you're working on the Adventure Works DW 2012 database. Then type in the following query and execute it:

```
SELECT
    { [Measures].[Reseller Order Count] } ON 0,
    NON EMPTY
    { [Promotion].[Promotion].MEMBERS }
    DIMENSION PROPERTIES
        [Promotion].[Promotion].[Discount Percent]
    ON 1
FROM
    [Adventure Works]
```

The preceding query returns 12 promotions and all the top-level promotions on the rows axis. The **DIMENSION PROPERTIES** keyword is used to get additional information about members – each promotion's discount percent. However, the property is not visible on either of the query axes and it can only be seen by double-clicking each promotion member on rows.

	Reseller Order Count
All Promotions	3,796
No Discount	3,782
Volume Discount 11 to 14	570
Volume Discount 15 to 24	347
Volume Discount 25 to 40	71
Volume Discount 41 to 60	2
Mountain-100 Clearance Sale	24
Sport Helmet Discount-2002	36
Road-650 Overstock	61
Sport Helmet Discount-2003	30
Touring-3000 Promotion	101
Touring-1000 Promotion	101
Mountain-500 Silver Clearance Sale	62

Our task is to exclude promotions with a discount percent of 0, 2, and 5.

How to do it...

To exclude promotions with a discount percent of 0, 2, and 5, is to say that we want the promotion members that are NOT IN the discount percent (0, 2, 5). Translating the NOT IN logic into the WHERE clause, we can use this pseudo code:

```
WHERE
    ( - { [member of Discount Percent 0],
          [member of Discount Percent 2],
             [member of Discount Percent 5] } )
```

All we need to do now is to find the three fully qualified member names.

Let us open a new query in SSMS against the Adventure Works DW 2012 database, and follow these steps:

1. Navigate to the **Promotion** dimension and expand it.

2. Expand the **Discount Percent** hierarchy and its level.

3. Take the first three members (with the names **0**, **2**, and **5**) and drag them one by one beneath the query, and then form a set of them using curly brackets.

4. Expand the query by adding the WHERE part.

5. Add the set with those three members using a minus sign in front of the set.

```
SELECT
    { [Measures].[Reseller Order Count] } ON 0,
    NON EMPTY
    { [Promotion].[Promotion].MEMBERS }
    DIMENSION PROPERTIES
        [Promotion].[Promotion].[Discount Percent]
    ON 1
FROM
    [Adventure Works]
WHERE
    ( - { [Promotion].[Discount Percent].&[0],
          [Promotion].[Discount Percent].&[2.E-2],
          [Promotion].[Discount Percent].&[5.E-2] } )
```

6. Execute the query and see how the results change. Double-click each promotion and verify that no promotion has discount percent equal to 0, 2, or 5 anymore.

How it works...

The initial query is not sliced by discount percentages. We can think of it as if all the members of that hierarchy exist there in the slicer:

```
WHERE ( { [Promotion].[Discount Percent]
                .[Discount Percent].MEMBERS } )
```

Of course, we don't have to write such expressions; the SSAS engine takes care of it by default. In other words, we're fine until the moment we want to change the slicer by either isolating or removing some members from that set. That's when we have to use that hierarchy in slicer.

Isolation of members is simply done by enumerating them in slicer. Reduction, the opposite operation, is performed using the `Except()` function:

```
WHERE ( Except( { [Promotion].[Discount Percent]
                        .[Discount Percent].MEMBERS },
                { [Promotion].[Discount Percent].&[0],
                  [Promotion].[Discount Percent].&[2.E-2],
                  [Promotion].[Discount Percent].&[5.E-2] }
              )
      )
```

The alternative for the `Except()` function is a minus sign, which brings us to the shorter version of the previous expression, the version that was used in this recipe.

Notice that the `Except()` function takes two sets, and the minus sign in our example has only one set after it, and has no set before it.

When a minus sign is used between two sets, it performs the same difference operation between those sets as `Except()` does. When the first set is missing, which is the case in our example, all the members of the second set are implicitly added as the first set. The difference between all members and the members of any set is the opposite set of that set. This is how you can perform the NOT IN logic on sets. Both variants work, but the one with the minus sign in front of the set is hopefully easier to remember.

There's more...

If we open the **Promotion** dimension inside **SQL Server Data Tools** (**SSDT**), we'll notice that the `Discount Percent` attribute has the `MemberValue` property defined. The value of that property is equal to a discount percentage and therefore in this particular case we could write an equivalent syntax:

```
WHERE
    ( { Filter( [Promotion].[Discount Percent]
              .[Discount Percent].MEMBERS,
              [Promotion].[Discount Percent]
              .CurrentMember.MemberValue >= 0.1 ) } )
```

The advantage of this expression is that it should filter out additional members with a percentage less than 10 percent, if they ever appear on that hierarchy. If we're not expecting such a case or if we strictly want to exclude certain, not necessarily consecutive, members from the hierarchy (Unknown Member, NA member, and so on), we should use the first example: the one with explicit members in the set.

See also

  ▶ The next recipe, *Implementing logical OR on members from different hierarchies* is based on a similar theme to this recipe.

Implementing the logical OR on members from different hierarchies

If we need to slice the data by only black color for products, we would put the `Black` member in the where clause, such as this:

```
WHERE
    ( [Product].[Color].&[Black] )
```

In the Adventure Works DW 2012 database, putting Reseller Order Quantity and Count on the columns, we would get this result:

	Reseller Order Quantity	**Reseller Order Count**
All Products	72,013	2,970
Cranksets	1,107	261
Gloves	11,553	991
Helmets	4,447	922
Mountain Bikes	12,771	1,119
Mountain Frames	5,604	736
Road Bikes	14,304	1,237
Road Frames	3,456	769
Shorts	8,946	758
Tights	4,562	470
Wheels	5,263	716

Similarly, to get only the products whose size is XL, we can put the member XL in the slicer as:

```
WHERE
    ( [Product].[Size Range].&[XL] )
```

What if we want to get the products whose size is XL in the same result set as the result set for black only?

Somehow, we need to combine the black member with the XL member. Simply by putting these two members together, it would not work. Putting two members from different hierarchies would form a tuple; a tuple implies logic AND in MDX, not logic OR.

On the other hand, in MDX implies a logic OR. However, we cannot simply put the preceding two members together to form a set, because they are not from the same hierarchy, or in MDX terms, they do not have the same dimensionality (they are from the same dimension though).

In this recipe, we will focus on how to implement logic OR on members from different hierarchies.

Getting ready

Start a new query in SSMS and check that you're working on the Adventure Works DW 2012 database. We will start with slicing by the black color first. Type in the following query and execute it:

```
SELECT
    { [Measures].[Reseller Order Quantity],
      [Measures].[Reseller Order Count] } ON 0,
    NON EMPTY
    { [Product].[Subcategory].MEMBERS } ON 1
FROM
    [Adventure Works]
WHERE
    ( [Product].[Color].&[Black] )
```

The query displays 10 product subcategories containing all black products, plus one row on the top level [All Products].

Next, open a new query window and execute the following query:

```
SELECT
    { [Measures].[Reseller Order Quantity],
      [Measures].[Reseller Order Count] } ON 0,
    NON EMPTY
    { [Product].[Subcategory].MEMBERS } ON 1
FROM
    [Adventure Works]
WHERE
    ( [Product].[Size Range].&[XL] )
```

It's a query similar to the previous one, but this one returns only product subcategories containing XL size range products. There's only one product subcategory in the result - **Jersey**.

Out task is to combine these queries so that we get the result of the OR operation on those two conditions, in a single query, of course.

How to do it...

Our goal is to combine these two members from different hierarchies and place them in the slicer.

```
[Product].[Color].&[Black]
[Product].[Size Range].&[XL]
```

To combine members from different hierarchies, we need to make sure that they have the same dimensionality.

1. Here is our solution; first we need to form two tuples that have the same dimensionality and then combine the two tuples with the same dimensionality to form a set. To form two tuples that have the same dimensionality, we add one more member expression `[Product].[Size Range].[All Products]` to each member, separating each member by a comma, and enclosing the tuple with a pair of parentheses. The pair of curly brackets indicates a set; each tuple in the set is separated by a comma; the member order in each tuple must be the same.

```
WHERE
    (
            { ( [Product].[Color].&[Black],
                [Product].[Size Range].[All Products] )

            ,
              ( [Product].[Color].[All Products],
                [Product].[Size Range].&[XL] ) }
```

2. Here is the final query:

```
SELECT
    { [Measures].[Reseller Order Quantity],
      [Measures].[Reseller Order Count] } ON 0,
    NON EMPTY
    { [Product].[Subcategory].MEMBERS } ON 1
FROM
    [Adventure Works]
WHERE
(
    { ( [Product].[Color].&[Black],
        [Product].[Size Range].[All Products] )

      ,
      ( [Product].[Color].[All Products],
        [Product].[Size Range].&[XL] ) }
)
```

3. Executing the preceding query, we would get the result as shown in the following screenshot. **Jerseys** is the only product that is picked up by the XL size range. Notice that the cell values for the All Products are also properly aggregated for all 12 products, including **Jerseys**.

	Reseller Order Quantity	Reseller Order Count
All Products	78,035	3,017
Cranksets	1,107	261
Gloves	11,553	991
Helmets	4,447	922
Jerseys	6,022	967
Mountain Bikes	12,771	1,119
Mountain Frames	5,604	736
Road Bikes	14,304	1,237
Road Frames	3,456	769
Shorts	8,946	758
Tights	4,562	470
Wheels	5,263	716

How it works...

The nature of a multidimensional database and its underlying structures has a direct consequence on how we should write the combinations of members. Some combinations are there by design, others require a bit of imagination.

For example, a set of two members of the same hierarchy (colors black and white) placed in a slicer automatically applies OR logic on the result. This means that the result will have data where the first, the second, or both of the members (or at least one of their descendants to be precise) occurred in the underlying fact table. In other words, where the product sold was either black or white. The emphasis is on two things: the set and the OR word. In other words, OR logic manifests in sets.

The other example is a tuple formed by two members from different hierarchies (that is color black and size XL). Once placed in the slicer, this tuple guarantees that the resulting rows will have data on that exact slice, meaning, on both members (and at least one of the descendants of each to be precise). Here, the emphasis is again on two things: the tuple and the AND word. In other words, AND logic manifests in tuples.

Let's summarize. In MDX, a set is by default the equivalent of logical OR while a tuple is by default the equivalent of logical AND. So where's the problem?

The problem is we can only put members of different hierarchies in a tuple and of the same hierarchy in a set. Which means we're missing two combinations, different hierarchies using OR and the same hierarchy using AND.

This recipe shows how to implement OR logic using members from different hierarchies. The next recipe in this chapter shows how to perform AND logic using members from the same hierarchy. It is recommended that you read both recipes.

Logical OR represents a set. Since we have members of different dimensionality, we must first convert them to tuples of the same dimensionality. That is done by expanding each with the other one's root member and enclosing the expression in brackets (which is how we convert a member to a tuple). Once we have compatible tuples, we can convert them into a set by separating them with a comma and adding curly brackets around the whole expression. This is the standard way that we enumerate members in single-dimensional sets. Multi-dimensional sets are no different except it's the tuples that we're enumerating this time.

There's more...

We can also use the UNION() function instead of enumerating members in the set. The union has an extra feature, an option to remove or preserve duplicates in the resulting set. While that feature is of little interest when the slicer is concerned, it might be interesting when the same logic is applied in calculations.

A special case of a non-aggregatable dimension

In case your dimension has no root member (eliminated by setting the property IsAggregatable to False) use its default member instead.

A very complex scenario

In this recipe we used two hierarchies of the same dimension because this is often the case in real life. However, the solution is applicable to any dimension and its hierarchies. For example, when you need to combine three different hierarchies you can apply the same solution, thereby expanding each member into a tuple with N-1 root members (here N=2) and creating a set of N such tuples.

In case you need to combine many members using OR logic, sometimes with even more than one of them on the same hierarchy and others on different hierarchies, you need to apply your knowledge about dimensionality – members of the same hierarchy should be enlisted in a set, and members of different dimensions should be combined with root members of other hierarchies. You just need to be careful with various brackets. The AsymmetricSet() function from the Analysis Services Stored Procedure Project may help to construct complex sets: http://tinyurl.com/AsymmetricSet

> ▸ The *Implementing NOT IN set operation* recipe is based on a similar theme to this recipe

> ▸ For more information on default members, take a look at the *Setting default member of a hierarchy in MDX script* recipe in *Chapter 1, Elementary MDX Techniques*

Implementing the logical AND on members from the same hierarchy

This recipe shows how to implement AND logic using members from the same hierarchy.

In the Adventure Works DW 2012 database, there are two members [New Product] and [Excess Inventory] in the [Promotion Type] hierarchy:

```
[Promotion].[Promotion Type].&[New Product]
[Promotion].[Promotion Type].&[Excess Inventory]
```

These two promotion types have reseller orders, but the only two months in which they both have reseller orders are July and August.

The idea is to have a single query that displays the reseller orders, where both of these promotion types occur in the same month. In other words, we want to show the reseller orders for July and August.

Our goal is to somehow combine these two members from the same hierarchy so that we perform logic AND along the [Month of Year] hierarchy on the Date dimension.

Getting ready

Start a new query in SSMS and make sure that you're working on the Adventure Works DW 2012 database.

Our first query will slice the cube by the [New Product] promotion type. The query is as follows. Let's execute it:

```
SELECT
    { [Measures].[Reseller Order Quantity],
      [Measures].[Reseller Order Count] } ON 0,
    NON EMPTY
    { [Date].[Month of Year].MEMBERS } ON 1
FROM
    [Adventure Works]
WHERE
    ( [Promotion].[Promotion Type].&[New Product] )
```

The query displays three months from the [Month of Year] hierarchy with the New Product promotion type, July, August and September, with the top level [All periods]. The result should be the same as shown in the following table.

For [New Product]:

	Reseller Order Quantity	Reseller Order Count
All Periods	2,323	116
July	513	24
August	811	39
September	999	53

Let's replace the new product with the Excess Inventory promotion type; we'll get one month less with only July and August. See the query and the result as shown:

```
SELECT
    { [Measures].[Reseller Order Quantity],
      [Measures].[Reseller Order Count] } ON 0,
    NON EMPTY
    { [Date].[Month of Year].MEMBERS } ON 1
FROM
    [Adventure Works]
WHERE
    ( [Promotion].[Promotion Type].&[Excess Inventory] )
```

For [Excess Inventory]:

	Reseller Order Quantity	Reseller Order Count
All Periods	304	61
July	135	24
August	169	37

The idea is to have a single query which displays the result where both of these promotion types occur in the same month. In other words, we want to show the values for July and August.

We have several ways of doing it, but this recipe will focus on the slicer-subselect solution. Other solutions will be mentioned in further sections of this recipe.

Our final result should be as follows:

	Reseller Order Quantity	Reseller Order Count
All Promotions	1,628	124
Excess Inventory	304	61
New Product	1,324	63

How to do it...

Our goal is to somehow combine these two members from the same hierarchy so that we perform logic AND along the [Month of Year] hierarchy on the Date dimension.

```
WHERE
    ( [Promotion].[Promotion Type].&[New Product] )
WHERE
    ( [Promotion].[Promotion Type].&[Excess Inventory] )
```

In order to perform an AND logic on different members from the same hierarchy, we must nest our conditions:

1. Here is our innermost condition, where we are using the Exists() function to get the month of year that has Reseller Sales for Excess Inventory. Notice that Reseller Sales is our measure group of interest. The Exists() function takes two set expressions and one measure group, and returns a set of tuples from the first set that exist with one or more tuples in the second set. The returned set of tuples must be associated with the measure group. This innermost condition will return July, August, and September in our example because they are the only three months that have reseller sales for New Product.

2. Also notice that we are using the **Month of Year** level (not hierarchy!) as the first parameter. Level has three-part syntax; hierarchy has two-part syntax. Don't omit the third part otherwise it won't work.

```
Exists(
{ [Date].[Month of Year].[Month of Year].MEMBERS },
{ [Promotion].[Promotion Type].&[New Product] },
"Reseller Sales"
)
```

3. We are going to use this inner condition as a nested condition, and wrap it with another Exists() function. The outer Exists() function also takes two sets and one measure group. With the first set being July, August, and September, and the second set being the excess inventory, only July and August are returned. September will be filtered out because it no longer has reseller sales for Excess Inventory.

```
WHERE
    (
    Exists(
        Exists(
{[Date].[Month of Year].[Month of Year].MEMBERS},
        {[Promotion].[Promotion Type].&[New Product]},
         "Reseller Sales"
         ),
         { [Promotion].[Promotion Type].&[Excess Inventory] },
        "Reseller Sales"
    )
    )
```

4. We have worked out the slicer so far. We also need a subselect with those two members `[New Product]` and `[Excess Inventory]` inside (see the subselect that follows):

```
FROM
(
   SELECT
       { [Promotion].[Promotion Type].&[New Product],
         [Promotion].[Promotion Type].&[Excess Inventory] } ON 0
     FROM
       [Adventure Works]
)
```

5. Here is the final query. Let's run it:

```
SELECT
    { [Measures].[Reseller Order Quantity],
      [Measures].[Reseller Order Count] } ON 0,
    NON EMPTY
    { [Promotion].[Promotion Type].MEMBERS } ON 1
FROM
    (
          SELECT
                  { [Promotion].[Promotion Type].&[New Product],
                    [Promotion].[Promotion Type].&[Excess Inventory]
} ON 0
          FROM
                  [Adventure Works]
    )
WHERE
    (
          Exists(
                  Exists( { [Date].[Month of Year].[Month of Year].
MEMBERS },
                                  { [Promotion].[Promotion Type].&[New
Product] },
                                  "Reseller Sales"
                          ),
                                  { [Promotion].[Promotion
Type].&[Excess Inventory] },
                                  "Reseller Sales"
                          )
    )
```

6. The result of the query shows the aggregate for July and August, the only two months where both promotion types occur.

	Reseller Order Quantity	Reseller Order Count
All Promotions	1,628	124
Excess Inventory	304	61
New Product	1,324	63

7. Compare these results with tables at the beginning of this recipe (showing a combination of promotion types and months) and you'll notice that the aggregates match the sum of individual values.

How it works...

In the introduction we stated that our goal is to have a single query that displays the reseller orders where both of these promotion types occur in the same month. Since there is no MDX expression that would work and return logic AND result using two members from the same hierarchy, the [Month of Year] hierarchy has become our base for performing the AND logic.

In order to perform an AND logic on the same hierarchy, we must cascade the conditions using an inner set and an outer set. The inner set is repeated here.

```
Exists( { [Date].[Month of Year].[Month of Year].MEMBERS },
                    { [Promotion].[Promotion Type].&[New
Product] },
                        "Reseller Sales"
              )
```

This inner set returns all the months that have the **New Product** promotion type (three months as seen on the initial screenshot).

The outer set restricts the inner set even more by filtering out all months that don't have the other promotion type as well. That leaves only two months, **July** and **August**.

We have chosen the [Month of Year] hierarchy as our base to perform the AND logic. In practice, we will need to decide which hierarchy and which level we want to use as the new base or granularity and adhere to some common-sense rules.

Firstly, the relationship between the new hierarchy's level members and the members for slicing should be many-to-many. This is always so in case of different dimensions (**Promotion** and **Date**), a case covered in this example. In case of the same dimension, the solution will work only for a single member that is related to both members in the AND operation. Whether that will be something other than the All member depends on the hierarchy and members selected for the AND operation. For example, two promotion types used in this example share only one ancestor – the All member, which can be verified in the **Promotions** user hierarchy of that dimension.

Secondly, the whole idea has to be valid. In practice, we can run multiple promotions in the same month. Therefore on the granularity of month, two different promotions can have intersections on the same order, and our idea is valid.

Which hierarchy to use? That usually becomes quite obvious once we ask ourselves the question behind the report. For example, the last query, as seen in the previous screenshot, returned the two promotion types we started with this recipe, promotion types that come together on a monthly basis. Two things are important here: **together** and **basis**. The term "together" represents the AND logic. The term "monthly basis" is in fact the new granularity for the report (that which goes in slicer).

That explains the slicer part of the solution. What about the subselect part? Why is it there?

The subselect part serves the purpose of adjusting the results. Without it, we would get the wrong total. Let me explain this in more detail.

If you remove the subselect part of the query and execute it again, it will return the result displayed in the following screenshot:

	Reseller Order Quantity	Reseller Order Count
All Promotions	46,429	603
Excess Inventory	304	61
New Product	1,324	63
No Discount	35,096	596
Seasonal Discount	1,172	66
Volume Discount	8.533	158

The cell numbers for **New Product** and **Excess Inventory** on this screenshot match the aggregated values displayed in the previous screenshot.

However, the query returned all promotion types because nothing limited them in the query. The slicer effectively limits the months only, not promotion types.

There are two things we can do to correct it, that is, to display the result for those two hierarchies only. One is to put them in slicer so that they cross join with the existing slicer. The other is to put them in a subselect. I prefer the second option because this way we can still have them on a query axis. Otherwise, we will have a conflict with the slicer (a hierarchy cannot appear in slicer and on an axis, but it can appear in the subselect and also on an axis). That's why we have chosen the subselect.

The subselect, as seen before, limits the promotion types that appear on an axis and adjusts their total so that it becomes the visual total for those two members. This is exactly what we need, the value for individual promotion types and their correct total.

To conclude, in order to implement AND logic, we have done two things. First, we have established a new granularity in slicer. Second, we used the subselect to adjust the total.

There's more...

This is not the only way to implement the AND logic. We can do it on an axis as well. In that case, all we have to do is put a construct from the slicer on the rows and leave the subselect as it is.

Where to put what?

Based on a request, the AND logic can be implemented on rows or in slicer. If there's a request to hide the hierarchy for which we're applying the AND logic, we should put the corresponding MDX expression in slicer. On the other hand, if there's an explicit request to show members on rows, we must put the construct on the rows. There we can cross join it with additional hierarchies if required.

A very complex scenario

In case of a more complex scenario where three different hierarchies need to be combined, we can apply the same solution, which in a general case should have N cascades in slicer and N members in the subselect. The N is the number of members from the same hierarchy.

In case we need to combine many members using AND logic, some of them originating from different hierarchies and some from the same, the solution becomes very complex.

You are advised to watch out for the order in the cascades and dimensionality of the potential tuples.

See also

▶ A recipe with a similar theme is *Implementing logical OR on members from different hierarchies*.

Iterating on a set in order to reduce it

Iteration is a very natural way of thinking for us humans. We set a starting point, we step into a loop, and we end when a condition is met. While we're looping, we can do whatever we want: check, take, leave, and modify items in that set.

In this recipe, we will start from a result set as shown in the following table, and iterate through the days in each fiscal month to count the number of days for which the growth was positive. By "to reduce", we mean the filtering effect; in our example, we need to "filter out" the days for which the growth was not positive. Our goal is still to only display the fiscal months on ROWS, not the days.

	Customer Count	Growth in Customer Base
July 2005	31	(null)
August 2005	31	0.00%
September 2005	13	-58.06%
October 2005	27	107.69%
November 2005	32	18.52%
December 2005	39	21.88%

Then we will look at a different approach that takes performance advantage of the block-mode calculation.

Getting ready

Start a new query in SSMS against the Adventure Works DW 2012 database. Then write the following query:

```
SELECT
    { [Measures].[Customer Count],
      [Measures].[Growth in Customer Base] } ON 0,
    NON EMPTY
    { [Date].[Fiscal].[Month].MEMBERS } ON 1
FROM
    [Adventure Works]
WHERE
    ( [Product].[Product Categories].[Subcategory].&[1] )
```

The query returns fiscal months on rows and two measures: a count of customers, and their growth compared to the previous month. Mountain bikes are in the slicer. The first few rows from the result set are shown in the preceding table.

Now let's see how we can get the number of days the growth was positive for each period.

How to do it...

We are going to use the `FILTER()` function to loop through the descendants of the fiscal month on leaves, and apply the `COUNT()` function to get the count of days. We will put the expression in the `WITH` clause and name it `[Measures].[Positive growth days]`. Finally, we place this new calculated member on the columns.

1. The final query is as follows:

```
WITH
MEMBER [Measures].[Positive growth days] AS
    Filter(
            Descendants([Date].[Fiscal].CurrentMember, , leaves),
            [Measures].[Growth in Customer Base] > 0
                ).Count
SELECT
    { [Measures].[Customer Count],
        [Measures].[Growth in Customer Base],
        [Measures].[Positive growth days] } ON 0,
    NON EMPTY
    { [Date].[Fiscal].[Month].MEMBERS } ON 1
FROM
    [Adventure Works]
WHERE
    ( [Product].[Product Categories].[Subcategory].&[1] )
```

2. Run the preceding query and observe if the results match the following screenshot:

	Customer Count	Growth in Customer Base	Positive growth days
April 2005	(null)	(null)	0
May 2005	(null)	(null)	0
June 2005	(null)	(null)	0
July 2005	31	(null)	2
August 2005	31	0.00%	7
September 2005	13	-58.06%	0
October 2005	27	107.69%	2
November 2005	32	18.52%	3
December 2005	39	21.88%	7
January 2006	36	-7.69%	3
February 2006	18	-50.00%	2

How it works...

Iteration is a technique that steps into a loop, checks or modifies items in the set, and then exits the loop when a condition is met.

Our goal is to count the number of days for which the growth was positive. Therefore, it might seem appropriate to perform iteration on days in each fiscal month. Iteration can be performed by using the `FILTER()` function.

First, since we do not want to have the days on rows, so we must use the `DESCENDANTS()` function to get all dates in the current context.

Second, in order to get the number of items that came up upon filtering, we use the `COUNT()` function.

Iteration works in this situation; however, if there's a way to manipulate the collection of members in block mode, without cutting that set into small pieces and iterating on individual members, we should use it.

There's more...

Filter function is an iterative function which doesn't run in block mode; hence it will slow down the query.

Let's see if we can find a way to work in the block mode. A keen eye will notice a "count of filtered items" pattern in this expression. That pattern suggests the use of a set-based approach in the form of a **SUM-IF** combination. The trick is to provide 1 for the true part of the condition taken from the `FILTER()` statement and null for the false part. The sum of one will be equivalent to the count of filtered items.

This is the same `WITH` clause, being rewritten by using the `SUM-IF` combination:

```
WITH
MEMBER [Measures].[Positive growth days] AS
    SUM(
            Descendants([Date].[Fiscal].CurrentMember, , leaves),
            IIF( [Measures].[Growth in Customer Base] > 0, 1, null)
            )
```

Execute the query using the new definition. Both the `SUM()` and the `IIF()` functions are optimized to run in the block mode, especially when one of the branches in `IIF()` is null. In this particular example, the impact on performance was not noticeable because the set of rows was relatively small. Applying this technique on large sets will result in drastic performance improvement as compared with the FILTER-COUNT approach.

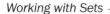

More information about this type of optimization can be found in Mosha Pasumansky's blog, at `http://tinyurl.com/SumIIF`.

Hints for query improvements

There are several ways in which we can avoid the `FILTER()` function in order to improve performance.

When you need to filter by non-numeric values (that is, properties or other metadata), you should consider creating an attribute hierarchy for often-searched items and then do one of the following:

- ▶ Use a tuple when you need to get a value sliced by that new member
- ▶ Use the `EXCEPT()` function when you need to negate that member on its own hierarchy (NOT or <>)
- ▶ Use the `EXISTS()` function when you need to limit other hierarchies of the same dimension by that member
- ▶ Use the `NONEMPTY()` function when you need to operate on other dimensions, that is, subcubes created with that new member
- ▶ Use the 3-argument `EXISTS()` function instead of the `NONEMPTY()` function, if you also want to get combinations with nulls in the corresponding measure group (nulls are available only when the `NullProcessing` property for a measure is set to `Preserve`)

When you need to filter by values and then count a member in that set, you should consider aggregate functions like `SUM()` with the `IIF()` part in its expression, as described earlier.

See also

- ▶ The next recipes, *Iterating on a set in order to create a new one* and *Iterating on a set using recursion*, deal with other methods of iteration.

Iterating on a set in order to create a new one

There are situations when we don't want to eliminate certain members from a set, but instead execute for each type of loop. This is done using the `GENERATE()` function. The `GENERATE()` function applies a set to each member of another set, and then joins the resulting sets by union. In this recipe we'll show you how to create a new set of members from the existing one.

Getting ready

Let's start a new query in SSMS against the Adventure Works DW 2012 database. Then write the following query:

```
SELECT
    NON EMPTY
    { [Date].[Calendar].[Calendar Year].MEMBERS *
      [Measures].[Sales Amount] } ON 0,
    NON EMPTY
    { [Sales Territory].[Sales Territory Country].MEMBERS }
    ON 1
FROM
    [Adventure Works]
```

The query returns four years on columns and six countries plus the top level `[All Sales Territories]` on rows. The result is shown as follows:

	CY 2005	CY 2006	CY 2007	CY 2008
	Sales Amount	Sales Amount	Sales Amount	Sales Amount
All Sales Territories	$11,331,808.96	$30,674,773.18	$41,993,729.72	$25,808,962.34
Australia	$1,309,047.20	$2,154,284.88	$3,881,215.18	$3,310,788.70
Canada	$1,660,189.26	$5,444,601.58	$6,187,089.89	$3,063,889.72
France	$180,571.69	$1,372,065.19	$3,400,129.00	$2,298,789.76
Germany	$237,784.99	$521,230.85	$2,157,272.42	$1,962,012.12
United Kingdom	$291,590.52	$1,433,344.61	$3,458,394.40	$2,487,391.50
United States	$7,652,625.30	$19,749,246.06	$22,909,628.84	$12,686,090.53

Our goal is to get a set of best months, one for each year. We will use the GENERATE () function to do a for-each type of loop to apply a set of calendar month to each member of the calendar year, and to get the best month for each year.

How to do it...

Follow these steps to create a new set from the initial one:

1. Cut the years from columns and define a named set using them.

2. Name that set `Best month per year`.

3. Wrap that set in the `Generate()` function so that the set of years becomes its first argument.

4. The second argument should be the `TopCount ()` function which uses the descendants of each year on the `Month` level and finds the best month according to the value of the measure `Sales Amount`.

5. Put the name of the new set on columns.

6. The final query should look as follows:

```
WITH
SET [Best month per year] AS
    Generate( [Date].[Calendar].[Calendar Year].MEMBERS,
               TopCount(
               Descendants( [Date].[Calendar].CurrentMember,
                            [Date].[Calendar].[Month],
                            SELF ),
               1,
               [Measures].[Sales Amount] )
            )
SELECT
    NON EMPTY
    { [Best month per year] *
      [Measures].[Sales Amount] } ON 0,
    NON EMPTY
    { [Sales Territory].[Sales Territory Country].MEMBERS } ON 1
FROM
    [Adventure Works]
```

7. Execute the query. Notice that each year is replaced with a single month, the month with the best sales result in that year:

| | November 2005 | August 2006 | December 2007 | June 2008 |
	Sales Amount	Sales Amount	Sales Amount	Sales Amount
All Sales Territories	$2,868,129.20	$4,147,192.18	$5,242,736.50	$5,364,840.18
Australia	$210,683.56	$149,740.46	$600,028.52	$711,086.98
Canada	$411,652.56	$725,785.42	$833,436.15	$717,837.71
France	$36,799.34	$304,422.34	$352,425.97	$316,740.80
Germany	$43,396.04	$34,224.00	$341,570.07	$349,467.10
United Kingdom	$26,966.90	$246,769.43	$644,990.00	$688,354.97
United States	$2,138,630.81	$2,686,250.54	$2,470,285.78	$2,581,352.62

How it works...

The `Generate()` function can be thought of as a for-each loop. Its syntax is:

```
Generate( Set_Expression1 , Set_Expression2 [ , ALL ] )
```

This means that we can iterate through each member of the first set and assign each member from the second set. This second set can have zero, one, or many members and this can vary during the iteration. In our example we're assigning a set with one member only, the best month in each year. That member is obtained using the `TopCount()` function where the first argument is months of the current year in iteration, the second argument is 1 (only one member to be returned), and the third argument is the `Sales Amount` measure – the criterion for deciding which month is the best. Months are obtained the standard way, using the `Descendants()` function.

Notice that a different best month is displayed for each year, and that the use of the `Generate()` function is the only way to get this result. Simply crossjoining calendar years and the set of top one calendar months will display the top one calendar month for all time, repeated for each year. We can think of the first set in the `Generate()` function as the context of the looping.

There's more...

The `CURRENTORDINAL` function is a special MDX function valid only in iterations. It returns the position of the current member (or tuple, to be precise) in the set in iteration (from 0 to N, where N is the total number of members in a set). In addition to that, there's also the `CURRENT` function. The `CURRENT` function returns the current tuple in a set being iterated. Again, it's only applicable during iterations.

Both of these functions can be used to detect the current tuple and to create various calculations with the current tuple and other tuples in that set. Reversing any initial set is one example of these manipulations. Comparing the value of the current tuple with the value of the previous tuple in the set (or any one before or after) in order to isolate certain tuples is another example.

Here's how you could reverse the set of months from the previous example. Out next query uses the `.CurrentOrdinal` function and will reverse the order of the months on the columns, as shown in the following screenshot:

	June 2008	December 2007	August 2006	November 2005
	Sales Amount	Sales Amount	Sales Amount	Sales Amount
All Sales Territories	$5,364,840.18	$5,242,736.50	$4,147,192.18	$2,868,129.20
Australia	$711,086.98	$600,028.52	$149,740.46	$210,683.56
Canada	$717,837.71	$833,436.15	$725,785.42	$411,652.56

```
SET [Best month per year reversed] AS
    Generate( [Date].[Calendar].[Calendar Year].MEMBERS
            AS MySetAlias,
            TopCount(
                Descendants(
```

```
                    MySetAlias.Item( MySetAlias.Count -
                              MySetAlias.CurrentOrdinal
                                 - 1 ).Item(0),
                [Date].[Calendar].[Month],
                SELF ),
            1,
            [Measures].[Sales Amount]  )
        )
```

A set alias (`MySetAlias` in this example) is defined for the initial set. That set alias is later used for navigation. The combination of `Count` and `CurrentOrdinal` gives us members from the end of the set to its beginning, progressively, while the `Item()` function serves as a pointer on members in that set.

Yes, the same operation could be done simply by sorting the months by their member key, in descending order. Nevertheless, the idea of this example was to show you the principle which can be applied on any set, especially those that can't be ordered easily.

The `CURRENTORDINAL` function can also be used in the `Filter()` function. There, tuples can be compared with each other progressively in order to see which one has a value higher than both of its neighboring members, which would signal that the current member is a relative peak. Or the opposite, whatever is more interesting in a particular case. However, the `Filter()` function doesn't add new members, it only limits its initial set and for that reason it is out of the scope of this recipe.

To summarize, both `Current ()` and `CurrentOrdinal ()` are powerful functions that allow us to perform the self-joining type of operations in MDX or make use of the existing relations between dimensions and measure groups. These functions are useful not only in the `Generate()` function, but also in other iterating functions as well, namely, the `Filter()` function.

Did you know

In MDX, there's no concept of the FOR loop. Iterations cannot be based on numbers (as in other languages or on other systems). They must always be based on a set. If we need to loop exactly N times, there are two basic ways we can achieve this. One is with the existing cube structure; the other is by expanding a cube with a utility dimension. The former means that we can use the date dimension and take N members from its start. Or it could be some other dimension, as long as it has enough members to loop on. The latter, using the utility dimension, will be explained later in *Chapter 7, Implementing the Tally Table Utility Dimension*.

See also

> ▶ The recipes *Iterating on a set using recursion* and *Iterating on a set in order to reduce it* show other methods of iteration

Iterating on a set using recursion

Recursion is sometimes the best way to iterate a collection. Why? Because iterations using set functions (including the `GENERATE()` function) require that we loop through the whole set. But what if that set is big and we only need to find something specific in it? Wouldn't it be great to be able to stop the process when we've found what we wanted? Recursion enables just that – to stop when we're done.

In this recipe we're going to see how to calculate the average of an average using recursion.

Getting ready

To get started, start a new query in SSMS and check that you're working in the right database. Then write the following query:

```
SELECT
    { [Measures].[Order Count] } ON 0,
    NON EMPTY
    { Descendants( [Date].[Fiscal Weeks].[All Periods],
                   1 , SELF_AND_BEFORE) } ON 1
FROM
    [Adventure Works]
```

It returns four fiscal years and their total on top for the `Order Count` measure. Now let's see how to calculate the average daily value on the week level and the average weekly level on the year level, which is based on the week level, not on the date level. In other words, each level will have the average value of members on the level immediately beneath.

How to do it...

Follow these steps to perform recursion over a set:

1. Define a new calculated measure and name it `Average of an average`.

2. Use the `IIF()` function and specify its true parameter as the initial measure (`Order Count`).

3. The value should be returned for the leaf level, so the condition in `IIF()` should test exactly that using the `ISLEAF()` function.

4. In the false parameter we should provide the calculation we want to repeat recursively. In this case it is the `AVG()` function used on the children of the current member.

5. The measure expression inside `AVG()` function should be the measure being defined.

6. Check if the measure is defined as follows:

```
WITH
MEMBER [Measures].[Average of an average] AS
    iif( IsLeaf( [Date].[Fiscal Weeks].CurrentMember ),
        [Measures].[Order Count],
        Avg( [Date].[Fiscal Weeks].CurrentMember.Children,
            [Measures].[Average of an average] )
    )
, FORMAT_STRING = '#,#'
```

7. Don't forget to include that measure as the second measure on columns.

8. Run the query. The results will look as follows. The first row, the one with the **All Periods** member, will have the average yearly value as result, that is, (56+84+435+195)/4=193. In turn, every year will have the average weekly value. The weekly values are not visible in this screenshot, but we can divide the **Order Count** values by 53, which is the number of weeks per year. That should give us the values for the **Average of an average** measure for each year shown in the second column:

	Order Count	Average of an average
All Periods	31,455	193
FY 2006	2,945	56
FY 2007	4,477	84
FY 2008	23,057	435
FY 2009	976	195

How it works...

Recursions are the most difficult iteration concept to apply. Their logic is very condensed. However, once you conquer them, you'll appreciate their power and efficiency. Let's see how that solution worked.

In order to start the recursive process, we have to specify an expression that uses the same calculated measure we're defining, thereby providing a different input parameter than the one which was being used in the current pass of recursive process. In order to stop the process, we must have a branch without the reference to that measure. On top of all that, we must perform some operation to collect values on the way. Complicated? Let's analyze our query.

It is helpful to examine the `[Fiscal Weeks]` hierarchy. In SSMS, starting a new MDX query, in the cube navigation pane, we can see the `[Fiscal Weeks]` hierarchy on the date dimension.

Notice that the **Fiscal Year** on rows is not the leaf level of the **Fiscal Weeks** user hierarchy. Therefore, the expression inside the `IIF()` statement evaluates as `False`. This leads us to the part where we have to calculate the average value for each child of the current member. With a small detail, the calculation should be performed using the same measure we're evaluating!

The evaluation for the current year member cannot be completed and is therefore delayed until the calculation for all its child members (weeks in this case) is performed. One by one, each week of the year in context is passed inside the definition of this measure and evaluated.

In the case of a leaf member, the **Order Count** measure would be evaluated and returned to the outer evaluation context. Otherwise, another turn of the child member's evaluation would occur. And so on until we would finally hit leaf-level members.

In this example, weeks are the leaf level of the hierarchy being used in the query. They would be evaluated using the `True` part of the condition. The `True` parameter is without reference to the measure we're calculating, which means the recursive path would be over. The value of the **Order Count** measure starting from the Week **1** of **FY 2006** would be collected and saved in a temporary buffer. The same process would be repeated for all weeks of that year. Only then would the average of them be calculated and returned as a value for FY 2006, after which the process would repeat for subsequent years on rows.

Let's also mention that the value for the root member (All years) is calculated with the recursion depth of two, meaning each year it is first evaluated as an average of its weeks and then the average of its years is calculated and returned as the final result.

There's more...

You might be wondering, how does one recognize when to use recursion and when to use other types of iteration? Look for some of these pointers: relative positions, relative granulation for calculation, and stop logic. If there's a mention of going back or forth from the current member in a set, but there's no fixed span, then that might be a good lead to use recursion. If there's a relative stopping point, that's another sign. Finally, if there's no explicit requirement to loop through the whole set, but moreover a requirement to stop at some point in the process, that's a definite sign to try to apply recursion as a solution to the problem.

In case no such signs exist, it's perhaps better and easier to use the simple types of iterations we covered in previous recipes. The other case when you should consider straightforward iteration is when the recursion would span over more than half of the members on a particular hierarchy, which pushes the SSAS engine into the slow cell-by-cell mode.

Earlier versions of SSAS

SSAS 2008 and later have better support for recursion than previous versions of SSAS. Optimizations have been added to the code in the form of unlimited recursion depth. Versions prior to that may suffer from memory limitations in some extreme cases.

See also

> ▸ The recipes *Iterating on a set in order to create a new one* and *Iterating on a set in order to reduce it* illustrate other ways of iteration

Dissecting and debugging MDX queries

When writing a query involving complex calculations, you might have a hard time trying to debug it, in case there is a problem inside the calculation. But there is a way. By breaking complex sets and calculations into smaller pieces and/or by converting those sets and members into strings, we can visually represent the intermediate results and thereby isolate the problematic part of the query.

True, there's no real debugger in the sense that you can pause the calculation process of the query and evaluate the variables. What you can do is to simulate that by concatenating intermediate results into strings for visual verification.

Getting ready

For this recipe we'll use the final query in the previous recipe, *Iterating on a set using recursion*. We have chosen this as our example because it's a relatively complex calculation and we want to check if we're doing the right thing.

How to do it...

Follow these steps to create a calculated measure that shows the evaluation of another calculation:

1. Start SSMS and execute the following query:

```
WITH
MEMBER [Measures].[Average of an average] AS
    iif( IsLeaf( [Date].[Fiscal Weeks].CurrentMember ),
        [Measures].[Order Count],
```

```
            Avg( [Date].[Fiscal Weeks].CurrentMember.Children,
                [Measures].[Average of an average] )
        )
    , FORMAT_STRING = '#,#'
SELECT
    { [Measures].[Order Count],
      [Measures].[Average of an average] } ON 0,
    NON EMPTY
    { Descendants( [Date].[Fiscal Weeks].[All Periods],
                    1 , SELF_AND_BEFORE) } ON 1
FROM
    [Adventure Works]
```

2. Create a new calculated measure and name it Proof.

3. Copy the definition of the Average of an average measure and paste it as the definition of the new calculated measure Proof.

4. Leave the True part as it is.

5. Modify the False part as shown in the next step.

6. Finally, wrap the whole expression with one IIF() statement that checks whether the original measure is empty. The definition of that measure should look like this:

```
MEMBER [Measures].[Proof] AS
    iif( IsEmpty( [Measures].[Order Count] ),
        null,
        iif( IsLeaf( [Date].[Fiscal Weeks].CurrentMember ),
            [Measures].[Order Count],
            '( ' +
            Generate( [Date].[Fiscal Weeks]
                        .CurrentMember.Children,
                    iif( IsEmpty( [Measures]
                            .[Average of an average] ),
                        '(null)',
                        CStr(
                            Round( [Measures]
                                .[Average of an average],
                                0 ) )
                    ),
                    ' + ' ) +
            ' ) / ' +
            CStr( NonEmpty( [Date].[Fiscal Weeks]
                            .CurrentMember.Children,
                        [Measures].[Order Count]
                    ).Count )
        )
    )
```

7. Add that measure onto the columns and execute the query. The result will look like:

	Order Count	Proof	Average of an average
All Periods	31,455	((null) + 56 + 84 + 435 + 195 + (null) + (null)) / 4	193
FY 2006	2,945	(47 + 28 + 28 + 38 + 38 + 111 + 34 + 31 + 37 + 101 +...	56
FY 2007	4,477	(61 + 58 + 59 + 48 + 197 + 57 + 68 + 72 + 165 + 42 +...	84
FY 2008	23,057	(322 + 122 + 104 + 124 + 429 + 343 + 370 + 355 + 5...	435
FY 2009	976	(158 + 227 + 221 + 215 + 155 + (null) + (null) + (null) +...	195

How it works...

The general idea of debugging MDX queries is to display some intermediate results, such as the current member names, their properties, position in a set, their descendants, and ancestors, that can help us with visual verification. Other times we'll convert the complete sets that we're operating with into a string, just to see the members inside, and their order. For numeric values, if they are formed using several subcalculations like in this example, we try to compose that evaluation as a string too. In short, we're displaying textual values of items we are interested in.

In our example, the main part that we want to verify is the `False` parameter of the inner `IIF()` function, that is, when the fiscal week hierarchy is not at the leaf level. Therefore, that's the place where we're building a concatenated string to show how the average of an average is calculated.

The preceding screenshot can help us to understand how the measure `Proof` is concatenated. It is a string representation of all individual values used to calculate each row of Average of an average. It is represented as a sum of N values, where N is the number of children of the current member, divided by their count. Additionally, null values are preserved and displayed as well in the string, but the count omits them.

Now, the calculation for the measure `Proof` itself. First, there's an open bracket in the form of a string. Then the `Generate()` function is applied, only this time it's the second version of that function, the one that returns not a set but a string. More information about it can be found at `http://tinyurl.com/MDXGenerate`.

The `Generate()` function has two different usages with two different syntaxes. We've seen its first usage in a previous recipe *Iterating on a set in order to create a new one*, where Generate is used to evaluate a complex set expression, such as `TopCount`, over a set of members. In this recipe, we've used its second syntax in which a string expression is evaluated over a set of members, and the strings are eventually concatenated and returned, separated by a delimiter of either plus sign or parentheses. The syntax is shown as follows:

```
Generate( Set_Expression1, String_Expression, Delimiter)
```

Partial strings generated during iteration need to be concatenated. For that reason the third argument of the `Generate()` function was used with the value "+".

The `Generate()` function, as explained in the recipe *Iterating on a set in order to create a new one,* is a type of loop. In this case, it takes each child of a current member of the **Fiscal Weeks** user hierarchy and tests whether it is empty or not. If it is, a constant string is used ('(null)'), if not; the value of the measure is rounded to zero decimals.

Which measure? That same measure we're calculating the result for. Hence, it's again a call for iteration, this time using each child, one by one, because they are in the context at the time of the call.

In the new pass, those members will be leaf members. They'll collect the value of measure `Order Count` and get out of that pass.

Once all the children are evaluated, the individual values will be concatenated using a " + " sign with a space on each side for better readability.

But the process is not over, only the recursion is.

Next, we have to close the bracket which we opened in the beginning of the process, and we have to calculate the denominator. Notice the measure inside the denominator is not calling for recursion. In order to get the count of members, we used the `NonEmpty()` function over the original measure. That returns the members which have values.

Finally, we haven't mentioned this specifically so far, but the outer `IIF()` statement checks if we're on a member that has no result. If so, we can skip that member. Remember, we had to do that because the inner part of the `Proof` measure is a string which is never null.

There's more...

In the process of dissecting, evaluating and debugging calculations and queries, various MDX functions can be used. Some of them are mentioned beneath. However, it is advised that you look for additional information on MSDN and other sources.

- String functions, namely `MembertToStr` and `SetToStr`, for converting members and sets into strings.
- Set functions, namely the `Generate()` function and especially its string variant, which is a very powerful method for iterating on a set, and for collecting partial calculations in the form of strings.
- Metadata functions (also known as hierarchy and level functions), for collecting information about members and their hierarchies.
- Logical functions, for testing on leaf level and emptiness.
- VBA functions, for handling errors (`IsError()`)and string manipulations.

[🔅💡 Don't forget to use the `AddCalculatedMembers()` function if you need to include calculated members.]

Useful string functions

Here's a list of VBA functions that can be used in MDX:

`http://tinyurl.com/MDXVBAFunction`

Here's a list of MDX functions grouped by types:

`http://tinyurl.com/MDXfunctions`

See also

> ▸ The recipe *Optimizing MDX queries using NonEmpty() function* shows how to keep only relevant members for debugging purposes and prevent all members of a hierarchy from being returned as the result.

3
Working with Time

In this chapter, we will cover:

- ► Calculating the YTD (Year-To-Date) value
- ► Calculating the YoY (Year-over-Year) growth (parallel periods)
- ► Calculating moving averages
- ► Finding the last date with data
- ► Getting values on the last date with data
- ► Calculating today's date using the string functions
- ► Calculating today's date using the `MemberValue` function
- ► Calculating today's date using an attribute hierarchy
- ► Calculating the difference between two dates
- ► Calculating the difference between two times
- ► Calculating parallel periods for multiple dates in a set
- ► Calculating parallel periods for multiple dates in slicer

Introduction

Time handling features are an important part of every BI system. Programming languages, database systems, they all incorporate various time-related functions and Microsoft SQL Server Analysis Services (SSAS) is no exception there. In fact, that's one of its main strengths.

The MDX language has various time-related functions designed to work with a special type of dimension called the **Time** and its typed attributes. While it's true that some of those functions work with any type of dimension, their usefulness is most obvious when applied to time-type dimensions. An additional prerequisite is the existence of multi-level hierarchies, also known as user hierarchies, in which types of levels must be set correctly or some of the time-related functions will either give false results or will not work at all.

Because of the reasons described earlier, and the fact that almost every cube will have one or more time dimensions, we've decided to dedicate a whole chapter to this topic, that is, for time calculations. In this chapter we're dealing with typical operations, such as year-to-date calculations, running totals, and jumping from one period to another. We go into detail with each operation, explaining known and less known variants and pitfalls.

We will discuss why some time calculations can create unnecessary data for the periods that should not have data at all, and why we should prevent it from happening. We will then show you how to prevent time calculations from having values after a certain point in time.

In most BI projects, there are always reporting requirements to show measures for today, yesterday, month-to-date, quarter-to-date, year-to-date, and so on. We have three recipes to explore various ways to calculate today's date, and how to turn it into a set and use MDX's powerful set operations to calculate other related periods.

Calculating date and time spans is also a common reporting requirement.

The chapter ends with two recipes explaining how to calculate the parallel period for a range of dates.

Calculating the YTD (Year-To-Date) value

In this recipe we will look at how to calculate the Year-To-Date value of a measure, that is, the accumulated value of all dates in a year up to the current member on the date dimension. An MDX function YTD() can be used to calculate the Year-To-Date value, but not without its constraints.

In this recipe, we will discuss the constraints when using the YTD() function and also the alternative solutions.

Getting ready

Start SQL Server Management Studio and connect to your SSAS 2012 instance. Click on the **New Query** button and check that the target database is **Adventure Works DW 2012**.

In order for this type of calculation to work, we need a dimension marked as `Time` in the `Type` property, in the **Dimension Structure** tab of SSDT. That should not be a problem because almost every database contains at least one such dimension and **Adventure Works** is no exception here. In this example, we're going to use the `Date` dimension. We can verify in SSDT that the `Date` dimension's `Type` property is set to `Time`. See the following screenshot from SSDT:

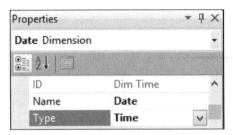

Here's the query we'll start from:

```
SELECT
    { [Measures].[Reseller Sales Amount] } ON 0,
    { [Date].[Calendar Weeks].[Calendar Week].MEMBERS } ON 1
FROM
    [Adventure Works]
```

Once executed, the preceding query returns reseller sales values for every week in the database.

How to do it...

We are going to use the `YTD()` function, which takes only one member expression, and returns all dates in the year up to the specified member. Then we will use the aggregation function `SUM()` to sum up the **Reseller Sales Amount**.

Follow these steps to create a calculated measure with YTD calculation:

1. Add the `WITH` block of the query.

2. Create a new calculated measure within the `WITH` block and name it `Reseller Sales YTD`.

3. The new measure should return the sum of the measure `Reseller Sales Amount` using the `YTD()` function and the current date member of the hierarchy of interest.

4. Add the new measure on axis `0` and execute the complete query:

```
WITH
MEMBER [Measures].[Reseller Sales YTD] AS
    Sum( YTD( [Date].[Calendar Weeks].CurrentMember ),
        [Measures].[Reseller Sales Amount] )
```

```
SELECT
    { [Measures].[Reseller Sales Amount],
      [Measures].[Reseller Sales YTD] } ON 0,
    { [Date].[Calendar Weeks].[Calendar Week].MEMBERS } ON 1
FROM
    [Adventure Works]
```

5. The result will include the second column, the one with the YTD values. Notice how the values in the second column increase over time:

	Reseller Sales Amount	Reseller Sales YTD
Week 1 CY 2008	$1,662,547.32	$1,662,547.32
Week 2 CY 2008	(null)	$1,662,547.32
Week 3 CY 2008	(null)	$1,662,547.32
Week 4 CY 2008	(null)	$1,662,547.32
Week 5 CY 2008	$2,699,300.79	$4,361,848.12
Week 6 CY 2008	(null)	$4,361,848.12
Week 7 CY 2008	(null)	$4,361,848.12
Week 8 CY 2008	(null)	$4,361,848.12
Week 9 CY 2008	$2,738,653.62	$7,100,501.74
Week 10 CY 2008	(null)	$7,100,501.74
Week 11 CY 2008	(null)	$7,100,501.74
Week 12 CY 2008	(null)	$7,100,501.74
Week 13 CY 2008	(null)	$7,100,501.74

How it works...

The YTD() function returns the set of members from the specified date hierarchy, starting from the first date of the year and ending with the specified member. The first date of the year is calculated according to the level [Calendar Year] marked as Years type in the hierarchy [Calendar Weeks]. In our example, the YTD() value for the member **Week 9 CY 2008** is a set of members starting from **Week 1 CY 2008** and going up to that member because the upper level containing years is of the Years type.

The set is then summed up using the SUM() function and the Reseller Sales Amount measure. If we scroll down, we'll see that the cumulative sum resets every year, which means that YTD() works as expected.

In this example we used the most common aggregation function, SUM(), in order to aggregate the values of the measure throughout the calculated set. SUM() was used because the aggregation type of the Reseller Sales Amount measure is **Sum**. Alternatively, we could have used the Aggregate() function instead. More information about that function can be found later in this recipe.

There's more...

Sometimes it is necessary to create a single calculation that will work for any user hierarchy of the date dimension. In that case, the solution is to prepare several YTD() functions, each using a different hierarchy, cross join them, and then aggregate that set using a proper aggregation function (Sum, Aggregate, and so on). However, bear in mind that this will only work if all user hierarchies used in the expression share the same year level. In other words, that there is no offset in years among them (such as exists between the fiscal and calendar hierarchies in Adventure Works cube in 2008 R2).

Why does it have to be so? Because the cross join produces the set intersection of members on those hierarchies. Sets are generated relative to the position when the year starts. If there is offset in years, it is possible that sets won't have an intersection. In that case, the result will be an empty space. Now let's continue with a couple of working examples.

Here's an example that works for both monthly and weekly hierarchies:

```
WITH
MEMBER [Measures].[Reseller Sales YTD] AS
    Sum( YTD( [Date].[Calendar Weeks].CurrentMember ) *
        YTD( [Date].[Calendar].CurrentMember ),
        [Measures].[Reseller Sales Amount] )
SELECT
    { [Measures].[Reseller Sales Amount],
      [Measures].[Reseller Sales YTD] } ON 0,
    { [Date].[Calendar Weeks].[Calendar Week].MEMBERS } ON 1
FROM
    [Adventure Works]
```

If we replace [Date].[Calendar Weeks].[Calendar Week].MEMBERS with [Date].[Calendar].[Month].MEMBERS, the calculation will continue to work. Without the cross join part, that wouldn't be the case. Try it in order to see for yourself! Just be aware that if you slice by additional attribute hierarchies, the calculation might become wrong.

In short, there are many obstacles to getting the time-based calculation right. It partially depends on the design of the time dimension (which attributes exist, which are hidden, how the relations are defined, and so on), and partially on the complexity of the calculations provided and their ability to handle various scenarios. A better place to define time-based calculation is the MDX script. There, we can define scoped assignments, but that's a separate topic which will be covered later in the recipe, *Using utility dimension to implement time-based calculations* in *Chapter 6, Business Analytics*.

In the meantime, here are some articles related to that topic:

```
http://tinyurl.com/MoshaDateCalcs
```

```
http://tinyurl.com/DateToolDim
```

Inception-To-Date calculation

A similar calculation is the Inception-To-Date calculation in which we're calculating the sum of all dates up to the current member, that is, we do not perform a reset at the beginning of every year. In that case, the `YTD()` part of the expression should be replaced with this:

```
Null : [Date].[Calendar Weeks].CurrentMember
```

Using the argument in the YTD() function

The argument of the `YTD()` function is optional. When not specified, the first dimension of the `Time` type in the measure group is used. More precisely, the current member of the first user hierarchy with a level of type `Years`.

This is quite convenient in the case of a simple `Date` dimension; a dimension with a single user hierarchy. In the case of multiple hierarchies or a role-playing dimension, the `YTD()` function might not work, if we forget to specify the hierarchy for which we expect it to work.

This can be easily verified. Omit the `[Date].[Calendar Weeks].CurrentMember` part in the initial query and see that both columns return the same values. The `YTD()` function is not working anymore.

Therefore, it is best to always use the argument in the `YTD()` function.

Common problems and how to avoid them

In our example we used the `[Date].[Calendar Weeks]` user hierarchy. That hierarchy has the level **Calendar Year** created from the same attribute. The type of attribute is `Years`, which can be verified in the **Properties** pane of **SSDT**:

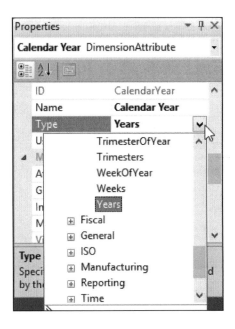

However, the Date dimension in the **Adventure Works** cube has fiscal attributes and user hierarchies built from them as well. The fiscal hierarchy equivalent to [Date].[Calendar Weeks] hierarchy is the [Date].[Fiscal Weeks] hierarchy. There, the top level is named Fiscal Year, created from the same attribute. This time, the type of the attribute is FiscalYear, not Year. If we exchange those two hierarchies in our example query, the YTD() function will not work on the new hierarchy. It will return an error:

	Reseller Sales Amount	Reseller Sales YTD
Week 1 FY 2008	$2,665,650.54	#Error
Week 2 FY 2008	(null)	#Error
Week 3 FY 2008	(null)	#Error
Week 4 FY 2008	(null)	#Error
Week 5 FY 2008	$4,212,971.51	#Error
Week 6 FY 2008	(null)	#Error
Week 7 FY 2008	(null)	#Error
Week 8 FY 2008	(null)	#Error
Week 9 FY 2008	$4,047,574.04	#Error
Week 10 FY 2008	(null)	#Error
Week 11 FY 2008	(null)	#Error

Query (3, 7) By default, a year level was expected. No such level was found in the cube.

The name of the solution is the PeriodsToDate() function.

YTD() is in fact a short version of the PeriodsToDate() function, which works only if the Year type level is specified in a user hierarchy. When it is not so (that is, some BI developers tend to forget to set it up correctly or in the case that the level is defined as, let's say, FiscalYear like in this test), we can use the PeriodsToDate() function as follows:

```
MEMBER [Measures].[Reseller Sales YTD] AS
    Sum( PeriodsToDate( [Date].[Fiscal Weeks].[Fiscal Year],
                        [Date].[Fiscal Weeks].CurrentMember ),
        [Measures].[Reseller Sales Amount] )
```

PeriodsToDate() might therefore be used as a safer variant of the YTD() function.

YTD() and future dates

It's worth noting that the value returned by a **SUM-YTD** combination is never empty once a value is encountered in a particular year. Only the years with no values at all will remain completely blank for all their descendants. In our example with the [Calendar Weeks] hierarchy, scrolling down to the **Week 23 CY 2008**, you will see that this is the last week that has reseller sales. However, the Year-To-Date value is not empty for the rest of the weeks for year 2008, as shown in the following screenshot:

	Reseller Sales Amount	Reseller Sales YTD
Week 20 CY 2008	(null)	$12,621,827.74
Week 21 CY 2008	(null)	$12,621,827.74
Week 22 CY 2008	$755.78	$12,622,583.53
Week 23 CY 2008	$3,415,479.07	$16,038,062.60
Week 24 CY 2008	(null)	$16,038,062.60
Week 25 CY 2008	(null)	$16,038,062.60
Week 26 CY 2008	(null)	$16,038,062.60
Week 27 CY 2008	(null)	$16,038,062.60
Week 28 CY 2008	(null)	$16,038,062.60

This can cause problems for the descendants of the member that represents the current year (and future years as well). The **NON EMPTY** keyword will not be able to remove empty rows, meaning we'll get YTD values in the future.

We might be tempted to use the NON_EMPTY_BEHAVIOR operator to solve this problem but it wouldn't help. Moreover, it would be completely wrong to use it, because it is only a hint to the engine which may or may not be used. It is not a mechanism for removing empty values, as explained in the previous chapter.

In short, we need to set some rows to null, those positioned after the member representing today's date. We'll cover the proper approach to this challenge in the recipe, *Finding the last date with data*.

▶ For the reasons explained in the last section of this recipe, you should take a look at the recipe, *Finding the last date with data*.

Calculating the YoY (Year-over-Year) growth (parallel periods)

This recipe explains how to calculate the value in a parallel period, the value for the same period in a previous year, previous quarter, or some other level in the date dimension. We're going to cover the most common scenario – calculating the value for the same period in the previous year, because most businesses have yearly cycles.

A `ParallelPeriod()` is a function that is closely related to time series. It returns a member from a prior period in the same relative position as a specified member. For example, if we specify June 2008 as the member, Year as the level, and 1 as the lag, the `ParallelPeriod()` function will return June 2007.

Once we have the measure from the prior parallel period, we can calculate how much the measure in the current period has increased or decreased with respect to the parallel period's value.

Getting ready

Start SQL Server Management Studio and connect to your SSAS 2012 instance. Click on the **New Query** button, and check that the target database is **Adventure Works DW 2012**.

In this example we're going to use the `Date` dimension. Here's the query we'll start from:

```
SELECT
    { [Measures].[Reseller Sales Amount] } ON 0,
    { [Date].[Fiscal].[Month].MEMBERS } ON 1
FROM
    [Adventure Works]
```

Once executed, the previous query returns the value of `Reseller Sales Amount` for all fiscal months.

How to do it...

Follow these steps to create a calculated measure with YoY calculation:

1. Add the `WITH` block of the query.

2. Create a new calculated measure there and name it `Reseller Sales PP`.

3. The new measure should return the value of the measure `Reseller Sales Amount` measure using the `ParallelPeriod()` function. In other words, the definition of the new measure should be as follows:

    ```
    MEMBER [Measures].[Reseller Sales PP] As
    ( [Measures].[Reseller Sales Amount],
    ParallelPeriod( [Date].[Fiscal].[Fiscal Year], 1,
    [Date].[Fiscal].CurrentMember ) )
    ```

4. Specify the format string property of the new measure to match the format of the original measure. In this case that should be the currency format.

5. Create the second calculated measure and name it `Reseller Sales YoY %`.

6. The definition of that measure should be the ratio of the current member's value against the parallel period member's value. Be sure to handle potential division by zero errors (see the recipe *Handling division by zero errors* in *Chapter 1, Elementary MDX Techniques*).

7. Include both calculated measures on axis `0` and execute the query, which should look like:

    ```
    WITH
    MEMBER [Measures].[Reseller Sales PP] As
        ( [Measures].[Reseller Sales Amount],
          ParallelPeriod( [Date].[Fiscal].[Fiscal Year], 1,
                          [Date].[Fiscal].CurrentMember ) )
        , FORMAT_STRING = 'Currency'
    MEMBER [Measures].[Reseller Sales YoY %] As
        iif( [Measures].[Reseller Sales PP] = 0, null,
             ( [Measures].[Reseller Sales Amount] /
               [Measures].[Reseller Sales PP] ) )
        , FORMAT_STRING = 'Percent'
    SELECT
        { [Measures].[Reseller Sales Amount],
          [Measures].[Reseller Sales PP],
          [Measures].[Reseller Sales YoY %] } ON 0,
        { [Date].[Fiscal].[Month].MEMBERS } ON 1
    FROM
        [Adventure Works]
    ```

8. The result will include two additional columns, one with the PP values and the other with the YoY change. Notice how the values in the second column repeat over time and that **YoY %** ratio shows the growth over time:

	Reseller Sales Amount	Reseller Sales PP	Reseller Sales YoY %
June 2007	$1,987,872.71	$1,001,803.77	198.43%
July 2007	$2,665,650.54	$2,393,689.53	111.36%
August 2007	$4,212,971.51	$3,601,190.71	116.99%
September 2007	$4,047,574.04	$2,885,359.20	140.28%
October 2007	$2,282,115.88	$1,802,154.21	126.63%
November 2007	$3,483,161.40	$3,053,816.33	114.06%
December 2007	$3,510,948.73	$2,185,213.21	160.67%
January 2008	$1,662,547.32	$1,317,541.83	126.19%
February 2008	$2,700,766.80	$2,384,846.59	113.25%
March 2008	$2,739,370.98	$1,563,955.08	175.16%
April 2008	$2,204,623.41	$1,865,278.43	118.19%
May 2008	$3,315,275.00	$2,880,752.68	115.08%
June 2008	$3,415,479.07	$1,987,872.71	171.82%
July 2008	(null)	$2,665,650.54	(null)

How it works...

The `ParallelPeriod()` function takes three arguments, a level expression, an index, and a member expression, and all three arguments are optional. The first argument indicates the level on which to look for that member's ancestor, typically the year level like in this example. The second argument indicates how many members to go back on the ancestor's level, typically one, as in this example. The last argument indicates the member for which the function is to be applied.

Given the right combination of arguments, the function returns a member that is in the same relative position as a specified member, under a new ancestor.

The value for the parallel period's member is obtained using a tuple which is formed with a measure and the new member. In our example, this represents the definition of the PP measure.

The growth is calculated as the ratio of the current member's value over the parallel period member's value, in other words, as a ratio of two measures. In our example, that was **YoY %** measure.

In our example we've also taken care of a small detail, setting the `FORMAT_STRING` to `Percent`.

There's more...

The `ParallelPeriod()` function is very closely related to time series, and typically used on date dimensions. However, it can be used on any type of dimension. For example, this query is perfectly valid:

```
SELECT
    { [Measures].[Reseller Sales Amount] } ON 0,
    { ParallelPeriod( [Geography].[Geography].[Country],
                      2,
                      [Geography].[Geography].[State-Province]
                        .&[CA]&[US] ) } ON 1
FROM
    [Adventure Works]
```

The query returns **Hamburg** on rows, which is the third state-province in the alphabetical list of states-provinces under **Germany**. **Germany** is two countries back from the **USA**, whose member **California**, used in this query, is the third state-province underneath that country in the `Geography.Geography` user hierarchy. We can verify this by browsing the **Geography** user hierarchy in the `Geography` dimension in SQL Server Management Studio, as shown in the following screenshot. The **UK** one member back from the **USA**, has only one state-province: **England**. If we change the second argument to 1 instead, we'll get nothing on rows because there's no third state-province under the **UK**. Feel free to try it:

All arguments of the `ParallelPeriod()` function are optional. When not specified, the first dimension of type `Time` in the measure group is used, more precisely, the previous member of the current member's parent. This can lead to unexpected results as discussed in the previous recipe. Therefore, it is recommended that you use all the arguments of the `ParallelPeriod()` function.

ParallelPeriod is not a time-aware function

The `ParallelPeriod()` function simply looks for the member from the prior period based on its relative position to its ancestor. For example, if your hierarchy is missing the first six months in the year 2005, for member January 2006, the function will find July 2005 as its parallel period (lagging by one year) because July is indeed the first month in the year 2005.

This is exactly the case in Adventure Works DW SSAS prior to 2012.

You can test the following scenario in Adventure Works DW SSAS 2008 R2.

In our example we used the `[Date].[Fiscal]` user hierarchy. That hierarchy has all 12 months in every year which is not the case with the `[Date].[Calendar]` user hierarchy where there's only six months in the first year. This can lead to strange results. For example, if you search-replace the word "Fiscal" with the word "Calendar" in the query we used in this recipe, you'll get this as the result:

	Internet Sales Amount	Internet Sales PP	Internet Sales YoY %
July 2005	$473,388.16	(null)	(null)
August 2005	$506,191.69	(null)	(null)
September 2005	$473,943.03	(null)	(null)
October 2005	$513,329.47	(null)	(null)
November 2005	$543,993.41	(null)	(null)
December 2005	$755,527.89	(null)	(null)
January 2006	$596,746.56	$473,388.16	126.06%
February 2006	$550,816.69	$506,191.69	108.82%
March 2006	$644,135.20	$473,943.03	135.91%
April 2006	$663,692.29	$513,329.47	129.29%
May 2006	$673,556.20	$543,993.41	123.82%
June 2006	$676,763.65	$755,527.89	89.57%
July 2006	$500,365.16	(null)	(null)
August 2006	$546,001.47	(null)	(null)
September 2006	$350,466.99	(null)	(null)
October 2006	$415,390.23	(null)	(null)
November 2006	$335,095.09	(null)	(null)
December 2006	$577,314.00	(null)	(null)

Notice how the values are incorrect for the year 2006. That's because the `ParallelPeriod()` function is not a time-aware function, it merely does what it's designed for taking the member that is in the same relative position. Gaps in your time dimension are another potential problem. Therefore, always make the complete date dimensions, with all 12 months in every year and all dates in them, not just working days or similar shortcuts. Remember, Analysis Services isn't doing the date math. It's just navigating using the member's relative position. Therefore, make sure you have laid a good foundation for that.

However, that's not always possible. There's an offset of six months between fiscal and calendar years, meaning if you want both of them as date hierarchies, you have a problem; one of them will not have all of the months in the first year.

The solution is to test the current member in the calculation and to provide a special logic for the first year, fiscal or calendar; the one that doesn't have all months in it. This is most efficiently done with a scope statement in the MDX script.

Another problem in calculating the YoY value is leap years. One possible solution for that is presented in this blog article: `http://tinyurl.com/LeapYears`

See also

  ▶   The `ParallelPeriod()` function operates on a single member. However, there are times when we will need to calculate the parallel period for a set of members. The recipes *Calculating parallel periods for multiple members in a set* and *Calculating parallel periods for multiple members in a slicer* deal with this more complex request.

Calculating moving averages

The moving average, also known as the rolling average, is a statistical technique often used in events with unpredictable short-term fluctuations in order to smooth their curve and to visualize the pattern of behavior.

The key to get the moving average is to know how to construct a set of members up to and including a specified member, and to get the average value over the number of members in the set.

In this recipe, we're going to look at two different ways to calculate moving averages in MDX.

Getting ready

Start SQL Server Management Studio and connect to your SSAS 2012 instance. Click on the **New Query** button and check that the target database is **Adventure Works DW 2012**.

In this example we're going to use the `Date` hierarchy of the `Date` dimension. Here's the query we'll start from:

```
SELECT
    { [Measures].[Internet Order Count] } ON 0,
    { [Date].[Date].[Date].MEMBERS} ON 1
FROM
    [Adventure Works]
```

Execute it. The result shows the count of Internet orders for each date in the `Date.Date` attribute hierarchy. Our task is to calculate the simple moving average (SMA) for dates in the year 2008 based on the count of orders in the previous 30 days.

How to do it...

We are going to use the `LastPeriods()` function with a 30 day moving window, and a member expression, `[Date].[Date].CurrentMember`, as two parameters, and also the `AVG()` function, to calculate the moving average of Internet order count in the last 30 days.

Follow these steps to calculate moving averages:

1. Add the `WHERE` part of the query and put the year `2006` inside using any available hierarchy.

2. Add the `WITH` part and define a new calculated measure. Name it `SMA 30`.

3. Define that measure using the `AVG()` and `LastPeriods()` functions.

4. Test to see if you get a managed query similar to this. If so, execute it:
    ```
    WITH
    MEMBER [Measures].[SMA 30] AS
    Avg( LastPeriods( 30, [Date].[Date].CurrentMember ),
    [Measures].[Internet Order Count] )
    SELECT
    { [Measures].[Internet Order Count],
    [Measures].[SMA 30] } ON 0,
    { [Date].[Date].[Date].MEMBERS } ON 1
    FROM
    [Adventure Works]
    WHERE
    ( [Date].[Calendar Year].&[2008] )
    ```

5. The second column in the result set will represent the simple moving average based on the last 30 days.

6. Our final result will look like the following screenshot:

	Internet Order Count	SMA 30
January 1, 2008	44	67
January 2, 2008	59	67
January 3, 2008	56	66
January 4, 2008	54	66
January 5, 2008	57	65
January 6, 2008	59	64
January 7, 2008	59	64
January 8, 2008	75	64
January 9, 2008	51	64
January 10, 2008	73	64
January 11, 2008	66	64

How it works...

The moving average is a calculation that uses the moving window of N items for which it calculates the statistical mean, that is, the average value. The window starts with the first item and then progressively shifts to the next one until the whole set of items is passed.

The function that acts as the moving window is the `LastPeriods()` function. It returns N items, in this example, 30 dates. That set is then used to calculate the average orders using the `AVG()` function.

Note that the number of members returned by the `LastPeriods()` function is equal to the span, 30, starting with the member that lags 30 - 1 from the specified member expression, and ending with the specified member.

There's more...

Another way of specifying what the `LastPeriods()` function does is to use a range of members with a range-based shortcut. The last member of the range is usually the current member of the hierarchy on an axis. The first member is the `N-1th` member moving backwards on the same level in that hierarchy, which can be constructed using the `Lag(N-1)` function.

The following expression employing the `Lag()` function and a range-based shortcut is equivalent to the `LastPeriods()` in the preceding example:

```
[Date].[Date].CurrentMember.Lag(29)  :  [Date].[Date].CurrentMember
```

Note that the members returned from the range-based shortcut are inclusive of both the starting member and the ending member.

We can easily modify the moving window scope to fit different requirements. For example, in case we need to calculate a 30-day moving average up to the previous member, we can use this syntax:

```
[Date].[Date].CurrentMember.Lag(30)  :  [Date].[Date].PrevMember
```

The `LastPeriods()` function is not on the list of optimized functions on this web page: `http://tinyurl.com/Improved2008R2`. However, tests show no difference in duration with respect to its range alternative. Still, if you come across a situation where the `LastPeriods()` function performs slowly, try its range alternative.

Finally, in case we want to parameterize the expression (for example, to be used in SQL Server Reporting Services), these would be generic forms of the previous expressions:

```
[Date].[Date].CurrentMember.Lag( @span - @offset )  :
```

```
[Date].[Date].CurrentMember.Lag( @offset )
```

And

```
LastPeriods( @span, [Date].[Date].CurrentMember.Lag( @offset ) )
```

The `@span` parameter is a positive value which determines the size of the window. The `@offset` parameter determines how much the right side of the window is moved from the current member's position. This shift can be either a positive or negative value. The value of zero means there is no shift at all, the most common scenario.

Other ways to calculate the moving averages

The simple moving average is just one of many variants of calculating the moving averages. A good overview of a possible variant can be found in Wikipedia:

```
http://tinyurl.com/WikiMovingAvg
```

MDX examples of other variants of moving averages can be found in *Mosha Pasumansky's* blog article:

```
http://tinyurl.com/MoshaMovingAvg
```

Moving averages and the future dates

It's worth noting that the value returned by the moving average calculation is not empty for dates in future because the window is looking backwards, so that there will always be values for future dates. This can be easily verified by scrolling down in our example using the `LastPeriods()` function, as shown in the following screenshot:

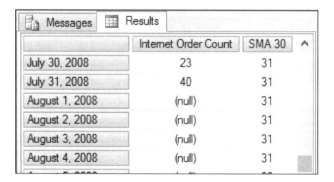

In this case the **NON EMPTY** keyword will not be able to remove empty rows.

We might be tempted to use `NON_EMPTY_BEHAVIOR` to solve this problem but it wouldn't help. Moreover, it would be completely wrong as explained in the previous chapter. We don't want to set all the empty rows to null, but only those positioned after the member representing today's date. We'll cover the proper approach to this challenge in the following recipes.

Finding the last date with data

In this recipe we're going to learn how to find the last date with data for a particular combination of members in the cube. We'll start with a general calculation, not dependent on the time context, and later show how to make it time-sensitive, if required so.

Getting ready

Open **SQL Server Data Tools** (**SSDT**) and then open **Adventure Works DW 2012** solution.
Double-click on the **Date** dimension found in the **Solution Explorer**. Select the `Date` attribute
and locate the property `ValueColumn` at the bottom of the **Properties** pane.

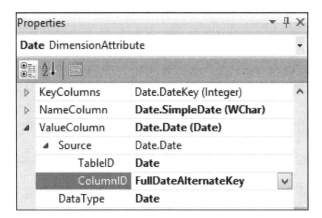

There's a value in that property. Column **FullDateAlternateKey**, of the **Date type**, is specified
as the `ValueColumn` of the key attribute property, the `Date` attribute. This check is important
because without that property filled correctly, this recipe won't work.

Next, start SQL Server Management Studio and connect to your SSAS 2012 instance. Click on
the **New Query** button and check that the target database is **Adventure Works DW 2012**.

In this example we're going to use the **Date** hierarchy of the `Date` dimension. Here's the query
we'll start from:

```
SELECT
    { [Measures].[Internet Order Count] } ON 0,
    { [Date].[Date].[Date].MEMBERS } ON 1
FROM
    [Adventure Works]
```

Execute it, and then scroll down to the end. By scrolling up again, try to identify the last date with data. It should be the **July 31, 2008** date, as highlighted in the following screenshot:

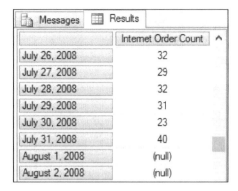

Now let's see how we can get this automatically, as the result of a calculation.

How to do it...

Follow these steps to create a calculated measure that returns the last date with data:

1. Add the WITH part of the query.

2. Create a new calculated measure there and name it Last date.

3. Use the Max() function with Date attribute members as its first argument.

4. The second argument should be the MemberValue() function applied on the current member of Date.Date.Date hierarchy, but only if the value of the Internet order count measure is not empty or 0.

5. Add the Last date measure on the columns axis.

6. Put the Promotion.Promotion hierarchy on rows instead.

7. Run the query which, should look like:

```
WITH
MEMBER [Measures].[Last date] AS
    Max( [Date].[Date].[Date].MEMBERS,
        iif( [Measures].[Internet Order Count] = 0,
            null,
            [Date].[Date].CurrentMember.MemberValue
        )
    )
SELECT
    { [Measures].[Internet Order Count],
      [Measures].[Last date] } ON 0,
    { [Promotion].[Promotion].MEMBERS } ON 1
FROM
    [Adventure Works]
```

8. The result will show the last date of Internet orders for each promotion as shown in the following screenshot:

	Internet Order Count	Last date
All Promotions	27,659	7/31/2008
No Discount	27,119	7/31/2008
Volume Discount 11 to 14	2,075	6/30/2008
Volume Discount 15 to 24	(null)	(null)
Volume Discount 25 to 40	(null)	(null)
Volume Discount 41 to 60	(null)	(null)
Volume Discount over 60	(null)	(null)
Mountain-100 Clearance Sale	(null)	(null)
Sport Helmet Discount-2002	(null)	(null)
Road-650 Overstock	(null)	(null)
Mountain Tire Sale	(null)	(null)
Sport Helmet Discount-2003	(null)	(null)
LL Road Frame Sale	(null)	(null)
Touring-3000 Promotion	20	9/28/2007
Touring-1000 Promotion	13	9/23/2007
Half-Price Pedal Sale	(null)	(null)
Mountain-500 Silver Clearance Sale	(null)	(null)

How it works...

The **Date** dimension in the **Adventure Works DW 2012** database is designed in such a way that we can conveniently use the MemberValue() function on the Date attribute in order to get the date value for each member in that hierarchy. This best practice act allows us to use that value inside the Max() function and hence get the member with the highest value, the last date.

The other thing we must do is to limit the search only to dates with Internet orders. The inner iif() statement, which provides null for dates with no Internet orders, not only takes care of that, but it also makes the set sparse and therefore allows for block-mode evaluation of the outer Max() function.

Since the data type of the ValueColumn property is defined as **Date** for the Date attribute, the result of the MemberValue() function is a typed value, that is, a date type. The role of this date type is two-fold in this recipe. One, it allow us to use the member value inside the Max() function, which returns the maximum value representing the last date. Two, it allows the calculated measure [Last date] to be nicely formatted as a date without any additional coding.

Finally, the outer Max() function evaluates all the date values returned from the MemberValue() function over the set of all members in the Date hierarchy, and returns the maximum date value, which represents the last date.

In case there was no `ValueColumn` property defined on the `Date.Date` attribute, we could use the `Name`, `Caption` or some other property to identify the last date or to use it in further calculations.

There's more...

In the previous example, the `Max()` function was used on all dates in the `Date.Date` hierarchy. As such, it is relatively inflexible. This means that it won't react to other hierarchies of the same dimension on axes which would normally reduce that set of dates. In other words, there are situations when the expression has to be made context-sensitive so that it changes in respect to other hierarchies of the same dimension. How do we achieve that? Using the `EXISTING` operator in front of the set!

For example, let us run the following query:

```
WITH
MEMBER [Measures].[Last date] AS
    Max( [Date].[Date].[Date].MEMBERS,
        iif( [Measures].[Internet Order Count] = 0,
            null,
            [Date].[Date].CurrentMember.MemberValue
        )
    )
MEMBER [Measures].[Last existing date] AS
    Max( EXISTING [Date].[Date].[Date].MEMBERS,
        iif( [Measures].[Internet Order Count] = 0,
            null,
            [Date].[Date].CurrentMember.MemberValue
        )
    )
SELECT
    { [Measures].[Internet Order Count],
      [Measures].[Last date],
      [Measures].[Last existing date] } ON 0,
    { [Date].[Calendar Year].MEMBERS } ON 1
FROM
    [Adventure Works]
WHERE
( [Sales Territory].[Sales Territory Country].&[France]    )
```

Now, values in the second column (the **Last date** measure) will all be the same – showing **07/29/2008**. On the other hand, values in the third column represent the last date for which we have Internet orders for each calendar year on the rows axis and therefore will differ, as seen in this screenshot:

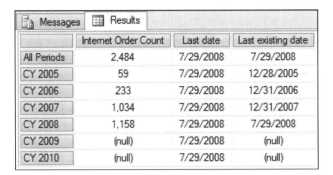

	Internet Order Count	Last date	Last existing date
All Periods	2,484	7/29/2008	7/29/2008
CY 2005	59	7/29/2008	12/28/2005
CY 2006	233	7/29/2008	12/31/2006
CY 2007	1,034	7/29/2008	12/31/2007
CY 2008	1,158	7/29/2008	7/29/2008
CY 2009	(null)	7/29/2008	(null)
CY 2010	(null)	7/29/2008	(null)

Those two types of calculation represent different things and should be used in the right context. In other words, if there is a need to get the last date no matter what, then that's a variant without the EXISTING part. In all other cases the EXISTING keywords should be used.

One thing is important to remember: the usage of the EXISTING keyword slows down the performance of the query. That's the cost we have to pay for having flexible calculations.

See also

▸ The next recipe, *Getting values on the last date with data* is relevant for this recipe because it shows how to return the value of measures on the last date with data.

Getting values on the last date with data

In this recipe we're going to learn how to get the value of a measure on the last date with data. If you haven't read the previous recipe, do so before reading this one as this recipe continues where the previous recipe stopped.

Getting ready

Start SQL Server Management Studio and connect to your SSAS 2012 instance. Click on the **New Query** button and check that the target database is **Adventure Works DW 2012**.

In this example we're going to use the simplified version of the query from the previous chapter, simplified in a sense that it has only one measure, the time-sensitive measure:

```
WITH
MEMBER [Measures].[Last existing date] AS
    Max( EXISTING [Date].[Date].[Date].MEMBERS,
            iif( [Measures].[Internet Order Count] = 0,
                null,
                [Date].[Date].CurrentMember.MemberValue
            )
        )
SELECT
    { [Measures].[Internet Order Count],
        [Measures].[Last existing date] } ON 0,
    { [Date].[Calendar Year].MEMBERS } ON 1
FROM
    [Adventure Works]
WHERE
( [Sales Territory].[Sales Territory Country].&[France]    )
```

The following screenshot shows the result of query execution:

	Internet Order Count	Last existing date
All Periods	2,484	7/29/2008
CY 2005	59	12/28/2005
CY 2006	233	12/31/2006
CY 2007	1,034	12/31/2007
CY 2008	1,158	7/29/2008
CY 2009	(null)	(null)
CY 2010	(null)	(null)

Now, let's see how to get the values on those last dates with data.

How to do it...

Follow these steps to get a measure's value on the last date with data:

1. Remove the `Last existing date` calculated measure from the `WITH` part of the query and from the columns axis.

2. Define a new calculated measure and name it `Value N`.

3. The definition of this new measure should be a tuple with two members, members we will identify or build in the following steps.

4. Use the `Internet Order Count` measure as one of the members in the tuple.

5. The other part of the tuple should be an expression which in its inner part has the `NonEmpty()` function applied over members of the `Date.Date` hierarchy and the measure `Internet Order Count`.

6. Use the `EXISTING` operator in front of the `NonEmpty()` function.

7. Extract the last member of that set using the `Tail()` function.

8. Convert the resulting set into a member using the `Item()` function.

9. The final query should look like:

```
WITH
MEMBER [Measures].[Value N] AS
    ( Tail( EXISTING
            NonEmpty( [Date].[Date].[Date].MEMBERS,
                      [Measures].[Internet Order Count] ),
            1
          ).Item(0),
      [Measures].[Internet Order Count] )
SELECT
    { [Measures].[Internet Order Count],
      [Measures].[Value N] } ON 0,
    { [Date].[Calendar Year].MEMBERS } ON 1
FROM
    [Adventure Works]
WHERE
( [Sales Territory].[Sales Territory Country].&[France]    )
```

10. Once executed, the result will show values of the measure `Internet Order Count` on the last dates with data, as visible in the following screenshot:

	Internet Order Count	Value N
All Periods	2,484	1
CY 2005	59	1
CY 2006	233	1
CY 2007	1,034	11
CY 2008	1,158	1
CY 2009	(null)	(null)
CY 2010	(null)	(null)

How it works...

The value of the last date with data is calculated from scratch. First, we have isolated dates with orders using the `NonEmpty()` function. Then we have applied the `EXISTING` operator in order to get dates relevant to the existing context. The `Tail()` function was used to isolate the last date in that set, while the `Item()` function converts that one-member set into a member.

Once we have the last date with data, we can use it inside the tuple with the measure of our interest, in this case, the `Internet Order Count` measure, to get the value in that coordinate.

There's more...

The `NonEmpty()` function we used in the earlier query for calculating the last date with data is not the only approach. We have several more options here, all of which make use of the `Last existing date` calculated measure from our previous recipe, *Finding the last date with data*, in which we've defined it as:

```
MEMBER [Measures].[Last existing date] AS
    Max( EXISTING [Date].[Date].[Date].MEMBERS,
            IIF( [Measures].[Internet Order Count] = 0,
                null,
                [Date].[Date].CurrentMember.MemberValue
            )
        )
```

Let's focus on a couple of other options that make use of the `Last existing date` calculated measure.

One approach is to use the `Filter()` function on all dates in order to find the one that has the same `MemberValue` as calculated in the measure Last existing date. However, that is the worst approach, the slowest one, and it shouldn't be used. The reason why it's slow is because the `Filter()` function needs to iterate over the complete set of dates in every cell in order to isolate a single date, the last one with data.

Since we already know the date we need, that is, the calculated measure `Last existing date`, you might think that we can simply form a tuple by putting together the `Last existing date` with `[Measures].[Internet Order Count]`. This will not work because `Last existing date` is a value, not a member. We cannot simply put a value in a tuple; we need a member because tuples are formed from members, not values.

The other approach is based on the idea that we might be able to convert that value into a member. Conversion can be done using the `StrToMember()` function, with the `CONSTRAINED` flag provided in it to enable faster execution of that function. Here are two expressions that work for the `Date` dimension in Adventure Works; they return the same result as shown in the previous screenshot:

```
MEMBER [Measures].[Value SN] AS
    iif( IsEmpty([Measures].[Last existing date]), null,
        ( StrToMember( '[Date].[Date].[' +
          Format( [Measures].[Last existing date],
                  "MMMM dd, yyyy" ) + ']', CONSTRAINED ),
          [Measures].[Internet Order Count] ) )
```

```
MEMBER [Measures].[Value SK] AS
    iif( IsEmpty([Measures].[Last existing date]), null,
        ( StrToMember( '[Date].[Date].&[' +
            Format( [Measures].[Last existing date],
                "yyyyMMdd" ) + ']', CONSTRAINED ),
            [Measures].[Internet Order Count] ) )
```

The first calculated measure (with the SN suffix) builds the member using its name, and the second one (with the SK suffix) using its key. The "S" stands for string-based solution; the "N" in the first solution in this recipe stands for nonempty-based solution.

Both expressions make use of the `Format()` function and apply the appropriate format for the date returned by the `Last existing date` calculated measure.

Since there might not be any date in a particular context, the `iif()` function is used to return null in those situations, otherwise the appropriate tuple is formed and its value is returned as the result of the expression.

Format members on the Date dimension properly

If you drag and drop any member from the `Date.Date.Date` level in the **Query Editor**, you will see its unique name. In case of **Adventure Works** cube, the unique name will look like:

```
[Date].[Date].&[20080701]
```

This is the key-based unique name for members on the `Date` dimension. To build a string, all you have to do is replace the part with the day, month, and year with the appropriate tokens in the format string. This web page might help in that: `http://tinyurl.com/FormatDate`

For the name-based member unique names you need to analyze the name of the member in the cube structure and match it with appropriate tokens in the format string. For the preceding key-based date member, the equivalent name-based member unique name is:
```
[Date].[Date].[July 1, 2008]
```

Optimizing time-non-sensitive calculation

Remember that in case you don't need a time-sensitive calculation, a calculation which evaluates the dates in each context (and hence is naturally slower because of that), you can use the same expressions provided in this recipe. Just remove the `EXISTING` operator in them.

Calculating today's date using the string functions

Calculating today's date is one of those problems every BI developer encounters sooner or later. It is also a repeatedly asked question on Internet forums; probably because books don't cover this topic at at all, or at least, not with concrete examples.

The `Date` dimension in the Adventure Works DW 2012 SSAS database has dates only up to December 31, 2010. If we are creating a current date expression that is after December 31, 2010, then the expression will not be valid. To overcome this little inconvenience, we will use string functions to only get the day and month of the current date, with the year being shifted to any year we need to.

In fact, this approach can not only explain the concept, well but also is generic enough so that you can apply it in your own SSAS database.

We are covering this intriguing topic in three recipes.

This recipe demonstrates the most intuitive technique of doing it, that is, generating today's date as a string and then converting that string into a dimension member. The other two recipes, following immediately after this one, show some not-so-intuitive but nevertheless perfectly valid and often better ways of performing the same thing. You are advised to read them all in order to get an overview of the possibilities.

Getting ready

Start SQL Server Management Studio and connect to your SSAS 2012 instance. Click on the **New Query** button and check that the target database is **Adventure Works DW 2012**.

Execute this query:

```
SELECT
    { } ON 0,
    { [Date].[Calendar].[Date].MEMBERS } ON 1
FROM
    [Adventure Works]
```

In this example we're using the `Calendar` hierarchy of the `Date` dimension. The result contains all the dates on rows and nothing on the columns. We've explained this type of query in the first recipe of the first chapter.

 Building the correct string for an Adventure Works cube is not a problem. Building the correct string for any database is almost impossible. The string has to be precise or it won't work. That's why we'll use the step-by-step approach here. We'll also highlight the important points for each step. Additionally, a step-by-step way is much easier to debug by visualizing which step is not calculating correctly. Hence, achieving the correct string for today's date becomes faster.

If you scroll down the results, you'll notice that there are only dates up to and including December 2010 and there is no date after that. As the last year that has sales amounts for the full year is 2007, we're going to build the current date for that year, for this recipe as well as for the next two recipes.

We'll also include a switch for shifting years which will allow you to apply the same recipe in any database.

How to do it...

Follow these steps to calculate today's date using VBA date time function `Now()` and string function `Format()`, and then finally using `StrToMember()` function to convert the string to a member on the Date dimension:

1. Add the `WITH` part in the query.

2. Define a new calculated measure using the VBA function `Now()` and try to match the name of date members. In case of Adventure Works cube, the required definition is this: `Format(Now(), 'MMMM dd, yyyy')`

3. Name the measure `Caption for Today` and include it in the query.

4. Execute the query and see how you matched the measure's value with the name of each member on rows. If it doesn't match, try to fix the format to fit your regional settings. This link provides detailed information about what each token represents: `http://tinyurl.com/FormatDate`

5. Add the second calculated measure with the following definition: `[Date].[Calendar].CurrentMember.UniqueName`

6. Name it `Member's Unique Name` and include it in the query.

7. Execute the query and notice the part of the measure's value that is not constant and that is changed in each row. Try to detect what the part is built from in terms of years, months, and dates or how it relates in general to dates on rows.

8. Add the third calculated measure by formatting the result of the `Now()` function based on the discoveries you made in the previous step. In other words, this: `Format(Now(), 'yyyyMMdd')`, because unique names are built using the yyyyMMdd sequence.

9. Name it `Key for Today` and include it in the query.

10. Execute the query. The value should repeat in every row giving you the current date formatted as yyyyMMdd.

11. In case of a database with no today's date in the `Date` dimension, such is the case here, add the fourth calculated measure. This measure should replace the year part with another year, already present in the `Date` dimension. That should be the year with all dates; otherwise, you'll get an error in subsequent steps of this recipe. The definition of that measure in case of the **Adventure Works** cube is this: `'2007' + Right([Measures].[Key for Today], 4)`.

12. Name it `Key for Today (AW)` and include it in the query.

13. Execute the query and find the row where that same key can be found as a part of the measure **Member's Unique Name**. If you can, that means you're doing everything fine so far.

14. Add the fifth calculated measure, name it `Today (string)` and define it by concatenating the fixed part of the unique name with the variable part defined as the measure `Key for Today` or `Key for Today (AW)`, depending on whether you have or don't have today's date in your `Date` dimension. In this example we'll use the latter because Adventure Works doesn't have it. This is the definition of the measure: `'[Date].[Calendar].[Date].&[' + [Measures].[Key for Today (AW)] + ']'`.

15. Include that fifth measure as well in the query and execute it. In that particular row mentioned earlier the value of this measure should match completely to the value of the measure **Member's Unique Name**.

16. Add a calculated set. Name it `Today` and define it using the `StrToMember()` function with the `CONSTRAINED` flag.

17. Execute the query. The set you just made represents today's date and can be used in all further calculations you make.

18. The final query is this:

```
WITH
MEMBER [Measures].[Caption for Today] AS
    Format(Now(), 'MMMM dd, yyyy')
MEMBER [Measures].[Member's Unique Name] AS
    [Date].[Calendar].CurrentMember.UniqueName
MEMBER [Measures].[Key for Today] AS
    Format(Now(), 'yyyyMMdd')
MEMBER [Measures].[Key for Today (AW)] AS
    '2007' + Right([Measures].[Key for Today], 4)
MEMBER [Measures].[Today (string)] AS
    '[Date].[Calendar].[Date].&[' +
  [Measures].[Key for Today (AW)] + ']'
SET [Today] AS
    StrToMember( [Measures].[Today (string)], CONSTRAINED )
SELECT
    { [Measures].[Caption for Today],
      [Measures].[Member's Unique Name],
    --[Measures].[Key for Today],
      [Measures].[Key for Today (AW)],
      [Measures].[Today (string)] } ON 0,
    { [Date].[Calendar].[Date].MEMBERS } ON 1
FROM
    [Adventure Works]
```

19. The result of your query should look like the following screenshot. There is one single row in which the `Today (string)` measure and the **Member's Unique Name** measure matches exactly, as visible in the screenshot. This row will differ from the row in your result since you are running the query on a different date. But you should nevertheless have such a row if you've followed the instructions carefully:

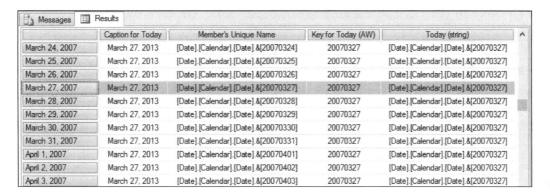

	Caption for Today	Member's Unique Name	Key for Today (AW)	Today (string)
March 24, 2007	March 27, 2013	[Date].[Calendar].[Date].&[20070324]	20070327	[Date].[Calendar].[Date].&[20070327]
March 25, 2007	March 27, 2013	[Date].[Calendar].[Date].&[20070325]	20070327	[Date].[Calendar].[Date].&[20070327]
March 26, 2007	March 27, 2013	[Date].[Calendar].[Date].&[20070326]	20070327	[Date].[Calendar].[Date].&[20070327]
March 27, 2007	March 27, 2013	[Date].[Calendar].[Date].&[20070327]	20070327	[Date].[Calendar].[Date].&[20070327]
March 28, 2007	March 27, 2013	[Date].[Calendar].[Date].&[20070328]	20070327	[Date].[Calendar].[Date].&[20070327]
March 29, 2007	March 27, 2013	[Date].[Calendar].[Date].&[20070329]	20070327	[Date].[Calendar].[Date].&[20070327]
March 30, 2007	March 27, 2013	[Date].[Calendar].[Date].&[20070330]	20070327	[Date].[Calendar].[Date].&[20070327]
March 31, 2007	March 27, 2013	[Date].[Calendar].[Date].&[20070331]	20070327	[Date].[Calendar].[Date].&[20070327]
April 1, 2007	March 27, 2013	[Date].[Calendar].[Date].&[20070401]	20070327	[Date].[Calendar].[Date].&[20070327]
April 2, 2007	March 27, 2013	[Date].[Calendar].[Date].&[20070402]	20070327	[Date].[Calendar].[Date].&[20070327]
April 3, 2007	March 27, 2013	[Date].[Calendar].[Date].&[20070403]	20070327	[Date].[Calendar].[Date].&[20070327]

How it works...

Basically, that's the query you get by following step-by-step instructions from the earlier example. With only one difference, the measure `Key for Today` is intentionally left out of the query, so that the result can fit the book size. You can leave it as is in your query, uncommented, to see its values.

The measure **Caption for Today** is there only to make you practice building the format string for dates; it has no significance for the final calculation. "MMMM" displays the full month name (that is **March**), "dd" displays the date using two digits (that is **27**), "yyyy" displays the 4-digit year.

The measure **Member's Unique Name** is here to show how the unique member's name is built, so that we can build the exact string using today's date as a variable part of that name. Again, it is not used in the final calculation; it's here just to help build the correct string.

The measure `Key for Today (AW)` is the one that's important. It is showing that the date dimension's key is an integer in the form of `yyyyMMdd`, built according to recommended best practice. In your real projects you might have a different key definition. There is no way of knowing in advance what the correct format should be for a particular `Date` dimension. Therefore, the second measure, **Member's Unique Name**, is here to enable us to identify the variable part of the unique name and to conclude how to build that part using date parts such as year, month, and date.

The measure `Today (string)` is the main part. Here we're actually building the final string. We're concatenating the fixed part of the unique name with the measure `Key for Today (AW)`.

Finally, we built a set named `Today` from that final string using the `StrToMember()` function.

The `CONSTRAINED` flag is used for two reasons. It automatically tells us if we've made a mistake in the string-building process. It also ensures that the evaluation is faster and hence the query performance will be faster as well.

The set `Today` can now be placed on the rows, replacing the members on the `Date` level of the `Date.Calendar` hierarchy in the previous query.

```
WITH
MEMBER [Measures].[Key for Today] AS
    Format(Now(), 'yyyyMMdd')
MEMBER [Measures].[Key for Today (AW)] AS
    '2007' + Right([Measures].[Key for Today], 4)
MEMBER [Measures].[Today (string)] AS
    '[Date].[Calendar].[Date].&[' +
  [Measures].[Key for Today (AW)] + ']'
SET [Today] AS
    StrToMember( [Measures].[Today (string)], CONSTRAINED )
SELECT
    { [Measures].[Key for Today],
      [Measures].[Key for Today (AW)],
      [Measures].[Today (string)] } ON 0,
    { [Today] } ON 1
FROM
    [Adventure Works]
```

The result will have only one row. The member on the row will be today's date with a shifted year.

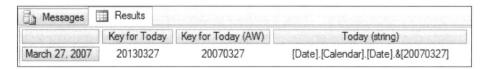

	Key for Today	Key for Today (AW)	Today (string)
March 27, 2007	20130327	20070327	[Date].[Calendar].[Date].&[20070327]

There's more...

A named set, contrary to a calculated member, preserves the original regular member. Regular members have a position in their level (also known as their ordinal), and they can have descendants, ancestors, and related members on other hierarchies of the same dimension. Sets can be placed in the slicer, or on columns or rows where they can interact with other dimensions. Calculated members do not have these features. They are placed as the last child of a regular member they are defined on and are not related to any other members except the root member of other hierarchies of the same dimension. The idea of creating a named set for today's date, not a calculated member, has opened up a lot of possibilities for us.

Another thing worth pointing out here is that using `Now()` in a calculated member stops the use of formula engine cache. See here for more info: `http://tinyurl.com/FormulaCacheChris`

The conversion from a set made of a single member to member, or shall we say, extraction of a single member in that set, is made relatively easy by using: `[Today].Item(0)`. Actually, we should specify `.Item(0).Item(0)`, but since there's only one hierarchy in the tuple forming that set, one `.Item(0)` is enough.

Defining new calculated measures is also easy. Today's sales measure would be defined like this: `([Today].Item(0), [Measures].[Internet Sales Amount] )`.

Relative periods

The opportunity doesn't stop there. Once we have a named set, **Today**, for today's date, all other relative periods follow easily. Here are some examples. Again, we're defining sets, not calculated members:

```
SET [Yesterday] AS [Today].Item(0).PrevMember
SET [This Month] AS [Today].Item(0).Parent
SET [Prev Month] AS [This Month].Item(0).PrevMember
SET [This Year] AS [Today].Item(0).Parent.Parent.parent.Parent
SET [Prev Year] AS [This Year].Item(0).PrevMember
SET [This Month Prev Year] AS [This Month].Item(0).Lag(12)
```

Moreover, you can anticipate the need for past or future relative periods and implement sets like `[Next month]`, `[1-30 days ahead]`, `[31-60 days ahead]`, and so on.

In the case of role-playing dimensions, you can build independent sets for each role-playing dimension, that is, `[Today]` and `[Due Today]` sets, each pointing to today's system date in its own dimension (and hierarchy).

Potential problems

Sets have many features that calculated members do not have. The ideal solution would be to construct the `Today` set, defining other relative periods as sets relative to the `Today` set. However, some SSAS frontend tools have problems working with sets. For example, you cannot put a named set on filters in an Excel 2007 or Excel 2010 PivotTable. If that's the case, you must be ready to make compromises by defining today's date instead as a calculated member, as explained earlier. You might also read the following recipes to find alternative solutions.

See also

▸ The recipes *Calculating today's date using the MemberValue function* and *Calculating today's date using an attribute hierarchy* provide an alternative solution to calculating today's date. You should read all of them in order to understand the pros and cons of each approach.

Calculating today's date using the MemberValue function

The second way to calculate today's date is by using the `MemberValue()` function. This is something we've already used in the *Finding the last date with data* recipe. In case you haven't read it yet, do so before continuing with this recipe, at least the part that shows the `ValueColumn` property.

Getting ready

Open SQL Server Data Tools (SSDT) and then open **Adventure Works DW 2012** solution. Double-click on the **Date** dimension found in the **Solution Explorer**. Select the `Date` attribute and locate the `ValueColumn` property. It should not be empty; otherwise this recipe won't work. It should have the `Date` type column from the underlying time dimension table.

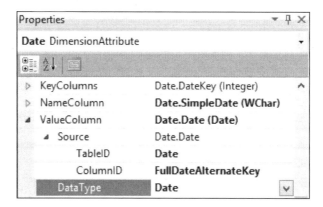

How to do it...

Follow these steps to calculate today's date using the `MemberValue` function:

1. Write and execute the following query in SQL Server Management Studio connected to the same cube mentioned earlier:

```
WITH
MEMBER [Measures].[Caption for Today] AS
    Format(Now(), 'MMMM dd, yyyy')
MEMBER [Measures].[Member Value] AS
    [Date].[Calendar].CurrentMember.MemberValue
MEMBER [Measures].[MV for Today] AS
    Format(Now(), 'M/d/yyyy')
MEMBER [Measures].[MV for Today (AW)] AS
    CDate( Left( [Measures].[MV for Today],
```

```
                    Len([Measures].[MV for Today]) - 4) + '2007'
        )
SET [Today] AS
    Filter( [Date].[Calendar].[Date].MEMBERS,
            [Measures].[Member Value] =
            [Measures].[MV for Today (AW)] )
SELECT
    { [Measures].[Caption for Today],
      [Measures].[Member Value],
      [Measures].[MV for Today],
      [Measures].[MV for Today (AW)] } ON 0,
    { [Date].[Calendar].[Date].MEMBERS } ON 1
FROM
    [Adventure Works]
```

2. Then use this query to test the `Today` set:

```
WITH
MEMBER [Measures].[Member Value] AS
    [Date].[Calendar].CurrentMember.MemberValue
MEMBER [Measures].[MV for Today] AS
    Format(Now(), 'M/d/yyyy')
MEMBER [Measures].[MV for Today (AW)] AS
    CDate( Left( [Measures].[MV for Today],
                 Len([Measures].[MV for Today]) - 4) + '2007'
          )
SET [Today] AS
    Filter( [Date].[Calendar].[Date].MEMBERS,
            [Measures].[Member Value] =
            [Measures].[MV for Today (AW)] )
SELECT
    { [Measures].[Member Value],
      [Measures].[MV for Today],
      [Measures].[MV for Today (AW)] } ON 0,
    { [Today] } ON 1
FROM
    [Adventure Works]
```

3. The result should contain only a single row with today's date.

	Member Value	MV for Today	MV for Today (AW)
March 28, 2007	3/28/2007	3/28/2013	3/28/2007

How it works...

The first query is used to build the `Today` set in a step-by-step fashion. The first measure **Caption for Today** is used for testing the behavior of various date part tokens. The next measure **Member Value** is used to extract the `MemberValue` from each date found on the rows and is later used in the set `Today`'s definition. The third measure, **MV for Today**, is the main measure. Its definition is obtained by deducing the correct format for the `MemberValue` from the observations made by analyzing the values in the previous measure **Member Value**. The step-by-step process is explained in the previous recipe, *Calculating today's date using the string functions*.

As the **Adventure Works** solution doesn't have the current date, we're forced to shift it to the year 2007. The day and month stay the same. This is implemented in the fourth measure: `MV for Today (AW)`. Finally, the set `Today` is defined using a `Filter()` function which returns only one member, the one where the `MemberValue` is equal to the `MV for Today (AW)` measure's value.

The second query is here to verify the result. It consists of three measures relevant to the set's condition and the set `Today` itself.

There's more...

The recipe *Calculating today's date using the string functions* explains how to enhance the cube design by adding relative periods in the form of additional sets. Look for the *Related periods* section of that recipe, which is also applicable to this recipe.

Using the ValueColumn property in the Date dimension

Many SSAS frontends use the so-called **Time Intelligence** implementation. That means they enable the usage of special MDX functions, such as `YTD()`, `ParallelPeriod()`, and others in their GUI. The availability of those functions is often determined by dimension type (has to be of the type `Date`) and by the existence of the `ValueColumn` property typed as `Date` on the key attribute of the dimension, or both. Specifically, Excel 2007 and Excel 2010 look for the latter. Be sure to check those things when you're working on your date dimension.

Here's a link to the document which explains how to design cubes for Excel:
`http://tinyurl.com/DesignCubesForExcel`

See also

> ▶ *Calculating today's date using the string functions* and *Calculating today's date using an attribute hierarchy* are the recipes which provide an alternative solution to calculating today's date. You should read both of them in order to understand the pros and cons of each approach.

Calculating today's date using an attribute hierarchy

The third way to calculate today's date is by using an attribute hierarchy. This is potentially the best way.

Instead of all the complexity with sets, strings, and other things in the previous two recipes, here we simply add a new column to the Date table and have the ETL maintain a flag for today's date. Then we slice by that attribute instead of using the Now() function in MDX. Plus, we don't have to wait to switch to "tomorrow" in MDX queries until the ETL completes and the cube is processed.

Getting ready

Open the **Adventure Works DW 2012** solution in SSDT. Double-click on the **Adventure Works DW** data source view. Locate the **Date** dimension in the left **Tables** pane and click on it.

How to do it...

Follow these steps to calculate today's date using an attribute hierarchy:

1. Right-click on the **Date** table and select **New Named Calculation**.

2. Enter Today for **Column Name** and this for the **Expression**:

```
case when convert(varchar(8), FullDateAlternateKey, 112) =
        convert(varchar(8), GetDate(), 112)
    then 'Yes'
    else 'No'
end
```

3. Close the dialog and explore that table. No record will have **Yes** in the last column.

4. Since we're on Adventure Works, which doesn't have the current date, we have to adjust the calculation by shifting it to the year 2007. Define the new **Named Calculation** using this formula and name it Today AW:

```
case when convert(varchar(8), FullDateAlternateKey, 112) =
        '2007' +
        right(convert(varchar(8), GetDate(), 112), 4)
    then 'Yes'
    else 'No'
end
```

5. Close the dialog and explore that table. You should notice that this time, one row in the year 2007 has **Yes** in the last column. It will be the row with the day and month the same as your system's day and month.

6. Save and close data source view.

7. Double-click on the **Date** dimension in the **Solution Explorer**.

8. Drag the **Today AW** column from the **Date** dimension table to the list of attributes on the left side. Leave the relation to the key attribute as it is flexible. This will be the only attribute of that kind in this dimension. All others should be rigid.

9. Save, deploy, and process the full **Date** dimension.

10. Double-click on the **Adventure Works** cube in the **Solution Explorer**, navigate to the **Browser** tab, and click on a button to process the cube.

11. Once it is processed, click on the **Reconnect** button and drag the **Internet Sales Amount** measure in data part of the browser.

12. Add the `[Date].[Calendar]` hierarchy onto the rows and expand it a few times. Notice that all the dates are here.

13. Add the `[Date].[Today AW]` hierarchy into the slicer and uncheck the **No** member in it. Notice that the result contains only the current date. You can do the same using any other hierarchy of the **Date** dimension; all will be sliced by our new attribute.

How it works...

This recipe depends on the fact that SSAS implements the so-called `auto-exists` algorithm. The main characteristic of it is that when two hierarchies of the same dimension are found in the query, the one in the slicer automatically reduces the other on the axis so that only some of the members remain there, those for which an intersection exists.

In other words, if we put the `Yes` member into the slicer, as we did a moment ago, only those years, months, quarters, days in the week, and so on, that are valid for today's date remain, meaning the current year, month, day in the week, and so on. Only one member from each hierarchy will remain.

The same query will give different results each day. That is exactly what we wanted to achieve. The usage is fairly simple – dragging the `Yes` member into slicer, which should be possible in any SSAS frontend.

The beauty of this solution lies not only in the elegance of creating queries, but in the fact that it is the fastest method for implementing the logic for today's date. Attribute relations offer better performance than string-handling functions and filtering.

There's more...

The solution doesn't have to stop with the `[Date].[Today AW]` hierarchy. We can add `Today` as a set in the MDX script. This time, however, we'll have to use the `Exists()` function in order to get the related members of other hierarchies. Later on we can use navigational functions to take the right part of the hierarchy.

For example, `Today` should be defined like this:

```
SET [Today] AS
    Exists( [Date].[Calendar].[Date].MEMBERS,
            [Date].[Today AW].&[Yes] )
```

Once we have the `Today` named set, other variants are easy to derive from it. We've covered some of them in the recipe *Calculating today's date using the string functions*.

However, be aware that named sets, when used inside aggregating functions like `Sum()` and others, will prevent the use of block evaluation. Here's a link to the page that talks about which things are improved and which aren't in SQL Server 2008 R2 Analysis Services: `http://tinyurl.com/Improved2008R2`

Member Yes as a default member?

Short and simple – DON'T! This might cause problems when other hierarchies of the **Date** dimension are used in slicer. That is, users of your cube might accidentally force a coordinate which does not exist.

For example, if they decide to put January in the slicer when the default **Yes** member implies the current quarter is not **Q1** but let's say **Q4**, they'll get an empty result without understanding what happened and why.

A solution exists, though. In such cases they should add the `All` member of the `[Date].`
`[Today AW]` hierarchy in the slicer as well, to remove restrictions imposed by the default member. The question is – will you be able to explain that to your users?

A better way is to instruct them to explicitly put the **Yes** member in the slicer whenever required. Yes, that's extra work for them, but this way they will have control over the context and not be surprised by it.

Other approaches

There's another method and that is using many-to-many relationships. The advantage of doing this over creating new attributes on the same dimension is that we only expose a single new hierarchy, even if it is on a new dimension.

See also

> ▶ The recipes *Calculating today's date using the string functions* and *Calculating today's date using the MemberValue function* are the ones which provide an alternative solution to calculating today's date. You should read both of them in order to understand the pros and cons of each approach.

Calculating the difference between two dates

This recipe shows how to calculate the difference between two dates. We're going to use promotions as an example, and calculate the time span of a promotion, from the start date to the end date.

Getting ready

Start SQL Server Management Studio and connect to your SSAS 2012 instance. Click on the **New Query** button and check that the target database is **Adventure Works DW 2012**. Then execute this query:

```
SELECT
    { [Measures].[Reseller Order Count] } ON 0,
    { [Promotion].[Start Date].[Start Date].MEMBERS *
    [Promotion].[End Date].[End Date].MEMBERS } ON 1
FROM
    [Adventure Works]
WHERE
    ( [Promotion].[Promotion Type].&[Discontinued Product] )
```

The query shows that the `Discontinued Product` promotion appeared twice with various time spans. Our task is to calculate how many days it lasted each time.

How to do it...

Follow these steps to calculate the difference between two dates:

1. Add the `WITH` part of the query.

2. Define two calculated measures that are going to collect the `ValueColumn` property of the `Start Date` and `End Date` hierarchies of the `Promotion` dimension.

3. Define the third calculated measure as `Number of days` using the VBA function `DateDiff()` and the two helper-calculated measures defined a moment ago. Be sure to increase the second date by one in order to calculate the duration, meaning that both start and end dates will count.

4. Include all three calculated measures on the columns and run the query, which should look like the following:

```
WITH
MEMBER [Measures].[Start Date] AS
    [Promotion].[Start Date].CurrentMember.MemberValue
MEMBER [Measures].[End Date] AS
```

```
        [Promotion].[End Date].CurrentMember.MemberValue
    MEMBER [Measures].[Number of days] AS
        DateDiff('d', [Measures].[Start Date],
                [Measures].[End Date] + 1)
    SELECT
        { [Measures].[Reseller Order Count],
          [Measures].[Start Date],
          [Measures].[End Date],
          [Measures].[Number of days] } ON 0,
        { [Promotion].[Start Date].[Start Date].MEMBERS *
          [Promotion].[End Date].[End Date].MEMBERS } ON 1
    FROM
        [Adventure Works]
    WHERE
        ( [Promotion].[Promotion Type].&[Discontinued Product] )
```

5. Check your result. It should look like this:

		Reseller Order Count	Start Date	End Date	Number of days
May 15, 2006	June 30, 2006	24	5/15/2006	6/30/2006	47
May 1, 2008	June 30, 2008	62	5/1/2008	6/30/2008	61

How it works...

DateDiff() is a VBA function. It can also be found in T-SQL. What we have to do is specify the time interval in which we'd like the difference to be expressed. In our case, we used the d token which corresponds to the day interval.

The duration is calculated as a difference plus one because both boundaries must be included. In the second row, it's easy to see that the 31 days in May and 30 days in June must equal 61.

There's more...

DateDiff() expects the date type items as its second and third arguments. Luckily, we had exactly the required type in the ValueColumn property. This can be checked by opening SSDT and analyzing the Start Date and End Date hierarchy on the Promotion dimension. If it weren't the case, we would have to convert them into Date type and use them in the DateDiff() function. Here are a couple of working examples using a VBA function CDate() to convert a valid date expression into a Date type:

```
CDate( '2013-03-28' )

CDate( [Promotion].[Start Date].CurrentMember.Name )
```

Dates in other scenarios

The example in this recipe highlighted a case where the two dates were found on two different hierarchies. That will not always be so. There will be situations when you'll only have a single date hierarchy or no dates at all.

There are two ways to get those dates. You can calculate them in the form of two measures as we did in this recipe or locate them on the `Date` hierarchy of your `Date` dimension.

The example illustrated in this recipe used the `DateDiff()` function, a good fit for the approach with measures since the two dates are from two different hierarchies. We should convert the value of measures (or expressions) to an appropriate date type (if it isn't already so), because the `DateDiff()` function requires dates.

The other approach is to locate the dates on one single `Date` hierarchy. For example, you can calculate the number of consecutive days with no change in quantity of products in the warehouse by locating a range of members on the `Date` hierarchy.

In that case, there's no need for `DateDiff()`. Simply form a range of members by employing the range-based shortcut, specifying the first date followed by a colon and then the second date. Finally, count the members in that set using the `Count()` function. Here is a working example of using the range-based shortcut and the `Count()` function:

```
Count([Date].[Date].&[20080101]:[Date].[Date].&[20080301])
```

Actually, the usage of the `Count()` function might turn off block computation, so use its `Sum()` alternative:

```
Sum( {<member1> : <member2> }, 1 )
```

Where `<member1>` and `<member2>` are placeholders for the range.

This will give you the same count of members in that range, but the `Sum()` function is optimized to work in block mode while `Count()` over a range is not.

When the members in that range are dates (which will typically be so), counting them will return the duration in days. If you need a different granularity (let's say the number of weeks, hours, or minutes), simply multiply the duration in days with the appropriate factor (1/7, 24 or 24*60, respectively). Additionally, for the `DateDiff()` function, you can provide the appropriate first argument. See here for options: `http://tinyurl.com/DateDiffExcel`

The problem of non-consecutive dates

A problem will arise if dates are not consecutive, that is, if some of them are missing in your date dimension. Here we are referring to weekends, holidays, and others which are sometimes left out of the date dimension guided by the thinking that there's no data in them, so why include them in the dimension? You should know that such a design is not recommended and the solution provided in this recipe will not work. Moreover, this will not be the only problem you'll encounter with this bad design. Therefore, consider redesigning your date dimension or look for alternative solutions listed in the **See also** section of this recipe.

See also

▶ When the dates are close to one another, you might want to calculate the time difference instead. This is described in the following recipe, *Calculating the difference between two times*.

Calculating the difference between two times

This recipe is similar to the previous one, but here we'll show how to calculate the difference in time and format the duration appropriately.

By time we mean everything on and beneath the day granularity. What is specific about time is that all periods are proportionally divided. A day has 24 hours, an hour has 60 minutes, and a minute has 60 seconds. On the other hand, the above-day granularity is irregular—days in a month vary throughout the year, and days in the year vary on leap years.

The nice thing about having proportional periods is that we can present the result in various units. For example, we can say that an event lasted for 48 hours but we can also say two days. On the other hand, we can say two days, but we cannot say 0.06 months because a month is not a constant unit of time.

This ability to format time duration in various units will be demonstrated in the following example as well.

Getting ready

The **Adventure Works** database doesn't contain any attribute or measure that has hours, minutes, or seconds. Hence we will create two calculated measures, one representing the start and the other representing the end of an event. Here are those measures:

```
WITH
MEMBER [Measures].[Start Time] AS
    CDate('2010-09-18 00:40:00')
MEMBER [Measures].[End Time] AS
    CDate('2010-09-21 10:27:00')
SELECT
    { } ON 0
FROM
    [Adventure Works]
```

How to do it...

Follow these steps to calculate the difference between two times:

1. Define a new calculated measure as a difference of two initial measures introduced earlier and name it `Duration in days`.

2. Put that new measure on axis 0 as a single measure and run the query which should look like:

```
WITH
MEMBER [Measures].[Start Time] AS
    CDate('2010-09-18 00:40:00')
MEMBER [Measures].[End Time] AS
    CDate('2010-09-21 10:27:00')
MEMBER [Measures].[Duration in days] AS
    [Measures].[End Time] - [Measures].[Start Time]
SELECT
    { [Measures].[Duration in days] } ON 0
FROM
    [Adventure Works]
```

3. The result represents the number of days between those two events.

How it works...

Each event has a starting point and an ending point. If those points in time are represented as dates, being the date type, then we can apply the simple operation of subtraction in order to get the duration of that event. In case those were not date type points, we should convert them into the date format, as shown in this example (string to date conversion using the `CDate()` VBA function).

There's more...

It is possible to shift the result into another time unit. For example, we can calculate the duration in hours by multiplying the initial expression with the number of hours in a day.

```
MEMBER [Measures].[Duration in hours] AS
    ([Measures].[End Time] - [Measures].[Start Time]) * 24
    , FORMAT_STRING = '#,##0.0'
```

Add this member into the initial query and observe the results.

Likewise, we can get the duration in minutes and seconds if required. Multiplications are by 60 and 3600, respectively, in addition to 24 already there for the number of hours.

Formatting the duration

Duration values can be formatted. Here's an example that shows how the original `Duration` in days calculation can be formatted so that the decimal part becomes displayed in a well-understood `hh:mm:ss` format, where `hh` stands for hours, `mm` for minutes, and `ss` for seconds:

```
MEMBER [Measures].[My Format] AS
    iif([Measures].[Duration in days] > 1,
        CStr(Int([Measures].[Duration in days])) +
 '"  "', '"0  "')
    + 'hh:mm:ss'

MEMBER [Measures].[Duration d  hh:mm:ss] AS
    ([Measures].[End Time] - [Measures].[Start Time])
    , FORMAT_STRING = [Measures].[My Format]
```

Add this member into the initial query and observe the results.

Here is the screenshot showing all three calculated measures:

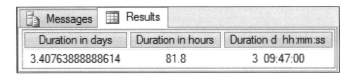

Notice that we've wrapped the expression for `FORMAT_STRING` in a separate calculated measure `My Format`. The reason for this is to improve the performance through caching. Only cell values are cached; expressions on the `FORMAT_STRING` are not cached. That's why it pays off to define them in separate measures.

Examples of formatting the duration on the web

Here are a few links with good examples of formatting the duration on the web:
`http://tinyurl.com/FormatDurationMosha`

`http://tinyurl.com/FormatDurationVidas`

Counting working days only

In case you're interested in counting working days only, Marco Russo, one of the reviewers of this book, presented his approach to this problem in his blog post: `http://tinyurl.com/WorkingDaysMarco`

See also

▶ When the dates are far from each other, you might want to calculate the date difference instead. This is described in the previous recipe, *Calculating the difference between two dates*.

Calculating parallel periods for multiple dates in a set

In the recipe *Calculating the YoY (Year-over-Year) growth (parallel periods)*, we've shown how the `ParallelPeriod()` function works and how it can be used to calculate the YoY growth. All we had to do is specify a member, ancestor's level, and an offset, and the parallel member was returned as a result.

OLAP works in discrete space and therefore many functions, `ParallelPeriod()` included, expect a single member as their argument. On the other hand, relational reports are almost always designed using a date range, with `Date1` and `Date2` parameters for many relational reports. As the relational reporting has a longer tradition than the multidimensional, people are used to thinking in ranges. They expect many multidimensional reports to follow the same logic. However, operating on a range is neither easy nor efficient. A cube designed with best practices can help, by eliminating the need for ranges and increasing the performance of the cube. A well-designed cube should have various attributes on the time dimension: months, weeks, quarters, and so on. They should cover common ranges and should be used instead of a range of random dates.

However, there are times when the cube design cannot cover all the combinations and the request for reports to operate on a range is quite legitimate. The question arises – can we do the same in OLAP as in relational reporting? Can we calculate the growth based on a range of members and not just a single member?

Yes, we can. The solution in MDX exists. This recipe shows how to calculate parallel periods with multiple dates defined as a set. The next recipe shows how to deal with a more complex case – when dates are present in the slicer.

Getting ready

We're going to make a simple query. We will analyze sales by colors for a date range that starts in December and ends just before Christmas. We'd like to analyze how we are doing in respect to the previous year, for the same period.

Start SQL Server Management Studio and connect to your SSAS 2012 instance. Click on the **New Query** button and check that the target database is **Adventure Works DW 2012**. Then execute this query:

```
WITH
MEMBER [Internet Sales CP] AS
    Sum( { [Date].[Calendar].[Date].&[20071201] :
           [Date].[Calendar].[Date].&[20071224] },
         [Measures].[Internet Sales Amount] )
SELECT
```

```
    { [Internet Sales CP] } ON 0,
    { [Product].[Color].MEMBERS } ON 1
FROM
    [Adventure Works]
```

The query has a date range. The aggregate of that range in the form of a sum is calculated in a calculated measure, which is then displayed for each color, and the total is included as the first row. The result is shown in the following screenshot:

	Internet Sales CP
All Products	$1,344,125.13
Black	$414,778.17
Blue	$199,369.56
Grey	(null)
Multi	$7,655.14
NA	$30,493.58
Red	$33,454.97
Silver	$249,941.51
Silver/Black	(null)
White	$395.56
Yellow	$408,036.64

The calculated measure **Internet Sales CP** tells us the sales for each product color during December just before Christmas in the year 2007, but it is not telling us how much better or worse we are doing. What we need is the sales during the same December date range, but in the previous year. With both sales during the same date range in two different years, we can then calculate the Year-over-Year percent values.

In the recipe *Calculating the YoY (Year-over-Year) growth (parallel periods)* in this chapter, we have learned about the `ParallelPeriod()` function. Our first attempt would be to write an expression such as:

```
( ParallelPeriod( [Date].[Calendar].[Calendar Year],
                  1,
                  [Date].[Calendar].CurrentMember ),
  [Measures].[Internet Sales Amount] )
```

This expression will only give us the sales for one date at a time. However, we have more than just one date. Our challenge in this recipe is to sum up the sales during all the dates in the previous year.

How to do it...

Follow these steps to calculate parallel periods for multiple dates in a set:

1. Define a new calculated measure, which returns the value for the same period but in the previous year. Name it `Internet Sales PP`, where `PP` stands for parallel period. The expression should look like:

```
MEMBER [Internet Sales PP] As
    Sum({ [Date].[Calendar].[Date].&[20071201] :
          [Date].[Calendar].[Date].&[20071224] },
        ( ParallelPeriod( [Date].[Calendar].[Calendar Year],
                          1,
                          [Date].[Calendar].CurrentMember ),
        [Measures].[Internet Sales Amount] )
      )
    , FORMAT_STRING = 'Currency'
```

2. Define another measure, `Internet Sales YoY %` as a ratio of the `PP` measure over `CP` measure. The expression should be as follows:

```
MEMBER [Internet Sales YoY %] As
    iif( [Internet Sales PP] = 0, null,
        ( [Internet Sales CP] / [Internet Sales PP] ) )
    , FORMAT_STRING = 'Percent'
```

3. Add both calculated measures to the query and execute it. The query should look like this:

```
WITH
MEMBER [Internet Sales CP] AS
    Sum( { [Date].[Calendar].[Date].&[20071201] :
           [Date].[Calendar].[Date].&[20071224] },
         [Measures].[Internet Sales Amount] )
MEMBER [Internet Sales PP] As
    Sum({ [Date].[Calendar].[Date].&[20071201] :
          [Date].[Calendar].[Date].&[20071224] },
        ( ParallelPeriod( [Date].[Calendar].[Calendar Year],
                          1,
                          [Date].[Calendar].CurrentMember ),
        [Measures].[Internet Sales Amount] )
      )
    , FORMAT_STRING = 'Currency'
MEMBER [Internet Sales YoY %] As
    iif( [Internet Sales PP] = 0, null,
        ( [Internet Sales CP] / [Internet Sales PP] ) )
    , FORMAT_STRING = 'Percent'
SELECT
```

```
     { [Internet Sales PP],
       [Internet Sales CP],
       [Internet Sales YoY %] } ON 0,
     { [Product].[Color].MEMBERS } ON 1
FROM
     [Adventure Works]
```

4. The results show that three colors had better results than before, one had worse
    (red), but the overall result is almost three times better. There were also four new
    colors in the current season:

	Internet Sales PP	Internet Sales CP	Internet Sales YoY %
All Products	$463,163.13	$1,344,125.13	290.21%
Black	$258,139.41	$414,778.17	160.68%
Blue	(null)	$199,369.56	(null)
Grey	(null)	(null)	(null)
Multi	(null)	$7,655.14	(null)
NA	(null)	$30,493.58	(null)
Red	$86,080.64	$33,454.97	38.86%
Silver	$84,928.20	$249,941.51	294.30%
Silver/Black	(null)	(null)	(null)
White	(null)	$395.56	(null)
Yellow	$34,014.88	$408,036.64	1199.58%

How it works...

In order to calculate the parallel period's value for a set of members (a range in this example),
we apply the same principle we use when calculating the value for the current season;
summarizing the value of a measure on that range by using the SUM() function.

The SUM() function takes a set expression and a numeric expression. The calculation for the
previous season differs only in the numeric expression. There we no longer use a measure
[Internet Sales Amount], but instead a tuple. That tuple is formed using the original
measure [Internet Sales Amount] combined with the parallel period's member. In other
words, we're reaching for the value in another coordinate and summing up those values.

The calculation for the YoY % ratio is very straightforward. We check the division by zero and
specify the appropriate format string.

There's more...

The other approach is to calculate another set, the previous season's range, and then apply the SUM() function. Here's the required expression:

```
MEMBER [Internet Sales PP] As
    Sum(
        Generate(
            { [Date].[Calendar].[Date].&[20071201] :
              [Date].[Calendar].[Date].&[20071224] },
            { ParallelPeriod( [Date].[Calendar]
                                       .[Calendar Year],
                              1,
                              [Date].[Calendar]
                                       .CurrentMember.Item(0) )
            } ),
        [Measures].[Internet Sales Amount] )
```

Here, we're iterating on the old set using the Generate() function in order to shift each member of that set to its parallel member.

Note that we deliberately skipped defining any named sets for this scenario because they, when used inside aggregating functions like Sum(), prevent the block evaluation. We should put the sets instead of named sets inside those functions.

One more thing for measures with non-linear aggregation functions (that is, the Distinct Count), the Aggregate() function should be used instead of Sum().

Parameters

The set of dates defined as a range can often be parameterized like this:

```
{ StrToMember( @Date1, CONSTRAINED ) :
  StrToMember( @Date2, CONSTRAINED ) }
```

This way, the query (or SSRS report) becomes equivalent to its relational reporting counterpart.

Reporting covered by design

▶ We mentioned in the introduction to this recipe that it is often possible to improve the performance of the queries operating on a range of members by modifying the cube design. How it's done is explained in more detail in *Using a new attribute to separate members on a level* recipe in *Chapter 7, When MDX is Not Enough*.

See also

▶ The recipes *Calculating the YoY (Year-over-Year) growth (parallel periods)* and *Calculating parallel periods for multiple dates in a slicer* deal with a similar topic.

▶ The `Generate()` function, very useful here, is also covered in the recipe *Iterating on a set in order to create a new one* in *Chapter 2, Working with Sets*.

Calculating parallel periods for multiple dates in a slicer

In the recipe *Calculating the YoY (Year-over-Year) growth (parallel periods)*, we've shown how the `ParallelPeriod()` function works when there's a single member involved. In *Calculating parallel periods for multiple dates in a set*, we've shown how to do the same, but on a range of members defined in a set. This recipe presents the solution to a special case, when the set of members is found in slicer.

Getting ready

We'll use the same case as in the previous recipe; we'll calculate the growth in the pre-Christmas season for each color of our products.

Start SQL Server Management Studio and connect to your SSAS 2012 instance. Click on the **New Query** button and check that the target database is **Adventure Works DW 2012**. Then execute this query:

```
SELECT
    { [Internet Sales Amount] } ON 0,
    { [Product].[Color].MEMBERS } ON 1
FROM
    [Adventure Works]
WHERE
    ( { [Date].[Calendar].[Date].&[20071201] :
        [Date].[Calendar].[Date].&[20071224] } )
```

The query returns the value of the **Internet Sales Amount** for each color. Notice that when the range is provided in slicer, there's no need to define new calculated measures as in the previous recipe; the SSAS engine automatically aggregates each measure using its aggregation function. Because of that, this is the preferred approach for implementing multi-select, although rarely found in SSAS frontends.

How to do it...

Follow these steps to calculate parallel periods for multiple dates in slicer:

1. Define a new calculated member. Name it `Internet Sales PP`. The definition for it should be the sum of the parallel period's values on existing dates of the `Date.Calendar` hierarchy.

```
MEMBER [Internet Sales PP] As
    Sum( EXISTING [Date].[Calendar].[Date].MEMBERS,
        ( ParallelPeriod( [Date].[Calendar].[Calendar Year],
                          1,
                          [Date Range].Current.Item(0) ),
        [Measures].[Internet Sales Amount] )
        )
    , FORMAT_STRING = 'Currency'
```

2. Add another calculated measure. Name it `Internet Sales YoY %` and define it as a ratio of the original **Internet Sales Amount** measure over the `Internet Sales PP` measure. Be sure to implement a test for division by zero.

3. Add both calculated measures on the columns axis.

4. The final query should look like this:

```
WITH
MEMBER [Internet Sales PP] As
    Sum( EXISTING [Date].[Calendar].[Date].MEMBERS,
        ( ParallelPeriod( [Date].[Calendar].[Calendar Year],
                          1,
                          [Date].[Calendar].CurrentMember ),
        [Measures].[Internet Sales Amount] )
        )
    , FORMAT_STRING = 'Currency'
MEMBER [Internet Sales YoY %] As
    iif( [Internet Sales PP] = 0, null,
        ( [Measures].[Internet Sales Amount] /
            [Internet Sales PP] ) )
    , FORMAT_STRING = 'Percent'
SELECT
    { [Internet Sales PP],
      [Internet Sales Amount],
      [Internet Sales YoY %] } ON 0,
    { [Product].[Color].MEMBERS } ON 1
FROM
    [Adventure Works]
WHERE
    ( { [Date].[Calendar].[Date].&[20071201] :
        [Date].[Calendar].[Date].&[20071224] } )
```

5. Execute it and observe the results. They should match the results in the previous recipe because the same date range was used in both recipes.

	Internet Sales PP	Internet Sales Amount	Internet Sales YoY %
All Products	$463,163.13	$1,344,125.13	290.21%
Black	$258,139.41	$414,778.17	160.68%
Blue	(null)	$199,369.56	(null)
Grey	(null)	(null)	(null)
Multi	(null)	$7,655.14	(null)
NA	(null)	$30,493.58	(null)
Red	$86,080.64	$33,454.97	38.86%
Silver	$84,928.20	$249,941.51	294.30%
Silver/Black	(null)	(null)	(null)
White	(null)	$395.56	(null)
Yellow	$34,014.88	$408,036.64	1199.58%

How it works...

For the purpose of the comparison between the solution in this recipe and that of the previous recipe, *Calculating parallel periods for multiple dates in a set*, we are repeating the calculated members here:

```
-- Sum up the sales over a set of dates from previous year
MEMBER [Internet Sales PP] As
    Sum( { [Date].[Calendar].[Date].&[20071201] :
           [Date].[Calendar].[Date].&[20071224] },
         ( ParallelPeriod( [Date].[Calendar].[Calendar Year],
                           1,
                           [Date].[Calendar].CurrentMember ),
           [Measures].[Internet Sales Amount] )
    )


-- Sum up the sales over a set of dates from previous year
-- when the set of dates for the current year is on the slicer
MEMBER [Internet Sales PP] As
    Sum( EXISTING [Date].[Calendar].[Date].MEMBERS,
         ( ParallelPeriod( [Date].[Calendar].[Calendar Year],
                           1,
                           [Date].[Calendar].CurrentMember ),
           [Measures].[Internet Sales Amount] )
    )
```

Note that the only difference is in the set expression for the SUM() function. To detect the multiple members, or a set, in the slicer, we have to use the EXISTING keyword. The EXISTING keyword forces the specified set, that is, the dates on the Calendar hierarchy to be evaluated within the current contexts in the slicer. It serves the purpose of collecting all the members on the leaf level, the Date level in this case, that are valid for the current context. Since the slicer is the part of a query which establishes the context, this is a way in which we can detect a currently selected range of members (or any current member on axes in general).

Once we know the dates from the slicer, we can use that range to sum the values of the measure in the parallel period.

Finally, the ratio **YoY %** is calculated using both measures, **Internet Sales Amount** and **Internet Sales PP**.

There's more...

We can never know exactly what was in the slicer, only "see the shadow" of it. Let's see why.

There are two MDX functions which serve the purpose of identifying members in the context. The first is the CurrentMember function. The function undoubtedly identifies single members, but it cannot be used for detecting multiple members in context. That's what the Existing function does. However, that one is not so precise. In other words, each of them has their purpose, advantages, and disadvantages.

Suppose the slicer contains the city **New York**, a member of the Geography.Geography user hierarchy. Using the CurrentMember function, we can immediately identify the exact member of that hierarchy. We know that the slicer contains **New York City**, not anything above, below, left, or right.

However, if there's also the **UK** country member, the usage of CurrentMember is inappropriate; it will result in an error.

In that case, we must use the Existing function. That function detects members of a level, not the hierarchy, which makes it less precise. If used on the **Country** level, it will return **USA** and **UK** although **USA** wasn't in the slicer, but one of its descendants **New York City**. If used on a State-Province level, it will return **New York** and all the children of the UK member.

The following screenshot can shed more light on it. It shows the members **New York**, **UK**, **USA** and their relative positions; the different levels they are on:

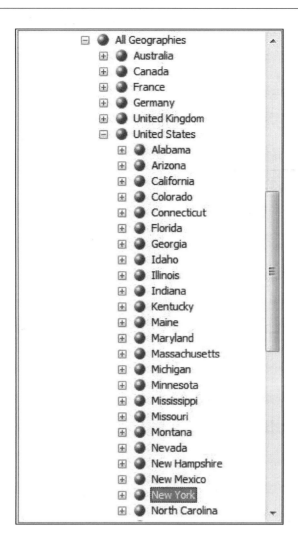

The problem with this is that we never know exactly which members were there. The only way to calculate this correctly is to use the leaf level of a hierarchy because only then can we be sure that our calculation is correct. This can have a serious impact on the performance; leaf level calculations are slow in OLAP.

The other problem with detecting the context is that neither the `Existing` function nor the `CurrentMember` function detects what's in the subselect part of the query. That is not a problem per se, because both the slicer and the subselect have their purpose. The subselect doesn't set the context and so there's no need to know what was in there. However, Excel 2007 and 2010 use subselect in many situations where the slicer should be used instead and that makes many calculations useless because they can't detect the context and adjust to it. Make sure to test calculations in your client tool of choice to see whether it also uses unnecessary subselects.

Here's a blog post by Mosha Pasumansky that shows how to use dynamically named sets to detect the contents of subselect: `http://tinyurl.com/MoshaSubselect`

The difference between them comes from the fact that the original period can be present in various places within an MDX query and that there are one or more dates the parallel period should be calculated for. Based on that, an appropriate recipe should be applied. Therefore, in order to understand and memorize the differences among them, it is suggested that you read all of the recipes dealing with parallel periods.

See also

▶ The recipes *Calculating the YoY (Year-over-Year) growth (parallel periods)* and *Calculating parallel periods for multiple dates in a set*, deal with a similar topic, how to calculate the set of dates in a parallel period.

4
Concise Reporting

In this chapter, we will cover:

- ▶ Isolating the best N members in a set
- ▶ Isolating the worst N members in a set
- ▶ Identifying the best/worst members for each member of another hierarchy
- ▶ Displaying a few important members, others as a single row, and the total at the end
- ▶ Combining two hierarchies into one
- ▶ Finding the name of a child with the best/worst value
- ▶ Highlighting siblings with the best/worst values
- ▶ Implementing bubble-up exceptions

Introduction

A crucial part of report design is determining what appropriate level of information will be presented to the business users. The appropriate level of information must be carefully matched to business requirements, with maximized benefit to the business and minimum performance impact.

Every analytical reporting project has different requirements. In this chapter we are going to focus on techniques that you can employ in your project to make analytical reports more compact and more concise, and therefore more efficient.

Recipes in this chapter can be implemented in pivot tables, the analytical component found in any SSAS frontend in one form or another. **SQL Server Reporting Services** (**SSRS**) report developers will also find these recipes very useful since they can implement these methods directly in an SSRS report.

The problem with pivot table style reports is that they tend to grow very large very quickly. All it takes is to include several hierarchies on rows, some on columns, and we will end up with a very large table to be analyzed.

The analysis of a large table can be very difficult. Even worse, when presenting a large amount of data in a chart, it might not be very readable when the number of items crosses a certain threshold.

The solution is to make reports compact; to focus on what is important to business users in your project. This chapter offers several techniques for reducing the amount of data reported without losing the crucial information.

We start with several recipes dealing with isolation of important members, whether they are from only one hierarchy, or from multiple hierarchies.

We also present a unique way of presenting data in one single report that includes three sections: the Top N members, the other members as a single row, and the total at the end.

The chapter also includes a trick to combine members from two different hierarchies into one column.

In the last three recipes, we cover techniques for presenting data at the higher granular level, but extracting additional information at the lower granular level, and color-coding the foreground and/or background of certain important cells.

Isolating the best N members in a set

Hierarchies can contain a lot of members. In this recipe we are going to show how to extract only the significant ones; members with the highest value for a certain measure.

This requirement is often necessary because not only does it allow end users to focus their efforts on a smaller set of members, but also the queries are also much faster.

We will base our example on the `TopCount()` function, a function that returns the exact number of members as specified. In addition to that function, MDX has two more similar functions, namely `TopPercent()` and `TopSum()`. Contrary to the `TopCount()` function, these functions return an unknown number of members. In other words, they are designed to return a set of members based on their contribution, in percentage or in absolute value, respectively.

Further similarities and differences between `TopCount()`, `TopSum()`, and `TopPercent()` functions will be covered in later sections of this recipe.

Getting ready

Start SQL Server Management Studio and connect to your SSAS 2012 instance. Click on the **New Query** button and check that the target database is **Adventure Works DW 2012**.

In this example we are going to use the `Reseller` dimension. Here is the query we will start from:

```
WITH
SET [Ordered Resellers] AS
    Order( [Reseller].[Reseller].[Reseller].MEMBERS,
           [Measures].[Reseller Sales Amount],
    BDESC )
SELECT
    { [Measures].[Reseller Sales Amount] } ON 0,
    { [Ordered Resellers] } ON 1
FROM
    [Adventure Works]
```

Once executed, this query returns reseller sales values for each individual reseller, where the resellers themselves are sorted in descending order of **Reseller Sales Amount**. Our task is to extract only five of them, those with the highest sales amount.

	Reseller Sales Amount
Brakes and Gears	$877,107.19
Excellent Riding Supplies	$853,849.18
Vigorous Exercise Company	$841,908.77
Totes & Baskets Company	$816,755.58
Retail Mall	$799,277.90
Corner Bicycle Supply	$787,773.04
Outdoor Equipment Store	$746,317.53
Thorough Parts and Repair Ser...	$740,985.83
Health Spa, Limited	$730,798.71
Fitness Toy Store	$727,272.65
Latest Sports Equipment	$724,299.64

How to do it...

We are going to use the `TopCount ()` function to return the top five resellers with the highest sales amount.

Follow these steps to create a named set with `TopCount()` function:

1. Create a new calculated set and name it `Top 5 Resellers`.

2. Define it using the `TopCount()` function where the first argument is the set of reseller members, the second is the number `5`, and the third is the measure `ResellerSalesAmount`.

3. Remove the `Ordered Resellers` set from the query and put the `Top 5 Resellers` on the rows instead.

4. The query should look like the following. Execute it.

```
WITH
SET [Top 5 Resellers] AS
TopCount( [Reseller].[Reseller].[Reseller].MEMBERS,
          5,
          [Measures].[Reseller Sales Amount] )
SELECT
{ [Measures].[Reseller Sales Amount] } ON 0,
{ [Top 5 Resellers] } ON 1
FROM
    [Adventure Works]
```

5. Only the five rows with the highest values should remain, as displayed in the following screenshot:

6. Compare the rows returned with the ones from the initial query in this recipe. They should be the same, in the exact same order, and with the exact same values, but with only the top 5 resellers returned.

How it works...

The `TopCount()` function takes three arguments. The first one is a set of members that is to be limited. The second argument is the number of members to be returned. The third argument is an expression to be used for determining the order of members.

In this example we asked for the five resellers with the highest value of the measure **Reseller Sales Amount**. Using the `TopCount()` function we got exactly that.

It's worth mentioning that the `TopCount()` function always sorts the returned items in descending order of the measure.

There's more...

The most important argument of the `TopCount()` function is the third argument. That is what determines how the members will be sorted internally so that only the top N of them remains afterwards. As mentioned earlier, the argument is an expression. This expression can be a single measure, an expression including several measures, a single tuple, multiple tuples, or anything that evaluates to a scalar value.

The top N member is evaluated in All Periods, not in the context of the opposite query axis

As seen in this example, returning the top N members is quite easy with the `TopCount()` function. However, in MDX, it is also relatively easy to make a mistake and return members we do not intend to.

Here is one scenario that can happen.

We would position a member of another hierarchy (for example, year 2007 from the calendar year hierarchy) on the opposite query axis (on columns), expecting the `TopCount()` function to include that in its third argument. In the following query, you might mistakenly expect that the `TopCount()` function will return top N members in the single year 2007. It will not.

```
WITH
SET [Top 5 Resellers] AS
TopCount( [Reseller].[Reseller].[Reseller].MEMBERS,
          5,
          [Measures].[Reseller Sales Amount] )
SELECT
{ [Measures].[Reseller Sales Amount] } *
{ [Date].[Calendar Year].&[2007] } ON 0,
{ [Top 5 Resellers] } ON 1
FROM
    [Adventure Works]
```

The result is shown in the following screenshot. The question is – what does it represent?

	Reseller Sales Amount
	CY 2007
Brakes and Gears	$361,627.85
Excellent Riding Supplies	$323,324.43
Vigorous Exercise Company	$252,613.29
Totes & Baskets Company	$328,615.66
Retail Mall	$291,364.58

The result contains the same top 5 resellers which are evaluated in the context of all years, with their sales amount in single year 2007 displayed on the columns. In other words, we got the best N members in all years but then displayed their sales amount for a single year, 2007.

The data itself is correct, but the result is not what we intended. Notice that the sales amount for the year 2007 in the preceding screenshot is not ordered in descending order. This should be the clue that we have made a mistake.

The query and its result beneath should also confirm that we have made a mistake in the preceding query. In the following query, we have placed the All Periods in the slicer, and queried the same top 5 resellers which are evaluated in the context of all years. We then displayed their sales amount for each year. Notice that only the first column All Periods is sorted in descending order. Also notice that the column CY 2007 shows the same sales amount as the previous screenshot:

```
WITH
SET [Top 5 Resellers] AS
TopCount ( [Reseller].[Reseller].[Reseller].MEMBERS,
           5,
             [Measures].[Reseller Sales Amount] )
SELECT
{ [Measures].[Reseller Sales Amount] } *
{ [Date].[Calendar Year].MEMBERS } ON 0,
{ [Top 5 Resellers] } ON 1
FROM
    [Adventure Works]
WHERE
( [Date].[Calendar].[All Periods] )
```

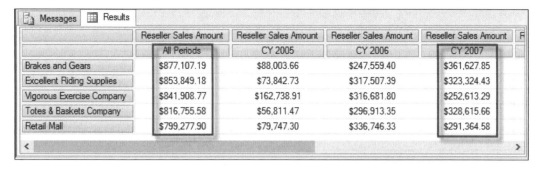

Can we somehow see that we have made such a mistake? Yes, although not necessarily always.

In most cases, it is a clue that something went wrong with the calculation when the results are not shown in descending order or when the number of rows is fewer than specified.

So, what is the reason for this kind of behavior?

The top N member will be evaluated in the context of the slicer

Axes are independent. Only the members in slicer are implicitly included in the third argument of the TopCount() function (which is a mechanism known as **Deep Autoexists**: http://tinyurl.com/AutoExists). To be precise, any outer MDX construct also sets the context, but here we didn't have such a case, so we can focus on the slicer and axes relation only. To conclude, only when the year 2007 is found in the slicer, then the third argument will be expanded into a tuple, and the result will be evaluated as the top N member in the year 2007.

Execute the following query and compare its result with the query that had the year 2007 on the opposite axis (visible in the previous screenshot).

```
WITH
SET [Top 5 Resellers] AS
TopCount( [Reseller].[Reseller].[Reseller].MEMBERS,
          5,
          [Measures].[Reseller Sales Amount] )
SELECT
{ [Measures].[Reseller Sales Amount] } ON 0,
{ [Top 5 Resellers] } ON 1
FROM
    [Adventure Works]
WHERE
( [Date].[Calendar Year].&[2007] )
```

Notice that the members on the rows have changed. These resellers are the top 5 resellers in the single year 2007. Also notice that their values are shown in descending order:

Use a tuple in the third argument of the TopCount() function to overwrite the member on the slicer

Now, let us take a look at another type of mistake. That is, when we want to override the context on the slicer but forget to do so in the third argument of the `TopCount()` function. For example, when the year 2007 is in the slicer, we want to get the top N members from the previous year, 2006.

Why would we want to do such a thing? Because we want to analyze how our last year's best resellers are doing this year.

If that's the case, we must provide a tuple as the third argument. The idea of the tuple is to overwrite the context set by the slicer with the member from the same hierarchy used inside the tuple. Remember, it has to be the same hierarchy or it will not work.

Following the previous example, where the year 2007 is on the slicer, we must change the third argument of the TopCount() function to include a tuple:

```
( [Measures].[Reseller Sales Amount],
            [Date].[Calendar Year].&[2006] )
```

The year 2006 is in the tuple in order to overwrite the year 2007 in the slicer.

Here is the final query:

```
WITH
SET [Top 5 Resellers in 2006] AS
   TopCount( [Reseller].[Reseller].[Reseller].MEMBERS,
              5,
              ( [Measures].[Reseller Sales Amount],
              [Date].[Calendar Year].&[2006] ) )
SELECT
   { [Measures].[Reseller Sales Amount] } ON 0,
   { [Top 5 Resellers in 2006] } ON 1
```

```
FROM
    [Adventure Works]
WHERE
    ( [Date].[Calendar Year].&[2007] )
```

Develop a habit of naming the top N sets that use tuples appropriately (see earlier). And remember that although the slicer or the outer MDX construct determines the context for the values to be displayed and for the functions to be evaluated, we can always override that in order to adjust the set we're after.

Testing the correctness of the result

The equivalent syntax of the `TopCount()` function is this:

```
Head( Order( [Reseller].[Reseller].[Reseller].MEMBERS,
             [Measures].[Reseller Sales Amount],
       BDESC ), 5 )
```

Although this construct can be useful for testing the correctness of the result, `TopCount()` is the preferred way of implementing the requirement of isolating the best N members. This is because the `Order()` function is a relatively slow MDX function because it materializes the set, and the query optimizer may not be successful in optimizing the query by recognizing the Head-Order construct as a `TopCount()` function.

Multidimensional sets

The first argument in the `TopCount()` function takes a set expression. In our examples, we only used a one-dimensional set that has only one hierarchy reseller. In this case, the second argument N determines the number of members from the one-dimensional set to be returned.

In the case of multidimensional sets that are made of more than one hierarchy, the second argument N determines the number of tuples to be returned. The returned tuples are also sorted in the descending order of the numeric expression.

TopPercent() and TopSum() functions

As we said in the introduction, `TopPercent()` and `TopSum()` are two functions similar to the `TopCount()` function. The first one returns an unknown number of members. In `TopPercent()`, the second argument determines the percentage of them to be returned, starting from the ones with the highest values, and ending when the total value of the members included compared to the total value of all members reaches the percentage specified in that function. The second one works on the same principle except that the absolute value and not the percentage is what is specified and compared. For example, `TopPercent()` with 80 means we want the top members who form 80 percent of the total result. `TopSum()` with 1,000,000 means we want members whose total forms that value, looking from the member with the highest value and adding all of them below until that value is reached.

The same principles, ideas, and warnings apply to all top-something functions.

> ▶ Refer to the *Isolating the worst N members in a set* and *Identifying the best/worst members for each member of another hierarchy* recipes in this chapter

Isolating the worst N members in a set

In the previous recipe we've shown how to identify members with the highest result. In this recipe we'll do the opposite and return those with the lowest result.

Getting ready

Start SQL Server Management Studio and connect to your SSAS 2012 instance. Click on the **New Query** button and check that the target database is **Adventure Works DW 2012**.

In this example we're going to use the `Reseller` dimension. Here's the query we'll start from:

```
WITH
SET [Ordered Resellers] AS
    Order( [Reseller].[Reseller].[Reseller].MEMBERS,
           [Measures].[Reseller Sales Amount],
    BASC )
SELECT
    { [Measures].[Reseller Sales Amount] } ON 0,
    { [Ordered Resellers] } ON 1
FROM
    [Adventure Works]
```

Once executed, that query returns resellers' sales values for every individual reseller, where the resellers themselves are sorted in the ascending order of the sales amount. Our task is to extract only the five with the worst sales amount.

How to do it...

We are going to use the `BottomCount()` function to return the bottom five resellers with the worst sales amount.

Follow these steps to create a named set with `BottomCount()` function:

1. Create a new calculated set and name it `Bottom 5 Resellers`.
2. Define it using the `BottomCount()` function where the first argument is the set of reseller members, the second is the number 5, and the third is the measure `ResellerSalesAmount`.

3. Apply the `NonEmpty()` function over the set specified as the first argument using the same measure as in the third argument of the `BottomCount()` function.

```
SET [Bottom 5 Resellers] AS
BottomCount(
NonEmpty( [Reseller].[Reseller].[Reseller].MEMBERS,
{ [Measures].[Reseller Sales Amount] } ),
        5,
        [Measures].[Reseller Sales Amount]
    )
```

4. Remove the `Ordered Resellers` set from the query and put the `Bottom 5 Resellers` on rows instead.

5. The query should look like the following. Execute it.

```
WITH
SET [Bottom 5 Resellers] AS
BottomCount(
NonEmpty( [Reseller].[Reseller].[Reseller].MEMBERS,
        [Measures].[Reseller Sales Amount] ),
        5,
        [Measures].[Reseller Sales Amount]
    )
SELECT
{ [Measures].[Reseller Sales Amount] } ON 0,
{ [Bottom 5 Resellers] } ON 1
FROM
    [Adventure Works]
```

6. Only the five rows with the lowest values should remain, as displayed in the following screenshot:

	Reseller Sales Amount
Mobile Outlet	$1.37
Parts Shop	$24.29
Eleventh Bike Store	$57.68
Large Bike Shop	$58.07
Essential Bike Works	$59.33

7. Compare the rows returned with the ones from the initial query in this recipe. If we ignore the empty rows from the initial rows, they should be the same, in the exact same order, and with the exact same values, only the new query returned only the lowest 5 resellers.

How it works...

The `BottomCount()` function takes three arguments. The first one is a set of members that is going to be limited. The second argument is the number of members to be returned. The third argument is the expression for determining the order of members.

In this example we asked for the five resellers with the lowest value of the measure `Reseller Sales Amount`. Using the `BottomCount()` function alone, without applying the inner `NonEmpty()` function on the following tuple, we would get five rows with empty values:

```
NonEmpty( [Reseller].[Reseller].[Reseller].MEMBERS,
                    [Measures].[Reseller Sales Amount] )
```

We can think of values, once sorted, being separated into four groups: positive values, zero values, null values, and negative values. Those groups appear in that particular order once sorted in descending order, and in the reverse order once sorted in ascending order.

In the `TopCount()` function covered in the previous recipe, we didn't experience the effect of null values because the results were all positive. In the `BottomCount()` function, this is something that needs to be taken care of, particularly if there are no negative values. The reason why we want to get rid of null values is because from a business perspective, those values represent no activity. What we are interested in is identifying members with activity.

That's the reason we applied the `NonEmpty()` function in the third step of this recipe. That action removed all members with a null value in that particular context, leaving only members with activity to the outer `BottomCount()` function.

It's worth mentioning that the `BottomCount()` function always sorts the rows in ascending order.

There's more...

`BottomPercent()` and `BottomSum()` are two functions similar to the `BottomCount()` function. They are the opposite functions of the `TopPercent()` and `TopSum()` functions explained in the last section of the previous recipe. The same principles, ideas, and warnings also apply here.

See also

> ▸ Refer to the *Isolating the best N members in a set* and *Identifying the best/worst members for each member of another hierarchy* recipes in this chapter

Identifying the best/worst members for each member of another hierarchy

Sales territory country and reseller are two different hierarchies in Adventure Works DW. To analyze sales, we might choose not to look at every reseller in every country. Instead, we often only need to look for the top or bottom N resellers per country.

In this case, we can view the country as the outer hierarchy, and the reseller as the inner hierarchy. Quite often we need to analyze the combination of hierarchies in a way that the top or bottom N members of the inner hierarchy are displayed for each member of the outer hierarchy.

Displaying only the top or bottom N members of the inner hierarchy for each member of the outer hierarchy is sort of a report reduction, where we preserve the important combinations of members and leave out the rest of the cross join.

This recipe shows how to create a `TopCount()` calculation to retrieve the top N resellers in each sales territory.

Getting ready

Start SQL Server Management Studio and connect to your SSAS 2012 instance. Click on the **New Query** button and check that the target database is **Adventure Works DW 2012**.

In this example we're going to use the `Sales Territory` dimension and the `Reseller` dimension. Here's the query we'll start from:

```
SELECT
    { [Measures].[Reseller Sales Amount] } ON 0,
    NON EMPTY
    { [Sales Territory].[Sales Territory Country].MEMBERS *
      [Reseller].[Reseller].[Reseller].MEMBERS } ON 1
FROM
    [Adventure Works]
```

Once executed, the earlier query returns reseller sales values for every individual reseller and country, where the resellers themselves are sorted in descending order of the sales amount for each country:

	Messages	Results	
			Reseller Sales Amount
All Sales Territories	Workout Emporium		$18,001.72
All Sales Territories	World Bike Discount Store		$4,918.52
All Sales Territories	World of Bikes		$278,568.57
All Sales Territories	Worthwhile Activity Store		$130,597.78
All Sales Territories	Year-Round Sports		$148,659.27
All Sales Territories	Yellow Bicycle Company		$77,468.59
Australia	Bike Part Wholesalers		$105,520.88
Australia	Budget Toy Store		$145,380.13
Australia	Cycle Parts and Accessories		$115,085.64
Australia	Eastside Cycle Shop		$2,669.11
Australia	Eastward Bike Accessories		$2,983.02
Australia	Fast Bike Works		$67,406.05
Australia	First Supplies		$30,845.61
Australia	Fitness Bike Accessories		$4,631.07
Australia	Fitness Discount Store		$3,405.07

Our task is to extract the five resellers with the best sales for each country. We would expect a different top 5 resellers in each country.

How to do it...

We are going to use the `Generate()` function together with the `TopCount()` function to return the top 5 resellers in each country.

Follow these steps to create a calculated set top 5 resellers per country:

1. Define a new calculated set; name it `Top 5 Resellers per Country`.

2. Use the `Generate()` function as a way of performing the iteration.

3. Provide the set of countries found on rows as the first argument of that `Generate()` function.

4. Provide the second argument of that function in the form of a cross join of the current member of countries hierarchy and the `TopCount()` function applied to the set of resellers.

5. Put that new calculated set on the rows, instead of having everything there.

6. Verify that the query looks like this, and then execute it.

```
WITH
SET [Top 5 Resellers per Country] AS
Generate(
        [Sales Territory].[Sales Territory Country].MEMBERS,
    { [Sales Territory].[Sales Territory Country]
            .CurrentMember } *
TopCount( [Reseller].[Reseller].[Reseller].MEMBERS,
                    5,
                [Measures].[Reseller Sales Amount] )
            )
SELECT
{ [Measures].[Reseller Sales Amount] } ON 0,
    NON EMPTY
{ [Top 5 Resellers per Country] } ON 1
FROM
    [Adventure Works]
```

7. The result is shown in the following screenshot. It returned different resellers for each country; they are the top 5 resellers relative to each country.

8. Notice that the results are ordered as descending inside each particular country.

How it works...

`Generate()` is a loop. Using that function, we can iterate over a set of members and create another set of members, as explained in the recipe, *Iterating on a set in order to create a new one* in Chapter 1, *Elementary MDX Techniques*.

In this recipe, we used it to iterate over a set of countries and to create another set, a set that is formed as a combination of the current country in the loop and the top 5 resellers in the context of that country.

Notice that we simply used the measure `[Reseller Sales Amount]` as the third argument for the `TopCount()` function. The loop sets the context, that's why we don't need to expand the third argument of the `TopCount()` function into a tuple. The following tuple would be redundant:

```
( [Sales Territory].[Sales Territory Country].CurrentMember,
    [Measures].[Reseller Sales Amount] )
```

That current member is already implicitly there, set by the outer loop, the `Generate()` function.

In order to display each country and its top 5 resellers on rows, we had to build a multidimensional set in advance using the cross-production of two sets as shown:

```
{ [Sales Territory].[Sales Territory Country].CurrentMember } *
    TopCount( [Reseller].[Reseller].[Reseller].MEMBERS,
            5,
            [Measures].[Reseller Sales Amount] )
        )
```

Because of the outer `Generate()` function, this multidimensional set is obtained in iteration, where the top 5 resellers are identified for each country.

There's more...

Was it really necessary to define such a complex syntax? Couldn't we have done something simpler instead? Let's see.

One idea would be to define `Top 5 Resellers` as we did in the first recipe of this chapter and use it on rows:

```
WITH
SET [Top 5 Resellers] AS
TopCount( [Reseller].[Reseller].[Reseller].MEMBERS,
            5,
            [Measures].[Reseller Sales Amount] )
SELECT
```

```
{ [Measures].[Reseller Sales Amount] } ON 0,
   NON EMPTY
{ [Sales Territory].[Sales Territory Country]
.[Sales Territory Country].MEMBERS *
     [Top 5 Resellers] } ON 1
FROM
   [Adventure Works]
```

When this query is run, it returns the total of 5 rows as seen in the following screenshot:

		Reseller Sales Amount
Canada	Vigorous Exercise Company	$841,908.77
Canada	Retail Mall	$799,277.90
United States	Brakes and Gears	$877,107.19
United States	Excellent Riding Supplies	$853,849.18
United States	Totes & Baskets Company	$816,755.58

The results are not sorted in any particular order, which is the first indicator that something is wrong. The number of returned items is fewer than expected. That's the second indicator.

In order to see what went wrong, we need to comment out the NONEMPTY keyword and execute the same query again. This time we can see more clearly what is going on:

		Reseller Sales Amount
Australia	Brakes and Gears	(null)
Australia	Excellent Riding Supplies	(null)
Australia	Vigorous Exercise Company	(null)
Australia	Totes & Baskets Company	(null)
Australia	Retail Mall	(null)
Canada	Brakes and Gears	(null)
Canada	Excellent Riding Supplies	(null)
Canada	Vigorous Exercise Company	$841,908.77
Canada	Totes & Baskets Company	(null)
Canada	Retail Mall	$799,277.90
France	Brakes and Gears	(null)
France	Excellent Riding Supplies	(null)
France	Vigorous Exercise Company	(null)

Resellers repeat in each country. The group of resellers marked in the preceding screenshot can be found above and below that country.

It wouldn't help to expand the third argument of the `TopCount()` function into a tuple either. The tuple below would not help.

```
( [Sales Territory].[Sales Territory Country].CurrentMember,
  [Measures].[Reseller Sales Amount] )
```

The reason why all this doesn't work is that calculated sets are evaluated once – after the slicer and before the iteration on cells. Therefore, the `TopCount()` function is evaluated in the context of the default country, the root member, not within the context of each country. That's why the resellers repeat in each country.

While calculated sets are evaluated only once before each cell is evaluated, calculated members, on the other hand, are evaluated for each cell. We cannot use a calculated member in this case, because we need a set of 5 members. The only thing that's left is to use the outer `Generate()` function to push each country into the set. By having everything in advance before the iteration on the cells begins, we can prepare the required multidimensional set of countries and their best resellers.

Support for the relative context and multidimensional sets in SSAS frontends

Frontends perform cross join operations while allowing end users to filter and isolate members of hierarchies in order to limit the size of the report. Some frontends even allow functions like `TopCount()` to be applied visually, without editing the actual MDX. The thing they rarely do is to allow the `TopCount()` function to be applied relatively to another hierarchy.

As we saw, without the relative component, top N members are calculated in the context of another hierarchy's root member, not individual members in the query. The only solution is to define a multidimensional set using the `Generate()` function. Then comes another problem – multidimensional sets (sets that contain members from more than one attribute) are not supported in many frontends, for example, in Excel 2007 and 2010.

Test the limitations of your tool in order to know whether you can use it as a front-end feature; implement it in a cube as a multidimensional set, or write an MDX query.

See also

> ▸ Refer to the *Isolating the best N members in a set* and *Isolating the worst N members in a set* recipes in this chapter

Displaying few important members, others as a single row, and the total at the end

There are times when isolating the best or worst members is not enough. In addition to the few important members, business users often want to see the total of all other not-so-important members, and also a single row representing the total of all the members.

An example of this type of reporting requirement is shown in the following table:

	Reseller Sales Amount
Top 1st Reseller	$877,107.19
Top 2nd Reseller	$853,849.18
Top 3rd Reseller	$841,908.77
Top 4thd Reseller	$816,755.58
Top 5th Reseller	$799,277.90
Other Resellers	$76,261,698.37
All Resellers	$80,450,596.98

In the first recipe in this chapter, *Isolating the best N members in a set*, we learned how to isolate the best members using the `TopCount()` function. The challenge in this recipe is to get only one row for the total of all Other Resellers, and only one row for the total of All Resellers. We will also need to make sure that the Top N Resellers, Other Resellers and All Resellers are all combined into one column. This recipe shows how to fulfill this type of reporting requirement.

Getting ready

Start SQL Server Management Studio and connect to your SSAS 2012 instance. Click on the **New Query** button and check that the target database is **Adventure Works DW 2012**.

In this example we're going to use the `Reseller` dimension. Here's the query we'll start from:

```
WITH
SET [Ordered Resellers] AS
    Order( [Reseller].[Reseller].[Reseller].MEMBERS,
            [Measures].[Reseller Sales Amount],
    BDESC )
SELECT
    { [Measures].[Reseller Sales Amount] } ON 0,
    { [Ordered Resellers] } ON 1
FROM
    [Adventure Works]
```

This query returns values of the **Reseller Sales Amount** measure for every single reseller. Notice that we purposely sorted the resellers in the descending order of the sales amount:

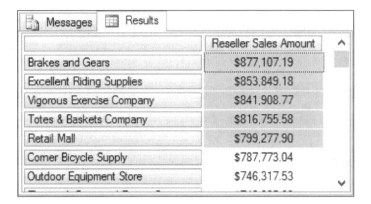

Our goal is to keep only the top 5 resellers highlighted in the preceding screenshot, with two additional rows. One of the additional rows is for other resellers, and the other one is for all resellers.

How to do it...

Follow these steps to return the Top 5 Resellers, followed by one row for Other Resellers and one row for All Resellers, all in one query:

1. Create a new calculated set and name it Top 5 Resellers.

2. Define it using the TopCount() function where the first argument is the set of reseller members, the second is the number 5, and the third is the measure ResellerSalesAmount. In short, the definition should be this:

```
SET [Top 5 Resellers] AS
TopCount( [Reseller].[Reseller].[Reseller].MEMBERS,
          5,
          [Measures].[Reseller Sales Amount] )
```

3. Remove the Ordered Resellers set from the query and put the Top 5 Resellers on the rows instead.

4. Execute the query. Only the five rows with the highest values should remain.

5. Next, create a new calculated member and name it Other Resellers. Use the following definition:

```
MEMBER [Reseller].[Reseller].[All].[Other Resellers] AS
Aggregate( - [Top 5 Resellers] )
```

6. Include that member on the rows, next to the set.

7. Finally, include the root member of the `Reseller.Reseller` hierarchy in a more generic way by adding its `[All]` level as the last set on the rows and run the query:

```
WITH
SET [Top 5 Resellers] AS
TopCount ( [Reseller].[Reseller].[Reseller].MEMBERS,
                5,
                [Measures].[Reseller Sales Amount] )
MEMBER [Reseller].[Reseller].[All].[Other Resellers] AS
Aggregate ( - [Top 5 Resellers] )
SELECT
{ [Measures].[Reseller Sales Amount] } ON 0,
{ [Top 5 Resellers],
    [Reseller].[Reseller].[All].[Other Resellers],
    [Reseller].[Reseller].[All] } ON 1
FROM
    [Adventure Works]
```

8. The result will display 7 rows: top five resellers, other resellers in a single row, and the total in the form of the root member:

	Reseller Sales Amount
Brakes and Gears	$877,107.19
Excellent Riding Supplies	$853,849.18
Vigorous Exercise Company	$841,908.77
Totes & Baskets Company	$816,755.58
Retail Mall	$799,277.90
Other Resellers	$76,261,698.37
All Resellers	$80,450,596.98

How it works...

The first part of the solution is to isolate top N members. This is done relatively easily, using the `TopCount ()` function. The more detailed explanation of this part is covered in the first recipe of this chapter.

The second part is what is special about this type of report. All other members are obtained using the negation of a set, which is written as a minus followed by that set. This is explained in the recipe, *Implementing NOT IN set logic*, in *Chapter 2, Working with Sets*.

Next, that negative set expression is wrapped inside the `Aggregate()` function, which compacts that set into a single calculated member. That calculated member is the row that follows top N members in the result.

Finally, the root member of that hierarchy comes as the last row which acts as a total of rows. Here it's worth noting that we didn't use the root member's name `[All Resellers]`; we've used its level name `[All]`. The reason for this is explained in the next section.

There's more...

The beauty of this solution is that the initial set, in this case `Top 5 Resellers`, can be any set. For example, the initial set can be the bottom N members, members that are a result of a `Filter()` function, existing members for the current context; pretty much anything. It doesn't matter how many members there are in the initial set. All the rest will be aggregated in a single row.

If we go one step further, to use a report parameter in the place of the `Reseller.Reseller` hierarchy, the query will work for any hierarchy without the need to change anything.

Another thing that makes this query generic is the way we referred to the root member. We didn't use its unique name (which would be different for different hierarchies), `[All Resellers]`. We used its level name `[All]` instead. `[All]` is a generic level name for every attribute hierarchy.

Notice that we created a calculated member for `Other Resellers`, but not for `All Resellers`. All resellers became the header for the last total row. To make this report a bit more user friendly, we could change the header to `Total`. We will need to create a calculated member for the root member in order to change the header for the last total row.

The root member, found in the `[All]` level, is usually named as `All` or `All Something`. In our example it's `All Resellers`. The following calculated member is named `Total`, which is an alias for the `All Resellers` member:

```
MEMBER [Reseller].[Reseller].[All].[Total] AS
       [Reseller].[Reseller].[All]
```

If we replace `[Reseller].[Reseller].[All]` with this calculated member on rows, the header for the last total row will be changed to `Total`.

Making the query even more generic

The query in this recipe referred to the `Reseller.Reseller` hierarchy. By replacing any reference to that hierarchy with a report parameter, we can make the query more generic. Of cause, that also means we should remove the word `Reseller` from `[Top 5 Resellers]` and `[Other Resellers]`.

We could then parameterize the whole query and insert any hierarchy and its level in it, in their corresponding places. While `Reseller.Reseller` is a unique name for a hierarchy, `Reseller.Reseller.Reseller` is the unique name of a level on that hierarchy. Therefore, any reference to the `Reseller.Reseller` hierarchy could be replaced by a parameter, say, `@HierarchyUniqueName`, and any reference to the `Reseller.Reseller.Reseller` level could be replaced by a parameter, say, `@LevelUniqueName`. Once such a query is built as a template, it can be executed as a regular query by passing dynamic parameters to it.

To provide meaningful results for the chosen hierarchy and its level, we can also parameterize the measure.

See also

▶ Refer to *Implementing NOT IN set logic, Isolating the best N members in a set*, and *Isolating the worst N members in a set recipes* in this chapter

Combining two hierarchies into one

The result of a query contains as many metadata columns as there were hierarchies on rows. For example, if we put two hierarchies on rows, color and size of products, there will be two columns of metadata information, one for each hierarchy. In the first column, we will have all colors and in the second column we will have all sizes. Depending on the relationship between those hierarchies, we will get either a full cross join for unrelated hierarchies (different dimensions) or a reduced set of valid combinations (in the case of the same dimension). In any case, there will be two columns.

We can think of this one hierarchy, which occupies one column type of report as a symmetric table. This type of report can grow very large very quickly because of the cross production of multiple hierarchies. It is not uncommon for business users to request placing data from different hierarchies into the same row or column, with the goal of reducing the size of the report.

The question is – can this be achieved in MDX? I know you've already guessed it; yes it can. This recipe shows the trick of how to make a report compact by combining two hierarchies in a single metadata column.

The example we will present in this recipe is to display the **Month of Year** on rows, the **Reseller Sales Amount** on columns, and then append only the **Last Week's** sales amount to the end of the report.

Getting ready

Start SQL Server Management Studio and connect to your SSAS 2012 instance. Click on the **New Query** button and check that the target database is **Adventure Works DW 2012**.

In this example we're going to use the `Date` dimension and its two incompatible hierarchies, months and weeks. We're going to show how to create a report that contains all months up to the "current" month and then how to add the last week of sales in the same column.

Here's the query we'll start from:

```
SELECT
    { [Measures].[Reseller Sales Amount] } ON 0,
    NON EMPTY
    { [Date].[Calendar].[Month].MEMBERS } ON 1
FROM
    [Adventure Works]
WHERE
    ( [Date].[Calendar Year].&[2008] )
```

Once executed, the query returns the values of the **Reseller Sales Amount** measure for six months of the year 2008:

	Reseller Sales Amount
January 2008	$1,662,547.32
February 2008	$2,700,766.80
March 2008	$2,739,370.98
April 2008	$2,204,623.41
May 2008	$3,315,275.00
June 2008	$3,415,479.07

The data in the **Adventure Works** cube ends with **June 2008**, which is the reason why we picked this example to simulate the "current" month in a year situation.

Our goal is to append one more row to the result, the last week's sales amount.

How to do it...

Follow these steps to create a calculated member last week and place it in the `Month of Year` hierarchy so last week can be displayed in the same column as `Month of Year`:

1. Replace the user hierarchy on rows with the appropriate attribute hierarchy to avoid problems with attribute relations. In this case that would be the `[Date].[Month of Year]` hierarchy.

2. Create a new calculated member in the `[Date].[Month of Year]` hierarchy and name it `Last week`. The definition of that member should include the 23rd week, the last week with the data, like:

```
MEMBER [Date].[Month of Year].[All Periods].[Last week] AS
( [Date].[Calendar Week of Year].&[23],
        [Date].[Month of Year].[All Periods] )
```

3. Include that member in rows as well and run the query which should look like:

```
WITH
MEMBER [Date].[Month of Year].[All Periods].[Last week] AS
( [Date].[Calendar Week of Year].&[23],
        [Date].[Month of Year].[All Periods] )
SELECT
{ [Measures].[Reseller Sales Amount] } ON 0,
   NON EMPTY
{ [Date].[Month of Year].[Month of Year].MEMBERS,
      [Date].[Month of Year].[All Periods].[Last week] } ON 1
FROM
   [Adventure Works]
WHERE
( [Date].[Calendar Year].&[2008] )
```

4. Verify that the result includes the new calculated member in the last row, as in the following screenshot:

How it works...

Different hierarchies don't add up in columns, they cross join and form multiple columns. In order to combine members from different hierarchies into the same column, we need to resolve the dimensionality issue first. In our example, we have chosen to display the top 5 months from the [Date]. [Month of Year] hierarchy. This hierarchy has become our "host" hierarchy. Our trick is to create a calculated member in this "host" hierarchy, that points to a member in another hierarchy, [Date].[Calendar Week of Year]. We named this new calculated member [Last week], which is hosted in the [Date]. [Month of Year] hierarchy, off the root member [All Periods]. Once the months and the last week have the same dimensionality, we can now have a single column for the result because we are using only one hierarchy.

Choosing a "host" hierarchy and forcing all the members into the same dimensionality is our first task. Notice that we also provided a tuple, not just a plain reference to the other hierarchy's member. This tuple, repeated, is formed using the root member of the "host" hierarchy, [All Periods] as follows:

```
( [Date].[Calendar Week of Year].&[23],
        [Date].[Month of Year].[All Periods] )
```

Why do we need to provide a tuple? Every expression is evaluated in its context. The current member of the [Date].[Month of Year] hierarchy is each month on the rows. Each single month of year has no intersection with the 23rd week (or any other week) and hence, the result of the expression without the root member in that tuple would return null. By forcing the root member into the tuple, we are actually saying we do not want the members from the month of year to interfere in the context. We are overriding the implicit query context in that expression with an explicit reference to the root member of the "host" hierarchy.

We need to validate our result before we wrap up this recipe. We have noticed that the result for the Last week member is the same as the result of the June member. Let us run the query below to validate this. This particular query simply cross joins two hierarchies, the Date and the Calendar Week of Year hierarchy. It shows us that the 23rd week started on June 1st and June 1st is the last date that has a sales amount. No wonder the month June and the last week have the same result because they both contains only one day's data, June 1st.

```
SELECT
    { [Measures].[Reseller Sales Amount] } ON 0,
    --NON EMPTY
    {   [Date].[Date].[Date].MEMBERS *
        [Date].[Calendar Week of Year].[Calendar Week of Year].MEMBERS
        } ON 1
FROM
    [Adventure Works]
WHERE
    ( [Date].[Calendar Year].&[2008] )
```

		Reseller Sales Amount	
May 26, 2008	CY Week 22	(null)	
May 27, 2008	CY Week 22	(null)	
May 28, 2008	CY Week 22	(null)	
May 29, 2008	CY Week 22	(null)	
May 30, 2008	CY Week 22	(null)	
May 31, 2008	CY Week 22	$755.78	
June 1, 2008	CY Week 23	$3,415,479.07	
June 2, 2008	CY Week 23	(null)	
June 3, 2008	CY Week 23	(null)	

There's more...

In our initial query, we used a user hierarchy, the [Calendar] hierarchy. However, in our final solution query, we used two attribute hierarchies, the [Month of Year] and the [Calendar Week of Year].The reason is that we need to take advantage of the attribute relations. The Date dimension is a very complex dimension with many related and unrelated attributes. It is a very challenging task to provide the proper tuple when the user hierarchy [Calendar] is on the rows in the original query because of all the relations among the members in the slicer, members on query axes, and the calculated member. A user hierarchy [Month of Year], on the other hand, requires that we use its root member only inside the tuple.

You should always look for a way to combine attribute hierarchies, not user hierarchies, whenever you are in a situation which requires that you combine two hierarchies in one column. The color and size on the Product dimension is another example of two attribute hierarchies that we can combine into one column by using the technique in this recipe.

Use it, but don't abuse it

If it has been explicitly stated that the report should combine different hierarchies in a single column, we can reach for this solution. It will be rare, but a possible case. In all other cases a much better solution is to have each hierarchy in its own column.

Limitations

Besides the aforementioned limitation with user hierarchies, there is another one. When more than one member should be "hosted" in the other hierarchy, all of them should be defined as calculated members, one by one. This can be an administrative burden and so it is advised that this solution is used only in cases with few members to be projected on the other hierarchy. Naturally, the hierarchy with more elements to be shown in the report should be the "hosting" one.

Finding the name of a child with the best/worst value

Sometimes there is a need to perform a for-each loop in order to get the top or bottom members in the inner hierarchy for each member in the outer hierarchy. The recipe *Identifying the best/worst members for each member of another hierarchy* deals with exactly that kind of topic.

Following the theme of the recipes in this chapter to reduce the size of the report to a manageable level, in this recipe, we will show another possibility for reducing the size of the result, by showing not all the descendant members, but only the best child member. We'll demonstrate how to identify the member with the best/worst value, only this time the member is not just from any other hierarchy, it will be from its children. We actually do not need the best/worst value from the child, and we are only going to return the name of the child in a calculated measure.

In our example, we will use the Product dimension. For every product subcategory, we are going to find the name of the product that has the best internet sales amount.

Getting ready

Start SQL Server Management Studio and connect to your SSAS 2012 instance. Click on the **New Query** button and check that the target database is **Adventure Works DW 2012**.

In this example we're going to use the Product dimension. Here's the query we'll start from:

```
WITH
MEMBER [Measures].[Subcategory] AS
iif(IsEmpty([Measures].[Internet Sales Amount] ),
null,
        [Product].[Product Categories]
        .CurrentMember.Parent.Name )
SELECT
{ [Measures].[Subcategory],
      [Measures].[Internet Sales Amount] } ON 0,
   NON EMPTY
{ Descendants( [Product].[Product Categories].[Category],
                2, SELF_AND_BEFORE ) } ON 1
FROM
   [Adventure Works]
```

Once executed, the query returns the values of the `Internet Sales Amount` measure for every product and subcategory. Part of the result is shown in the following screenshot. The measure serves as a validation point for each product and subcategory. That result can be used later for verification purposes.

	Subcategory	Internet Sales Amount
Accessories	All Products	$539,727.51
Bike Racks	Accessories	$30,240.00
Hitch Rack - 4-Bike	Bike Racks	$30,240.00
Bike Stands	Accessories	$31,959.00
All-Purpose Bike Stand	Bike Stands	$31,959.00
Bottles and Cages	Accessories	$43,804.40
Mountain Bottle Cage	Bottles and Cages	$15,404.58
Road Bottle Cage	Bottles and Cages	$12,037.61
Water Bottle - 30 oz.	Bottles and Cages	$16,362.21
Cleaners	Accessories	$5,453.70
Bike Wash - Dissolver	Cleaners	$5,453.70

How to do it...

Follow these steps to return the best product's name for each product subcategory:

1. Modify the query so that it returns only subcategories on rows. In other words, specify 1 and `SELF` as arguments of the `Descendants()` function.

2. Remove the first calculated measure from the query.

3. Define a new calculated member and name it `Best child`. Its definition should test whether we're on a leaf member or not. If so, we should provide null.

4. If not, we should again test whether the `Internet Sales Amount` is null. If so, we should provide null. Otherwise, we should calculate the top 1 child based on the measure `Internet Sales Amount`, and return the name of that child.

5. Include that calculated measure on columns as the second measure.

6. The final query should look like:

```
WITH
MEMBER [Measures].[Best child] AS
iif(IsLeaf( [Product].[Product Categories]
                .CurrentMember ),
null,
iif(IsEmpty([Measures].[Internet Sales Amount] ),
```

```
null,
TopCount ( [Product].[Product Categories]
                    .CurrentMember.Children,
                    1, [Measures].[Internet Sales Amount]
                    ).Item(0).Name
            )
        )
SELECT
{ [Measures].[Internet Sales Amount],
      [Measures].[Best child] } ON 0,
    NON EMPTY
{ Descendants( [Product].[Product Categories].[Category],
                    1, SELF ) } ON 1
FROM
    [Adventure Works]
```

7. The results will look like:

	Internet Sales Amount	Best child
Bike Racks	$30,240.00	Hitch Rack - 4-Bike
Bike Stands	$31,959.00	All-Purpose Bike Stand
Bottles and Cages	$43,804.40	Water Bottle - 30 oz.
Cleaners	$5,453.70	Bike Wash - Dissolver
Fenders	$35,585.62	Fender Set - Mountain
Helmets	$172,500.70	Sport-100 Helmet, Red
Hydration Packs	$31,344.30	Hydration Pack - 70 oz.
Tires and Tubes	$188,839.79	HL Mountain Tire
Mountain Bikes	$8,215,396.25	Mountain-200 Black, 46
Road Bikes	$12,546,132.15	Road-150 Red, 48
Touring Bikes	$2,955,090.63	Touring-1000 Blue, 46
Caps	$14,950.37	AWC Logo Cap
Gloves	$26,767.57	Half-Finger Gloves, M
Jerseys	$131,210.72	Long-Sleeve Logo Jersey, L
Shorts	$53,682.33	Women's Mountain Shorts, L
Socks	$3,946.61	Racing Socks, M
Vests	$27,876.50	Classic Vest, M

How it works...

Leaf members don't have children. That's why we provided a branch in the definition of the calculated member and eliminated them from the start by returning a NULL value.

In the case of a non-leaf member, that is, a subcategory, a single child product with the highest measure is returned using the `TopCount()` function. Actually, we only returned the child's name by first retrieving the only member using the `.item(0)` function, and then using the `.name` function.

The inner `iif()` function took care of empty values and preserved them as empty whenever the initial measure, the `Internet Sales Amount` measure, was null. This way the `NONEMPTY` operator was able to exclude the same number of empty rows as in the initial query.

There's more...

Now that we have the name of the best child, we can include additional information.

For example, the following query shows how to display the child's value as well as its percentage:

```
WITH
MEMBER [Measures].[Best child] AS
iif(IsLeaf( [Product].[Product Categories]
               .CurrentMember ),
null,
iif(IsEmpty([Measures].[Internet Sales Amount] ),
null,
TopCount( [Product].[Product Categories]
                    .CurrentMember.Children,
                 1, [Measures].[Internet Sales Amount]
               ).Item(0).Name
       )
     )
MEMBER [Measures].[Best child value] AS
iif(IsLeaf( [Product].[Product Categories]
               .CurrentMember ),
null,
iif(IsEmpty([Measures].[Internet Sales Amount] ),
null,
( TopCount( [Product].[Product Categories]
                      .CurrentMember.Children,
                   1, [Measures].[Internet Sales Amount]
                 ).Item(0),
              [Measures].[Internet Sales Amount] )
       )
     )
   , FORMAT_STRING = 'Currency'
MEMBER [Measures].[Best child %] AS
```

```
    [Measures].[Best child value]
     /
    [Measures].[Internet Sales Amount]
     , FORMAT_STRING = 'Percent'
SELECT
{ [Measures].[Internet Sales Amount],
      [Measures].[Best child],
      [Measures].[Best child value],
      [Measures].[Best child %] } ON 0,
   NON EMPTY
{ Descendants( [Product].[Product Categories].[Category],
                  1, SELF ) } ON 1
FROM
    [Adventure Works]
```

A child's value is obtained on the same principle as the child's name, except this time the tuple was used in order to get the value in that particular coordinate.

The percentage is calculated in a standard way.

Once executed, the preceding query returns this result:

	Internet Sales Amount	Best child	Best child value	Best child %
Bike Racks	$30,240.00	Hitch Rack - 4-Bike	$30,240.00	100.00%
Bike Stands	$31,959.00	All-Purpose Bike Stand	$31,959.00	100.00%
Bottles and Cages	$43,804.40	Water Bottle - 30 oz.	$16,362.21	37.35%
Cleaners	$5,453.70	Bike Wash - Dissolver	$5,453.70	100.00%
Fenders	$35,585.62	Fender Set - Mountain	$35,585.62	100.00%
Helmets	$172,500.70	Sport-100 Helmet, Red	$60,007.85	34.79%
Hydration Packs	$31,344.30	Hydration Pack - 70 oz.	$31,344.30	100.00%
Tires and Tubes	$188,839.79	HL Mountain Tire	$37,800.00	20.02%
Mountain Bikes	$8,215,396.25	Mountain-200 Black, 46	$768,821.65	9.36%
Road Bikes	$12,546,132.15	Road-150 Red, 48	$1,080,637.54	8.61%
Touring Bikes	$2,955,090.63	Touring-1000 Blue, 46	$343,306.08	11.62%
Caps	$14,950.37	AWC Logo Cap	$14,950.37	100.00%
Gloves	$26,767.57	Half-Finger Gloves, M	$9,477.63	35.41%
Jerseys	$131,210.72	Long-Sleeve Logo Jersey, L	$17,146.57	13.07%
Shorts	$53,682.33	Women's Mountain Shorts, L	$18,897.30	35.20%
Socks	$3,946.61	Racing Socks, M	$2,040.73	51.71%
Vests	$27,876.50	Classic Vest, M	$9,715.50	34.85%

Variations on a theme

Using the same principle, it is possible to get the member with the worst value. We have to be careful and apply `NonEmpty()` first in order to ignore empty values, as explained in the recipe *Isolating the worst N members in a set*.

Displaying more than one member's caption

It is possible to display several names inside the same cell. If that is the case, we must use the `Generate()` function in conjunction with its third syntax, to start the iteration. Once the iteration is in place, everything else remains the same.

See also

▶ *Isolating the best N members in a set*

▶ *Isolating the worst N members in a set*

▶ *Identifying the best/worst members for each member of another hierarchy*

▶ *Displaying a few important members, others as a single row, and the total at the end*

Highlighting siblings with the best/worst values

Data analysis becomes easier once we provide more information than a simple black and white grid allows us to. One way of doing this is to color code some cells. In this recipe, we'll show how to highlight the cells with the minimum and the maximum values among siblings and how to color code them based on their values relative to their siblings' values.

Getting ready

Start SQL Server Management Studio and connect to your SSAS 2012 instance. Click on the **New Query** button and check that the target database is **Adventure Works DW 2012**.

In this example we're going to use the `Product` dimension. Here's the query we'll start from:

```
SELECT
{ [Measures].[Internet Sales Amount] } ON 0,
  NON EMPTY
{ Descendants( [Product].[Product Categories].[Category],
             1, SELF ) } ON 1
FROM
  [Adventure Works]
```

Once executed, the query returns the value of the `Internet Sales Amount` measure for every single product subcategory. Part of the result is shown in the following screenshot:

We have two goals: one is to find the category that each subcategory belongs to; the other is to color code the best and worst subcategories in each category.

How to do it...

Follow these steps to color code the best and worst subcategories in each category:

1. Define a calculated measure that will show the name of the parent for each subcategory. Name it `Category`.

2. Be sure to provide the `null` value whenever the initial measure is `null` and then include that measure on columns as well, as the first of the two.

3. Define a cell calculation for the `Internet Sales Amount` measure and name it `Highlighted Amount`.

4. Define the `BACK_COLOR` property for the `Highlighted Amount` cell calculation. Use an expression that tests whether the current value is a max/min value.

5. Provide the adequate RGB values: green for max, red for min, and null for everything else.

6. Include the `CELLPROPERTIES` required to display the color information of a cell at the end of the query.

7. When everything is done, the query should look like:

```
WITH
MEMBER [Measures].[Category] AS
iif(IsEmpty( [Measures].[Internet Sales Amount] ),
null,
        [Product].[Product Categories]
        .CurrentMember.Parent.Name )
CELL CALCULATION [Highlighted Amount]
FOR '{ [Measures].[Internet Sales Amount] }' AS
   [Measures].[Internet Sales Amount]
   , BACK_COLOR =
iif( [Measures].CurrentMember =
Max( [Product].[Product Categories]
                .CurrentMember.Siblings,
                [Measures].CurrentMember ),
RGB(128,242,128), // green
iif( [Measures].CurrentMember =
Min( [Product].[Product Categories]
                    .CurrentMember.Siblings,
                    [Measures].CurrentMember ),
RGB(242,128,128), // red
null )
        )
SELECT
{ [Measures].[Category],
[Measures].[Internet Sales Amount] } ON 0,
   NON EMPTY
{ Descendants( [Product].[Product Categories].[Category],
                1, SELF ) } ON 1
FROM
   [Adventure Works]
CELL PROPERTIES
   VALUE,
   FORMATTED_VALUE,
   FORE_COLOR,
   BACK_COLOR
```

8. Once executed, the query returns the result presented on the following screenshot:

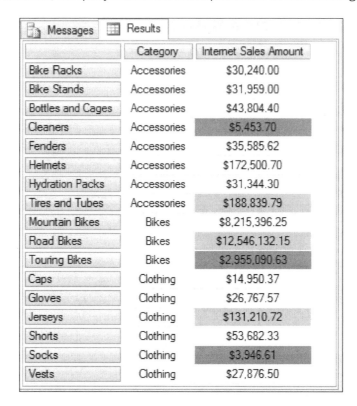

	Category	Internet Sales Amount
Bike Racks	Accessories	$30,240.00
Bike Stands	Accessories	$31,959.00
Bottles and Cages	Accessories	$43,804.40
Cleaners	Accessories	$5,453.70
Fenders	Accessories	$35,585.62
Helmets	Accessories	$172,500.70
Hydration Packs	Accessories	$31,344.30
Tires and Tubes	Accessories	$188,839.79
Mountain Bikes	Bikes	$8,215,396.25
Road Bikes	Bikes	$12,546,132.15
Touring Bikes	Bikes	$2,955,090.63
Caps	Clothing	$14,950.37
Gloves	Clothing	$26,767.57
Jerseys	Clothing	$131,210.72
Shorts	Clothing	$53,682.33
Socks	Clothing	$3,946.61
Vests	Clothing	$27,876.50

9. Notice that the highest value in a category is highlighted with light green and the lowest value per category is highlighted with light red. That's the visual cue we're after.

How it works...

Siblings are members that are under the same parent. In our earlier result, the first eight subcategories are all siblings that are under one category, accessories. We deliberately created a calculated measure [Measures].[Category] using the .Parent function. We can now visually identify all the siblings under each category, and are able to validate our color-coding calculation.

The BACK_COLOR property controls the color of the background of a cell. It can be defined as a constant value, but it can also be an expression. In this case, we used a combination – conditional formatting using fixed values for two colors, green and light red.

We had to use the `iif()` function in the definition of the calculated measure `[Measures].` `[Category]` because a calculated measure is evaluated as a string, which is never null. Therefore we have bound the calculated measure to the original measure `[Internet Sales Amount]` so that it returns values only for rows with data.

In the `BACK_COLOR` property expression, we used two nested `iif()` functions, with the `Max()` function in the outer `iif()` and `Min()` function in the inner `iif()`. The `Max()` and `Min()` functions return the highest and the lowest value in the specified set of sibling members. The current measure's value, which is the sales amount for each subcategory is compared to the maximum and minimum values respectively. In case of a match, the appropriate color is chosen (green for the max and red for the min values).

Finally, because the measure `[Measures].[Internet Sales Amount]` already existed, we used the `CELLCALCULATION` syntax to define (or overwrite) additional properties for it, such as the `BACK_COLOR` property in this example. The `CELLCALCULATION` is one of the three elements that can be defined in the `WITH` part of the query. It is analogous to the `SCOPE` statement inside the MDX script. In other words, it can be used to define or overwrite a value inside a particular subcube or to define or overwrite cell properties such as `BACK_COLOR`.

There's more...

It is also possible to color code any measure in a different way. For example, it is possible to provide a range of colors, so that the cell with the highest value has one color, the cell with the lowest value another color, and all in between a gradient of those colors. See for yourself by running this query and observing the result afterwards:

```
WITH
MEMBER [Measures].[Category] AS
iif(IsEmpty( [Measures].[Internet Sales Amount] ),
null,
        [Product].[Product Categories]
        .CurrentMember.Parent.Name )
MEMBER [Measures].[Rank in siblings] AS
iif(IsEmpty( [Measures].[Internet Sales Amount] ),
null,
Rank( [Product].[Product Categories].CurrentMember,
NonEmpty( [Product].[Product Categories]
                        .CurrentMember.Siblings,
                    [Measures].[Internet Sales Amount] ),
            [Measures].[Internet Sales Amount] )
    )
MEMBER [Measures].[Count of siblings] AS
Sum( [Product].[Product Categories]
        .CurrentMember.Siblings,
    iif(IsEmpty( [Measures].[Internet Sales Amount] ),
```

```
null, 1 )
        )
MEMBER [Measures].[R] AS
iif(IsEmpty( [Measures].[Internet Sales Amount] ),
null,
        255 / ( [Measures].[Count of siblings] - 1 ) *
( [Measures].[Count of siblings] -
        [Measures].[Rank in siblings] ) ) -- all shades
    , FORMAT_STRING = '#,#'
    , VISIBLE = 1
MEMBER [Measures].[G] AS
iif(IsEmpty( [Measures].[Internet Sales Amount] ),
null, 0 ) -- fixed dark green
    , VISIBLE = 1
MEMBER [Measures].[B] AS
iif(IsEmpty( [Measures].[Internet Sales Amount] ),
null,
        100 / [Measures].[Count of siblings] *
        [Measures].[Rank in siblings] ) -- dark shades
    , FORMAT_STRING = '#,#'
    , VISIBLE = 1
CELL CALCULATION [Highlighted Amount]
FOR '{ [Measures].[Internet Sales Amount] }' AS
    [Measures].[Internet Sales Amount]
    , BACK_COLOR =
RGB( [Measures].[R],
            [Measures].[G],
            [Measures].[B] )
    , FORE_COLOR = RGB( 255, 255, 255 ) -- white
SELECT
{ [Measures].[Category],
    [Measures].[Rank in siblings],
      [Measures].[Internet Sales Amount],
    [Measures].[R],
    [Measures].[G],
    [Measures].[B] } ON 0,
  NON EMPTY
{ Descendants( [Product].[Product Categories].[Category],
                1, SELF ) } ON 1
FROM
    [Adventure Works]
CELL PROPERTIES
    VALUE,
    FORMATTED_VALUE,
    FORE_COLOR,
    BACK_COLOR
```

The previous query, once executed, returns the result presented in the following screenshot:

	Category	Rank in siblings	Internet Sales Amount	R	G	B
Bike Racks	Accessories	7	$30,240.00	36	0	88
Bike Stands	Accessories	5	$31,959.00	109	0	63
Bottles and Cages	Accessories	3	$43,804.40	182	0	38
Cleaners	Accessories	8	$5,453.70	(null)	0	100
Fenders	Accessories	4	$35,585.62	146	0	50
Helmets	Accessories	2	$172,500.70	219	0	25
Hydration Packs	Accessories	6	$31,344.30	73	0	75
Tires and Tubes	Accessories	1	$188,839.79	255	0	13
Mountain Bikes	Bikes	2	$8,215,396.25	128	0	67
Road Bikes	Bikes	1	$12,546,132.15	255	0	33
Touring Bikes	Bikes	3	$2,955,090.63	(null)	0	100
Caps	Clothing	5	$14,950.37	51	0	83
Gloves	Clothing	4	$26,767.57	102	0	67
Jerseys	Clothing	1	$131,210.72	255	0	17
Shorts	Clothing	2	$53,682.33	204	0	33
Socks	Clothing	6	$3,946.61	(null)	0	100
Vests	Clothing	3	$27,876.50	153	0	50

The **Category** calculated measure is the same as in the previous query.

Rank in siblings is a measure that returns the rank of an individual subcategory when compared with the results of its siblings. This measure is included in the columns so that the verification becomes relatively easy.

Count of siblings is a measure which returns the number of sibling members and is used to establish the boundaries as well as the increment in the color gradient.

The R, G, and B values are calculated measures used to define the background color for the **Internet Sales Amount** measure. The gradient is calculated using the combination of rank and count measures with additional offsets so that the colors look better (keeping them relatively dark). In addition to that, the FORE_COLOR property is set to white so that proper contrast is preserved. The three calculated measures are displayed last in the result just to show how the values change. You can freely hide those measures and remove them from columns axis. The VISIBLE property is there to remind you about that.

It's worth mentioning that one component of the color should decrease as the other increases. Here it is implemented with the rank and count-rank expressions. As one increases, the other decreases.

For more complex color coding, an appropriate stored procedure installed on the SSAS server is another solution, unless the frontend and its pivot table grid already supports these features.

Troubleshooting

Don't forget to include the required cell properties, namely BACK_COLOR and FORE_COLOR, or the recipe solution won't work. The same applies for the frontend you're using. If you don't see the effect, check whether there's an option to turn those cell properties on.

See also

> ▶ *Applying conditional formatting on calculations*, a recipe in *Chapter 1*, *Elementary MDX Techniques*, and the next recipe, *Implementing bubble-up exceptions*

Implementing bubble-up exceptions

In the previous recipe we dealt with highlighting the cells based on their results in comparison with sibling members, which can be visualized in a horizontal direction. In this recipe we'll take a look at how to do the same but in a vertical direction, using the descendants of members in the report.

Bubble-up exceptions are a nice way of visualizing the information about descendants of a member without making reports huge. By coding the information about the result of descendants, we can have compact reports on a higher level while still having some kind of information about what's going on below.

The information we are going to "bubble-up" will be presented in the form of color coding the cells.

Getting ready

Start SQL Server Management Studio and connect to your SSAS 2012 instance. Click on the **New Query** button and check that the target database is **Adventure Works DW 2012**.

In this example we're going to use the Product dimension. Here's the query we'll start from:

```
SELECT
{ [Measures].[Reseller Sales Amount],
    [Measures].[Reseller Gross Profit Margin] } ON 0,
  NON EMPTY
{ Descendants( [Product].[Product Categories].[Category],
                1, BEFORE ) } ON 1
FROM
    [Adventure Works]
WHERE
( [Date].[Fiscal].[Fiscal Year].&[2007] )
```

Once executed, the query returns the value of the `Reseller Sales Amount` and `Reseller Gross Profit Margin` measures in the fiscal year `2007` for each product category.

We are going to analyze the product subcategory, which is the descendant of the product category, and color-code the category if at least one of its subcategories has a negative profit margin. We will do this in one query without displaying the subcategories.

How to do it...

Follow these steps to color code the product categories if at least one of its subcategories has a negative profit margin:

1. Create a new calculated measure that will serve as an alias for the `Reseller Gross Profit Margin` measure. Name it `Margin with Bubble-up`.

2. Define the `FORE_COLOR` property of that measure so that it turns red when at least one descendant on the lower level has negative values for the margin.

3. Include that new measure on the columns, as the third measure there.

4. Include the `CELLPROPERTIES` part of the query and enlist the `FORE_COLOR` property as one of them to be returned by the query.

5. Execute the query, which should look like:

```
WITH
MEMBER [Measures].[Margin with Bubble-up] AS
    [Measures].[Reseller Gross Profit Margin]
    , FORE_COLOR =
iif(
Min( Descendants( [Product].[Product Categories]
                        .CurrentMember,
                        1, SELF ),
                [Measures].CurrentMember )< 0,
RGB( 255, 0, 0 ), -- red
null
            )
SELECT
{ [Measures].[Reseller Sales Amount],
    [Measures].[Reseller Gross Profit Margin],
    [Measures].[Margin with Bubble-up] } ON 0,
    NON EMPTY
{ Descendants( [Product].[Product Categories].[Category],
                    1, BEFORE ) } ON 1
FROM
    [Adventure Works]
WHERE
```

```
( [Date].[Fiscal].[Fiscal Year].&[2007] )
CELL PROPERTIES
    VALUE,
    FORMATTED_VALUE,
    FORE_COLOR,
    BACK_COLOR
```

6. Verify that the new measure is red in two rows, **Bikes** and **Clothing**:

	Reseller Sales Amount	Reseller Gross Profit Margin	Margin with Bubble-up
Accessories	$124,433.35	29.23%	29.23%
Bikes	$22,417,419.69	1.64%	1.64%
Clothing	$750,716.33	23.46%	23.46%
Components	$4,629,101.14	12.40%	12.40%

How it works...

As mentioned earlier, the new measure is just an alias for the original measure, [Reseller Gross Profit Margin]; there's nothing special in its definition. Its real value is in the additional cell property expressions, namely, the FORE_COLOR property used in this example. It could have been the BACK_COLOR property if we had preferred; what matters in this recipe is the expression we used in the conditional color coding of the calculated measure.

In that expression, we are analyzing descendants of the current member and extracting only the ones with a negative result for the current measure, the Margin with Bubble-up measure. As that measure is an alias for the Reseller Gross Profit Margin measure, we are actually testing the latter measure.

We applied the MIN() function to the tuple, and used the outer iif() function to determine whether the minimum Reseller Gross Profit Margin is a negative value. If that's a negative number, we turn the color to red. If not, we leave it as it is.

The red color for the two rows, **Bikes** and **Clothing**, tells us that at least one of the subcategories under bikes and clothing has a negative profit margin.

There's more...

On the query axis on the rows, we could have directly used the level `[Category]`, without using the construct `Descendants([Product].[Product Categories].[Category],` `1, BEFORE)`, which is essentially just another way of specifying that we want to see product categories there. However, the advantage of this construct is that it allows us to make a small change in the query, maybe using a report parameter, and to be able to drill down one level below.

The part that needs a change is the second argument of the `Descendants()` function on the rows. The value of that argument was `1`, signaling that we want only product categories and nothing else.

If we change that argument to `2`, we will get the result as displayed in the following screenshot:

	Reseller Sales Amount	Reseller Gross Profit Margin	Margin with Bubble-up
Helmets	$94,693.44	28.67%	28.67%
Locks	$16,225.22	30.98%	30.98%
Pumps	$13,514.69	31.05%	31.05%
Bikes	$22,417,419.69	1.64%	1.64%
Mountain Bikes	$9,184,858.57	9.40%	9.40%
Road Bikes	$13,232,561.12	-3.75%	-3.75%
Clothing	$750,716.33	23.46%	23.46%
Bib-Shorts	$166,739.71	30.74%	30.74%
Caps	$11,698.80	-3.00%	-3.00%
Gloves	$155,267.18	27.15%	27.15%
Jerseys	$133,279.01	-2.22%	-2.22%
Shorts	$81,898.62	30.93%	30.93%
Tights	$201,833.01	30.08%	30.08%
Components	$4,629,101.14	12.40%	12.40%
Forks	$77,931.69	25.90%	25.90%
Handlebars	$77,104.06	25.96%	25.96%
Headsets	$60,942.20	25.35%	25.35%
Mountain Frames	$1,728,121.66	11.18%	11.18%

In other words, now the query includes both product categories and product subcategories on rows.

What's good about it is that our measure reacts in this scenario as well. Two subcategories, Bikes and Clothing, remained in red. The change also captures a few more negative values. Now the color coding calculation not only captured the descendants that have negative value, but also the member itself if it is negative.

The reason this worked is because our color coding expression for our calculated measure also used a relative depth for descendants. The Descendants expression is repeated here. The relative depth we used was 1.

```
Descendants( [Product].[Product Categories].CurrentMember,
        1, SELF )
```

If it is required, we can specify an absolute level, not a relative one. We would do this by specifying the name of a particular level instead of the number. For example, if we want our expression to detect negative values only in the subcategories, we should specify it like:

```
Descendants( [Product].[Product Categories].CurrentMember,
             [Product].[Product Categories].[Subcategory],
    SELF )
```

If we want the expression to work on the lowest level only, we should use this construct:

```
Descendants( [Product].[Product Categories].CurrentMember, ,
    LEAVES )
```

In short, there are a lot of possibilities and you are free to experiment.

Practical value of bubble-up exceptions

Members colored in red signal that some of the members on the lower level have negative margins. With the visual indicator, end users can save a lot of their precious time by drilling down to the next level only if a cell gives them a visual clue. On the other hand, without the visual indicator, they might miss opportunities if the data at the more granular level is not examined.

Potential problems

On very large hierarchies, there can be problems with performance if the bubble-up exceptions are set at a granular level that is too low.

See also

> ▶ Refer to the preceding recipe, *Highlighting siblings with the best/worst values*

5
Navigation

In this chapter, we will cover:

- ▶ Detecting a particular member in a hierarchy
- ▶ Detecting the root member
- ▶ Detecting members on the same branch
- ▶ Finding related members in the same dimension
- ▶ Finding related members in another dimension
- ▶ Calculating various percentages
- ▶ Calculating various averages
- ▶ Calculating various ranks

Introduction

One of the advantages of multidimensional cubes is their rich metadata model backed up with a significant number of MDX functions that enable easy navigation and data retrieval from any part of the cube. We can easily navigate through levels, hierarchies, dimensions, and cubes.

The goal of this chapter is to show common tasks and techniques related to navigation and data retrieval relative to the current context. We will show how to take control of and fine-tune the query context and how to achieve query optimization.

The first three recipes illustrate how to test whether the current context is the one we're expecting or not.

Then we will continue on to two recipes where we illustrate how to find related members, whether the related members are on different hierarchies in the same dimension, or they are from totally different dimensions.

Finally, building on the knowledge of detecting specific members and navigating through any parts of the cube, we run a series of relative calculations of percentage, average and rank. We provide examples for relative calculations that take the current context and compare its value to some other related context, such as parents, children, siblings, members on the same level or same hierarchy, and so on. Examples of such calculations are percentage of parent, percentage of total, average on a level, average on leaves, rank among siblings, rank on a level, and so on.

Multidimensional cubes are conceptually enormous structures filled with empty space, with no data at all in all but a few combinations. There are times when the Analysis Services engine takes care of that by utilizing various algorithms that compact the cube space, but there are times when we have to do that by ourselves.

The MDX language incorporates functions that enable fast retrieval of related members, to move from one hierarchy to another, from one dimension to another, and to get only members valid in the current context. This technique improves query performance because the engine is not forced to calculate on non-relevant space. There are several recipes in this chapter covering that topic.

Let's start!

Detecting a particular member in a hierarchy

We frequently encounter situations where we need to include or exclude a certain member in a calculation. Our first step is to determine if the member exists in a hierarchy.

When iterating through a set of hierarchy members, at each step in the iteration, the member being operated upon is the current member. This recipe shows how to determine if the current member in the query context is a particular member that we are interested in.

Getting ready

Start SQL Server Management Studio and connect to your SSAS 2012 instance. Click on the **New Query** button and check that the target database is **Adventure Works DW 2012**.

In this example we're going to use the `Product` dimension. Here's the query we'll start from:

```
SELECT
    { } ON 0,
    { [Product].[Color].AllMembers } ON 1
FROM
    [Adventure Works]
```

Once executed, the query returns all product colors including the root member. The preceding query will return products in rows, with nothing in columns. This type of query that has nothing on columns is explained in the recipe *Skipping axis* in *Chapter 1, Elementary MDX Techniques*.

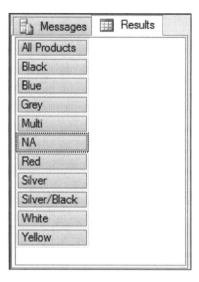

Our task is to detect the member **NA**. Once the specific member is detected, we can perform calculations that either include this member or exclude this member. In this recipe we are focusing only on how to perform the detection.

How to do it...

Follow these steps to detect the **NA** member:

1. Add the `WITH` block of the query.

2. Create a new calculated measure and name it `Member is detected`.

3. Define it as `True` for the `NA` member and `null`, not `False`, in all other cases.

4. Add this calculated measure on axis `0`.

5. Execute the query, which should look like:

```
WITH
MEMBER [Measures].[Member is detected] AS
    iif( [Product].[Color].CurrentMember Is
        [Product].[Color].&[NA],
        True,
        null
    )
SELECT
```

```
    { [Measures].[Member is detected] } ON 0,
    { [Product].[Color].AllMembers } ON 1
FROM
    [Adventure Works]
```

6. Verify that the result matches the following screenshot:

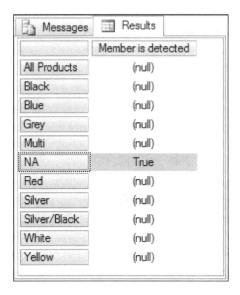

How it works...

When a MDX query is executed, part of the standard query execution is iterating through a set of hierarchy members on query axes. The current member changes on a hierarchy used on an axis in a query. In the iteration phase we can detect the current context on an axis in the query using the `CurrentMember` function. This function returns the member of the hierarchy on the query axis we are currently operating upon.

The `IS` operator performs a logical comparison on two object expressions, and is often used to determine whether two tuples or members are exactly equivalent. By comparing the current member with a particular member of the same hierarchy, we can know when we have hit the row or column with that member in it.

There's more...

The solution presented here is good in situations when there is a *temporary* need to isolate a particular member in the query. The emphasis is on the word "temporary." Typical examples of this type of "temporary" need include highlighting the rows or columns of a report or providing two calculations for a single measure based on the context.

In case the required behavior has a more *permanent* characteristic, defining the member in MDX script or using the `Scope()` statement are better approaches.

Take a look at the following script, which can be added in the MDX script of the Adventure Works cube:

```
Create Member CurrentCube.[Measures].[Member is detected]
As null;

Scope( ( [Product].[Color].&[NA],
         [Measures].[Member is detected] ) );
    This = True;
End Scope;
```

First, the measure is defined as `null`. Then, the scope is applied to it in the context of `NA` color. When the scope becomes active, it will provide `True` as the result. In all other cases, the initial definition of the measure `null` will prevail.

The `Scope()` statement is basically doing the same thing as the `iif()` statement in a calculated member, with one important difference – the scope statement itself is evaluated (resolved) only once, when the first user connects to the cube. That goes for named sets and left side of assignments too, which can easily be verified by observing the *Execute MDX Script Begin/End* events in SQL Server Profiler. More about this is in the recipe *Capturing MDX queries generated by SSAS frontends* in *Chapter 9, On the Edge*.

The right side of assignments (here, the value `True`) is evaluated at query time and hence it makes no difference if the expression on that side was used in an MDX script or in a query. However, as the scope statement gets evaluated only once, it may be reasonable to put a complex expression in scope instead of the `iif()` function.

Important remarks

The earlier `Create Member` statement did not use the Boolean value `False` as the result of the negative branch. Instead, the value of null was provided in order to keep the calculation sparse and hence preserve performance. The `iif()` function is optimized to work in block mode if one of the branches is null.

Comparing members versus comparing values

We have used the Is keyword to compare the current member on the `[Color]` hierarchy with `[Product].[Color].&[NA]`, which is a key-based fully qualified member on the same hierarchy. It is important to differentiate the comparison of members from the comparison of values. The first is performed using the `Is` keyword, the latter using the = sign. It is essential that you learn and understand that difference. Otherwise, you will not get correct results from your logical comparison.

When you do need to compare values using the = sign, try to compare members using their unique names whenever you can. The following logical comparison using the member's unique name is equivalent to using the `Is` keyword to compare two member object expressions.

```
[Product].[Color].CurrentMember.Uniquename = '[Product].[Color].&[NA]'
```

We should avoid comparing member properties such as name. The following logical comparison will work, but it will not give you the best possible performance:

```
[Product].[Color].CurrentMember.Name =    'NA'
```

The other reason you should avoid comparing names is that names can repeat, especially in multi-level user hierarchies. For example, the `Geography.Geography` hierarchy has `New York` the state and `New York` the city. Obviously, using the following code to compare the current member to that member by its name would be a bad choice:

```
[Geography].[Geography].CurrentMember.name = 'New York'
```

Detecting complex combination of members

When the business logic is complex it might be required to detect several members, not just one of them. In that case apply the same principles described in this recipe. Your only concern in that case is to handle the logic correctly. The MDX language offers various logical functions for that scenario.

In the case of OR logic, here are few additional hints:

▶ You can define a set of members and use the `Intersect()` function to test whether the set formed from the current member has intersection with the predefined set.

▶ In case of poor performance, you might want to consider creating a new attribute hierarchy based on a Yes/No value in the field derived using the case statement in your DW/DSV, as explained in recipe *Using a new attribute to separate members on a level* from *Chapter 7, When MDX is Not Enough*. This way you can have pre-aggregated values for those two members.

▶ In case of very complex logic you'd be better off defining a new column in your fact table and creating a dimension from it. That way you are pushing the logic in DW and using SSAS cubes for what they do best – slicing and aggregation of the data.

See also

▶ The recipe *Detecting the root member* covers a similar topic, but in a much more narrow case. It is worth reading right after this recipe because of the additional insights it provides.

Detecting the root member

The root member is the topmost member of a hierarchy. It is present in all hierarchies (in user hierarchies as well as in attributes hierarchies) as long as the `IsAggregatable` property is enabled, as in its default state.

The root member represents the highest level of granularity within a hierarchy the data can be aggregated up to. When calculating the percentage of a total, we need to detect whether the current member in the query context is pointing to the root member of a hierarchy or not. Based on the detection result, we can make our calculation of the percentage of a total response differently to the root member.

Although we have the real-world application of the root member detection in mind, this recipe shows only how to detect the root member.

Getting ready

Start SQL Server Management Studio and connect to your SSAS 2012 instance. Click on the **New Query** button and check that the target database is **Adventure Works DW 2012**.

In this example we're going to use the same `Color` hierarchy of the `Product` dimension like in the previous recipe, *Detecting a particular member of a hierarchy*. Here's that query:

```
SELECT
    { } ON 0,
    { [Product].[Color].AllMembers } ON 1
FROM
    [Adventure Works]
```

Once executed, the query returns all product colors including the root member. The preceding query will return products on rows, with noting on columns. This special type of query is explained in the recipe *Skipping axis* in *Chapter 1, Elementary MDX Techniques*.

In the previous recipe, *Detecting a particular member in a hierarchy*, we showed you how to detect a member NA. Our task in this recipe is to detect the root member in the [Color] hierarchy.

How to do it...

Follow these steps to create a calculated member that detects the root member:

1. Add the WITH block of the query.

2. Create a new calculated measure and name it `Root member detected`.

3. Define it as True for the branch where the detection occurs and null for the other part.

4. Add this measure on axis 0.

5. Execute the query which should look like:

```
WITH
MEMBER [Measures].[Root member detected] AS
    iif( [Product].[Color].CurrentMember Is
        [Product].[Color].[All Products],
        True,
        null
    )
SELECT
    { [Measures].[Root member detected] } ON 0,
    { [Product].[Color].AllMembers } ON 1
FROM
    [Adventure Works]
```

6. Verify that the result matches the following screenshot:

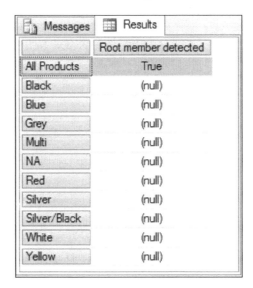

How it works...

The CurrentMember function returns the member we are currently operating on in a particular hierarchy. We then compare this current member to the root member of the [Color] hierarchy, [Product].[Color].[All Products], to detect if the current member on the query axis is the root member.

The condition in our IIF() expression evaluates to the Boolean value True when the root member is detected. In all other cases, the returned value is null.

There's more...

In the preceding query, we have hard-coded the root member, by referencing it as `[Product].[Color].[All Products]`. However, the name of the root member can change over time. We should try to avoid referencing the root member using its name.

Instead of using the reference to the root member, we can use the reference to its internal alias `All`. The calculated measure can be changed to:

```
MEMBER [Measures].[Root member detected] AS
    iif( [Product].[Color].CurrentMember Is
         [Product].[Color].[All],
         True,
         null
       )
```

With the changed name of the root member to `[Product].[Color].[All]` our calculation still works. That is because the internal alias for the root member `All` works the same way as the actual name of the root member. However, anything other than the correct name of the root member and its alias will result in an error. Depending on a particular configuration of SSAS cube, the error will be reported or bypassed. Mostly it will be bypassed, because it is the default option.

This trick will work on any hierarchy, but may not work in future SSAS versions based on the fact that it isn't documented anywhere.

There are, of course, other ways to detect the root member. One is to test the level of a hierarchy by retrieving the ordinal number of the current member. The `Ordinal` function returns a zero-based ordinal value associated with a level. The calculated measure can be changed to:

```
MEMBER [Measures].[Root member detected] AS
    iif( [Product].[Color].CurrentMember.Level.Ordinal = 0,
         True,
         null
       )
```

Ordinal value of a level in a hierarchy can be from 0 to n, where n is the number of user-defined levels in that hierarchy. An ordinal value of zero represents the topmost level, the root member.

One potential problem with this calculation is that any calculated member defined on the hierarchy itself (not on another regular member) will also be positioned on the topmost level. Its level ordinal will be zero too. However, if you exclude calculated members in our calculation, the preceding expression will work.

To avoid hard-coding the name of a root member, we have another way to detect the topmost regular member (as opposed to calculated members) using the `Root()` function. The calculated measure can be changed to:

```
MEMBER [Measures].[Root member detected] AS
    iif( [Product].[Color].CurrentMember Is
        Extract(Root([Product]),
[Product].[Color]).item(0),
        True,
        null
    )
```

In the preceding expression, we used the `Root()` function which takes the dimension `[Product]` as the argument and returns a tuple that contains the top-level member (or the default member if the `All` member does not exist) from each attribute hierarchy in the `[Product]` dimension based on the context of the current member. Since we are only interested in the attribute hierarchy `[Color]`, we used the `Extract()` function to isolate the single hierarchy and its members in that tuple. The `Item()` function converts the set of members into a single member. That's the topmost regular member of that hierarchy extracted from the tuple.

The scope-based solution

All the calculations for `[Root member detected]` so far are query-based, being part of a MDX expression in MDX queries. In case the calculations are shared by many different users, sessions and applications, we should define the calculation in MDX script, either using the `Scope()` statement or using the `CREATE MEMBER` statement only without the `Scope()` statement. This scoped-based solution is a better approach than the query-based `iif()` statement.

The following MDX script is equivalent to the query-based calculation. Define it in the MDX script of the Adventure Works cube using SSDT, deploy, and then verify its result in the cube browser using the same hierarchy `[Color]`:

```
Create Member CurrentCube.[Measures].[Root member detected]
As null;

Scope( ( [Product].[Color].[All],
        [Measures].[Root member detected] ) );
    This = True;
End Scope;
```

One more thing: detection of this kind is usually done so that another calculation can exploit it. In MDX script, it is possible to directly specify the scope for an existing measure, such as [Internet Sales Amount], and to provide a scoped-based calculation for it. The following MDX script is an example that returns the average [Internet Sales Amount] for all colors at the topmost level using the Scope() statement to detect the All level:

```
Scope( ( [Product].[Color].[All],
          [Measures].[Internet Sales Amount] ) );
    This = Avg( [Product].[Color].[All].Children,
                [Measures].CurrentMember );
End Scope;
```

See also

▸   The recipe *Detecting a particular member of a hierarchy*

Detecting members on the same branch

So far we've covered cases when there is a need to isolate a single member in the hierarchy, whether it is a root member or any other member in the hierarchy. This recipe deals with detecting the ascendants or descendants of a member in a hierarchy. As a matter of fact, the detection does not need to go all the way to the top level or to the leaf level; it can detect only a certain cascading branch in a hierarchy.

Multi-levels are often found in user hierarchies. For a certain member, we might need to apply certain calculations to its ascendants only, or its descendants only, or to only part of a cascading branch in the hierarchy. Let's illustrate this with a couple examples.

Suppose we want to analyze dates. There's a concept of the current date, but since that date is usually found in a multilevel user hierarchy, we can also talk about the current month, current quarter, current year, and so forth. They are all ascendants of the current date member. For the month of April 2008, we might have needs to detect all its parents, Q2 CY 2008, H1 CY 2008, and CY 2008, and apply some special calculations to them.

Another example is the Customer Geography user hierarchy. There we can detect whether a particular customer is living in a particular city, or if that city is in the state or country in the context. In other words, we can test above and below, as long as there are levels to be detected in each direction.

In this recipe we are going to use the Product Categories user hierarchy and a particular member **Touring Bikes** on the **Subcategory** level. The reason we picked the subcategory level is because it is a middle level in the Product Categories user hierarchy. We want to demonstrate how to check if a particular member in a middle level is on the selected drill-up/down part in the hierarchy.

Getting ready

Open the **SQL Server Data Tools** (SSDT) and then open the **Adventure Works DW 2012** solution. Double-click on the **Adventure Works** cube and go to **Calculations** tab. Choose **Script View**. Position the cursor at the end of the script.

We'll base the example for this recipe on providing a special calculation for **Touring Bikes**.

How to do it...

Follow these steps to detect members on the same branch:

1. Add the Scope() statement.

2. Specify that you want **Touring Bikes** and all of their descendants included in this scope:

```
Scope( Descendants(
            [Product].[Product Categories].[Subcategory].&[3], ,
            SELF_AND_AFTER
                    )
      );
      [Measures].[Internet Sales Amount] = 1;
End Scope;
```

3. Save and deploy the script (or just press the **Deploy MDX Script** icon if you're using **BIDS Helper**).

4. Go to the **Cube Browser** tab and optionally re-connect.

5. Click on the icon **Analyze in Excel** on top, and choose the **Adventure Works** perspective. When the pivot table is open, select the measure **Internet Sales Amount** from the field list.

6. Select the **[Product Categories]** user hierarchy from the field list, and expand it until you see all the touring bikes, as displayed in the following screenshot:

	A	B
1	Row Labels ▼	Internet Sales Amount
2	⊞ Accessories	$539,727.51
3	⊟ Bikes	$20,761,529.39
4	⊞ Mountain Bikes	$8,215,396.25
5	⊞ Road Bikes	$12,546,132.15
6	⊟ Touring Bikes	1
7	Touring-1000 Blue, 46	1
8	Touring-1000 Blue, 50	1
9	Touring-1000 Blue, 54	1
10	Touring-1000 Blue, 60	1
11	Touring-1000 Yellow, 46	1
12	Touring-1000 Yellow, 50	1
13	Touring-1000 Yellow, 54	1
14	Touring-1000 Yellow, 60	1
15	Touring-2000 Blue, 46	1
16	Touring-2000 Blue, 50	1
17	Touring-2000 Blue, 54	1
18	Touring-2000 Blue, 60	1
19	Touring-3000 Blue, 44	1
20	Touring-3000 Blue, 50	1
21	Touring-3000 Blue, 54	1
22	Touring-3000 Blue, 58	1
23	Touring-3000 Blue, 62	1
24	Touring-3000 Yellow, 44	1
25	Touring-3000 Yellow, 50	1
26	Touring-3000 Yellow, 54	1
27	Touring-3000 Yellow, 58	1
28	Touring-3000 Yellow, 62	1
29	⊞ Clothing	$258,434.10
30	Grand Total	$21,559,691.00

7. Verify that the result for all touring bikes, including their total, is **1**, as defined in the scope statement.

8. Bring another measure, for example, **Reseller Sales Amount** and verify that this measure remains intact; the scope is not affecting it.

How it works...

The `Scope()` statement is used to isolate a particular part of the cube, also called the subcube, in order to provide a special calculation for that space. It starts with the `Scope` keyword followed by the subcube and ends with the `End Scope` phrase. Everything inside is valid only for that particular scope.

In this case, we formed the subcube by using the `Descendants()` function to get all the descendants of the member **Touring Bikes** and the member **Touring Bikes** itself. There are various ways that we can collect members on a particular branch using the `Ascendants()` and `Descendants()` function. These ways will be covered in the later sections of this recipe.

Once we have set our subcube correctly, we can provide various assignments inside that scope. Here we have specified that the value for the **Internet Sales Amount** measure is to be 1 for every cell in that subcube.

It is worth noticing that the **Touring Bikes Total** is not calculated as an aggregate of its children. This is because we have used the flag `SELF_AND_AFTER` in the `Descendants()` function, therefore, the member representing that total was included in the scope. Therefore, a constant value of 1 has been assigned to it, the same way it was assigned to its children. Consequently, the **Touring Bikes** member contributes with its own value, 1, as the **Touring Bikes Total**.

If the `AFTER` flag had been used in the `Descendants()` function, the **Touring Bikes** member would have been left out of that scope. In that case, its value would be equal to the sum of its children, that is, 22. The aggregate value of 22 would be used as its contribution to the **Touring Bikes Total**.

It is worth noting that regular measures roll up their children's values using aggregate functions (`Sum`, `Max`, `Min`, and others) that are specified in the measure property `AggregateFunction`. Calculated measures do not roll up. They are calculated by evaluating their expression for every single member, be it parent or child.

There's more...

The earlier example showed how to isolate a lower part of a hierarchy, a part below a particular member. In this section we're going to show that the opposite is not so easy, but still possible.

In case we need to scope a part of the hierarchy above the current member, we might be tempted to do the obvious, to use the opposite MDX function, the `Ascendants()` function. However, that would result in an error because the subcube wouldn't be compact any more. The term arbitrary shape represents a subcube formed by two or more smaller subcubes of different granularity, something that is not allowed in the scopes. The solution is to break the bigger subcube into many smaller ones, so that each can be considered compact, with data of consistent granularity. More about which shape is arbitrary and which is not can be found in Appendix and on this site: `http://tinyurl.com/ArbitraryShapes`

Here's an example for the **Mountain Bikes** member in which we show how to set the value to
2 for all of its ancestors.

```
Scope ( Ancestors (
        [Product].[Product Categories].[Subcategory].&[1],
          1    )
    );
    [Measures].[Internet Sales Amount] = 2;
End Scope;

Scope ( Ancestors (
        [Product].[Product Categories].[Subcategory].&[1],
          2    )
    );
    [Measures].[Internet Sales Amount] = 2;
End Scope;
```

This is the result:

	A	B
1	Row Labels ▼	Internet Sales Amount
2	⊞ Accessories	$539,727.51
3	⊟ Bikes	2
4	⊞ Mountain Bikes	$8,215,396.25
5	⊞ Road Bikes	$12,546,132.15
6	⊟ Touring Bikes	1
7	Touring-1000 Blue, 46	1
8	Touring-1000 Blue, 50	1
9	Touring-1000 Blue, 54	1
10	Touring-1000 Blue, 60	1
11	Touring-1000 Yellow, 46	1
12	Touring-1000 Yellow, 50	1
13	Touring-1000 Yellow, 54	1
14	Touring-1000 Yellow, 60	1
15	Touring-2000 Blue, 46	1
16	Touring-2000 Blue, 50	1
17	Touring-2000 Blue, 54	1
18	Touring-2000 Blue, 60	1
19	Touring-3000 Blue, 44	1
20	Touring-3000 Blue, 50	1
21	Touring-3000 Blue, 54	1
22	Touring-3000 Blue, 58	1
23	Touring-3000 Blue, 62	1
24	Touring-3000 Yellow, 44	1
25	Touring-3000 Yellow, 50	1
26	Touring-3000 Yellow, 54	1
27	Touring-3000 Yellow, 58	1
28	Touring-3000 Yellow, 62	1
29	⊞ Clothing	$258,434.10
30	Grand Total	2

The value **1** for **Touring Bikes** and its children is from the previous scope script. But, notice the value **2** in the **Bikes Total** row. The same value can be seen in the **Grand Total** row, highlighted in the bottom of the image. Both the **Bikes Total** and **Grand Total** are the ancestors of member **Mountain Bikes**. The calculation worked as expected.

The query-based alternative

These two scope-based calculations can easily be turned into query-based calculations in case that the calculation is not required to persist in all queries.

Here's the query that returns exactly the same thing as those scope statements we've covered so far, one in the initial example and two in the *There's more* section:

```
WITH
MEMBER [Measures].[Branch detected on member or below] AS
    iif( IsAncestor(
            [Product].[Product Categories].[Subcategory].&[3],
            [Product].[Product Categories].CurrentMember
                )
        OR
        [Product].[Product Categories].[Subcategory].&[3] Is
        [Product].[Product Categories].CurrentMember,
        True,
        null
    )
MEMBER [Measures].[Branch detected on member or above] AS
    iif( Intersect(
            Ascendants(
                [Product].[Product Categories].[Subcategory].&[3]
                    ),
                [Product].[Product Categories].CurrentMember
                    ).Count > 0,
        True,
        null
    )
SELECT
    { [Measures].[Branch detected on member or above],
      [Measures].[Branch detected on member or below] } ON 0,
    NON EMPTY
    { [Product].[Product Categories].AllMembers } ON 1
FROM
    [Adventure Works]
```

The first calculated measure detects ascendants of the current member. It uses the `IsAncestor()` function and detects whether the current member is beneath the selected member in the hierarchy. That function returns `False` for the member itself. Therefore, we have to incorporate additional logic in the form of testing for the presence of a particular member, which is explained in the first recipe of this chapter, *Detecting a particular member in a hierarchy*.

The second calculation detects the descendants of the current member. It uses the `Ascendants()` function to get all the members above and including the selected one. When that set is obtained, we test if the current member is in the set of ascendants. The test is performed using the `Intersect()` and `Count` functions.

Here's another query-based alternative, this time using a CELL CALCULATION:

```
WITH
CELL CALCULATION [Touring Bikes]
FOR '( [Measures].[Internet Sales Amount],
        Descendants( [Product].[Product Categories]
                                .[Subcategory].&[3], ,
                   SELF_AND_AFTER
                 )
       )'
AS 1
SELECT
    { [Measures].[Internet Sales Amount] } ON 0,
    Descendants(
          [Product].[Product Categories].[Subcategory].&[3], ,
          SELF_AND_AFTER
                ) ON 1
FROM
    [Adventure Works]
```

As you can see, a cell calculation does the same thing a `Scope()` statement does in MDX script – it provides an expression for a particular subcube. A CELL CALCULATION is one of the three elements that can be defined using the `WITH` keyword in MDX query. Here's more information about it: `http://tinyurl.com/CellCalculations`

Now, what happens if we want to exclude the selected member in those calculations?

The first calculation in the query we started this section with is easy. We simply have to omit the part next to the OR statement, keeping only the `IsAncestor()` part of the expression.

The second calculation is a bit more complex but it can also be done. All we have to do is extract the selected member from the set of ascendants. This can be done relatively easily using the `Except()` function:

```
Except(
    Ascendants(
        [Product].[Product Categories].[Subcategory].&[3]
            ),
    [Product].[Product Categories].CurrentMember )
```

Other parts of the calculation remain the same.

In the query with the `CELL CALCULATION`, we have to change the `SELF_AND_AFTER` flag into the `AFTER` flag. We don't have to do the same for the set on rows, only in cell calculation, where this behavior is defined.

Children() will return empty sets when out of boundaries

Under certain conditions, some MDX functions generate empty sets as their result; others always return a non-empty set. It is therefore good to know which one is preferred in which scenario, because an empty set will result in an empty value and this may cause problems in some calculations.

The `Descendants()` function will almost always return a result. If there are no children under the member or the set defined as the first argument, then it will return the member or the set itself. On the other hand, the `Children` function will return an empty set when applied to members on the leaf level.

The `Ascendants()` function behaves pretty much the same as the `Descendants()` function. If the specified member is at the top level, it will return the member itself. On the other hand, the `Parent` function when applied to the root member or a top level calculated member returns an empty set. The same is true for the `Ancestors()` and the `Ancestor()` functions. When out of boundaries, they return an empty set as well.

Based on how you want your calculation to react, you should use the function that is most appropriate in a particular case.

Various options of the Descendants() function

The following link provides more information about the `Descendants()` function and how to use its arguments: `http://tinyurl.com/MDXDescendants`

See also

- ▶ The recipes *Detecting a particular member of a hierarchy* and *Detecting the root member* cover a similar topic and are worth reading because of the additional insights they provide.

Finding related members in the same dimension

The dimensionality of a cube equals to the number of hierarchies used in it. This encompasses all the user and attribute hierarchies, including a special hierarchy Measures, visible or not, as long as they are enabled. A cube with 10 dimensions, each having 10 attribute hierarchies is a 101D object! Comparing that to any 3D objects in your environment, such as a Rubik's cube, you will immediately be amazed by the space a typical SSAS cube forms. The number of coordinates, or shall we say cells, in that space is simply beyond our imagination.

Fortunately, a great deal of that space is empty and the SSAS engine has ways to optimize that. It even exposes some of the optimization features to us through several MDX functions we can use when needed.

In this recipe, we are going to look at two hierarchies, Color and Subcategory, and find the number of available colors in each of the product subcategories. Although these two hierarchies are from the same Product dimension, the number of all the possible combinations of Color and Subcategory can still be enormous. Our goal is to find only the existing colors for each product subcategory.

Because of the enormous possible combinations of the hierarchies, from the same dimension or not, in a typical cube, we should always pay attention to optimization. In this recipe, we will cover a type of optimization that is related to combining hierarchies from the same dimension. In the next recipe, we will cover a type of optimization that is related to optimizing the combination of hierarchies from different dimensions.

Getting ready

Start SQL Server Management Studio and connect to your SSAS 2012 instance. Click on the **New Query** button and check that the target database is **Adventure Works DW 2012**.

Here's the query we'll start from:

```
SELECT
    { [Measures].[Internet Order Count] } ON 0,
    { [Product].[Subcategory].[Subcategory].Members *
      [Product].[Color].[Color].Members } ON 1
FROM
    [Adventure Works]
```

Once executed, the query returns all product subcategories cross-joined with product colors. Scroll down your result and compare it with the following screenshot:

		Internet Order Count
Road Bikes	Black	3,030
Road Bikes	Red	2,719
Road Bikes	Yellow	2,319
Road Frames	Black	(null)
Road Frames	Red	(null)
Road Frames	Yellow	(null)
Saddles	NA	(null)
Shorts	Black	1,019
Socks	White	568
Tights	Black	(null)
Tires and Tubes	NA	9,867
Touring Bikes	Blue	1,283
Touring Bikes	Yellow	884
Touring Frames	Blue	(null)
Touring Frames	Yellow	(null)
Vests	Blue	562
Wheels	Black	(null)

It is worth noticing that the result is not a Cartesian product of those two hierarchies. With over 30 different subcategories and 10 different colors in the `Product` dimension, a Cartesian product of these two hierarchies would return over 300 different combinations. The engine, however, has automatically reduced the two-dimensional set on rows to a set of existing combinations only. The reason why this was possible follows.

The two hierarchies `Color` and `Subcategory` belong to the same dimension `Product`. A dimension originates from the underlying table (or a set of them in a snowflake model). The columns on the underlying table become attribute hierarchies. There are only a finite number of various combinations of attributes, and that number is almost always less than a Cartesian product of those attributes. The engine merely has to read that table and return the set of distinct combinations of the attributes for a particular case.

Of course, that is not exactly how it is done, but you get a good idea of how the multidimensional space is automatically shrunk whenever possible.

Notice also that this is not a result of the NON EMPTY keyword on rows because we didn't put it there. That keyword does something else, it removes empty fact rows. As seen in the preceding screenshot, we have many rows with the value of null in them. We deliberately didn't use that keyword to show the difference between what is known as the `auto-exists` algorithm and what NON EMPTY does.

Now, let's get back to the solution and see how to get the number of colors per subcategory without displaying colors on the query axis.

How to do it...

Follow these steps to find related members in the same dimension:

1. Add the `WITH` part of the query.

2. Create a new calculated measure and name it `Number of colors`.

3. Remove the set with `[Product].[Color]` hierarchy from rows and move it inside the definition of the new measure. Only product subcategories should remain on rows.

4. Use the `EXISTING` function before the set of color members and wrap everything in the `Count()` function.

5. Add this calculated measure on axis `0`, next to the existing measure.

6. Execute the query which should look like:

```
WITH
MEMBER [Measures].[Number of colors] AS
    Count( EXISTING [Product].[Color].[Color].Members )
SELECT
    { [Measures].[Internet Order Count],
      [Measures].[Number of colors] } ON 0,
    { [Product].[Subcategory].[Subcategory].Members
                } ON 1
FROM
    [Adventure Works]
```

7. Scroll down to the end and verify that the result matches the following screenshot:

	Internet Order Count	Number of colors
Road Bikes	8,068	3
Road Frames	(null)	3
Saddles	(null)	1
Shorts	1,019	1
Socks	568	1
Tights	(null)	1
Tires and Tubes	9,867	1
Touring Bikes	2,167	2
Touring Frames	(null)	2
Vests	562	1
Wheels	(null)	1

How it works...

By default, sets are evaluated within the context of the cube, not within the current context. The EXISTING keyword forces the succeeding set to be evaluated in the current context. Without it, the current context would be ignored and for each subcategory we would get 10 colors, which are all the distinct colors on the Product dimension table.

After that, we apply the Count() function in order to get the dynamic count of colors, a value calculated for each row separately.

There's more...

There might be situations when you'll have multiple hierarchies of the same dimension in the context, but you'll only want some of them to have an impact on the selected set. In other words, there could have been sizes from the [Size] attribute next to product Subcategories on rows. If you use the EXISTING keyword on colors, you'll get the number of colors for each combination of the subcategory and the site. In case you need your calculation to ignore the current size member and get the number of colors per subcategory only, you will have to take another approach. If you're wondering why you would do such a thing, just imagine you need an indicator which gives you a percentage of the color per size and subcategory. That indicator would have an unusual expression in its denominator and the usual expression in its numerator.

OK, so what's the solution in this case and how do we make such a calculation?

The Exists() function comes to the rescue. In fact, that function does the same thing as the EXISTING keyword, but it requires a second argument in which we need to specify the context for the evaluation.

Here's an example query:

```
WITH
MEMBER [Measures].[Number of colors] AS
    Count( EXISTING [Product].[Color].[Color].Members )
MEMBER [Measures].[Number of colors per subcategory] AS
    Count( Exists( [Product].[Color].[Color].Members,
                   { [Product].[Subcategory].CurrentMember } )
         )
SELECT
    { [Measures].[Internet Order Count],
      [Measures].[Number of colors],
      [Measures].[Number of colors per subcategory] } ON 0,
    { [Product].[Subcategory].[Subcategory].Members *
      [Product].[Size Range].[Size Range].Members } ON 1
FROM
    [Adventure Works]
```

Once run, this query returns two different color-count measures. The first is unique to each row, the second changes by subcategory only. Their ratio, not present but easily obtainable in the query, would return the percentage of color coverage. For example, in the following screenshot it is obvious that there's only 33 percent color coverage for 38-40 CM Road Bikes, which may or may not be a signal to fill the store with additional colors for that subcategory. The important thing is that we were able to control the context and fine-tune it.

		Internet Order Count	Number of colors	Number of colors per subcategory
Pedals	NA	(null)	1	1
Pumps	NA	(null)	1	1
Road Bikes	38-40 CM	782	1	3
Road Bikes	42-46 CM	2,235	3	3
Road Bikes	48-52 CM	3,091	3	3
Road Bikes	54-58 CM	1,355	2	3
Road Bikes	60-62 CM	605	2	3
Road Frames	38-40 CM	(null)	1	3
Road Frames	42-46 CM	(null)	3	3
Road Frames	48-52 CM	(null)	3	3
Road Frames	54-58 CM	(null)	2	3
Road Frames	60-62 CM	(null)	2	3
Saddles	NA	(null)	1	1
Shorts	L	363	1	1

We can also turn it the other way around. The EXISTING keyword is in fact a shortcut, a shorter version of the Exists() function which says, "take everything available as the second argument, don't force me to specify everything." The EXISTING keyword is therefore a more flexible, generic variant which handles any context. When we want to take control over the context, we can step back to the Exists() function.

Tips and trick related to the EXISTING keyword

Another way of specifying the EXISTING keyword is by using the MDX function with the same name. The following expression using the Existing() function is the same as using the EXISTING keyword:

```
Existing( [Product].[Color].[Color].Members )
```

This may come in handy with cross-joins because the cross-join operator * has precedence over the EXISTING keyword. In the following pseudo expression, the EXISTING keyword will be applied to the cross-joined set, and not the first set in the cross-join.

```
EXISTING set_expression1 * set_expression2
```

In order to apply the `EXISTING` to the first set, wrap the first set including the `EXISTING` keyword in curly brackets, like:

```
{ EXISTING set_expression1 } * set_expression2
```

We can also use the alternative `Existing()` function for the first set:

```
Existing ( set_expression1 ) * set_expression2
```

Filter() versus Exists(), Existing(), and EXISTING

Never iterate on a set unless you really have to because iteration is slow. Use specialized functions which operate on sets whenever possible. They are designed to leverage the internal structures and therefore operate much faster.

A `Filter()` function filters a specified set based on a search condition by iterating through each tuple in the specified set. This recipe hopefully showed there's no need to filter a set of members if that set is related to the current context, in other words, that it belongs to the same dimension as explained in the introduction. The `Exists()`, `Existing()`, or `EXISTING` keyword are better choices because they are functions optimized to work in block mode.

A friendly warning

After reading the subsequent recipe about finding related members on a different dimension, you might be tempted to use the technique described in that recipe here as well. The idea of not having to memorize each approach separately is an attractive one. A unique, all-purpose way of finding related a member no matter where is.

You should know that, although it would work, it would be an inefficient solution. The performance could suffer greatly.

The reason for this lies in the fact that if you stick with the solution presented in this recipe, the SSAS engine will be able to perform a fast auto-exist operation on a single dimension table. The solution presented in the subsequent chapter relies on a join between the dimension table and the fact table. Now, all of a sudden, the engine has N times larger a table to scan. That could be a very costly operation if the engine is not optimized to reduce the unnecessary complexity involved here. Such complexity is not needed at all in this scenario! Therefore, try to make a difference in your mind between finding related members in the same dimension and finding related members in another dimension, and approach each case using a different, but appropriate technique.

The procedure mentioned earlier serves the purpose of illustrating the concept; it doesn't necessarily represent the actual implementation in the engine.

See also

▸ Other aspects of the EXISTING keyword are covered in the recipe *Optimizing MDX query using the NonEmpty() function* in *Chapter 1, Elementary MDX Techniques*. You may gain a better understanding of that keyword by reading that recipe.

▸ Also, read the recipe *Finding related members in another dimension* in order to understand the difference between finding related members in the same dimension and in different dimensions.

Finding related members in another dimension

As mentioned in the introduction of the previous recipe, *Finding related members in the same dimension*, this recipe deals with a slightly different scenario. It explains how to find the related members from two or more different dimensions.

Before we start, please keep in mind that when we say a **dimension**, we mean any hierarchy in that dimension from now on.

Dimensions, unlike hierarchies of the same dimension, are unrelated and therefore independent objects. Without a third table in the form of a third fact table, they are unrelated, at least in the dimensional modeling sense. When a fact table is inserted among them, the many-to-many relationship comes into existence.

There are two different types of combination we can make with the dimensions. One type is the **Cartesian product** because they are unrelated. It is obtained by cross-joining members in both dimensions. In relational terms, that would represent the CROSS JOIN of two tables. Since those tables are two independent objects, we get a real Cartesian product.

The other combination is a combination over a fact table, an intermediate table for two or more dimensions. This fact table can serve as a filter. We can use it to get members in the second dimension, members which have associated records, or non-empty values in the fact table for the valid members in the first dimension. A typical example would be "find me products that are available on a particular territory, are bought by a particular customer, or are shipped on a particular date". The first dimension in this case contains the territory, customers and dates respectively; the second one is the product dimension; the fact table or the measure group could be the sales orders or any measure group of our interest.

The previous requirement example can be accomplished by cube design in SSAS alone. All we have to do is position the selected member or more of them in slicer, turn the NON EMPTY keyword on rows, provide a set of members from the other dimension on rows and a measure of our interest on columns. The result would meet our requirement. This type of operation is natural for any SSAS client, and it is available for ad-hoc analysis.

However, as we've learned quite a few times throughout this book, there are always situations when we need to have a control over certain calculations, and the controlled calculations might need to get not all but only the related members, in another dimension. Is there a way to support this? Yes, this recipe shows how.

In this recipe we are going to use the `Reseller` dimension and we are going to find how many `subcategories` each of the top 100 resellers is ordering.

`Reseller` and `Subcategory` are two hierarchies from two different dimensions. Our goal is to find their combinations that have associated rows in the fact table of the specified measure group **Reseller Orders**.

Getting ready

Start SQL Server Management Studio and connect to your SSAS 2012 instance. Click on the **New Query** button and check that the target database is **Adventure Works DW 2012**.

Here's the query we'll start from:

```
SELECT
    { [Measures].[Reseller Order Count] } ON 0,
    { TopCount( [Reseller].[Reseller].[Reseller].Members,
                100,
                [Measures].[Reseller Order Count] ) *
      [Product].[Subcategory].[Subcategory].Members } ON 1
FROM
    [Adventure Works]
```

Once executed, the query returns the top 100 resellers based on their ordering frequency combined with product subcategories. The NON EMPTY keyword is omitted intentionally in order to show a Cartesian product in action.

Combining 100 customers with 37 subcategories makes 3700 rows. The result is a Cartesian product of `Reseller` and `Subcategory`, which are from two different dimensions.

Scroll down to the last row, highlight it, and check the status bar of SSMS. That extra row, 3701th, is the column header row.

It is easy to notice that many combinations of `Reseller` and `Subcategory` produces NULL reseller order. We have two goals in this recipe. The first is to show `Reseller` only on the rows. The second is to count the number of `Subcategory` for each `Reseller` with a condition that the combination actually has associated rows in the reseller order fact table.

The key part of the solution is to find combinations from two different dimensions that have associated rows in the fact table of the specified measure group:

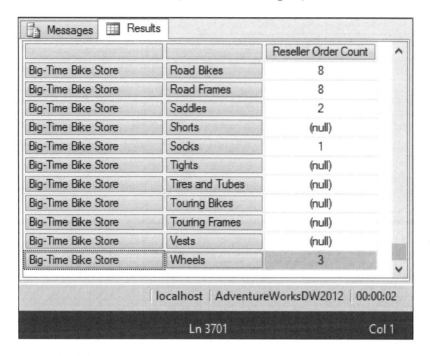

	Messages	Results

		Reseller Order Count
Big-Time Bike Store	Road Bikes	8
Big-Time Bike Store	Road Frames	8
Big-Time Bike Store	Saddles	2
Big-Time Bike Store	Shorts	(null)
Big-Time Bike Store	Socks	1
Big-Time Bike Store	Tights	(null)
Big-Time Bike Store	Tires and Tubes	(null)
Big-Time Bike Store	Touring Bikes	(null)
Big-Time Bike Store	Touring Frames	(null)
Big-Time Bike Store	Vests	(null)
Big-Time Bike Store	Wheels	3

localhost AdventureWorksDW2012 00:00:02

Ln 3701   Col 1

How to do it...

Follow these steps to find related members from `Reseller` and `Subcategory` through the fact table of the measure group **Reseller Orders**:

1. Add the `WITH` part of the query.

2. Create a new calculated measure and name it `Count of SubCategory - Exists`.

3. Remove the set with the `[Product].[Subcategory]` hierarchy from rows and move it inside the definition of the new measure. Only the resellers should remain on rows.

4. Use the variant of the `Exists()` function which has the third argument, the measure group name. In this case, you should use the measure group containing the measure `Reseller Order Count`. The name of that measure group is `Reseller Orders`.

5. Finally, wrap everything with the `Count()` function.

6. Add this calculated measure on axis `0`, next to the existing measure.

7. Execute the query which should look like:

```
WITH
MEMBER [Measures].[Count of SubCategory - Exists] AS
    Count( Exists(
                [Product].[Subcategory].[Subcategory].Members, ,
                'Reseller Orders' ) )
SELECT
    { [Measures].[Reseller Order Count],
      [Measures].[Count of SubCategory - Exists] } ON 0,
    { TopCount( [Reseller].[Reseller].[Reseller].Members,
              100,
              [Measures].[Reseller Order Count] ) *
      [Product].[Subcategory].[Subcategory].Members } ON 1
FROM
    [Adventure Works]
```

8. Verify that the result matches the following screenshot:

	Reseller Order Count	Count of SubCategory - Exists
Advanced Bike Components	12	22
Area Bike Accessories	12	19
Basic Sports Equipment	12	18
Better Bike Shop	12	21
Bike Dealers Association	12	22
Bike Goods	12	8
Brakes and Gears	12	13
Brightwork Company	12	17

How it works...

To find the related members from two different dimensions through a fact table we used the `Exists()` function. The `Exists()` function has three variants, as shown:

```
Exists( Set_Expression1, Set_Expression2)
Exists( Set_Expression1, Set_Expression2, MeasureGroupName )
Exists( Set_Expression1, , MeasureGroupName )
```

The first variant without the third argument `Measure Group Name` is useful for intersecting related attributes from the same dimension as shown in the previous recipe, *Finding related members in the same dimension*. The second variant with the third argument `Measure Group Name` is ideal for combining dimensions across a fact table. In SSAS, a measure group represents a fact table.

The third variant omits the second argument for a set expression. What this variant does is instructs the engine to return distinct members from the first set that have valid combinations with the current member in context, that is the combinations have associated rows in the fact table of the specified measure group.

In our example, we have used the third variant, omitting the second set argument. The current member in context is every reseller on rows. This query context is established in the evaluation phase of the query. There's no need to use the current member as the second set; that member will be there implicitly.

Once we get a set of distinct members from the `Subcategory` hierarchy, all we have to do is count them using the `Count ()` function.

There's more...

The alternative, although not exactly the same solution, would be to use the `NonEmpty ()` function. Here's the query which, when run, shows that both count measures return the same results for each reseller.

```
WITH
MEMBER [Measures].[Count of SubCategory - Exists] AS
    Count ( Exists (
                [Product].[Subcategory].[Subcategory].Members, ,
                'Reseller Orders') )
MEMBER [Measures].[Count of SubCategory - NonEmpty] AS
    Count ( NonEmpty (
                [Product].[Subcategory].[Subcategory].Members,
                { [Measures].[Reseller Order Count] } ) )
SELECT
    { [Measures].[Reseller Order Count],
      [Measures].[Count of SubCategory - Exists],
      [Measures].[Count of SubCategory - NonEmpty] } ON 0,
    { TopCount ( [Reseller].[Reseller].[Reseller].Members,
                100,
                [Measures].[Reseller Order Count]
            ) } ON 1
FROM
    [Adventure Works]
```

Since we've given a hint that this alternative of using NonEmpty() function is not exactly the same as the solution using the Exists(), now's the time to shed more light upon that.

The difference between the third variant of the Exists() function and the NonEmpty() function is subtle. They differ only on measures for which the NullProcessing property is set to Preserve. NonEmpty() is a more destructive function in this case, because it ignores fact records with nulls while Exists() preserves them. In the case where the measure's NullProcessing property is set to Preserve, we can have two different counts and use the one that best meets our reporting requirements. The other subtle difference is that the Exists() function ignores the MDX script and simply does a storage engine query. For example, if the MDX script nulls out a measure, the Exists() function will still return values.

The queries in this recipe so far have illustrated the concept behind the Exists() and NonEmpty() functions. These functions can be used to isolate related members on other dimensions. However, from the performance perspective, they are not great when you need to count members on other dimensions because the count-exists and the count-nonempty combinations are not optimized to run in block mode. The sum-iif combination, on the other hand, is optimized to run in block mode. Therefore, whenever you need to do something more than simply isolating related members on other dimensions (such as counting, and so on), consider using a combination of functions that you know run in block mode.

Here's the query that outperforms the two queries shown so far in this recipe:

```
WITH
MEMBER [Measures].[Count of SubCategory - SumIIF] AS
    Sum( [Product].[Subcategory].[Subcategory].MEMBERS,
         iif( IsEmpty( [Measures].[Reseller Order Count] ),
              null,
              1 )
       )
SELECT
    { [Measures].[Count of SubCategory - SumIIF] } ON 0,
    { TopCount( [Reseller].[Reseller].[Reseller].MEMBERS,
                100,
                [Measures].[Reseller Order Count] ) *
      [Product].[Subcategory].[Subcategory].MEMBERS } ON 1
FROM
    [Adventure Works]
```

Leaf and non-leaf calculations

The examples in this and the previous recipe are somewhat complex from a technical perspective, but they are perfectly valid in many reporting requirements. From an analytical perspective, it is often required to get the count of existing members on a non-leaf level, such as at the subcategory level in our example.

When it's required to get the count of members on a leaf level, designing a distinct count measure using the dimension key in the fact table might be a better option. It will work by the cube design in SSAS; there is no code maintenance and it's much faster than its MDX counterpart. Therefore, look for a by-design solution whenever possible; don't assume that things should be handled in MDX just because this recipe indicated such. *Chapter 7, When MDX is Not Enough* deals with that in more detail.

When it is required to get the count on a non-leaf attribute, that's the time when MDX calculations and relations between hierarchies and dimensions come in to play as valid solutions. Because either you are going to include that higher granularity attribute in your fact table (not likely, especially on large fact tables) and then build a distinct count measure from it, or you can build a new measure group at the non-leaf grain, or you will look for an MDX alternative like we did in this example and the one in the previous chapter. Additionally, the non-leaf levels will typically, although not always, have much lower cardinality than the leaf level, which means that MDX calculations will perform significantly better than they would on a leaf level.

This section serves the purpose of a reminder when it comes to the choice between cube design and MDX calculations. Knowing the pros and cons you should be well on your way to make the right decision.

See also

▸ Other aspects of the `NonEmpty()` function are covered in the recipe *Optimizing MDX queries using the NonEmpty() function, Chapter 1, Elementary MDX Techniques*. You may gain a better understanding of that function by reading that recipe.

▸ Also, read the recipe *Finding related members in the same dimension* in order to understand the difference between finding related members in the same dimension and in the different dimensions.

Calculating various percentages

This recipe and the next two recipes show how to calculate relative percentages, averages, and ranks. We are starting with percentages in this recipe.

Having a ratio of a current member's value over their parent's value is an often-required calculation. It's a form of normalizing the hard-to-grasp values in the table. When the individual amounts become percentages, it immediately becomes clear where the good or bad values are.

There are many kinds of percentages or shares, but we'll take the typical three and present them in this recipe. These are: percentage of parent's value, percentage of level's total, and the percentage of the hierarchy's total.

This recipe will show how to calculate them using the ragged `Sales Territory` hierarchy of the `Sales Territory` dimension. Unlike a balanced (or standard) hierarchy, whose branches all have the same level (or depth) with each member's parent being at the level immediately above the member, a ragged (or unbalanced) hierarchy is a hierarchy whose branches can have inconsistent depths. A typical example of a ragged hierarchy is an organization chart. The levels within the organizational structure are unbalanced, with some branches in the hierarchy having more levels than others.

In Adventure Works cube, the **Sales Territory** hierarchy is a ragged hierarchy. This can be seen by browsing the **Sales Territory** hierarchy in SQL Server management Studio, as shown in the following screenshot. The member **United States** is the only country in that hierarchy which has children, the regions. No other country in that hierarchy has them. This has created inconsistent depths in the hierarchy.

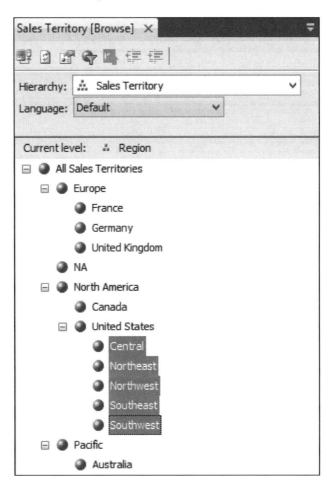

So, let's start!

Getting ready

Start SQL Server Management Studio and connect to your SSAS 2012 instance. Click on the **New Query** button and check that the target database is **Adventure Works DW 2012**.

Here's the query we'll start from:

```
WITH
MEMBER [Measures].[Level] AS
    [Sales Territory].[Sales Territory]
    .CurrentMember.Level.Ordinal
SELECT
    { [Measures].[Level],
        [Measures].[Reseller Sales Amount] } ON 0,
    { [Sales Territory].[Sales Territory].AllMembers } ON 1
FROM
    [Adventure Works]
```

Once executed, the query returns the hierarchized territories in rows:

	Level	Reseller Sales Amount
All Sales Territories	0	$80,450,596.98
Europe	1	$10,870,534.80
France	2	$4,607,537.94
Germany	2	$1,983,988.04
United Kingdom	2	$4,279,008.83
NA	1	(null)
North America	1	$67,985,726.81
Canada	2	$14,377,925.60
United States	2	$53,607,801.21
Central	3	$7,906,008.18
Northeast	3	$6,932,842.01
Northwest	3	$12,435,076.00
Southeast	3	$7,867,416.23
Southwest	3	$18,466,458.79
Pacific	1	$1,594,335.38
Australia	2	$1,594,335.38

In the columns we have a little helper, the level ordinal displayed in a form of a measure. This level ordinal number helps us to see how the members are arranged and ordered in a hierarchy, with the **All Sales Territories** at the top, followed by the level 1 members and their children at level 2. We can also observe that only level 2 member **United States** has children at level 3.

Now we are ready to calculate three percentages for the **Reseller Sales Amount** measure. For each member in the rows, we will calculate its percentage of parent's value, the percentage of the level's total, and the percentage of the hierarchy's total.

How to do it...

Follow these steps to calculate various percentages:

1. Create the first calculated measure for the percentage of parent's value, name it `Parent %` and provide the following definition for it:

```
MEMBER [Measures].[Parent %] AS
    iif( [Sales Territory].[Sales Territory].CurrentMember Is
        [Sales Territory].[Sales Territory].[All],
        1,
        [Measures].[Reseller Sales Amount] /
        (
          [Measures].[Reseller Sales Amount],
          [Sales Territory].[Sales Territory]
          .CurrentMember.Parent
        )
    ), FORMAT_STRING = 'Percent'
```

2. Create the second calculated measure for the percentage of level's total value, name it `Level %` and provide the following definition for it:

```
MEMBER [Measures].[Level %] AS
        [Measures].[Reseller Sales Amount] /
    Aggregate( [Sales Territory].[Sales Territory]
.CurrentMember.Level.Members,
                [Measures].[Reseller Sales Amount] )
    , FORMAT_STRING = 'Percent'
```

3. Create the third calculated measure for the percentage of hierarchy's total value, name it `Hierarchy %` and provide the following definition for it:

```
MEMBER [Measures].[Hierarchy %] AS
        [Measures].[Reseller Sales Amount] /
        ( [Sales Territory].[Sales Territory].[All],
            [Measures].[Reseller Sales Amount] )
        , FORMAT_STRING = 'Percent'
```

4. Include all three calculated measures in columns, execute the query, and verify that the result matches the following screenshot:

	Level	Reseller Sales Amount	Parent %	Level %	Hierarchy %
All Sales Territories	0	$80,450,596.98	100.00%	100.00%	100.00%
Europe	1	$10,870,534.80	13.51%	13.51%	13.51%
France	2	$4,607,537.94	42.39%	5.73%	5.73%
Germany	2	$1,983,988.04	18.25%	2.47%	2.47%
United Kingdom	2	$4,279,008.83	39.36%	5.32%	5.32%
NA	1	(null)	(null)	(null)	(null)
North America	1	$67,985,726.81	84.51%	84.51%	84.51%
Canada	2	$14,377,925.60	21.15%	17.87%	17.87%
United States	2	$53,607,801.21	78.85%	66.63%	66.63%
Central	3	$7,906,008.18	14.75%	14.75%	9.83%
Northeast	3	$6,932,842.01	12.93%	12.93%	8.62%
Northwest	3	$12,435,076.00	23.20%	23.20%	15.46%
Southeast	3	$7,867,416.23	14.68%	14.68%	9.78%
Southwest	3	$18,466,458.79	34.45%	34.45%	22.95%
Pacific	1	$1,594,335.38	1.98%	1.98%	1.98%
Australia	2	$1,594,335.38	100.00%	1.98%	1.98%

How it works...

The Parent % measure returns the ratio of the current member's value over its parent's value. The parent's value is calculated relative to the current member, using the following tuple. In other words, the ratio returns a different value for each territory.

```
( [Measures].[Reseller Sales Amount],
    [Sales Territory].[Sales Territory].CurrentMember.Parent )
```

One additional thing we have to take care of is handling the problem of the nonexisting parent of the root member. There's no such thing as the parent of the root member, meaning, the calculation would result in an error for that cell. In order to take care of that, we've wrapped the calculation in an additional iif() statement. In it, we've provided the value of 1 (100% later) when the root member becomes the current member during the iteration phase on rows.

Similarly, we've defined the other two calculated measures.

For the `Level %` measures, we have used the following tuple to get the aggregated value of all the members at the same level as the current member as the denominator of the ratio:

```
Aggregate( [Sales Territory].[Sales Territory].CurrentMember.Level.
Members,
            [Measures].[Reseller Sales Amount] )
```

For the `Hierarchy %` measures, we have directly used the coordinate with the root member because the following tuple represents the total value of the hierarchy:

```
( [Sales Territory].[Sales Territory].[All],
    [Measures].[Reseller Sales Amount] )
```

It is easy to notice that, the `Level %` and the `Hierarchy %` measures return the same ratio at all levels except at level 3. This is because the aggregate of level 0, 1 or 2 would be practically the same as the value of the root member. If you add up the sales amount for all level 1 members, you would get $80,450,596.98, which is the sales amount of the root member. Same with all level 2 members. However, the aggregated sales amount for the members on the third level is only $53,607,801.21. This is because other level 2 members do not have children except the member, United States.

There's more...

The examples in this recipe so far should give you a good start for percentage calculations. If you have reporting requirements for other types of percentage calculation, the following techniques might come in handy for you.

First, you can use the `SCOPE` statement within an MDX script if you need to calculate the percentage only for a part of your hierarchy.

Next, if you need only a single member in a denominator's tuple, use the `Ancestor()` function and provide the appropriate level. Otherwise, you will have to aggregate the set of members using the `Aggregate()` function, as shown in our example for the `Level %` calculation.

Finally, remember to take care of division by zero problems and problems related to nonexisting members in the hierarchy. One such example is the `Parent %` calculation where we were detecting the root member because that's the only member in that hierarchy without a parent.

Use cases

The `Parent %` measure is the most requested and useful one. It is applicable in any hierarchy and gives an easy way to comprehend information about members in the hierarchy.

`Hierarchy` `%` is useful in the parent-child hierarchy to calculate the individual percentages of members scattered in various positions and levels of a parent-child hierarchy. In addition to that, this calculation is useful in user hierarchies when there is a need to calculate the percentage of members in lower levels with respect to hierarchy's total, because the immediate parents and ancestors break the result into a series of `100%` contributions.

Finally, the `Level` `%` measure is also useful in parent-child hierarchies.

Besides ragged hierarchies, the difference between the `Level` `%` and the `Hierarchy` `%` will manifest in other non-symmetrical structures, those are hierarchies with custom roll-ups and special scopes applied to them. Financial structures (dimensions) like P&L and balance sheet are examples of these special types of hierarchies. In those scenarios you might want to consider having both percentages.

The `Hierarchy` `%` calculated measure is performance-wise a better measure because it picks a coordinate in the cube directly. Moreover, that coordinate is the coordinate with the root member, something we can expect to have an aggregate for. Unless the situation really requires both of these measures, use the `Hierarchy` `%` measure only.

The alternative syntax for the root member

We have used the `All` level to get the root member in our example:

```
[Sales Territory].[Sales Territory].[All]
```

There is an alternative syntax for the root, and it is safe enough that we do not need to worry about possible errors. That definition is this:

```
Tail(
Ascendants(
        [Sales Territory].[Sales Territory].CurrentMember
            )
  ).Item(0)
```

The expression basically says, "take the last of the ascendants of the current member and extract it from that set as a member."

The ascendants are always arranged in a hierarchy which means that the last member in the set of ascendants is the root we're after. Once we have that set, we can use the `Tail()` function to get the last member of that set. If we omit the second argument of the `Tail()` function, the value of 1 is implicitly applied.

The result of that function is still a set so we have to use the `Item()` function in order to convert that single-member set into as a member object. Only then can we use it in our tuple.

The case of nonexisting [All] level

In SSAS, the (All) level is an optional, system-generated level. When the `IsAggregatable` property of a hierarchy is set to `False`, the hierarchy will have no (All) level. For example, in Adventure Works cube the `Organizations` hierarchy on the `Organization` dimension has the `IsAggregatable` property set to `False`. In this case, the following expression for the root member using the `[All]` level will return an empty object:

```
[Organization].[Organizations].[All]
```

However, the `Tail-Ascendants` expression in this case will correctly return the top level member:

```
Tail( Ascendants( [Organization].[Organizations].CurrentMember )
).Item(0)
```

The percentage of leaf member values

The percentage on leaves is the fourth type of the percentage we can calculate. The reason we didn't is that an aggregate on leaves is almost always the same value as the value in the root member. If you have a different situation, use the following calculation:

```
MEMBER [Measures].[Leaves %] AS
    [Measures].[Reseller Sales Amount] /
    Aggregate(
        Descendants( [Sales Territory].[Sales Territory]
                                        .[All], ,
                    leaves ),
        [Measures].[Reseller Sales Amount] )
    , FORMAT_STRING = 'Percent'
```

This calculation takes all leaf members and then applies an aggregate of them in respect to the measure provided. Because of this, it might be significantly slower.

See also

> ▶ The following recipes are part of the three-part series of recipes in this chapter dealing with the topic of relative calculations: *Calculating various averages* and *Calculating various ranks*. It is recommended that you read all of them in order to get a more thorough picture.

Calculating various averages

This is the second recipe in our series of relative calculations. In the previous recipe, *Calculating various percentages*, we created calculated measures for the `Parent` %, the `Level` %, the `Hierarchy` % and the `Leaves` %. We used the ragged `Sales Territory` hierarchy of the `Sales Territory` dimension. There is a good introduction to ragged hierarchy in the previous recipe.

In this recipe, we will continue to use the ragged `Sales Territory` hierarchy of the `Sales Territory` dimension. We are going to show how to calculate the average among siblings, average in the level, average in the entire hierarchy, and average on leaves.

Getting ready

Start SQL Server Management Studio and connect to your SSAS 2012 instance. Click on the **New Query** button and check that the target database is **Adventure Works DW 2012**.

Here is the same initial query we used in the previous recipe for calculating various percentages:

```
WITH
MEMBER [Measures].[Level] AS
    [Sales Territory].[Sales Territory]
    .CurrentMember.Level.Ordinal
SELECT
    { [Measures].[Level],
      [Measures].[Reseller Sales Amount] } ON 0,
    { [Sales Territory].[Sales Territory].AllMembers } ON 1
FROM
    [Adventure Works]
```

Once executed, the query returns hierarchized territories on rows. Please refer back to the screenshot in the previous recipe.

On columns we have a little helper, the level ordinal displayed in a form of a measure. This level ordinal number helps us to see how the members are arranged and ordered in a hierarchy, with the **All Sales Territories** at the top, followed by the level 1 members and their children at level 2. We can also observe that only the level 2 member **United States** has children at level 3.

In addition to the ordinal number for each level, we also have the main measure, the **Reseller Sales Amount** measure. That's the measure we'll use to calculate four different averages: **Siblings AVG**, **Level AVG**, **Hierarchy AVG** and **Leaves AVG**.

How to do it...

Follow these steps to calculate these averages:

1. Create the first calculated measure for the average among the siblings, name it `Siblings AVG`, and provide the definition for it using the `Avg()` function and the `Siblings` function:

   ```
   MEMBER [Measures].[Siblings AVG] AS
       Avg( [Sales Territory].[Sales Territory]
           .CurrentMember.Siblings,
           [Measures].[Reseller Sales Amount] )
   ```

2. Create the second calculated measure for the average on level, name it `Level AVG`, and provide the definition for it using the `Avg()` function and the Level function:

   ```
   MEMBER [Measures].[Level AVG] AS
       Avg( [Sales Territory].[Sales Territory]
           .CurrentMember.Level.Members,
           [Measures].[Reseller Sales Amount] )
   ```

3. Create the third calculated measure for the average on hierarchy, name it `Hierarchy AVG`, and provide the definition for it using the `Avg()` function.

   ```
   MEMBER [Measures].[Hierarchy AVG] AS
       Avg( [Sales Territory].[Sales Territory].Members,
           [Measures].[Reseller Sales Amount] )
   ```

4. Create the fourth calculated measure for the average on leaves, name it `Leaves AVG`, and provide the definition for it using the `Avg()` function and the version of the `Descendants()` function which returns leaves:

   ```
   MEMBER [Measures].[Leaves AVG] AS
       Avg( Descendants( [Sales Territory].[Sales Territory]
                                           .[All], ,
                   Leaves ),
           [Measures].[Reseller Sales Amount] )
   ```

5. Include all four calculated measures on columns, execute the query, and verify that the result matches the following screenshot:

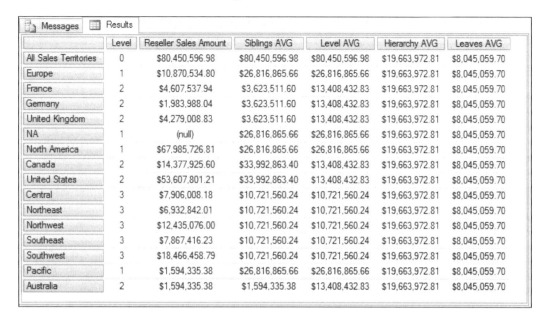

	Level	Reseller Sales Amount	Siblings AVG	Level AVG	Hierarchy AVG	Leaves AVG
All Sales Territories	0	$80,450,596.98	$80,450,596.98	$80,450,596.98	$19,663,972.81	$8,045,059.70
Europe	1	$10,870,534.80	$26,816,865.66	$26,816,865.66	$19,663,972.81	$8,045,059.70
France	2	$4,607,537.94	$3,623,511.60	$13,408,432.83	$19,663,972.81	$8,045,059.70
Germany	2	$1,983,988.04	$3,623,511.60	$13,408,432.83	$19,663,972.81	$8,045,059.70
United Kingdom	2	$4,279,008.83	$3,623,511.60	$13,408,432.83	$19,663,972.81	$8,045,059.70
NA	1	(null)	$26,816,865.66	$26,816,865.66	$19,663,972.81	$8,045,059.70
North America	1	$67,985,726.81	$26,816,865.66	$26,816,865.66	$19,663,972.81	$8,045,059.70
Canada	2	$14,377,925.60	$33,992,863.40	$13,408,432.83	$19,663,972.81	$8,045,059.70
United States	2	$53,607,801.21	$33,992,863.40	$13,408,432.83	$19,663,972.81	$8,045,059.70
Central	3	$7,906,008.18	$10,721,560.24	$10,721,560.24	$19,663,972.81	$8,045,059.70
Northeast	3	$6,932,842.01	$10,721,560.24	$10,721,560.24	$19,663,972.81	$8,045,059.70
Northwest	3	$12,435,076.00	$10,721,560.24	$10,721,560.24	$19,663,972.81	$8,045,059.70
Southeast	3	$7,867,416.23	$10,721,560.24	$10,721,560.24	$19,663,972.81	$8,045,059.70
Southwest	3	$18,466,458.79	$10,721,560.24	$10,721,560.24	$19,663,972.81	$8,045,059.70
Pacific	1	$1,594,335.38	$26,816,865.66	$26,816,865.66	$19,663,972.81	$8,045,059.70
Australia	2	$1,594,335.38	$1,594,335.38	$13,408,432.83	$19,663,972.81	$8,045,059.70

How it works...

The averages are calculated using the standard MDX function called `Avg()`. That function takes a set of members and calculates the average value of the measure provided as the second argument of that function throughout that set of members. The only thing we have to take care of is to provide a good set of members, the one we need the average to be calculated on.

The set of members for the average among siblings calculation is obtained using the `Siblings` function. The set of members for the average on level calculation is obtained using the `Level` function. The set of members for the average on hierarchy calculation is obtained using the `Members` function only, applied directly to the hierarchy, not an individual level. That construct returns all members in that hierarchy, starting from the root member and ending with all leaf members. Finally, the set of members for the average on leaves calculation is obtained by isolating the leaf members using the `Descendants()` function.

There's more...

Most of these averages measures are not intended to be displayed in a grid as we've done here. They are more frequently used as a denominator in various ratios or other types of calculations. For example, it might be interesting to see the discrepancy of each value against one or more average values. That way we can separate members performing below the average from those above the average, particularly if we apply additional conditional formatting to the foreground or the background colors of the cells.

The first two average calculations, the `Siblings AVG` and the `Level ANG`, are applicable to any hierarchy. The `Hierarchy AVG` and the `Leaves AVG` measures are more applicable in parent-child hierarchies and other types of non-symmetrical hierarchies. The `Employee.Employees` hierarchy is another example where the calculation of `Hierarchy AVG` and `Leaves AVG` measures makes perfect business sense.

The `Employee.Employees` hierarchy is a parent-child hierarchy. Employees are found on all levels in that hierarchy. It makes sense to calculate the average value for all employees, no matter which level they are found at, so that we can compare each employee's individual value against the average value of all employees. This is the calculation of `Hierarchy AVG`.

The same process can be restricted to employees that have no one underneath them in the corporate hierarchy. That is, employees which are located as leaves in that hierarchy. It makes sense to calculate their individual contribution against the average value of all such leaf employees. This way we could notice and promote those above average employees by hiring new ones as their subordinates. This is the calculation of `Leaves AVG`.

Preserving empty rows

The average is rarely an empty value. In other words, it's a dense type of calculation in general.

The consequence of making a dense calculation is that we need to identify the situations where it makes sense to set it to the `null` value.

Take a look at the screenshot with the results again and you'll notice there's a row with the null value for the `Reseller Sales Amount`, but the averages are not null themselves. That's what a dense calculation is.

We normally do not want the rows where the original measure is `null`. We generally tend to use the `NON EMPTY` keyword on axes in order to remove the entire empty rows. In this example, we've deliberately omitted that keyword in order to demonstrate this issue, but in a real situation we would have applied it on rows.

The issue we have is that `NON EMPTY` works only when the complete row is empty. Any calculated measures that come from the dense calculations can spoil that.

In order to deal with this issue, we can wrap all calculations for averages in an outer `iif()` statement and detect empty value for the original measure there. This way we will be able to return `null` when the original measure is empty, and applying the NON EMPTY keyword on axes will be able to remove the empty rows. As mentioned in many examples in this book, the `iif()` function is optimized to perform well when one of the branches is null. To detect an empty value for the original measure we will use the `IsEmpty()` function.

Here's an example of how to correct previous calculations:

```
MEMBER [Measures].[Siblings AVG] AS
    iif( IsEmpty( [Measures].[Reseller Sales Amount] ),
         null,
         Avg( [Sales Territory].[Sales Territory]
             .CurrentMember.Siblings,
             [Measures].[Reseller Sales Amount]
           )
       )
```

We could do the same for the rest of the calculated measures, including the `Level` measure.

Other specifics of average calculations

The `Avg()` function returns the average value of non-empty cells only. If you want to create something like a rolling three-month average where some of the months may be empty, you will need to modify or adjust your calculation.

One way of doing this is to break the calculation in two so that the numerator calculates the sum of a set and denominator calculates the count of members (or tuples in general) in that set. The `Count()` function counts empty cells by default. But you can always set its optional second flag to INCLUDEEMPTY to count all members in a set.

The other solution is to modify the second argument in the `Avg()` function so that the expression is never null, either by using the `CoalesceEmpty()` function or by using a dense calculated measure, which is never empty. The sum over count approach is the preferred approach because it preserves the format of measures.

Here you can find more information about MDX functions mentioned in this section and their specifics, including examples: `http://tinyurl.com/AvgInMDX` and `http://tinyurl.com/CountInMDXhttp://tinyurl.com/CoalesceEmptyInMDX`

The **Sum-Count** approach is also the best approach when you need the average on granularity, when you need an aggregation function to calculate the average sales amount or similar. Notice there's no `Avg` aggregation function, only `Sum`, `Count`, `Max`, `Min`, `DistinctCount`, and those semi-aggregatable functions available only in the Enterprise version of SQL Server Analysis Services. In other words, the average aggregation is done by creating two regular measures, one that sums the value and another one that counts the rows, and then a calculated measure as their ratio.

You can always create various scope statements inside the MDX script, thereby breaking the complexity of the requested functionality into a subset of smaller, more compact calculations.

See also

▸ The following recipe is part of the three-part series of recipes in this chapter dealing with the topic of relative calculations: *Calculating various percentages* and *Calculating various ranks*. It is recommended that you read all of them in order to get a more thorough picture.

Calculating various ranks

This is the final recipe in our series of relative calculations. In this recipe, we're going to show how to calculate the rank among siblings, the rank on a level, and the rank in the entire hierarchy. A good introduction is given in the first recipe of this series, *Calculating various percentages*. Therefore it is recommended that you read all three recipes in this series in order to get a better picture of the possibilities and specifics of calculating relative percentages, averages, and ranks.

Getting ready

Start SQL Server Management Studio and connect to your SSAS 2012 instance. Click on the **New Query** button and check that the target database is **Adventure Works DW 2012**.

Here's the query we'll start from:

```
WITH
MEMBER [Measures].[Level] AS
    [Sales Territory].[Sales Territory]
    .CurrentMember.Level.Ordinal
SELECT
    { [Measures].[Level],
      [Measures].[Reseller Sales Amount] } ON 0,
    { [Sales Territory].[Sales Territory].AllMembers } ON 1
FROM
    [Adventure Works]
```

Once executed, the query returns the complete [Sales Territory].[Sales Territory] user hierarchy on rows.

In columns we have a little helper, the level ordinal, displayed in the form of a measure. In addition to that, we have the main measure, the `Reseller Sales Amount` measure. That's the measure we're going to use to calculate the ranks.

This is the same initial query we used in the previous two recipes in this series. Please refer back to the screen shot in the previous two recipes.

We are going to calculate three different ranks: `Siblings Rank`, `Level Rank`, and `Hierarchy Rank`.

How to do it...

Follow these steps to create these three rank calculations:

1. Create the first calculated measure, name it `Siblings Rank`, and provide the definition for it using the `Rank()` function and the `Siblings` function.

```
MEMBER [Measures].[Siblings Rank] AS
    Rank( [Sales Territory].[Sales Territory].CurrentMember,
        [Sales Territory].[Sales Territory]
        .CurrentMember.Siblings,
        [Measures].[Reseller Sales Amount] )
```

2. Create the second calculated measure, name it `Level Rank`, and provide the definition for it using the `Rank()` function and the `Level` function.

```
MEMBER [Measures].[Level Rank] AS
    Rank( [Sales Territory].[Sales Territory].CurrentMember,
        [Sales Territory].[Sales Territory]
        .CurrentMember.Level.Members,
        [Measures].[Reseller Sales Amount] )
```

3. Create the third calculated measure, name it `Hierarchy Rank`, and provide the definition for it using the `Rank()` function. This time, use a named set for the second argument. Name that set `Hierarchy Set`.

```
MEMBER [Measures].[Hierarchy Rank] AS
    Rank( [Sales Territory].[Sales Territory].CurrentMember,
        [Hierarchy Set],
        [Measures].[Reseller Sales Amount] )
```

4. Define that set above all calculated measures as a set of all hierarchy members:

```
SET [Hierarchy Set] AS
    [Sales Territory].[Sales Territory].Members
```

5. Include all three calculated measures on columns and execute the query.

6. Verify that the result matches the following screenshot:

	Level	Reseller Sales Amount	Siblings Rank	Level Rank	Hierarchy Rank
All Sales Territories	0	$80,450,596.98	1	1	1
Europe	1	$10,870,534.80	2	2	7
France	2	$4,607,537.94	1	3	11
Germany	2	$1,983,988.04	3	5	13
United Kingdom	2	$4,279,008.83	2	4	12
NA	1	(null)	4	4	16
North America	1	$67,985,726.81	1	1	2
Canada	2	$14,377,925.60	2	2	5
United States	2	$53,607,801.21	1	1	3
Central	3	$7,906,008.18	3	3	8
Northeast	3	$6,932,842.01	5	5	10
Northwest	3	$12,435,076.00	2	2	6
Southeast	3	$7,867,416.23	4	4	9
Southwest	3	$18,466,458.79	1	1	4
Pacific	1	$1,594,335.38	3	3	14
Australia	2	$1,594,335.38	1	6	14

How it works...

The `Rank()` function has two variants, one with two arguments, and one with a third numeric expression:

```
Rank(Member_Expression, Set_Expression)
Rank(Member_Expression, Set_Expression, Numeric Expression)
```

When using the first syntax, where a numeric expression is not specified, the `Rank()` function simply returns the one-based ordinal position of the first member in the second set argument.

When using the second syntax, where a third numeric expression is specified, the `Rank()` function determines the one-based rank for the specified member in the set according to the results of evaluating the specified numeric expression against the member.

In our example, we have used the second syntax. Let us discuss some specifics of the second syntax and how we used in our example.

When the third numeric argument is supplied to the `Rank()` function, the `Rank()` function evaluates the numeric expression for the member specified as the first argument and compares it to the members of the set specified as the second argument. The function then determines the 1-based rank of the member in that set according to the results.

All three ranks are for the current member on the rows. Therefore, we have used the same member expression as the first argument to the `Rank()` function.

    [Sales Territory].[Sales Territory].CurrentMember

We have also provided the same numeric expression, `[Measures].[Reseller Sales Amount]`, to the `Rank()` function as the third argument.

The only difference in the three calculations is in the second set expression we provided to the `Rank()` function.

The `Siblings Rank` is calculated against the current member's siblings, or children of the same parent. This is the set expression to get all the current member's siblings:

    [Sales Territory].[Sales Territory].CurrentMember.Siblings

The `Level Rank` is calculated against all members in the same level as the current member's level. This is the set expression to get all members at the current member's level:

    [Sales Territory].[Sales Territory].CurrentMember.Level.Members

Finally, the third rank, the `Hierarchy Rank`, is calculated against all members in that hierarchy. This is the set expression to get all the members in the hierarchy:

    [Sales Territory].[Sales Territory].Members

That is also the only set not dependent on the current context. Notice that we have created a named set, `[Hierarchy Set]`. By creating a named set that is independent of the current context, we have essentially moved it outside the iteration. The query performance has been improved. Notice that we did not do this for the `Siblings Rank` and the `Level Rank` because we couldn't.

The rules are relatively simple. Whenever there's a set that doesn't depend on the current context, it is better to extract it from the calculation and define it as a named set. That way it will be evaluated only once, after the evaluation of the subselect and slicer, and before the evaluation of axes. During the process of cell evaluation, which is the next phase in the query execution, such set acts like a constant which makes the calculations run faster.

On the other hand, when the set's definition references the current context, that is, current members of the hierarchies on columns or rows, we must leave the set inside the calculation, or else our calculation will not be dynamic.

There's more...

In the first variant of the `Rank()` function, where the third numeric expression is not provided, the order of members in the set supplied as the second argument plays a crucial role. The function returns the ordinal position of the first member in the second set.

It is important to remember that, in either variant, the Rank() function will not do the sorting for us. If we want the function to return the ranks in a sorted order, then it is up to us to supply a pre-sorted set of members and use it as the second argument.

Tie in ranks

While the three-argument version of the Rank() function can produce tied ranks, the two-argument version will never have tied ranks because the two-argument version determines the ordinal order of members in a set and there's never a tie in the ordinal order; all ordinal positions are unique. However, in the three-argument version, the rank position depends on the value of the numeric expression. Occasionally, that value can repeat which is why the ties exist.

For example, the last two rows of the Hierarchy Rank column in the previous screenshot both have the value 14 as their rank. Consequently, there's no rank 15 in that column; the sequence continues with 16.

Preserving empty rows

Ranks are never null. They are a dense type of calculation. The consequence is that we need to handle rows where the original measure is empty.

Take a look at the screenshot with the results again and you'll notice that there is a row with the null value for the Reseller Sales Amount, but the ranks themselves are not null. This is something we need to take care of.

First, we can use the iif() statement to handle empty rows, just like we did in the previous recipe. Here's an example of how we can correct rank calculations so that they skip rows with empty values:

```
MEMBER [Measures].[Siblings Rank] AS
    iif( IsEmpty( [Measures].[Reseller Sales Amount] ),
        null,
        Rank( [Sales Territory].[Sales Territory]
            .CurrentMember,
            [Sales Territory].[Sales Territory]
            .CurrentMember.Siblings,
            [Measures].[Reseller Sales Amount]
        )
    )
```

This extra layer in our calculation does indeed eliminate the rows where the original measure is empty, making it a good approach. The problem is that the solution is still not a good enough one. Not yet, and we're about to find out why.

The problem lies in the fact that ranks can have holes; they might not be consecutive. A subtle surprise we may not notice at first, but a perfectly understandable behavior once we realize that ranks are actually calculated on a whole set of members, not just the non-empty ones.

While calculating the rank on all members may or may not be what we want, it is more often that we do not want that. In that case, there's still something we can do.

We can make the set in the second argument more compact. We can eliminate all extra members so that our ranks are consecutive and our calculation is faster, because it will operate on a smaller set.

The magic happens in the `NonEmpty()` function. Here's how the modified query could look:

```
WITH
SET [Hierarchy Set] AS
    NonEmpty( [Sales Territory].[Sales Territory].Members,
                { [Measures].[Reseller Sales Amount] } )
MEMBER [Measures].[Level] AS
    iif( IsEmpty( [Measures].[Reseller Sales Amount] ),
        null,
        [Sales Territory].[Sales Territory]
        .CurrentMember.Level.Ordinal
    )
MEMBER [Measures].[Siblings Rank] AS
    iif( IsEmpty( [Measures].[Reseller Sales Amount] ),
        null,
        Rank( [Sales Territory].[Sales Territory]
            .CurrentMember,
            NonEmpty( [Sales Territory].[Sales Territory]
                .CurrentMember.Siblings,
                { [Measures].[Reseller Sales Amount] }
            ),
            [Measures].[Reseller Sales Amount] )
    )
MEMBER [Measures].[Level Rank] AS
    iif( IsEmpty( [Measures].[Reseller Sales Amount] ),
        null,
        Rank( [Sales Territory].[Sales Territory]
            .CurrentMember,
            NonEmpty( [Sales Territory].[Sales Territory]
                .CurrentMember.Level.Members,
                { [Measures].[Reseller Sales Amount] }
            ),
            [Measures].[Reseller Sales Amount] )
    )
MEMBER [Measures].[Hierarchy Rank] AS
    iif( IsEmpty( [Measures].[Reseller Sales Amount] ),
        null,
```

```
            Rank( [Sales Territory].[Sales Territory]
                .CurrentMember,
                [Hierarchy Set],
                [Measures].[Reseller Sales Amount] )
        )
SELECT
    { [Measures].[Level],
      [Measures].[Reseller Sales Amount],
      [Measures].[Siblings Rank],
      [Measures].[Level Rank],
      [Measures].[Hierarchy Rank] } ON 0,
    { [Sales Territory].[Sales Territory].AllMembers } ON 1
FROM
    [Adventure Works]
```

From the preceding query, it's evident that we've added the outer iif() clause in each calculated member. That's the part that handles the detection of empty rows.

Additionally, we wrapped all sets in a NonEmpty() function, specifying that the second argument of that function should be the Reseller Sales Amount measure. Notice that we've done it in the named set too, not just for inner sets in Rank() functions, but in that case we applied the NonEmpty() function in the set, not inside the Rank() function. This is important because, as we said before, the set is invariant to the context and it makes sense to prepare it in full in advance.

Now, the effect of the NonEmpty() function may not be visible in three-part variants of the Rank() function, especially if there are no negative values, because the negative values come after the zeros and nulls. It is immediately clear when we have discontinuous ranks. Therefore, we're going to make another example, a really simple example using the product colors.

Write the following query:

```
WITH
SET [Color Set] AS
    [Product].[Color].[Color].Members
SET [Color Set NonEmpty] AS
    NonEmpty( [Product].[Color].[Color].Members,
              { [Measures].[Internet Sales Amount] } )
MEMBER [Measures].[Level Rank] AS
    iif( IsEmpty( [Measures].[Internet Sales Amount] ),
         null,
         Rank( [Product].[Color].CurrentMember,
               [Color Set] )
       )
MEMBER [Measures].[Level Rank NonEmpty] AS
    iif( IsEmpty( [Measures].[Internet Sales Amount] ),
```

```
            null,
            Rank( [Product].[Color].CurrentMember,
                  [Color Set NonEmpty] )
        )
    SELECT
        { [Measures].[Internet Sales Amount],
          [Measures].[Level Rank],
          [Measures].[Level Rank NonEmpty] } ON 0,
        { [Product].[Color].[Color].Members } ON 1
    FROM
        [Adventure Works]
```

This query displays all product colors and their corresponding sales values. The query also contains two named sets, one having all product colors, the other having only the colors with sales. The two calculated measures return ranks, one using the first set and the other using the second named set.

Now execute that query and observe the results:

	Internet Sales Amount	Level Rank	Level Rank NonEmpty
Black	$7,363,689.27	1	1
Blue	$1,760,058.30	2	2
Grey	(null)	(null)	(null)
Multi	$80,887.18	4	3
NA	$335,882.51	5	4
Red	$6,993,774.57	6	5
Silver	$4,226,772.02	7	6
Silver/Black	(null)	(null)	(null)
White	$3,946.61	9	7
Yellow	$3,749,770.18	10	8

In the preceding screenshot the highlighted section shows the adjusted ranks.

The left rank runs from 1 to 10 and occasionally doesn't display the result. The right rank runs from 1 to 8 because the empty rows are excluded in the named set used as its second argument.

Now, imagine we apply the NON EMPTY operator to rows. That action would eliminate the grey and silver/black colors. In this situation, only the right rank would return the results as expected in most cases. Now you know how to make the rank work this way, so do it.

One more thing: in the previous query, there was a set of members in rows, including all product colors. Notice that the same set appears in both named sets.

The first named set is defined exactly as the set in rows. The second named set contains non-empty colors only. That definition is actually the equivalent of what we would get in rows if the NON EMPTY operator was applied. In short, we can put one of the named sets in rows instead and have a more manageable code.

Ranks in multidimensional sets

The first argument of the Rank() function can in fact be a tuple, not just a member, which enables calculation of ranks for multidimensional sets.

What we need to be extra careful about in this case is the dimensionality of first two arguments. The dimensionality must match. In other words, the order of hierarchies in a tuple must match the order of hierarchies in a set.

Everything that's been said for one-dimensional sets applies here too.

The pluses and minuses of named sets

When named sets are used in calculations, the performance can either benefit from it or suffer because of it. The latter is more often the case. However, this certainly doesn't classify sets in MDX as bad per se. Quite the opposite, sets are a very valuable mechanism in MDX, just like the fire in our ordinary life. If you learn to tell the difference between when to use them and when to not, you're safe with named sets and sets in general.

Currently, the SSAS engine is not optimized to run in block computation mode when sets (named sets or set aliases, that is, sets defined inline in MDX expressions) are used as an argument of functions that perform the aggregation of values. Typical examples are the Sum() and the Count() functions. Those functions are optimized to run in block mode but if you provide a named set or set alias as their argument, you will turn this optimization off and those functions will run in a much slower cell-by-cell mode. This lack of support may change in future releases of SSAS but for the time being you should avoid using named sets and set aliases in those functions unless the situation really requires so. This requirement will rarely be mentioned for named sets, but it may be a valid scenario for set aliases if you need to achieve very flexible and dynamic calculations and you're ready to make a compromise in performance as a tradeoff.

On the other hand, other functions like the Rank() function can profit from using named sets. This is because a different execution pattern is applied in their case. Let's illustrate this with an example.

Let's suppose that the Sum() and Count() functions iterate along a vertical line in cell-by-cell mode and compress that line in a dot when operating in the block mode. Naturally, returning a value in a single point is a much faster operation than iterating along the line.

The rank has to be evaluated for each cell; it does not run in block mode. In other words, it has to go along that vertical line anyway. Unfortunately, that's not the entire issue. Along the way, the `Rank()` function has to evaluate the set on which to perform the rank operation, a set which can be visualized as yet another, this time a horizontal line. The problem is that this new line can change per each dot on the vertical line which means the engine can anticipate nothing but an irregular surface on which to calculate rank values. This is slow because all of a sudden we have two loops, one for the vertical path and the other for the horizontal. Could this be optimized? Yes, by removing the unnecessary loop again, which in this case is the inner loop. Here's how.

When we define a named set and use it inside the `Rank()` function, we're actually telling the SSAS engine that this set is invariant to the current context and as such can be treated as constant. That is, we declare there's a rectangle, not an irregular surface. This way the engine can traverse the vertical line and not bother with evaluating the horizontal line, which is a kind of block optimization again. In other words, it can perform much better.

Other situations when you might want to use named sets is when you're not aggregating values but instead applying set operations like the difference or intersection of sets. In those situations sets also perform well, much better than using the `Filter()` function to do the same thing, for example.

To conclude, named sets are a mixed bag, use them but with caution. Don't forget you can always test which version of your calculation performs better, the one with named sets or the one without them. The recipe *Capturing MDX queries generated by SSAS frontends* in *Chapter 9, On the Edge* will show you how to test that.

See also

- The two recipes prior to this are part of the three-part series of recipes in this chapter dealing with the topic of relative calculations: *Calculating various percentages* and *Calculating various averages*. It is recommended that you read all of them in order to get a more thorough picture.

6

Business Analytics

In this chapter, we will cover:

- ▶ Forecasting using linear regression
- ▶ Forecasting using periodic cycles
- ▶ Allocating nonallocated company expenses to departments
- ▶ Analyzing fluctuation of customers
- ▶ Implementing ABC analysis

Introduction

In the first part of this chapter we will focus on how to perform some of the typical business analyses such as forecasting, allocating values, and calculating the number of days from last sale date.

To forecast future business we frequently use linear regression to calculate the trend line which can tells us how the business will be likely doing in the future, if everything continues the same. Many businesses have a cyclic behavior, and the cycle period can be a year, a month, a week, and so on. If we can calculate the values for the next cycle using the trend line from the previous cycle, we will have a better approximation of the future results than we would be able to get from simply using a linear trend. We will learn how to do forecasting using both the linear regression and the periodic cycles.

Businesses can have unallocated expenses, such as **Operating Expenses** that are charged to corporate, but not allocated to individual departments. The key to allocating theses expenses to individual departments is to calculate a percentage of an expense value of each member department against the aggregate of all the other sibling departments. This percentage can then be used to spread the unallocated expenses to individual departments. In the third recipe in this chapter, we will learn the allocation scheme to calculate the allocation percentages (ratios) and to effectively allocate any measures to any coordinate.

The second half of this chapter shows how to determine the behavior of individual members. These are the last two recipes.

One recipe performs analysis on customers to determine new, returning (loyal), and lost customers. It illustrates an approach which becomes useful when we need to track fluctuations in periods.

In the last recipe, we turn our focus from customer analysis to item grouping. ABC analysis is a method of identifying and classifying items, based on their contribution, into three groups: A, B, and C. In our example, we will use a 30/50/20 ratio as an extension to the "80-20" rule, putting the top 80 percent of product members into two segments of 30 percent and 50 percent.

Let's start!

Forecasting using the linear regression

This recipe illustrates the method of estimating the future values based on the linear trend. The linear trend is calculated using the least-square distance, a statistical method of determining the line that fits the best through the set of values in the chart, as displayed in the following figure:

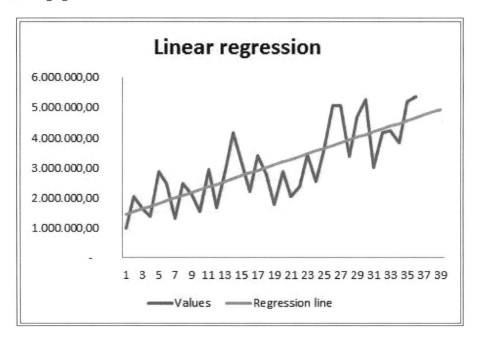

Mathematically, linear regression can be represented by a regression line, $y = ax + b$, where y is the value of the y-intercept for a particular value of x.

Linear regression is often used in a way that "x" is a period and "y" is the value in a particular time period, for example, a month.

Most importantly, the regression line is used to forecast values outside the initial period. For example, we can use a period of 60 months and forecast the value for each of the following 12 months.

This recipe shows how to estimate the values of the two months subsequent to the period of 36 months that were used in the calculation. The screenshot you saw in the introduction of this recipe shows the regression line and forecasted values for those two months.

Getting ready

Start **SQL Server Management Studio** and connect to your SSAS 2012 instance. Click on the **New Query** button and check that the target database is **Adventure Works DW 2012**.

In this example we're going to use the Date dimension. Here's the query we'll start from:

```
SELECT
    { [Measures].[Sales Amount] } ON 0,
    { [Date].[Fiscal].[Month].MEMBERS } ON 1
FROM
    [Adventure Works]
```

Once executed, the query returns 72 months, from January 2005 to December 2010, with no gaps in between. However, not every month has sales amount. The first month with data is July 2005, and the last month with data is June 2008.

> The Date dimension in the Adventure Works DW 2012 database does follow the best practice guideline which says that all months should be consecutive with no holes inside the year. If you are working on the Adventure Works DW 2008R2 database, you might have noticed that this best practice guideline is not strictly followed. The month starts from July 2005 to August 2008, with one extra month in the year 2010, November as the next member in the hierarchy, which is in fact more than two years apart.

Our task will be to forecast the sales amount beyond the three fiscal years period from July 2005 to June 2008, all based on the sales of three fiscal years. As explained in the introduction, we'll use the linear regression method in this recipe while the next recipe will show how to do the same using another approach – the method of periodic cycles.

How to do it...

Follow these steps to add the linear regression code to your MDX:

1. Add the `WITH` part of the query.

2. Create two named sets. One named `Full Period` and the other named `Input Period`. The definition for the first set should be the same set that is on the axis 1. The definition of the second set should be a range of months up to and including `June 2008`. Don't forget to use the `Fiscal` hierarchy.

3. Create several calculated members. The first, `Input X`, is a measure that determines the rank of the current fiscal member in the named set `Input Period`.

4. The second, `Input Y`, is a measure that is an alias for the `Sales Amount` measure.

5. The third, `Output X`, is a measure similar to `Input X`, only this time we're determining the rank in the first set, `Full Period`.

6. Finally, the fourth calculated member, `Forecast`, will be a measure that contains the formula which combines all the previous calculated members and sets and calculates the regression line using the `LinRegPoint()` function:

```
LinRegPoint(
        [Measures].[Output X],
                [Input Period],
        [Measures].[Input Y],
        [Measures].[Input X]
        )
```

7. Specify `$#,##0.00` as a format string of the `Forecast` measure.

8. Add the `Forecast` measure on axis 0, next to the `Sales Amount` measure.

9. Verify that your query looks like the following one. Execute it:

```
WITH
SET [Full Period] AS
    [Date].[Fiscal].[Month].MEMBERS
SET [Input Period] AS
    { null : [Date].[Fiscal].[Month].&[2008]&[6] }
MEMBER [Measures].[Input X] AS
    Rank( [Date].[Fiscal].CurrentMember, [Input Period] )
MEMBER [Measures].[Input Y] AS
    [Measures].[Sales Amount]
MEMBER [Measures].[Output X] AS
    Rank( [Date].[Fiscal].CurrentMember, [Full Period] )
MEMBER [Measures].[Forecast] AS
                // = Output Y
    LinRegPoint(
        [Measures].[Output X],
```

```
            [Input Period],
        [Measures].[Input Y],
        [Measures].[Input X]
        )
        , FORMAT_STRING = '$#,##0.00'
SELECT
    { [Measures].[Sales Amount],
      [Measures].[Forecast] } ON 0,
    { [Date].[Fiscal].[Month].MEMBERS } ON 1
FROM
    [Adventure Works]
```

10. Verify that the result matches the following screenshot. The highlighted cells contain the forecasted values:

	Sales Amount	Forecast
February 2008	$4,163,246.63	$4,004,744.94
March 2008	$4,220,276.16	$4,085,414.57
April 2008	$3,813,373.94	$4,166,084.20
May 2008	$5,193,592.51	$4,246,753.83
June 2008	$3,460,129.77	$4,327,423.46
July 2008	(null)	$4,408,093.09
August 2008	(null)	$4,488,762.72
September 2008	(null)	$4,569,432.35
October 2008	(null)	$4,650,101.98
November 2008	(null)	$4,730,771.61
December 2008	(null)	$4,811,441.24
January 2009	(null)	$4,892,110.86
February 2009	(null)	$4,972,780.49
March 2009	(null)	$5,053,450.12
April 2009	(null)	$5,134,119.75

How it works...

In this example we've used a few more calculated members and sets than necessary. We've defined two named sets and three calculated members before we came to the main part of the query: the fourth calculated member, which contains the formula for forecasting values based on the linear trend. We did this extra bit of work in order to have a simple and easy-to-memorize expression for the otherwise complicated `LinRegPoint()` function.

The `LinRegPoint()` function has four parameters. Names used in this example suggest what these parameters represent. The key to use this function is to provide these four parameters correctly. So, let's repeat the function and the four parameters from our previous query:

```
LinRegPoint (
        [Measures].[Output X],
                    [Input Period],
        [Measures].[Input Y],
        [Measures].[Input X]
        )
```

As the names suggest, the last three parameters (`Input Period`, `Input X`, and `Input Y`) are all inputs used to determine the regression line $y = a \cdot x + b$. Here we've specified a set of members (July 2005 – June 2008 period), their ordinal positions in that set (values 1 – 36 obtained using the `Rank()` function on that period), and their corresponding values (measuring the sales amount). We've prefixed all of them with "Input" in order to emphasize that these parameters are used as the input for the calculation of the regression line.

Once the regression line is calculated internally, it is used in combination with the first parameter, `Output X`. This two-step process is a composition of functions where the result of the inner one is used as the argument in the outer one. This is what makes the `LinRegPoint()` function difficult to understand and remember. Hopefully, by making a distinction between parameters, that is, prefixing them as input and output parameters, the function becomes less difficult to understand.

Here is the calculation we used for `Input X`. Notice that for input, we have included only the periods that have sale amount.

```
Rank( [Date].[Fiscal].CurrentMember, [Input Period] )
```

Now starts the second phase, the invisible outer function.

The first parameter (`Output X`) is used to specify the ordinal position of the member which we want to calculate the value for. Here is the calculation for `Output X`:

```
Rank( [Date].[Fiscal].CurrentMember, [Full Period] )
```

Notice we've used `[Full Period]`, which is a different set than what we used for the parameter `Input X` because our primary need was to get the value for members whose positions are beyond June 2008.

Notice also that the measure `Forecast` represents the `Output Y` value which was hinted at in the code. In other words, for a given regression line (based on the "Input" parameters), we have calculated the y value for any given x, including, but not limited to the initial set of members. That was step two in the evaluation of the `LinRegPoint()` function.

There's more...

The `LinRegPoint()` is not the only MDX function which can be used to calculate the values based on the regression line. Remember we said this function evaluates in a two-step process. The result of the inner step is not one but actually two numbers. One is the slope, the other intercept. In other words, the a and b in the y = a · x + b equation.

You might feel more comfortable using the slope (a) and the intercept (b) in order to forecast a value. If that's the case then here's the add-on to the previous example.

Add this part of the code in the previous query, and then add those three calculated members on axis 0 and run the query:

```
MEMBER [Measures].[Slope] AS // = a
    LinRegSlope(
                    [Input Period],
        [Measures].[Input Y],
        [Measures].[Input X]
        )
        , FORMAT_STRING = '#,#'
MEMBER [Measures].[Intercept] AS // = b
    LinRegIntercept(
                    [Input Period],
        [Measures].[Input Y],
        [Measures].[Input X]
        )
        , FORMAT_STRING = '#,#'
MEMBER [Measures].[Verify y = a * x + b] AS
    [Measures].[Slope] * [Measures].[Output X] +
    [Measures].[Intercept]
    // y = a * x + b
        , FORMAT_STRING = '$#,##0.00'
```

The result will look like the following screenshot:

	Sales Amount	Forecast	Slope	Intercept	Verify y = a * x + b
February 2008	$4,163,246.63	$4,004,744.94	80,670	939,299	$4,004,744.94
March 2008	$4,220,276.16	$4,085,414.57	80,670	939,299	$4,085,414.57
April 2008	$3,813,373.94	$4,166,084.20	80,670	939,299	$4,166,084.20
May 2008	$5,193,592.51	$4,246,753.83	80,670	939,299	$4,246,753.83
June 2008	$3,460,129.77	$4,327,423.46	80,670	939,299	$4,327,423.46
July 2008	(null)	$4,408,093.09	80,670	939,299	$4,408,093.09
August 2008	(null)	$4,488,762.72	80,670	939,299	$4,488,762.72
September 2008	(null)	$4,569,432.35	80,670	939,299	$4,569,432.35
October 2008	(null)	$4,650,101.98	80,670	939,299	$4,650,101.98
November 2008	(null)	$4,730,771.61	80,670	939,299	$4,730,771.61
December 2008	(null)	$4,811,441.24	80,670	939,299	$4,811,441.24
January 2009	(null)	$4,892,110.86	80,670	939,299	$4,892,110.86
February 2009	(null)	$4,972,780.49	80,670	939,299	$4,972,780.49
March 2009	(null)	$5,053,450.12	80,670	939,299	$5,053,450.12

The three extra measures were the `Slope`, `Intercept`, and `Verify y = a * x + b` measures. The first two were defined using the `LinRegSlope()` and `LinRegIntercept()` functions respectively. The same last three parameters were used here as in the `LinRegPoint()` function. What `LinRegPoint()` does extra is that it takes one step further and combines those two values with an additional parameter in order to calculate the final `y`.

From the previous screenshot it is clear that the `LinRegSlope()` and `LinRegIntercept()` can be used instead of the `LinRegPoint()` function – the values are exactly the same. All it takes is to combine them in the equation `y = a · x + b`. Therefore, it is up to you to choose the preferred way for you to forecast the value based on the regression line.

Tips and tricks

The `Rank()` function is used to determine the ordinal position of a member in a set. Here we've used it twice: to calculate the position of members in the `Input Period` set and to calculate the position of members in the `Full Period` set.

`Rank()` performs better if we extract the set used as the second argument and define it as a separate named set, which we did. This is because in that case the set is evaluated only once and not repeatedly for each cell.

Where to find more information?

For more information, please refer to the following MSDN links:

`http://tinyurl.com/LinRegPoint`

`http://tinyurl.com/LinRegSlope`

`http://tinyurl.com/LinRegIntercept`

Also, *Mosha Pasumansky* has a blog on using the MDX linear regression functions for forecasting: `http://tinyurl.com/MoshaLinReg`

See also

▸ The recipe *Forecasting using the periodic cycles* covers a similar topic

Forecasting using the periodic cycles

Linear trend, covered in the recipe *Forecasting using the linear regression*, is just an overview of how the business is going. The regression line serves us merely as an indicator of where we will be in the future if everything continues the same. What it doesn't tell us, at least not well enough, is what the individual values on that path will be. The values that method returns are too simplified, too imprecise.

Of course, there are other ways of forecasting the future values, i.e. using polynomial curves or similar, which, generally speaking, will fit better to the shape of achieved business values and therefore represent future values more precisely. However, we won't make an example using them; we will use something simple but effective as well.

The characteristic of many businesses is that events tend to repeat themselves after some time. In other words, many of them have a cyclic behavior whether that period is a year, a month, a week, a day, or whatever.

The simplification can be summarized like this: there's an envelope of events taking place during a cycle and there is a linear trend which says how much better or worse the next period is going to be compared to the previous one. When we say "the envelope", we mean a shape of events and their values. For example, there might be a spike in the curve for the Spring/Autumn parts when people buy shoes, there might be a spike in the activity in the end of the month when people need to finish their reports, there might be a spike in the middle of the week because people are more business-focused in that part of the week, or there might even be a spike in the early morning or late afternoon because that's when people travel to and from the work. All in all, things are not flat and moreover, the shape of their non-flatness more or less looks the same in every cycle.

If we calculate the values for the next cycle using the trend line but keep the shape of the events in the cycle, we will have a better approximation and estimation of the future results than by simply using a linear trend. It's not that we'll replace it with something else. No, we're just going to improve it by adjusting the stiffness of the regression line.

Getting ready

Open **SQL Server Data Tools** (SSDT) and then open **Adventure Works DW 2012** solution. Double-click on **Adventure Works** cube and go to **Calculations** tab. Choose **Script View**. Position the cursor at the end of the script where you'll create a calculated measure `Sales`, `null` by default, and then scope that measure so that only the values up to the **December 2007** are not null.

```
Create Member CurrentCube.[Measures].[Sales] As null;

Scope( ( { null : [Date].[Fiscal].[Month].&[2007]&[12] },
         [Measures].[Sales] ) );
    This = [Measures].[Sales Amount];
End Scope;
```

We are going to use this measure to forecast its values for the next half of the year. We've deliberately used a calculated measure being equal to the original measure, `Sales Amount`, because the latter one already has values in that period. In other words, we'll be able to test how good our forecasting expression is.

Once you're done, deploy the changes, preferably using the **BIDS Helper**, if not SSDT itself.

Then start **SQL Server Management Studio** and connect to your SSAS 2012 instance. Click on the **New Query** button and check that the target database is **Adventure Works DW 2012**.

Write this query:

```
SELECT
    { [Measures].[Sales] } ON 0,
    { Descendants( [Date].[Fiscal].[Fiscal Year].&[2008],
                   [Date].[Fiscal].[Month] ) } ON 1
FROM
    [Adventure Works]
```

Once executed, the query returns 12 months of the fiscal year 2008. Half of them have values, the other half are blank:

	Sales
July 2007	$3,552,319.38
August 2007	$5,060,385.02
September 2007	$5,057,832.17
October 2007	$3,362,565.46
November 2007	$4,680,142.51
December 2007	$3,574,001.32
January 2008	(null)
February 2008	(null)
March 2008	(null)
April 2008	(null)
May 2008	(null)
June 2008	(null)

Now let's see if we can predict the values for those empty six months based on the previous years and the shape of the curve in those previous fiscal years on a monthly granularity.

How to do it...

We're going to define six calculated measures and add them to the columns axis.

1. Add the WITH part of the query.

2. Create the calculated measure Sales PP and define it as the value of the measure Sales in the parallel period.

3. Create the calculated measure Sales YTD and define it as a year-to-date value of the Sales measure.

4. Create the calculated measure Sales PP YTD and define it as a year-to-date value of the Sales measure in the parallel period. The YTD value should only be calculated up to the parallel period of the last month with the data. For this you might need some help, so here's the syntax:

```
Sum(
    PeriodsToDate( [Date].[Fiscal].[Fiscal Year],
        ParallelPeriod( [Date].[Fiscal].[Fiscal Year], 1,
            Tail( NonEmpty( { null :
                                [Date].[Fiscal].CurrentMember },
                            [Measures].[Sales] ),
                1 ).Item(0) ) ),
        [Measures].[Sales] )
```

5. Define a calculated measure `Ratio` being equal to the ratio of YTD value versus PP YTD value. Don't forget to take care of division by zero.

6. Define a calculated measure `Forecast` being equal to the parallel period's value of the measure `Sales` corrected (multiplied) by the measure `Ratio`.

7. Define a calculated measure `Forecast YTD` being equal to the sum of year-to-date values of the measures `Sales` and `Forecast`, but only for months when `Sales` is null.

8. Add all those measures on columns of the query and verify that your query looks like the following one:

```
WITH
MEMBER [Measures].[Sales PP] AS
    ( ParallelPeriod( [Date].[Fiscal].[Fiscal Year], 1,
                      [Date].[Fiscal].CurrentMember ),
      [Measures].[Sales] )
    , FORMAT_STRING = '$#,##0.00'
MEMBER [Measures].[Sales YTD] AS
    Sum(
        PeriodsToDate( [Date].[Fiscal].[Fiscal Year],
                       [Date].[Fiscal].CurrentMember ),
        [Measures].[Sales] )
    , FORMAT_STRING = '$#,##0.00'
MEMBER [Measures].[Sales PP YTD] AS
    Sum(
        PeriodsToDate( [Date].[Fiscal].[Fiscal Year],
            ParallelPeriod( [Date].[Fiscal].[Fiscal Year], 1,
                Tail( NonEmpty( { null :
                                  [Date].[Fiscal].CurrentMember },
                                [Measures].[Sales] ),
                    1 ).Item(0) ) ),
        [Measures].[Sales] )
    , FORMAT_STRING = '$#,##0.00'
MEMBER [Measures].[Ratio] AS
    iif( [Measures].[Sales PP YTD] = 0,
         null,
         [Measures].[Sales YTD] / [Measures].[Sales PP YTD] )
    , FORMAT_STRING = '#,##0.00'
MEMBER [Measures].[Forecast] AS
    iif( IsEmpty( [Measures].[Sales] ),
         [Measures].[Ratio] * [Measures].[Sales PP],
         null )
    , FORMAT_STRING = '$#,##0.00'
MEMBER [Measures].[Forecast YTD] AS
    iif( IsEmpty( [Measures].[Sales] ),
```

```
        Sum (
            PeriodsToDate( [Date].[Fiscal].[Fiscal Year],
                           [Date].[Fiscal].CurrentMember ),
            [Measures].[Sales] +
            [Measures].[Forecast] ),
        null )
      , FORMAT_STRING = '$#,##0.00'
SELECT
    { [Measures].[Sales],
      [Measures].[Sales PP],
      [Measures].[Sales YTD],
      [Measures].[Sales PP YTD],
      [Measures].[Ratio],
      [Measures].[Forecast],
      [Measures].[Forecast YTD]
    } ON 0,
    { Descendants( [Date].[Fiscal].[Fiscal Year].&[2008],
                   [Date].[Fiscal].[Month] ) } ON 1
FROM
    [Adventure Works]
```

9. Execute the query.

10. Verify that the result matches the following screenshot. The highlighted cells represent the forecasted values:

	Sales	Sales PP	Sales YTD	Sales PP YTD	Ratio	Forecast	Forecast YTD
July 2007	$3,552,319.38	$2,894,054.68	$3,552,319.38	$2,894,054.68	1.23	(null)	(null)
August 2007	$5,060,385.02	$4,147,192.18	$8,612,704.40	$7,041,246.87	1.22	(null)	(null)
September 2007	$5,057,832.17	$3,235,826.19	$13,670,536.57	$10,277,073.06	1.33	(null)	(null)
October 2007	$3,362,565.46	$2,217,544.45	$17,033,102.02	$12,494,617.50	1.36	(null)	(null)
November 2007	$4,680,142.51	$3,388,911.41	$21,713,244.54	$15,883,528.92	1.37	(null)	(null)
December 2007	$3,574,001.32	$2,219,811.82	$25,287,245.86	$18,103,340.74	1.40	(null)	(null)
January 2008	(null)	$1,756,407.01	$25,287,245.86	$18,103,340.74	1.40	$2,453,397.77	$27,740,643.63
February 2008	(null)	$2,873,936.93	$25,287,245.86	$18,103,340.74	1.40	$4,014,394.40	$31,755,038.03
March 2008	(null)	$2,049,529.87	$25,287,245.86	$18,103,340.74	1.40	$2,862,839.88	$34,617,877.90
April 2008	(null)	$2,371,677.70	$25,287,245.86	$18,103,340.74	1.40	$3,312,824.85	$37,930,702.76
May 2008	(null)	$3,443,525.25	$25,287,245.86	$18,103,340.74	1.40	$4,810,011.08	$42,740,713.83
June 2008	(null)	$2,542,671.93	$25,287,245.86	$18,103,340.74	1.40	$3,551,674.32	$46,292,388.15

How it works...

The first calculated measure, `Sales PP`, represents a value of the measure `Sales` in the parallel period, the previous year in this case. This value will serve as a basis for calculating the value of the same period in the current year later on. Notice that the measure `Sales PP` has values in each month.

The second calculated measure, `Sales YTD`, is used as one of the values in the `Ratio` measure, the measure which determines the growth rate and which is subsequently used to correct the parallel period value by the growth ratio. Notice that the `Sales YTD` values remain constant after **December 2007** because the values of the measure it depends on, `Sales`, are empty in the second half of the fiscal year.

The third calculated measure, `Sales PP YTD`, is a bit more complex. It depends on the `Sales PP` measure and should serve as the denominator in the growth rate calculation. However, values of the `Sales PP` measure are not empty in the second half of the fiscal year which means that the cumulative sum would continue to grow. This would corrupt the ratio because the ratio represents the growth rate of the current period versus the previous period, the year-to date of each period. If one stops, the other should stop too. That's why there's an additional part in the definition which takes care of finding the last period with data and limiting the parallel period to the exact same period. This was achieved using the `Tail-NonEmpty-Item` combination where the `NonEmpty()` function looks for non-empty members up to the current period, `Tail()` takes the last one, and the `Item()` function converts that into a single member. Notice in the previous screenshot that it works exactly as planned. `Sales PP YTD` stops growing when `Sales YTD` stops increasing, all because `Sales` is empty.

Once we have that fixed, we can continue and build a ratio measure which, as stated earlier, represents the growth rate between all the periods in the current fiscal year so far versus the same periods in the previous year. As both of the year-to-date measures become constant at some point in time, the ratio also becomes constant as visible in the previous screenshot.

The `Forecast` measure is where we take the value of the same period in the previous year and multiply it by the growth rate in form of the `Ratio` measure. That means we get to preserve the shape of the curve from the previous year while we increase or decrease the value of it by an appropriate factor. It is important to notice that the ratio is not constant, it changes in time, and it adjusts itself based on all the year-to-date values, as long as they exist. When there aren't any, it becomes a constant.

Finally, the last calculated measure, `Forecast YTD`, is here to show what would have happened to the `Sales YTD` measure if there were values in the last six months of that fiscal year. Of course, it does that by summing the year-to-date values of both the `Sales` and `Forecast` measures.

The following figure illustrates the principle behind the periodic cycles' calculation quite easily:

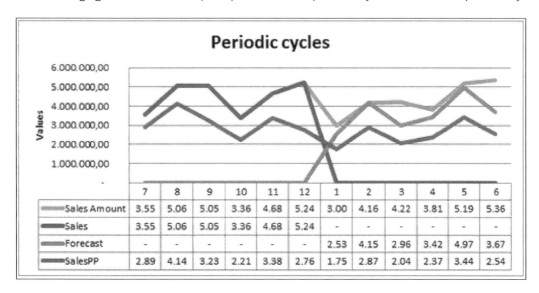

The **Sales Amount** series represents values of the original measure, the one we used in the scope. The **Sales** series represents values of the calculated measure which has the same value as the original `Sales Amount` measure, which stops in December, as visible in the previous image. The Forecast series continues where the **Sales** series stops and takes the shape of the last series, the **SalesPP** series, which represents the values of the `Sales Amount` measure in the previous year's months.

The **Sales** series versus the **Sales PP** series determines the ratio. Once there is no data, the **Forecast** series takes the shape of the **Sales PP** series, but multiplied by the ratio.

The previous image illustrates that the forecasted values are not exact with the actual **Sales Amount** data, the measure that contains real values, but they are much better than they would be using the linear regression only. There's certainly a possibility to improve the formula for the ratio calculation in a way that it incorporates many previous periods and not just the previous year as in this example, in addition to adding more weight to the recent years, perhaps. You are encouraged to experiment with this recipe in order to get more accurate forecasts of the data.

Other approaches

The technique described in this recipe will fail to achieve good values when applied to non-periodic business processes or processes with periodic cycles but irregular events inside the cycles. The recipe *Calculating moving averages* in *Chapter 3, Working with Time* might be a good starting point in those situations.

If you find this recipe interesting, here's another variant in a blog article by *Chris Webb*, one of the reviewers of this book: `http://tinyurl.com/ChrisSeasonCalcs`

Finally, **Data Mining** and its **Time Series** algorithm can be a more accurate way of forecasting future values, but that's outside the scope of this book. If you're interested in learning more about it, here are two links to get you started in that direction. One explains what the Time Series algorithm is and the second is *Chris Webb's* application of it: `http://tinyurl.com/DataMiningTimeSeries`

`http://tinyurl.com/ChrisDataMiningForecast`

See also

▸ The recipe *Forecasting using the linear regression* deals with a similar topic

Allocating the nonallocated company expenses to departments

There are two types of expenses, direct and indirect. It is relatively easy for any company to allocate a direct expense to a corresponding department because it actually happens in that department and is in no way associated with other departments. This type of expense is usually allocated in real-time, at the moment it enters the system. An example of such an expense is salaries.

The other type of expense is an indirect expense, for example, electricity or heating bill. These expenses are usually entered in the system using a special department like the corporation itself, a common expense department, or simply nothing (a null value). The company, in order to have a clear picture of how each department is doing, usually wants to allocate these expenses to all departments. Of course, there are many ways of achieving this and none of them are perfect. Because of that, the allocation is usually done at the later stage, not in the real-time.

For example, the allocation can be implemented in the **ETL** (**Extract, Transform, Load**) phase. In that case, the modified data enters the **Data Warehouse** (**DW**) and later the cube. The other approach is to leave the data as it is in the DW and use the MDX script in the cube to modify it. The first scenario will have better performance, the second more flexibility.

Flexibility means that the company can apply several calculations and choose which set of allocation keys fits the best in a particular case, a sort of what-if analysis. It also means that the company may decide to use multiple allocation schemes at the same time, one for each business process. However, the allocation keys can change in time. Maintaining complex scope statements can become difficult. The performance of such scopes will degrade too. In short, each approach has its advantages and disadvantages.

In this recipe, we'll focus on the second scenario, the one where we apply MDX. After all, this is a book about MDX and its applications. Here, you'll learn how to perform the scope type allocation, how to allocate the values from one member in the hierarchy on its siblings so that the total remains the same. Once you learn the principle, you will be able to choose any set of allocation keys and apply it whenever and wherever required.

Getting ready

In this example, we're going to use the measure **Amount** and two related dimensions, **Account** and **Department**.

Open **SQL Server Data Tools** (SSDT) and then open **Adventure Works DW 2012** solution. Double-click on **Adventure Works** cube. Locate the measure **Amount** in the **Financial Reporting** measure group. Go to the next tab, **Dimension Usage**, and check that the two dimensions mentioned previously are related to this measure group.

Now, go to the **Cube Browser** tab and click on the **Analyze in Excel** button on top to create a pivot which shows accounts and departments on rows and the value of the measure **Amount** in the data part. Expand the accounts until the member **Operating Expenses** located under **Net Income | Operating Profit** is visible. Expand the departments until all of them are visible. Once you're done, you'll see the following screenshot:

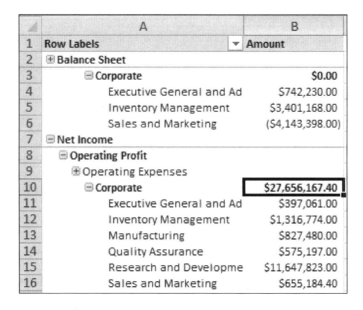

	A	B
1	Row Labels	Amount
2	⊞ Balance Sheet	
3	⊟ Corporate	$0.00
4	Executive General and Ad	$742,230.00
5	Inventory Management	$3,401,168.00
6	Sales and Marketing	($4,143,398.00)
7	⊟ Net Income	
8	⊟ Operating Profit	
9	⊞ Operating Expenses	
10	⊟ Corporate	$27,656,167.40
11	Executive General and Ad	$397,061.00
12	Inventory Management	$1,316,774.00
13	Manufacturing	$827,480.00
14	Quality Assurance	$575,197.00
15	Research and Developme	$11,647,823.00
16	Sales and Marketing	$655,184.40

Notice a strange thing in the result. The total for the **Corporate** department in the **Operating Expenses** account (the highlighted 27+ million) is not equal to the sum of the individual departmental values. Roughly 12 million is missing. Why is that?

Double-click on the **Department** dimension in the **Solution Browser** pane. Select the attribute that represents the parent key and check its property `MembersWithData` found under the **Parent-Child** group of properties. Notice that it's bold, which means the property has a non-default value. The option that was selected is `NonLeafDataHidden`. That means this parent-child hierarchy hides members which represent the data members of the non-leaf members. In this case there's only one, the **Corporate** member, found on the first level in that hierarchy.

Change the value of this property to `NonLeafDataVisible` and deploy the solution, preferably using the **Deploy Changes Only** deployment mode (configurable in the **Project Properties** form) in order to speed up the process.

Now, return to the **Cube Browser** and reconnect to the cube, and click on the **Analyze in Excel** button on top to create a pivot again in Excel.

A new member will appear on the second level, **Corporate**. This member is not the same as the member on the first level. It is a special member representing its parent's individual value that, together with the value of other siblings, goes into the final value of their parent, the **Corporate** member on the first level. This hidden **Corporate** member, sometimes called the `datamember`, has a value of 12+ million which is now clearly visible in the pivot. The exact amount, highlighted in the following screenshot, was missing in our equation a moment ago:

	A	B
1	Row Labels	Amount
2	⊞ Balance Sheet	
3	⊟ Corporate	$0.00
4	Executive General and Administration	$742,230.00
5	Inventory Management	$3,401,168.00
6	Sales and Marketing	($4,143,398.00)
7	⊟ Net Income	
8	⊟ Operating Profit	
9	⊞ Operating Expenses	
10	⊟ Corporate	$27,656,167.40
11	Corporate	$12,236,648.00
12	Executive General and Administration	$397,061.00
13	Inventory Management	$1,316,774.00
14	Manufacturing	$827,480.00
15	Quality Assurance	$575,197.00
16	Research and Development	$11,647,823.00
17	Sales and Marketing	$655,184.40

This new member will represent the unallocated expenses we will try to spread to other departments.

OK, let's start.

Double-click on the **Adventure Works** cube and go to the **Calculations** tab. Choose **Script View**. Position the cursor at the end of the script and follow the steps in the next section.

How to do it...

The solution consists of one calculated measure, two scopes one inside the other, and modifications of the previously defined calculated measure inside each scope:

1. Create a new calculated measure in MDX script named Amount alloc and set it equal to the measure Amount. Be sure to specify $#,##0.00 as the format of that measure and place it in the same measure group as the original measure:

```
Create Member CurrentCube.[Measures].[Amount alloc]
As [Measures].[Amount]
, Format_String = '$#,##0.00'
, Associated_Measure_Group = 'Financial Reporting'
```

2. Create a scope statement in which you'll specify this new measure, the level two department members, the Operating Expenses account, and all of its descendants.

```
Scope( ( [Measures].[Amount alloc],
         [Department].[Departments]
                     .[Department Level 02].MEMBERS,
         Descendants( [Account].[Accounts].&[58] ) ) );
```

3. The value in this subcube should be increased by a percentage of the value of the **Corporate** datamember. The percentage of the allocation key that is being used here is going to be the percentage of the individual department in respect to its parents' value. Specify this using the following expression:

```
This = [Measures].[Amount] +
       ( [Department].[Departments].&[1].DATAMEMBER,
         [Measures].[Amount] ) *
       ( [Department].[Departments].CurrentMember,
         [Measures].[Amount] ) /
       Aggregate(
        Except( [Department].[Departments]
                            .[Department Level 02].MEMBERS,
                [Department].[Departments]
                            .&[1].DATAMEMBER ),
        [Measures].[Amount] );
```

4. Create another scope statement in which you'll specify that the value of the **Corporate** datamember should be null once all allocation is done:

```
Scope( [Department].[Departments].&[1].DATAMEMBER );
    This = null;
```

5. Provide two End Scope statements to close the scopes.

6. The complete code should look like:

```
Create Member CurrentCube.[Measures].[Amount alloc]
As [Measures].[Amount]
, Format_String = '$#,##0.00'
, Associated_Measure_Group = 'Financial Reporting' ;

Scope( ( [Measures].[Amount alloc],
          [Department].[Departments]
                     .[Department Level 02].MEMBERS,
          Descendants( [Account].[Accounts].&[58] ) ) );
    This = [Measures].[Amount] +
           ( [Department].[Departments].&[1].DATAMEMBER,
             [Measures].[Amount] ) *
           ( [Department].[Departments].CurrentMember,
             [Measures].[Amount] ) /
           Aggregate(
             Except( [Department].[Departments]
                                .[Department Level 02]
                                .MEMBERS,
                     [Department].[Departments]
                                .&[1].DATAMEMBER ),
             [Measures].[Amount] );
    Scope( [Department].[Departments].&[1].DATAMEMBER );
        This = null;
    End Scope;
End Scope;
```

7. Deploy the changes using the BIDS Helper 2012 or SSDT itself.

8. Go to the **Cube Browser**, reconnect, and add the new measure in the pivot.

9. Verify that the result matches the following screenshot. The highlighted cells are the cells for which the value is changed. The **Corporate** member has no value while the individual members are increased in proportion to their initial value. Beneath, the total remained the same:

	A	B	C
1	Row Labels ▼	Amount	Amount alloc
2	⊞ Balance Sheet		
3	⊟ Corporate	$0.00	$0.00
4	Executive General and Administration	$742,230.00	$742,230.00
5	Inventory Management	$3,401,168.00	$3,401,168.00
6	Sales and Marketing	($4,143,398.00)	-$4,143,398.00
7	⊟ Net Income		
8	⊟ Operating Profit		
9	⊞ Operating Expenses		
10	⊟ Corporate	$27,656,167.40	$27,656,167.40
11	Corporate	$12,236,648.00	
12	Executive General and Administration	$397,061.00	$712,161.33
13	Inventory Management	$1,316,774.00	$2,361,741.71
14	Manufacturing	$827,480.00	$1,484,152.96
15	Quality Assurance	$575,197.00	$1,031,662.80
16	Research and Development	$11,647,823.00	$20,891,321.86
17	Sales and Marketing	$655,184.40	$1,175,126.73

How it works...

The new calculated measure is used for allocating the values; the original measure preserves its values. This is not the only way how to perform the allocation, but it's the one that suits us at the moment because it allows us to easily compare the original and the new values. If you're interested in the other approach, skip to the next section which illustrates how to allocate values directly in the original measure.

The new calculated measure is defined to be an alias for the **Amount** measure, meaning it will return the exact same values.

The scope statement is used for specifying the subcube for which we want to apply a different evaluation of the cells. This subcube is formed using the new measure, the **Operating Expenses** account and all of its descendants, and finally, all the departments in the level two of the Department.Departments hierarchy. Once we have established this scope, we can apply the new calculation.

The new calculation basically says this: take the original **Amount** measure's value for the current context of that subcube and increase it by a percentage of the Amount measure's value of the **Corporate** datamember. The sum of all the percentages should naturally be 1 in order for the total to remain the same.

The percentage is a ratio of the current member's value versus the aggregated value of all its siblings except the **Corporate** datamember. We're skipping that member because that's the member whose value we're dividing among its siblings. We don't want some of it to return to that member again. Actually, we're not deducing its value by this expression; we're merely evaluating a proper percentage of it which we're using later on to increase the value of each sibling. That's why there was a need for the last statement in that scope. That statement resets the value of the **Corporate** datamember.

There's more...

The other way around is to use an existing measure while keeping the original value in the separate calculated measure. Here's how the MDX script would look like in that case:

```
Create Member CurrentCube.[Measures].[Amount preserve]
As [Measures].[Amount]
, Format_String = '$#,##0.00'
, Associated_Measure_Group = 'Financial Reporting' ;

Freeze( ( [Measures].[Amount preserve] ) );

Scope( ( [Measures].[Amount],
         [Department].[Departments]
                     .[Department Level 02].MEMBERS,
         Descendants( [Account].[Accounts].&[58] ) ) );
    This = [Measures].[Amount preserve] +
           ( [Department].[Departments].&[1].DATAMEMBER,
             [Measures].[Amount preserve] ) *
           ( [Department].[Departments].CurrentMember,
             [Measures].[Amount preserve] ) /
           Aggregate(
             Except( [Department].[Departments]
                                  .[Department Level 02].MEMBERS,
                     [Department].[Departments]
                                  .&[1].DATAMEMBER ),
             [Measures].[Amount preserve] );
    Scope( [Department].[Departments].&[1].DATAMEMBER );
        This = null;
    End Scope;
End Scope;
```

At first, it looks like the regular and calculated measures have just switched their positions inside the code. However, there's more to it; it's not that simple.

A calculated measure referring to another measure is in fact a **pointer** to that measure's value, not a constant. In order to evaluate its expression, the referred measure has to be evaluated first.

The assignment inside the `Scope()` statement (the first `This` part) uses the calculated measure which requires the value of the original `Amount` measure to be evaluated. But, the `Amount` measure is used in the very same scope definition, so in order to evaluate the `Amount` measure, the engine has to enter the scope and evaluate the calculated measure specified in the assignment in that scope. Now we're in the same position we started from, which means we've run into an infinite recursion. Seen from that perspective, it becomes obvious we have to change something in the script.

Just before the `Scope()` statement, we have added a `Freeze()` statement. The MDX `Freeze()` statement locks the cell value of the **Amount** so that changes to other cells in the subsequent `SCOPE()` statement have no effect to the **Amount**. The `Freeze()` statement takes a snapshot of the subcube which is provided as its argument and the snapshot was taken at the particular position in the MDX script. Using `Freeze()`, we have prevented the reevaluation of the calculated measure in all subsequent expressions. Therefore, the `Scope()` statement will not end up in infinite recursion. The assignment inside the scope takes the snapshot value of the calculated measure; it doesn't trigger its reevaluation. In other words, there's no infinite recursion with the use of the `Freeze()` statement.

Here's the screenshot of the **Analyze in Excel** in this case:

	A	B	C
1	Row Labels ▼	Amount	Amount preserve
2	⊞ Balance Sheet		
3	⊟ Corporate	$0.00	$0.00
4	Executive General and Administration	$742,230.00	$742,230.00
5	Inventory Management	$3,401,168.00	$3,401,168.00
6	Sales and Marketing	($4,143,398.00)	-$4,143,398.00
7	⊟ Net Income		
8	⊟ Operating Profit		
9	⊞ Operating Expenses		
10	⊟ Corporate	$27,656,167.40	$27,656,167.40
11	Corporate		$12,236,648.00
12	Executive General and Administration	$712,161.33	$397,061.00
13	Inventory Management	$2,361,741.71	$1,316,774.00
14	Manufacturing	$1,484,152.96	$827,480.00
15	Quality Assurance	$1,031,662.80	$575,197.00
16	Research and Development	$20,891,321.86	$11,647,823.00
17	Sales and Marketing	$1,175,126.73	$655,184.40

By looking at highlighted rows, it looks like the measures have switched places, but now we know the required expressions in MDX script are not done that way. We had to use the `Freeze()` statement because of the difference between regular and calculated measures and how they get evaluated.

If you want to learn more about the `Freeze()` statement, here's a link to the MSDN site: `http://tinyurl.com/MDXFreeze`

 Although this approach allows for drill through (because we're not using a calculated measure), the values returned will not match the cube's data. This is because allocations have been implemented in the MDX script, not in the original DW data.

Choosing a proper allocation scheme

This recipe showed how to allocate the values based on the key which is calculated as a percentage of the value of each member against the aggregate of all the other siblings to be increased. Two things are important here: we've used the same measure **Amount** and we've used the same coordinate **Departments** in the cube. However, this doesn't have to be the case.

We can choose any measure we want, any that we find appropriate. For example, we might have allocated the values based on the **Sales Amount**, **Total Product Cost**, **Order Count**, or anything similar. We might have also taken another coordinate for the allocation. For example, there is a Headcount member in the `Account.Accounts` hierarchy. We could have allocated **Operating Expense** according to the number of headcounts.

To conclude, it is totally up to you to choose your allocation scheme as long as the sum of the allocation percentages (ratios) remains 1.

Analyzing fluctuation of customers

Every company takes care of its customers, or at least it should, because it is relatively easy to lose one while it's much harder to acquire a new one.

There are many ways to perform analysis on customers. In this recipe, we are going to highlight a few techniques that allow us to get some easy to understand indicators:

- The number of loyal customers
- The number of new customers
- The number of lost customers
- Which customers are in a particular group

The idea is pretty simple to understand, so let's start.

Getting ready

Start **SQL Server Management Studio** and connect to your SSAS 2012 instance. Click on the **New Query** button and check that the target database is **Adventure Works DW 2012**.

In this example we're going to use the `Customer` and `Date` dimensions and the measure `Customer Count` which can be found in the `Internet Customers` measure group. Here's the query we'll start from:

```
SELECT
    { [Measures].[Customer Count] } ON 0,
    { [Date].[Fiscal].[Fiscal Quarter].MEMBERS } ON 1
FROM
    [Adventure Works]
```

Once executed, the query returns 24 quarters on rows.

Our task in this recipe is to make the necessary calculation in order to have indicators of customer flow. In other words, our task is to get the count of new, loyal, and lost customers as an expression that works in any period or context in general.

How to do it...

The solution consists of five calculated measures that we need to define in the query and then use on the columns.

1. Add the `WITH` part of the query.

2. Create the first calculated measure, name it `Agg TD` and define it as an inception-to-date calculation of the measure `Customer Count`.

3. Create the second calculated measure, name it `Agg TD prev` and define it similarly to the previous measure, only this time, limit the time range to the member that is previous to the current member.

4. Create the `Lost Customers` calculated measure and define it as the difference between the `Agg TD` measure and the `Customer Count` measure.

5. Create the `New Customers` calculated measure and define it as the difference between the `Agg TD` measure and the `Agg TD prev` measure.

6. Finally, create the `Loyal Customers` calculated measure and define it as the difference between the `Customer Count` measure and the `New Customers` measure.

7. Include all the calculated measures on the columns axis of the query.

8. Verify that the query looks like the following:

```
WITH
MEMBER [Measures].[Agg TD] AS
    Aggregate( null : [Date].[Fiscal].CurrentMember,
                [Measures].[Customer Count] )
MEMBER [Measures].[Agg TD prev] AS
    Aggregate( null : [Date].[Fiscal].PrevMember,
                [Measures].[Customer Count] )
MEMBER [Measures].[Lost Customers] AS
```

```
    [Measures].[Agg TD] - [Measures].[Customer Count]
MEMBER [Measures].[New Customers] AS
    [Measures].[Agg TD] - [Measures].[Agg TD prev]
MEMBER [Measures].[Loyal Customers] AS
    [Measures].[Customer Count] - [Measures].[New Customers]
SELECT
    { [Measures].[Customer Count],
      [Measures].[Agg TD],
      [Measures].[Agg TD prev],
      [Measures].[Lost Customers],
      [Measures].[New Customers],
      [Measures].[Loyal Customers] } ON 0,
    { [Date].[Fiscal].[Fiscal Quarter].MEMBERS } ON 1
FROM
    [Adventure Works]
```

9. Run the query and observe the results, especially the last three calculated measures. It is obvious that in the initial phase of this company there was a problem with retaining the existing customers.

	Customer Count	Agg TD	Agg TD prev	Lost Customers	New Customers	Loyal Customers
Q3 FY 2005	(null)	(null)	(null)	(null)	(null)	(null)
Q4 FY 2005	(null)	(null)	(null)	(null)	(null)	(null)
Q1 FY 2006	448	448	(null)	(null)	448	(null)
Q2 FY 2006	565	1,013	448	448	565	(null)
Q3 FY 2006	558	1,571	1,013	1,013	558	(null)
Q4 FY 2006	635	2,206	1,571	1,571	635	(null)
Q1 FY 2007	732	2,938	2,206	2,206	732	(null)
Q2 FY 2007	752	3,690	2,938	2,938	752	(null)
Q3 FY 2007	788	4,478	3,690	3,690	788	(null)
Q4 FY 2007	950	5,428	4,478	4,478	950	(null)
Q1 FY 2008	3,486	7,952	5,428	4,466	2,524	962
Q2 FY 2008	5,090	11,388	7,952	6,298	3,436	1,654
Q3 FY 2008	5,237	14,496	11,388	9,259	3,108	2,129
Q4 FY 2008	6,052	17,918	14,496	11,866	3,422	2,630
Q1 FY 2009	931	18,484	17,918	17,553	566	365
Q2 FY 2009	(null)	18,484	18,484	18,484	(null)	(null)
Q3 FY 2009	(null)	18,484	18,484	18,484	(null)	(null)
Q4 FY 2009	(null)	18,484	18,484	18,484	(null)	(null)
Q1 FY 2010	(null)	18,484	18,484	18,484	(null)	(null)
Q2 FY 2010	(null)	18,484	18,484	18,484	(null)	(null)
Q3 FY 2010	(null)	18,484	18,484	18,484	(null)	(null)
Q4 FY 2010	(null)	18,484	18,484	18,484	(null)	(null)
Q1 FY 2011	(null)	18,484	18,484	18,484	(null)	(null)
Q2 FY 2011	(null)	18,484	18,484	18,484	(null)	(null)

How it works...

The expressions used in this example are relatively simple expressions, but that doesn't necessarily mean that they are easy to comprehend. The key to understanding how these calculations work is in realizing that a distinct count type of measure was used. What's special about that type of aggregation is that it is not an additive aggregation. The measure `Customer Count` is a distinct type of measure. You can verify that by checking the `AggregateFunction` property of the measure, which is `DistinctCount` as shown in the following screenshot:

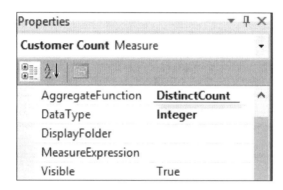

In this recipe we've taken advantage of their non-additive behavior and managed to get really easy-to-memorize formulas.

We're starting with the two special calculated measures. The first one `[Agg TD]` calculates the inception-to-date value of the `Customer Count` measure. For an ordinary measure with `Sum` as an aggregated function, this would mean we want to sum all the values up to the current point in time. However, for this non- additive `Distinct Count` type of measures, this means we want to get the count of distinct customers up to the current point in time. Because this calculated measure aggregates across the Internet customers fact data in a particular time period, this is not a sum of all customers. As a matter of fact, this is a value that can be greater or equal to the number of customers who have internet orders in any period and less than or equal to the total number of customers.

The second calculated measure `[Agg TD prev]` does the same thing except that it stops in the previous time period.

Combining those two measures with the original `Customer Count` measure leads to the solution for the other three calculated measures.

The `Lost Customers` measure gets the value obtained by subtracting the count of customers in the current period from the count of customers so far. The `New Customers` measure gets the value that is equal to the difference between those first two calculated measures. Again, this evaluates to the number of customers so far minus the number of customers up to the previous period. What's left are those that were acquired in the current time period.

Finally, the `Loyal Customers` calculated measure is defined as the count of customers in the current period minus the new customers; everything that's in the current period is either a new or a loyal customer.

The two special calculated measures are not required to be in the query or visible at all. They are used here only to show how the evaluation takes place.

There's more...

It makes sense to put those definitions in the MDX script so that they can be used in the subsequent calculations by all users. Here's what should go in the MDX script:

```
Create Member CurrentCube.[Measures].[Agg TD] AS
    Aggregate( null : [Date].[Fiscal].CurrentMember,
               [Measures].[Customer Count] )
    , Format_String = '#,#'
    , Visible = 0
    , Associated_Measure_Group = 'Internet Customers';

Create Member CurrentCube.[Measures].[Agg TD prev] AS
    Aggregate( null : [Date].[Fiscal].PrevMember,
               [Measures].[Customer Count] )
    , Format_String = '#,#'
    , Visible = 0
    , Associated_Measure_Group = 'Internet Customers';

Create Member CurrentCube.[Measures].[Lost Customers] AS
    [Measures].[Agg TD] - [Measures].[Customer Count]
    , Format_String = '#,#'
    , Associated_Measure_Group = 'Internet Customers';

Create Member CurrentCube.[Measures].[New Customers] AS
    [Measures].[Agg TD] - [Measures].[Agg TD prev]
    , Format_String = '#,#'
    , Associated_Measure_Group = 'Internet Customers';

Create Member CurrentCube.[Measures].[Loyal Customers] AS
    [Measures].[Customer Count] - [Measures].[New Customers]
    , Format_String = '#,#'
    , Associated_Measure_Group = 'Internet Customers';
```

This allows us to identify the customers in those statuses (lost, loyal, and new).

Identifying loyal customers in a particular period

The period we'll use in this example will be **Q1 FY 2008**. We want to find out which were our first loyal customers. Perhaps we want to reward them or analyze their behavior further in order to determine what made them stay with us. We'll choose to further analyze their behavior. We have prepared the following query to gather all sorts of measures about those customers:

```
WITH
SET [Loyal Customers] AS
        NonEmpty( [Customer].[Customer].[Customer].MEMBERS,
                  [Measures].[Customer Count] ) -
    (
        NonEmpty( [Customer].[Customer].[Customer].MEMBERS,
                  [Measures].[Agg TD] ) -
        NonEmpty( [Customer].[Customer].[Customer].MEMBERS,
                  [Measures].[Agg TD prev] )
    )
SELECT
    { [Measures].[Internet Order Count],
      [Measures].[Internet Order Quantity],
      [Measures].[Internet Sales Amount],
      [Measures].[Internet Gross Profit],
      [Measures].[Internet Gross Profit Margin],
      [Measures].[Internet Average Sales Amount],
      [Measures].[Internet Average Unit Price] } ON 0,
    { [Loyal Customers] } ON 1
FROM
    [Adventure Works]
WHERE
    ( [Date].[Fiscal].[Fiscal Quarter].&[2008]&[1] )
```

The preceding query has **Q1 FY 2008** in slicer and several measures on columns. The set on rows [Loyal Customers] is defined as the difference among three sets.

The expression for the Loyal Customers set is in the form of Y = A - (B - C), which is similar to how we calculate the Loyal Customers measure in our initial solution.

Here we are repeating the logic we used in the initial solution for calculating the Loyal Customers measure:

```
[Loyal Customers] = [Customer Count] - [New Customers]

[New Customers] = [Customers Inception-to-date (Agg TD)] - [Customers
previous to the current member (Agg TD prev)]
```

The logic is similar; the difference is that we are now doing the set operation. To get the set A, B and C, we used the `NonEmpty()` function and the following three calculated measures as the second argument of the `NonEmpty()` function.

```
[Measures].[Customer Count]
[Measures].[Agg TD]
[Measures].[Agg TD prev]
```

Yes, using these three sets we got 962 loyal customers. Here's the screenshot with their values:

	Internet Order Count	Internet Order Quantity	Internet Sales Amount	Internet Gross Profit	Inter
Aaron C. Diaz	1	2	$2,451.30	$893.38	
Aaron M. Young	1	5	$2,445.46	$1,132.91	
Aaron V. Wang	1	3	$2,366.46	$1,083.46	
Abby L. Sai	1	2	$2,439.99	$1,129.49	
Abby Subram	1	4	$620.46	$246.71	
Abigail Howard	1	4	$2,369.97	$1,089.95	
Abigail R. Foster	1	2	$2,414.99	$1,118.13	
Adam Hill	1	2	$2,478.34	$910.31	
Adam Lal	1	3	$848.47	$395.59	
Adam Ross	1	4	$2,363.96	$1,064.80	
Adrian C. Richardson	1	2	$839.48	$393.53	
Adrian K. Ramirez	1	4	$2,359.46	$1,079.08	
Adriana A. Sai	1	2	$819.48	$361.21	
Adriana Chandra	1	3	$2,428.05	$926.10	

It's worth mentioning that you can build several dynamic sets in the MDX script which would represent the customers in the particular status. Here's the expression for the dynamic `Loyal Customers` set:

```
Create Dynamic Set CurrentCube.[Loyal Customers] AS
    NonEmpty( [Customer].[Customer].[Customer].MEMBERS,
            [Measures].[Customer Count] ) -
    (
        NonEmpty( [Customer].[Customer].[Customer].MEMBERS,
                [Measures].[Agg TD] ) -
        NonEmpty( [Customer].[Customer].[Customer].MEMBERS,
                [Measures].[Agg TD prev] )
    );
```

 If you're wondering whether this applies only to the customer analysis, the answer is – no! It doesn't have to be the customer dimension, it can be any dimension. The principles apply in the same way.

More complex scenario

There are other options we can do with the customer analysis. For example, we might want to combine two or more periods.

We know there were 962 loyal customers in the first fiscal quarter of the year 2008. A perfectly logical question arises – what happens to them afterwards? Are they still loyal in Q4 of the same year? How many of them?

Let's find out:

```
SELECT
    { [Measures].[Internet Order Count],
      [Measures].[Internet Order Quantity],
      [Measures].[Internet Sales Amount],
      [Measures].[Internet Gross Profit],
      [Measures].[Internet Gross Profit Margin],
      [Measures].[Internet Average Sales Amount],
      [Measures].[Internet Average Unit Price] } ON 0,
    { Exists( [Loyal Customers],
              ( [Measures].[Customer Count],
                [Date].[Fiscal].[Fiscal Quarter].&[2008]&[4] ),
              'Internet Customers' ) } ON 1
FROM
    [Adventure Works]
WHERE
    ( [Date].[Fiscal].[Fiscal Quarter].&[2008]&[1] )
```

The query is similar to the previous one except here we have an extra construct using the `Exists()` function, the variant with the measure group name. What this function does is that it takes `Loyal Customers` and reduces it to a set of members who also have values in the Q4 of the same fiscal year.

The result shows 96 customers out of 962 who are identified as loyal customers in Q1 2008:

	Internet Order Count	Internet Order Quantity	Internet Sales Amount	Internet Gross Profit	Internet Gross Profit Margin	Inte
Abby Subram	1	4	$620.46	$246.71	39.76%	
Adriana L. Gonzalez	2	4	$4,891.40	$1,830.59	37.42%	
Alan Zheng	1	3	$854.97	$403.22	47.16%	
Alejandro Beck	1	3	$2,405.47	$1,107.88	46.06%	
Amy C. Sun	1	1	$2,294.99	$1,043.01	45.45%	
Ariana D. Gray	1	5	$2,501.96	$1,168.28	46.69%	
Audrey Blanco	1	1	$539.99	$196.34	36.36%	
Billy J. Munoz	1	2	$777.34	$302.81	38.95%	
Brad She	1	1	$2,443.35	$888.40	36.36%	
Brandi D. Gill	3	8	$7,219.32	$2,890.65	40.04%	

The alternative approach

Chris Webb has an alternative solution for customer analysis on his blog: `http://tinyurl.com/ChrisCountingCustomers`

Implementing the ABC analysis

ABC analysis is a method of identifying and classifying items, based on their impact, into three regions: A, B, and C. It's an extension of the "80-20" rule, also known as **Pareto** principle, which states that for many events, roughly 80 percent of the effects come from 20 percent of the causes. In one definition of the ABC analysis, the top 20 percent of the causes, the important part, are further divided in two subgroups: A (the top 5 percent) and B (the subsequent 15 percent), and the 80 percent of effects they contribute to into segments of 30 percent and 50 percent. These are the ratios we're going to use in this recipe. There are, of course, other definitions like 10/20/70. It really depends on the user needs and you're free to change it and experiment.

ABC analysis is a very valuable tool which can be found mostly in highly specialized applications, for example, in an inventory management application. This recipe will demonstrate how to perform the ABC analysis on the cube.

Getting ready

Start **SQL Server Management Studio** and connect to your SSAS 2012 instance. Click on the **New Query** button and check that the target database is **Adventure Works DW 2012**.

In this example we're going to use the `Product` dimension. Here's the query we'll start from:

```
SELECT
    { [Measures].[Internet Gross Profit] } ON 0,
    NON EMPTY
    { [Product].[Product].[Product].MEMBERS } ON 1
FROM
    [Adventure Works]
WHERE
    ( [Product].[Status].&[Current],
      [Date].[Fiscal Year].&[2008] )
```

Once executed, the query returns all active products and their profit in Internet sales for the fiscal year 2008. The result shows 102 active products.

Now, let's see how we can classify them.

How to do it...

The solution consists of two calculated measure and four named sets. The last measure returns the group A, B, or C.

1. Add the `WITH` part of the query.

2. Define a new calculated measure as an alias for the measure on columns and name it `Measure for ABC`.

3. Define a named set `Set for ABC` which returns only products for which the Internet profit is not null using the previously defined alias measure:

   ```
   NonEmpty( [Product].[Product].[Product].MEMBERS,
             [Measures].[Measure for ABC] )
   ```

4. Using the following syntax, define three named sets, A, B, and C:

   ```
   SET [A] AS
       TopPercent( [Set for ABC], 30,
                   [Measures].[Measure for ABC] )
   SET [B] AS
       TopPercent( [Set for ABC], 80,
                   [Measures].[Measure for ABC] ) - [A]
   SET [C] AS
       [Set for ABC] - [A] - [B]
   ```

5. Finally, define a calculated measure `ABC group` which returns the letter A, B, or C based on the contribution of each product. Use the following expression:

   ```
   iif( IsEmpty( [Measures].[Measure for ABC] ), null,
        iif( Intersect( [A],
                        [Product].[Product].CurrentMember
                      ).Count > 0,
           'A',
           iif( Intersect( [B],
                           [Product].[Product].CurrentMember
                         ).Count > 0,
              'B',
              'C'
              )
           )
        )
   ```

6. Add that last calculated measure on columns and replace the existing measure with the `Measure for ABC` calculated measure.

7. Run the query which should now look like:

```
WITH
MEMBER [Measures].[Measure for ABC] AS
    [Measures].[Internet Gross Profit]
SET [Set for ABC] AS
    NonEmpty( [Product].[Product].[Product].MEMBERS,
              [Measures].[Measure for ABC] )
SET [A] AS
    TopPercent( [Set for ABC], 30, [Measures].[Measure for ABC] )
SET [B] AS
    TopPercent( [Set for ABC], 80, [Measures].[Measure for ABC] ) -
    [A]
SET [C] AS
    [Set for ABC] - [A] - [B]
MEMBER [Measures].[ABC Group] AS
    iif( IsEmpty( [Measures].[Measure for ABC] ), null,
        iif( Intersect( [A],
                        [Product].[Product].CurrentMember
                      ).Count > 0,
            'A',
            iif( Intersect( [B],
                            [Product].[Product].CurrentMember
                          ).Count > 0,
                'B',
                'C' ) ) )
SELECT
    { [Measures].[Measure for ABC],
      [Measures].[ABC Group] } ON 0,
    NON EMPTY
    { [Product].[Product].[Product].MEMBERS } ON 1
FROM
    [Adventure Works]
WHERE
    ( [Product].[Status].&[Current],
      [Date].[Fiscal Year].&[2008] )
```

8. Verify that the result matches the following screenshot:

	Measure for ABC	ABC Group
Long-Sleeve Logo Jersey, M	$3,828.73	C
Long-Sleeve Logo Jersey, S	$3,725.25	C
Long-Sleeve Logo Jersey, XL	$3,667.77	C
ML Mountain Tire	$16,539.63	C
ML Road Tire	$10,966.23	C
Mountain Bottle Cage	$9,643.21	C
Mountain Tire Tube	$7,384.43	C
Mountain-200 Black, 38	$345,235.88	A
Mountain-200 Black, 42	$342,106.85	A
Mountain-200 Black, 46	$349,407.91	A
Mountain-200 Silver, 38	$348,996.64	A
Mountain-200 Silver, 42	$317,365.52	B
Mountain-200 Silver, 46	$336,344.19	A
Mountain-400-W Silver, 38	$38,817.99	C
Mountain-400-W Silver, 40	$33,922.03	C
Mountain-400-W Silver, 42	$30,774.62	C
Mountain-400-W Silver, 46	$39,517.41	C
Mountain-500 Black, 40	$9,325.59	C

How it works...

The alias for the measure `Internet Gross Profit` in form of the calculated measure `Measure for ABC`, together with the alias for the set on rows `Set for ABC` enables us to have a flexible and readable query. The query is flexible because we can change the measure in a single spot and have the query running another ABC analysis, for example, the analysis of the revenue or the number of orders. It is readable because we're using short but informative names in it instead of the long MDX-specific names for members and levels. I addition, we are keeping the syntax short by not having to repeat some expressions. As for the set on rows, we're not making the query completely flexible; there are still some parts of the query where the mention of a specific hierarchy was not replaced by something more general.

Anyway, let's analyze the main part of the query: sets A, B, and C and the calculated measure `ABC Group`.

The `TopPercent()` function, in combination with a set and a measure, returns top members from that set. The threshold, required as the second argument of that function, determines which members are returned.

That's a pretty vague description of what this function does because it is not clear which members get returned or how many top members will be returned. Let's see the more detailed explanation.

The behavior of that function can be explained using the list of members sorted in descending order. We don't know in advance how many of them the function will return; the only thing we know is that it will stop at some point.

The members are included up to the point where the ratio (in form of the percentage) of the cumulative sum versus the total becomes equal to the value provided as the second argument. In our example we had two such values, 30 and 80. 80 because the second segment is 50 and the sum of 30 and 50 is 80. The function would use all top members up to the point where their sum reaches 30 percent or 80 percent, respectively, of the total value of the set.

So, set A will contain the top products that form 30 percent of the total.

Set B gets calculated as even more, 80 percent of the total. However, that would include also members of the set A. That's why we had to exclude them. Set B contains the next 50 percent of the total.

Set C can eventually be calculated as all the rest, meaning, the complete set of members excluding members in both set A and set B. Set C contains the bottom 20 percent of the total.

The calculated measure ABC Group basically takes the current member on rows and checks in which set of three named sets it is. This is done using the combination of the `Intersect()` function and the `.Count` function. If there's an intersection, the count will show 1.

When the iteration on cells starts, each member gets classified as either A, B, or C, based on its score and in which of the three predefined groups it can be found.

There's more...

There are many ways to calculate A, B, or C. I'd like to believe I've shown you the fastest one.

Here's another example to explain what I meant by that.

Use the same query as before, but replace the measure ABC group with these two calculations:

```
MEMBER [Measures].[Rank in set] AS
    iif( IsEmpty( [Measures].[Measure for ABC] ), null,
        Rank( [Product].[Product].CurrentMember,
            [Set for ABC],
```

```
                    [Measures].[Measure for ABC] ) )
        , FORMAT_STRING = '#,#'


   MEMBER [Measures].[ABC Group] AS
       iif( IsEmpty( [Measures].[Measure for ABC] ), null,
           iif( [Measures].[Rank in set] <= [A].Count,
               'A',
               iif( [Measures].[Rank in set] <= { [A] + [B] }.Count,
                   'B', 'C' ) ) )
```

Run the query and observe the results. They should match the results from the previous query. What changes is the execution time.

In Adventure Works that change in time is not so obvious, especially in the context of this query. If you want to experience a more noticeable change, use the reseller dimensions. There you'll see a small difference.

Why is the second approach slower?

The initial example illustrates a classic case of set-based thinking. First we've defined the set A, then we've used it in the definition of set B and finally, we've defined the third set using the previous two. Therefore, we've used a simple and effective set operation – the difference between the sets.

That's not all there is to it. Something else is important. Sets evaluate before the iteration on cells starts. This means by the time the engine starts to evaluate the expression in the measure ABC Group, sets are already evaluated and therefore sort of a constant. When the iteration starts, the engine compares each member with maximum two of those sets. That comparison is again performed using a fast set operation – intersection of two sets. In short, we completely avoided any iteration in this approach.

Now, consider the second example, the one which uses the Rank function.

The idea is to have a rank which tells us how good each member was – which position it took. We can use this rank and compare it with the count of members in set A or count of members in both sets A and B. If the rank is a smaller number, we get a match and the member gets the corresponding class as a result of the calculation.

True, sets A, B, and C are static again, pre-evaluated, but the rank operation, together with the process of counting the number of items in a particular set, takes time. Here we're not applying the set-based thinking; we're iterating, although internally, on a set to get the rank while we don't really need that rank at all.

Remember to always look for a set-based alternative if you catch yourself using iteration. Sometimes it will be possible, sometimes not. If you have a large cube, it's certainly worth a try.

Tips and tricks

Always look if you can move everything that was on axis to a named set. Your calculations will be easier.

Consider defining everything in the MDX script because of the advantages of centrally-based calculations (speed, cache, availability).

See also

▸ The recipe *Isolating the best N members in a set* in *Chapter 4, Concise Reporting* covers the `TopPercent()` function in more detail.

7
When MDX is Not Enough

In this chapter, we will cover:

- ▶ Using a new attribute to separate members on a level
- ▶ Using a distinct count measure to implement histograms over existing hierarchies
- ▶ Using a dummy dimension to implement histograms over nonexisting hierarchies
- ▶ Creating a physical measure as a placeholder for MDX assignments
- ▶ Using a new dimension to calculate the most frequent price
- ▶ Using a utility dimension to implement flexible display units
- ▶ Using a utility dimension to implement time-based calculations

Introduction

So far we've been through the basics of MDX calculations. We learned few tricks regarding time calculations, practiced making concise reports, navigated hierarchies, and analyzed data by applying typical business calculations. As we're approaching the end of the book, more and more of the special topics arrive.

This is a book that follows the cookbook approach, the main topic being the MDX. In this chapter, however, we're going to discover that MDX calculations are not always the place to look for a solution to a problem. It is only one of the possible layers we can start from. The other two layers are the cube design and the underlying data warehouse (DW) model. One thing depends on the other. A good data model will enable a good cube design which in turn will enable simple MDX calculations.

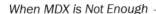

Whenever we are given a request to get something from the cube, it is not only a request to make an adequate MDX query or calculation and then to return the data, it is something much deeper – a challenge to our cube design and the underlying dimensional model. If the MDX becomes too complex, that's a potential sign there's something wrong with the layers below and that they, perhaps, can be improved.

This chapter illustrates several techniques to optimize the query response times with a relatively simple change in cube structure, to simplify the cube maintenance and further MDX calculations, to enable new analysis or even to make the so-far impossible ones possible. The types of changes we're talking about here are adding new measures or attributes, and even adding a complete dimension.

Calculations are performed by the formula engine at query time. Using regular measures we can avoid a query-time performance decrease. Regular measures have other advantages over the calculated ones which are discussed in this chapter.

Attributes not only enhance the dimension design allowing users to avoid multi-select and problems related to it, they are a potential place for aggregations and therefore a candidate for optimization of reports.

Utility dimensions play a vital role in providing powerful calculations that are easy to maintain in contrast to potential chaos with calculated measures. A variant of the utility dimensions, the dummy dimension, is a convenient structure which enables iteration, allocation, and other useful activities.

Finally, if you find yourself running a lot over leaves in your calculations, you should know that cubes are not designed to do that. Maybe a different granularity for the fact table should be applied or a new dimension should be considered.

These are the things we'll encounter in this chapter. If you can create the calculations in the DSV/DW layer or prepare data there without compromising the cube's flexibility, do it. That way whatever you implement will be resolved only once, during processing, instead of during every query execution. The idea is to push things down to the lower layers as much as possible so that queries run faster.

By the way, don't worry about MDX, there's still plenty of it here. The only difference is that in contrast to the previous chapters, here the focus is on other aspects, not just MDX.

Let's start slowly.

Using a new attribute to separate members on a level

In reporting and analysis, there are situations when a certain member (often named NA, Unknown, or similar) corrupts the analysis. It makes it hard for end users to focus on the rest of the data. It distracts them by making them think what this member represents, why it is here, and why it has data associated to it. Other times, the reason may be that the end users need a total without that member. In both of these situations, they remove that member from the result which generates a new MDX query.

It is true, that a combination of a named set without that member and a calculated member as an aggregate of that set can be created in MDX script to simplify the rest of the calculations and the usage of that hierarchy in general. However, this is not the optimal solution.

Is there a better way? Yes, but it requires a dimension redesign. If that's applicable in your case, read on because this recipe shows how to keep your cube design simple and effective, all at the price of a bit of your time invested in the preparation of data.

Getting ready

Open the **SQL Server Data Tools** (SSDT) and then open the **Adventure Works DW 2012** solution. Once it loads, double-click on the **Product** dimension, the dimension where the problematic member will be in this example.

We're going to use the `Color` attribute of the `Product` dimension. If you browse the dimension in the **Browser** tab, you'll see there are 10 colors, one of which is NA. The idea is to somehow exclude this color from the list of colors and keep it separate. To do this, we'll need another attribute to separate colors in two groups: colors with the exact name in one group and the NA color in another.

Attributes are built from one or more columns in the underlying dimension table or view. The preferred place for introducing this change is the data warehouse (DW), a view that represents the dimension table from which this dimension is built. Having all logic in one place increases the maintainability of the overall solution. However, in order to keep things simple and focus on what's important, we're going to disregard the best practice here and use the data source view (DSV) instead.

How to do it...

Follow these steps to add a new attribute that will be used to separate members on another attribute.

1. Double-click on the **Adventure Works DW** data source view.

2. Locate the **Product** dimension in the **Tables** pane on the left, then right-click and select **New Named Calculation**.

3. Enter `ColorGroupKey` for the **Column** name and this code for the expression:

   ```
   CASE Color WHEN 'NA' THEN 1 ELSE 0 END
   ```

4. Close the dialog and repeat the process for another column. This time name it `ColorGroupName` and use the following definition:

   ```
   CASE Color WHEN 'NA' THEN 'Unknown colors' ELSE 'Known colors' END
   ```

5. Close the dialog again and explore the **Product** table to see the result of those two new columns. They should be visible at the end of the table. If everything's OK, close the **Explore Product Table** tab.

6. Now return to the **Product** dimension again where you should see two new calculated columns in the end of that table in the **Data Source View** pane on the right.

7. Drag the `ColorGroupKey` column to the left and drop it in the **Attributes** pane.

8. Rename it to `Color Group`, then navigate to the `NameColumn` property and select the `ColorGroupName` column for that.

9. Set the `OrderBy` property to **Key** in order to preserve the order by key.

10. Drag the newly created `Color Group` attribute to the **Hierarchies** pane following by the `Color` attribute underneath it. The idea is to create a new user hierarchy.

11. Name the hierarchy `Product Colors` and set the `AllMemberName` in the **Properties** pane to **All Products**.

12. Notice the yellow warning sign. Go to the **Attributes Relationships** tab and set the correct relation between the `Color` and `Color Group` attributes. In SSDT for SSAS 2012, you can click on the **New Attribute Relationship** icon on top. If you are using BIDS for SSAS 2008 R2, you can drag the `Color` attribute over the `Color Group` attribute and release it.

13. Select the arrow that points to the `Color Group` attribute and change the `RelationshipType` property from **Flexible** to **Rigid** in the **Properties** pane. The tip of the arrow should turn black, just like in the following figure:

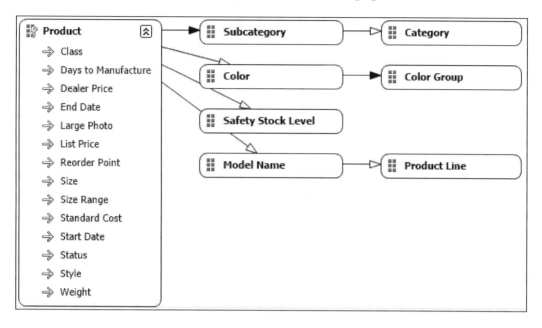

14. Return to the **Dimension Structure** tab and check that the warning sign is gone.

15. Select the **Product Colors** user hierarchy and set the `DisplayFolder` property to **Stocking**.

16. Select the `Color Group` attribute and set its visibility to `False` using the `AttributeHierarchyVisible` property.

17. Process the dimension. When it's done, go to the **Browser** tab, reconnect, and verify that the new **Product Colors** user hierarchy works as expected, that colors are separated in two new nodes, **Known colors** and **Unknown colors**.

18. Now process the **Adventure Works** cube, reconnect and go to the **Browser** tab to click on the **Analyze in Excel** icon on top to open Excel to make a report using the new **Product Colors** user hierarchy which you'll find under the `Stocking` folder of the `Product` dimension.

	A	B	C	D	E
1	Row Labels ▼	Order Quantity	Average Unit Price	Sales Amount	Gross Profit
2	⊟ Known colors	226,488	$640.29	$108,709,970.29	$12,084,542.62
3	Black	81,856	$610.08	$38,236,124.06	$4,971,374.95
4	Blue	23,659	$534.43	$9,602,850.97	$605,893.01
5	Multi	25,059	$27.07	$649,030.25	$13,160.89
6	Red	29,187	$990.68	$21,597,890.81	$2,720,764.26
7	Silver	25,023	$936.10	$19,777,339.95	$3,239,562.63
8	Silver/Black	3,931	$37.35	$147,483.91	$38,250.97
9	White	5,217	$6.85	$29,745.13	$12,163.31
10	Yellow	32,556	$731.52	$18,669,505.22	$483,372.60
11	⊟ Unknown colors	48,288	$18.44	$1,099,303.91	$466,823.63
12	NA	48,288	$18.44	$1,099,303.91	$466,823.63
13	Grand Total	274,776	$465.18	$109,809,274.20	$12,551,366.25

How it works...

The new attribute `Color Group` plays several roles. It enables natural, by-design subtotals, easy navigation, easy filtering, and keeps further MDX calculations simple and effective.

In order to create it, we've extended the **Product** table with two new columns, `ColorGroupKey` and `ColorGroupName`. We did that in the **Data Source View** (**DSV**), although we could have done the same in the dimension table in **Data Warehouse** (**DW**). In fact, it might have been a better decision to go to the DW. However, in order to keep things the way how Adventure Works database is done, we have chosen to use calculated columns in the DSV. In your real project, you should add those calculated columns to the dimension table in the DW.

Why did we use the Key-Name pair instead of using the name field alone? We have designed the Key-Name pair for a good reason. By carefully planning the key column value, and setting the `OrderBy` property to `Key`, we have met our needs for ordering. In this example, we've deliberately placed the `Known` colors value first using the lower key value and ordering the attribute by key instead of by name.

In the process of dimension redesign we did one extra step. We created a natural user hierarchy, **Product Colors**. A natural user hierarchy is beneficial from the perspective of both performance and data navigation.

We also did something else that is important and should not be forgotten – defining relations between the new attribute `Color Group` and an existing one `Color`. Attribute relationships define hierarchical dependencies between attributes. These relationships between attributes can be used by the Analysis Services engine to optimize performance.

Other things we did were more or less cosmetic.

Dimensional processing was required because the structure has changed. The same goes for the cube.

You should also consider redesigning your aggregations. The new attribute has only two members, therefore the aggregation wizard may look for including it in many combinations with other hierarchies. In other words for the same amount of space dedicated for aggregations, a low-cardinality attribute can generate more aggregations than the one with more members in it. The more aggregations, the greater the chance of hitting one of them in queries that uses this new attribute.

There's more...

Notice that once you redesign your dimension like that, you can do many things relatively easily. One of those things we've already shown is natural subtotals and ordering of the members in user hierarchy. The next thing is the filtering of members.

If you need to show only known colors, you can put that single member in slicer. Having a single member is a much better solution than using multi-select. Not only the performance could be better, but you also avoid problems with tools that have problems with multi-select. Therefore, think about this solution in a much broader sense, not only as a way of isolating unwanted members, but also as a way of avoiding problems with multi-select, and to have simple MDX calculations.

So when should we consider creating a new attribute?

Well, you know that sometimes a modification like this is just not possible. You can't anticipate all the possible multi-selects that users may want, or you are not allowed to change the dimension structure, or to have the cube down for a certain amount of time. Yes, this can be handled, but your current configuration may be preventing you from doing that smoothly.

Redesigning the aggregations could be beneficial, but it's totally optional. It doesn't have to put you off from implementing a new attribute. The existing aggregations on the `Color` attribute (if any) should be leveraged because of the established attribute relationships.

Nevertheless, the idea of this recipe was to show you how to do it. The final decision of whether you'll do it or not in the end is entirely yours. Weigh the pros and cons, especially if you have a development environment where you can play and make a decision based on your findings.

So, where's the MDX?

There isn't any! At least not in this recipe. Remember, the best thing is to keep things simple. This recipe presented a way how making a small investment in the redesign of your dimension pays off by not having complex MDX calculations. Even better, by not having MDX at all sometimes!

It follows the main idea of the chapter that the solution isn't to make the best possible MDX calculation or query. Oftentimes it is better to look for an alternative in either a cube/dimension design or even further, in the dimensional model. The general rule of thumb is to always prefer a built-in Analysis Services feature over writing MDX. This was the first recipe in a series of recipes that showed how. The others follow, so read on.

Typical scenarios

Every time you catch yourself using functions like `Except()`, `Filter()`, or similar functions too often in your calculations, you should step back and consider whether that's a repeating behavior and whether it would pay off to have an attribute to separate the data you've been separating using MDX calculations. If it has a repeating pattern and it's not something unpredictable, there's your candidate.

Once you have a member (or more) separating two or more parts of the set, you can simply use them in the calculations. You can even call upon their children or other descendants. You could make ratios the easier way. Everything becomes simplified.

Using a distinct count measure to implement histograms over existing hierarchies

Histograms are an important tool in data analysis. They represent the distribution of frequencies of an entity or event. In OLAP, those terms translate to dimensions and their attributes.

This recipe illustrates how to implement a histogram over an attribute `Color`. The histogram needs to tell us the product count for each `Color` in each `Fiscal Year`.

In order to create a histogram, we need a measure that can count distinct members of an attribute for any given context.

There are two solutions to this problem. One is to use a calculated measure; the other is to use a regular measure with the distinct count type of the aggregation.

Many BI developers might lean towards the first option. The calculated measure might be an easy to implement solution because deploying the MDX script doesn't require reprocessing the cube.

Like most things in life, a shortcut is usually not an optimal solution. Depending on various factors like the cube and dimension sizes, the calculation can turn out to be slow in certain scenarios or contexts.

The second option of creating a **Distinct count** type of measure is a better choice in terms of performance. In this recipe, we will discuss how to implement an attribute-based histogram using the second option, that is, to create a **Distinct count** type of measure over a dimension key column in the fact table.

Getting ready

Open the **SQL Server Data Tools** (SSDT) and then open the **Adventure Works DW 2012** solution. Once it loads, double-click on the **Adventure Works** cube.

In this example we're going to analyze products based on their characteristics. We're going to show how many red, green and blue products are present in a particular subcube.

How to do it...

Follow these steps to create a distinct count measure:

1. Create a new **Distinct count** type of measure using the column `ProductKey` in the **Sales Summary Facts** table:

2. Name it `Product Count` and set the format string as `#,#` (without quotes) in the **Properties** pane.

3. The best practice for distinct count measures is to have them in a separate measure group. Notice how SSDT ensures this is done. Name the new measure group `Sales Products`.

4. Process the cube. Once it's done, go to the **Cube Browser** tab and reconnect. Click on the **Analyze in Excel** icon on top to open Excel.

5. Test this new measure using any attribute of the `Product` dimension or any other dimension, for example, the `Date` dimension as seen in the following screenshot. The measure aggregation function adjusts itself returning the distinct number of products in each cell:

	A	B	C	D	E	F
1	Product Count	Fiscal Year ▼				
2	Color ▼	FY 2006	FY 2007	FY 2008	FY 2009	Grand Total
3	Black	19	53	39	7	111
4	Blue	1	1	26	4	28
5	Multi	4	7	5	5	16
6	NA		12	35	18	47
7	Red	26	19	5	1	50
8	Silver	8	6	30	1	44
9	Silver/Black			7		7
10	White	2		2	2	4
11	Yellow		9	34	4	43
12	Grand Total	60	107	183	42	350

How it works...

Attribute-based histograms are relatively easy to implement. All we need is a `Distinct` count type of measure over a dimension key column in the fact table. After that, everything is pretty straightforward; the new measure reacts to every attribute, directly or indirectly related to that fact table.

There's more...

Here's the calculation that can produce the same result as to the `Distinct` count type of measure we have implemented in this recipe:

```
Create MEMBER CurrentCube.[Measures].[Product Count calc orig] AS
    Count ( EXISTING
            Exists( [Product].[Product].[Product].MEMBERS, ,
                    'Sales Summary' ) )
    , Visible = 0
    , Format_String = '#,#'
    , Associated_Measure_Group = 'Sales Summary'
    , Display_Folder = 'Histograms'
    ;


Create MEMBER CurrentCube.[Measures].[Product Count calc] AS
    iif( [Measures].[Product Count calc orig] = 0, null,
         [Measures].[Product Count calc orig] )
    , Format_String = '#,#'
    , Associated_Measure_Group = 'Sales Summary'
    , Display_Folder = 'Histograms'
    ;
```

What we're doing here is creating two calculated measures. One, hidden, returns the count of products relevant to the existing context which has data in the `Sales Summary` measure group. The other, visible, converts zeros to null because the result of the first calculated measure is never null and we don't want zeros in our result. We'd like to keep the data sparse.

As we have mentioned in the introduction, calculated measure might be easy to implement, but a regular measure offers better performance, especially on very large dimensions. In scenarios where the distinct count column (`ProductKey`) has millions of distinct values, a distinct count measure may be a much, much faster solution than an MDX calculation.

We should also keep in mind that an additional measure does come at the cost of having to process and store it.

In scenarios where `ProductKey` has few distinct values (that is 100,000 members or less), another good approach might be to build a `ProductKey` grain measure group and add a many-to-many relationship on all the other dimensions in the `Sales Summary` measure group. Essentially, any distinct count can be reformulated as a many-to-many relationship which is explained in detail in *Marco Russo's, Many-to-Many dimensional modeling* paper: `http://tinyurl.com/M2Mpaper`

See also

> ▸ The next recipe, *Using a dummy dimension to implementing histograms over nonexisting hierarchies* covers a similar topic.

Using a dummy dimension to implement histograms over nonexisting hierarchies

As seen in the previous recipe, Analysis Services supports attribute-based histograms by design. All it takes is a distinct count measure and we're good to go.

This recipe illustrates how to implement more complex type of histograms — histograms over nonexisting hierarchies.

The complexity comes from the fact that the hierarchy which we'd like to base the calculation on does not exist. That's a big issue where a multidimensional cube is concerned.

OLAP cubes operate on predetermined structures. It is not possible to build items on-the-fly. In other words, it is not possible to create a new hierarchy based on a calculation and use it the way we would use any other hierarchy. In OLAP, every hierarchy must be prepared in advance and must already be a part of the cube, otherwise it can't exist.

In this recipe, we're interested in the fact table. The fact table represents a series of events that are taking place and are being recorded in a very consistent manner. Every row tells a story of an event. Various columns in that row represent dimensions related to those events.

In the previous recipe, where we calculated histograms over attributes, we created a measure based on one of the dimension columns in the fact table. That measure counted distinct dimension member keys that occur in a part of the fact table, the part determined by other dimensions in context. Those other dimensions limit the size of the fact table acting like a filter to it.

This time we're interested in something else. We're interested in combining several dimensions, for example counting the number of the distinct members of one of those dimensions inside the other.

Let's illustrate this with an example. Take resellers and their orders. We might be interested in orders only, as in the number of orders a particular reseller made in a certain period. The possible values are 0, 1, 2, 3, and so on, up to the maximum number of orders a single reseller ever made. If we want to analyze that, then that's a measure, the `Reseller Order Count` measure in the Adventure Works cube, to be precise. Resellers are simply a dimension we want to use on an axis in this case.

But what if we want to analyze both the resellers and the orders but neither of them is on rows or columns? That's a different story. For example, we want to know how many resellers made 0 orders in a given time frame, how many of them made 1, 2, or more. That sequence of numbers (0, 1, 2, and so on) is what should go on rows (or columns), something we will iterate on. The measure in this case would be the `Reseller Count` measure, a measure showing the distinct count of resellers in a particular context. The only problem is – neither this special dimension exists, nor the distinct count measure does.

While it is relatively easy to make a distinct count type of measure, either using a calculated measure or a regular measure with the distinct count aggregation, creating a dimension takes preparation and cannot be done on-the-fly.

Now that we've explained the problem, let's see how it can be solved.

Getting ready

Open the **SQL Server Data Tools** (SSDT) and then open the **Adventure Works DW 2012** solution. Once it loads, double-click on the **Adventure Works DW** data source view.

In this example we're going to analyze resellers based on the frequency of their orders. In other words, we're going to show how many resellers made zero, one, two, three, and so on orders in a given time frame and for given conditions.

How to do it...

Follow these steps to implement the histogram over the hierarchy that doesn't exist in the cube.

1. Create a new named query Reseller Order Frequency with the following definition:

```
SELECT 0 AS Interval
UNION ALL
SELECT
    TOP (
        SELECT
            MAX(Frequency) AS Interval
        FROM
            ( SELECT
                ResellerKey,
                COUNT(SalesOrderNumber) AS Frequency
              FROM
                ( SELECT
                    DISTINCT
                    ResellerKey,
                    SalesOrderNumber
                  FROM
                    dbo.FactResellerSales
                ) AS t1
              GROUP BY
                ResellerKey
            ) AS t2
    ) ROW_NUMBER()
        OVER (ORDER BY ResellerKey) AS Interval
FROM
    dbo.FactResellerSales
```

2. Turn off the **Show/Hide Diagram Pane** and **Show/Hide Grid Pane** and execute the previous query in order to test it.

An error might pop up when you run this type of query or when you open the named query to change it. The error basically says that this type of query cannot be represented visually using the diagram pane because it contains the OVER SQL clause. That's the reason why we've turned that pane off. If for whatever reason you see that error anyway, just acknowledge it and continue with the recipe. It is merely information, not a problem

3. Once executed, the query returns 13 rows with numbers, the first one being zero and the last one being the maximum number of orders for a customer (here 12).

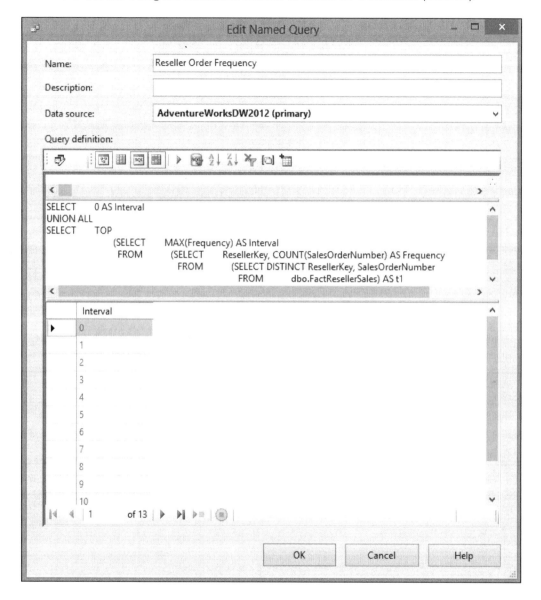

4. Close the named query editor, locate the **Reseller Order Frequency** named query, and mark the **Interval** column as a **Logical Primary Key**.

5. Create a new dimension using the previously defined named query and name it `Reseller Order Frequency`.

6. Use the **Interval** column for both the `KeyColumn` and the `ValueColumn` properties:

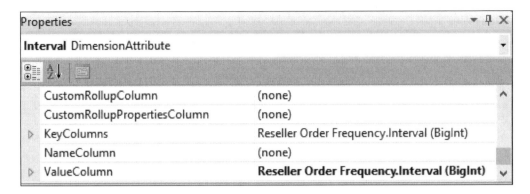

7. Name the `All` member `All Intervals`.

8. Process-full that dimension.

9. Open the **Adventure Works** cube and add that dimension without linking it to any measure group.

10. Deploy the changes by right-clicking on the project name (in the **Solution Explorer** pane) and by choosing the **Deploy action**. Then choose the **Process** action to process the cube.

11. Go to the **Calculations** tab and add the following code to the end of the MDX script:

```
Create MEMBER CurrentCube.[Measures].[RO Frequency] AS
    Sum( EXISTING [Reseller].[Reseller].[Reseller].MEMBERS,
            iif( [Reseller Order Frequency].[Interval]
                 .CurrentMember.MemberValue =
                 [Measures].[Reseller Order Count],
                 1,
                 null
               )
        )
, Format_String = '#,#'
, Associated_Measure_Group = 'Reseller Orders'
, Display_Folder = 'Histograms'
;

Scope( ( [Measures].[RO Frequency],
         [Reseller Order Frequency].[Interval].[All Intervals] )
);
    This = Sum( [Reseller Order Frequency].[Interval]
                .[Interval].MEMBERS,
                [Measures].[RO Frequency]
              );
End Scope;
```

12. Deploy the solution.

13. Go to the **Cube Browser** tab and click on the **Analyze in Excel** icon on top to open Excel to build a pivot using the new **RO Frequency** measure. Then place the `Reseller Order Frequency` dimension on the opposite side from measures, on rows. Finally, add another dimension to the columns, the `Date` dimension, to test if the calculation works for hierarchies on both axes. As seen in the following screenshot, values don't repeat which is a sign that our calculation works. They represent the number of resellers who in a particular time period (years, in this case) made as many orders as shown in the hierarchy on rows. The distribution of customers and their orders is in fact the histogram we've been looking for:

	A	B	C	D	E	F	G	H	I
1	RO Frequency	Fiscal Year ▼							
2	Interval ▼	FY 2005	FY 2006	FY 2007	FY 2008	FY 2009	FY 2010	FY 2011	Grand Total
3	0	701	493	336	208	701	701	701	66
4	1		10	30	37				30
5	2		19	34	16				20
6	3		25	47	43				38
7	4		154	254	390				235
8	5				1				20
9	6				3				21
10	7				3				34
11	8								145
12	9								10
13	10								8
14	11								10
15	12								64
16	Grand Total	701	701	701	701	701	701	701	701

How it works...

There are several important things in this recipe. We'll explain them one by one.

The solution starts with a particular T-SQL query that was used as a named query in the data source view. The purpose of that query is to return the maximum number of orders for any customer and all the integers up to that number, starting from zero.

The maximum frequency number is obtained by combining the distinct occurrence of the `ResellerKey` and `SalesOrderNumber` columns in the `ResellerSales` fact table and by taking the count of the orders for each reseller. That's the essence of that query.

As we saw, the query returns 13 rows, with numbers starting from zero and ending with 12. Those values in turn become members of a new dimension which we'll build afterwards. The dimension is in no way associated with any fact table or dimension in that cube. What's the purpose then?

We should remember that our initial goal is to show how many distinct customers fall into each segment: zero orders, one order, two orders, and so on. That requirement is contradictory in OLAP terms because it would require two measures: one with the distinct number of customers and the other with the distinct number of orders, both somehow used one against the other in a pivot. The problem is that OLAP supports measures on one axis only. Actually, that's true for any hierarchy.

So, what's the solution?

The idea is to build a special dimension and use it on one axis while we're keeping the other measure on another axis. The only thing this dimension has to have is a sequence of numbers so that we can assign values to them, somehow.

Now we've come to the calculations; the MDX script.

The first part of the calculation is the main part. That's where the assignment takes place. The idea is to use the `MemberValue` property value of the current member of the `Reseller Order Frequency` dimension and increment the measure **RO Frequency** only when `MemberValue` equals the number of orders a particular reseller made in the current slice. In other words, we're descending to the granularity of the resellers where we're counting how many of them be equal to the condition. The condition says that the number of orders must match the utility dimension member's value we're currently on. That way each reseller is thrown in one of the buckets, one of the members of that new dimension. Once we're done with the process, each bucket tells us how many resellers made that many orders. In other words, we have a complex histogram, a histogram based on an up-to-now non-existent dimension.

Each member of the utility dimension got its value using the techniques described earlier except for the `All` member. No value was assigned to it because the calculation operated only on individual members. That's why there was a requirement to use another statement where we're basically saying, "Collect all the individual values obtained during the allocation process and aggregate them."

There's more...

The example presented here was using a dedicated utility dimension named `Reseller Order Frequency`. It had exactly 13 members. However, they were not fixed; they were the consequence of the data in the fact table. Meaning the number of members can grow with time. It will always be a sequence of natural numbers up to the maximum number of occurrences for the entire fact table.

It is quite reasonable to expect multiple event-based histograms in the same cube. One way to handle this would be to build a separate named query for each combination of dimensions we'd like to analyze, each returning different number of rows which are eventually translated to dimension members. But there's another approach to it.

It is possible to build a single utility dimension which contains enough members so that it can cover any, or most, types of histograms. The idea is to build the tally table – a table with numbers starting from zero and ending with some big number. How big depends on your preference, it could be 100, 1000, or more.

The name of the corresponding dimension should be unique, something neutral like the Frequency dimension.

The code presented in this recipe applies, but it must be modified to include the new dimension name. It can be repeated many times, once for each new distinct count type measure.

The only downside is that we have more members now than before, for a particular distinct count type measure. The query results and charts might look bad because of this. For example, if the dimension contains 100 members and we only have 13 frequencies like in the example presented in this recipe, most of the cells would be empty.

Turning the NON EMPTY switch wouldn't help either. It would only do damage by removing some of the members in the range. What we need is a list of numbers starting from zero and ending with the max value. If some of the members inside that range are empty, they must be preserved. The idea is to show the full range, and not shrink it into something more compact by removing empty values.

How can we solve this problem?

There are several solutions. One is to use the named sets defined in the MDX script defined as a range, 0 – max. Here's the example:

```
Create SET CurrentCube.[RO Frequency Set] AS
    { null : Tail( NonEmpty( [Frequency]
                        .[Interval].[Interval].MEMBERS,
                        [Measures].[RO Frequency] ),
                1 ).Item(0)
```

In some tools, the set can be used on rows or columns instead of the complete Frequency dimension.

The other solution is to provide another scope in which you would convert nulls into zeros for members that form the range. Others would be null. That solution would work with NON EMPTY then.

DSV or DW?

The initial T-SQL query could have been implemented in the relational DW database instead. After all, it is the best practice to keep everything related to business logic in one place and that place is the data warehouse (DW). However, the concept of the utility dimension is purely SSAS-related and hence falls in the domain of a BI developer, not a DW developer. He's the one who creates it, knows what it's for, and modifies it when required. That's the reason we've used the data source view (DSV) instead. Does it have to be DSV then? No, it is up to you to decide which view is better for your situation. Just be consistent.

More calculations

Here's another calculation you may consider helpful. It calculates the percentage in total:

```
Create MEMBER CurrentCube.[Measures].[RO Frequency Total] AS
    ( [Measures].[RO Frequency],
        [Reseller Order Frequency].[Interval].DefaultMember )
  , Visible = 0
  , Format_String = '#,#'
  , Associated_Measure_Group = 'Reseller Orders'
  , Display_Folder = 'Histograms'
  ;


Create MEMBER CurrentCube.[Measures].[RO Frequency %] AS
    iif( [Measures].[RO Frequency Total] = 0,
        null,
        [Measures].[RO Frequency] /
        [Measures].[RO Frequency Total]
      )
  , Format_String = 'Percent'
  , Associated_Measure_Group = 'Reseller Orders'
  , Display_Folder = 'Histograms'
  ;
```

The result looks like:

	A	B	C	D	E	F	G	H	I
1		Business Type ▼							
2		⊕ Specialty Bike Shop		⊕ Value Added Reseller		⊕ Warehouse		Total RO Frequency	Total RO Frequency %
3	Interval ▼	RO Frequency	RO Frequency %	RO Frequency	RO Frequency %	RO Frequency	RO Frequency %		
4	0	31	13.42%	22	9.24%	13	5.60%	66	9.42%
5	1	13	5.63%	11	4.62%	6	2.59%	30	4.28%
6	2	8	3.46%	7	2.94%	5	2.16%	20	2.85%
7	3	14	6.06%	14	5.88%	10	4.31%	38	5.42%
8	4	71	30.74%	76	31.93%	88	37.93%	235	33.52%
9	5	6	2.60%	7	2.94%	7	3.02%	20	2.85%
10	6	10	4.33%	3	1.26%	8	3.45%	21	3.00%
11	7	10	4.33%	12	5.04%	12	5.17%	34	4.85%
12	8	44	19.05%	50	21.01%	51	21.98%	145	20.68%
13	9	1	0.43%	5	2.10%	4	1.72%	10	1.43%
14	10	1	0.43%	4	1.68%	3	1.29%	8	1.14%
15	11	5	2.16%	1	0.42%	4	1.72%	10	1.43%
16	12	17	7.36%	26	10.92%	21	9.05%	64	9.13%
17	Grand Total	231	100.00%	238	100.00%	232	100.00%	701	100.00%

As you can see, calculations work for other dimensions as long as they are related to the measure group of the `Reseller Order Count` measure, the measure used in the calculations.

Other examples

The following link is a page describing the same thing in another way: `http://tinyurl.com/OLAPHistograms`

See also

▸ The recipe *Using a distinct count measure to implementing histograms over existing hierarchies* covers a similar topic. *Creating a physical measure as a placeholder for MDX assignments* is directly related to this recipe and has an improved version of MDX assignments presented in this recipe.

Creating a physical measure as a placeholder for MDX assignments

There can be many problems regarding calculated members. First, they don't aggregate up like regular members; we have to handle that by ourselves. Next, the drill through statements and security restrictions are only allowed for regular members. Not to mention the limited support for them in various client tools, for example in Excel. Finally, regular measures often noticeably beat their calculated measures counterparts in terms of performance or the ability to work with subselect.

On the other hand, calculated members can be defined and/or deployed very easily. They don't require any drastic change of the cube or the dimensions and therefore are good for testing, debugging, as a temporary solution, or even a permanent one. Anything goes as long as they don't become a serious obstacle in any of the ways mentioned earlier. When that happens, it's time to look for an alternative.

In the previous recipe, *Using a dummy dimension to implement histograms over nonexisting hierarchies*, we used the `EXISTING` operator in the assignment made for the calculated measure `RO Frequency`. First, that expression tends to evaluate slowly which becomes noticeable on large dimensions. The `Reseller` dimension is not a large dimension and therefore, the provided expression will not cause significant performance issues there. However, the second problem is that the `EXISTING` operator will not react to the subselect and will therefore evaluate incorrectly if the subselect is used. That might become an issue with tools like Excel that extensively use subselect whenever multiple members are selected in the filter area.

This recipe illustrates the alternative approach. It shows how a dummy physical measure can be used as a placeholder for calculations assigned to a calculated measure. In other words, how a calculated measure can be turned into a regular measure to solve a particular problem. As explained a moment ago, subselect is just one of the reasons we look for the alternative, which means the idea presented in this recipe can be applied in other cases too.

Getting ready

This recipe depends heavily on the previous recipe; therefore you should implement the solution it presents. If you have read and practiced the recipes sequentially, you're all set. If not, simply read and implement the solution explained in the previous recipe in order to be able to continue with this one.

Once you have everything set up, you're ready to go with this one.

How to do it...

Follow these steps to implement a physical measure as a placeholder for MDX assignments:

1. Double-click on the **Adventure Works DW** data source view in the **Adventure Works DW 2012** solution opened in the **SQL Server Data Tools** (SSDT).

2. Locate the **Reseller Sales Fact** table in the pane with the list of tables on the left side.

3. Right-click it and add a new column by selecting **New Named Calculation** option.

4. The definition of the column should be:

   ```
   CAST( null AS int )
   ```

5. Name the column `NullMeasure`. Save the data source view.

6. Double-click on the **Adventure Works** cube and locate the `Reseller Sales` measure group.

7. Add a new physical measure in that measure group using the newly-added column in the underlying fact table and name it `RO Frequency DSV`.

8. Specify **Histograms** for its `DisplayFolder` property and provide #, # for the `FormatString` property.

9. Use the `Sum` for the `AggregateFunction` and set the `NullProcessing` property (available inside the `Source` property) to `Preserve`.

10. Deploy the changes. Process the **Adventure Works** cube.

11. Go to the **Calculations** tab and provide the adequate scope statement and MDX assignment for the new regular measure:

    ```
    Scope( [Measures].[RO Frequency DSV],
           [Reseller Order Frequency].[Interval].[Interval].Members,
           [Reseller].[Reseller].[Reseller].Members
    ```

```
        );
    This = iif( [Reseller Order Frequency].[Interval]
                .CurrentMember.MemberValue =
                [Measures].[Reseller Order Count],
                1,
                null
              );
End scope;
```

12. The `Reseller Order Frequency` dimension is not related to any fact table and automatic aggregations cannot work. Because of this, we have to perform additional steps, including providing the assignment for the `All` member of the dummy dimension `Reseller Order Frequency`:

```
Scope( [Measures].[RO Frequency DSV],
       [Reseller Order Frequency].[Interval].[All Intervals]
     );
    This = Sum( [Reseller Order Frequency].[Interval]
                .[Interval].MEMBERS,
                [Measures].[RO Frequency DSV]
              );
End Scope;
```

13. Deploy the changes made in the MDX script.

14. Now, go to the **Cube Browser** tab. Open **Excel** by clicking on the **Analyze in Excel** icon on top to build a pivot using the `Reseller Order Frequency` dimension on rows and both the new **RO Frequency DSV** measure and the old one, the **RO Frequency** measure on columns:

	A	B	C
1	Interval ▼	RO Frequency	RO Frequency DSV
2	0	66	66
3	1	30	30
4	2	20	20
5	3	38	38
6	4	235	235
7	5	20	20
8	6	21	21
9	7	34	34
10	8	145	145
11	9	10	10
12	10	8	8
13	11	10	10
14	12	64	64
15	**Grand Total**	701	701

15. As you can see in the preceding screenshot, the calculation works.

16. Now, add the `Business Type` attribute hierarchy of the `Reseller` dimension in the report filer area, and select **Specialty Bike Shop** for the **Filter Expression** there. The following screenshot shows how it should look like:

17. This screenshot shows the result with the report filter.

	A	B	C
1	Reseller Type	Specialty Bike Shop 🔽	
2			
3	Interval 🔽	RO Frequency	RO Frequency DSV
4	0	31	31
5	1	13	13
6	2	8	8
7	3	14	14
8	4	71	71
9	5	6	6
10	6	10	10
11	7	10	10
12	8	44	44
13	9	1	1
14	10	1	1
15	11	5	5
16	12	17	17
17	Grand Total	231	231

18. Notice that the values for both **RO Frequency DSV** measure and **RO Frequency** measure adjusted to the new context.

19. Next, we are going to write a MDX query with explicit subselect to prove that the **RO Frequency DSV** measure will adjust to the new context and the **RO Frequency** measure will not.

20. In the following MDX query, we put the **Business Type** filter in the subselect on purpose. We will prove that calculated measures using the `EXISTING` keyword will not respond to subselect, and physical measures will respond to subselect.

```
SELECT
    { [Measures].[RO Frequency],
      [Measures].[RO Frequency DSV]
    } ON 0,
    [Reseller Order Frequency].[Interval].[Interval] ON 1
FROM
    (
            SELECT
                    [Reseller].[Business Type].&[Specialty Bike Shop]
ON 0
            FROM
                    [Adventure Works]
    )
```

21. Execute the preceding query, and the result should look like the following screenshot.

	RO Frequency	RO Frequency DSV
0	66	31
1	30	13
2	20	8
3	38	14
4	235	71
5	20	6
6	21	10
7	34	10
8	145	44
9	10	1
10	8	1
11	10	5
12	64	17

22. Notice that the values for the **RO Frequency DSV** adjusted to the new context in subselect while the values of the **RO Frequency** measure (highlighted in the screenshot) remained unchanged. The alternative approach with a physical measure worked!

How it works...

A column, defined with the value of null, is created in the fact table and later used as a new cube measure. By default, the Analysis Services would turn the value of null into zero; however, we have prevented that by providing the **Preserve** option in the `NullProcessing` property. This produced a regular measure that is always null, in any context.

Now let's take a look at the definition of the measure from the previous recipe and see how it changed to the adequate scope statement. We'll repeat them here.

The calculated measure from the previous recipe is defined like this:

```
Create MEMBER CurrentCube.[Measures].[RO Frequency] AS
    Sum( EXISTING [Reseller].[Reseller].[Reseller].MEMBERS,
        iif( [Reseller Order Frequency].[Interval]
            .CurrentMember.MemberValue =
            [Measures].[Reseller Order Count],
            1,
            null
        )
    )
, Format_String = '#,#'
, Associated_Measure_Group = 'Reseller Orders'
, Display_Folder = 'Histograms'
;
```

The new measure from this recipe is scoped like:

```
Scope( [Measures].[RO Frequency DSV],
        [Reseller Order Frequency].[Interval].[Interval].Members,
        [Reseller].[Reseller].[Reseller].Members
    );
    This = iif( [Reseller Order Frequency].[Interval]
            .CurrentMember.MemberValue =
            [Measures].[Reseller Order Count],
            1,
            null
        );
End scope;
```

Notice the important difference in them. In our new physical measure implementation, we first passed the burden of detecting existing resellers to the server by adding the set of resellers inside the definition of the scope. We also passed the burden of summarizing the values across the existing resellers to the server. In other words, the server does all the heavy work for us. Another benefit we get from using a dummy regular measure is that the calculation will also work with the subselect, as shown in the example.

There's more...

However, the improvement comes with a price. In this case it is manifested in the form of all the modifications you have to perform and maintain later, as well as the increased cube size because of the new measure. Because of that, it is up to you to decide whether it pays off to implement this alternative or not in your particular case. Hopefully you'll have the chance to test it in parallel to the existing solution and measure the costs/benefits ratio of the new solution.

Additional information can be found in *Teo Lachev's* article: `http://tinyurl.com/TeoCalcAsRegular`

Associated measure group

The same format string and display folder used for the calculated measure can be specified in the process of creating new measure. The only exception we made is that we used the `Reseller Sales` measure group. That's because the `Reseller Orders` measure group, the one which the calculated measure was associated with, has a distinct count measure and distinct count measures should not be mixed with other regular measures.

We've decided to put the calculated measure in the best place we thought it should be. It made sense to put it in the same measure group as the `Reseller Orders Count` measure because they both count something related to resellers. Just for the record, we could have easily defined it on any measure group, it wouldn't make much difference.

See also

▸   Reading and implementing the recipe *Using a distinct count measure to implement histograms over existing hierarchies* is a prerequisite for this recipe

Using a new dimension to calculate the most frequent price

In this recipe we're going to analyze the products and their prices. The requirement is to find the most frequent price, or **Mode Price**, in any context.

Finding the price for a particular product doesn't look like a problem. We can either read it in its properties if the price is available as a product member property or we can calculate the average price based on the sales amount and the quantity sold.

Member properties are static and therefore choosing the first approach would be wrong. For example, the price in form of the member property doesn't change in time or with the territory. What we need is a dynamic expression.

The other option is to calculate the average price, but that's also not good enough. We need to know the exact price for each transaction, not the average value.

If we go low enough with the granularity of the query, the average price will eventually become the price used in the transaction, however, cubes are not optimized to be queried on leaf level. All in all, it's pretty obvious we need some help here. This can't be solved in MDX only.

The solution is to create a new dimension based on the price column in the fact table. That way we can have prices as an object we can use and manipulate within MDX calculations.

In addition to that, we need a measure that counts rows, but that's already there (or can be easily added) in every measure group (as long it's not the one with the distinct count measure). That measure can be used to isolate the price with the maximum number of rows for a given context. After that, we need to extract this price member's value which becomes the price we're after.

Let's see how it's done in this recipe.

Getting ready

Open the **SQL Server Data Tools** (SSDT) and then open the **Adventure Works DW 2012** solution. Once it loads, double-click on the **Adventure Works DW** data source view.

How to do it...

Follow these steps to change the model the cube is built from which in turn will enable simple and effective MDX calculations.

1. Create a new named query. Name it `Price` and use the following definition for it:

```
SELECT
    DISTINCT
    UnitPrice
FROM
    dbo.FactResellerSales
```

2. Execute the query in order to test it. It should return 233 rows.

3. Mark sure you've selected a single column in that table and then mark it as a **Logical Primary Key**.

4. Locate the **Reseller Sales** diagram in the **Diagram Organizer** pane.

5. Drag and drop the `Price` named query in the free area of that diagram and link the **Reseller Sales Facts** fact table to it using the `UnitPrice` columns in both objects.

6. Then create a new dimension using the previously defined `Price` named query and name it `Price`.

7. Use the `UnitPrice` column for the `KeyColumn`.

8. Name the attribute `Price`.

9. Once you finish with the wizard, the **Dimension Editor** will show.

10. Verify that the `OrderBy` property is set to `Key`.

11. Set the `ValueColumn` to `UnitPrice` column.

12. Name the `All` member `All Prices`.

13. Process-full the dimension.

14. When it's done, verify the dimension in the **Browser** tab of **Dimension Editor**. The prices should be sorted in ascending order.

15. Now, open the **Adventure Works** cube and go to the **Dimension Usage** tab of the cube to add the `Price` dimension.

16. Once added, the dimension will be automatically related to two measure groups: `Reseller Sales` and `Reseller Orders`. Verify that and then set its `Visible` property to `False` in the **Properties** pane.

17. Deploy the changes. When the processing is over, you're ready to write calculations.

18. Go to the **Calculations** tab and position the cursor in the end of the MDX script.

19. Enter the calculation for the `Mode Price`:

```
Create MEMBER CurrentCube.[Measures].[Mode Price] AS
        iif( IsEmpty( [Measures].[Reseller Transaction Count] ),
              null,
              TopCount( [Price].[Price].[Price].MEMBERS,
                        1,
                        [Measures].[Reseller Transaction Count]
                      ).Item(0).MemberValue
            )
    , Format_String = 'Currency'
    , Display_Folder = 'Statistics'
    , Associated_Measure_Group = 'Reseller Sales';
```

20. Deploy the changes in the MDX script and then go to the **Cube Browser** tab. Open **Excel** by clicking on the **Analyze in Excel** icon on top.

21. A comparison of the **Mode Price** and the **Reseller Average Unit Price** measures across the products subcategories can be seen in the following screenshot:

	A	B	C
1	Category ▼	Reseller Average Unit Price	Mode Price
2	⊞ Accessories	$21.67	$20.19
3	⊟ Bikes	$882.72	$469.79
4	⊞ Mountain Bikes	$1,085.21	$647.99
5	⊞ Road Bikes	$779.14	$469.79
6	⊞ Touring Bikes	$841.25	$1,430.44
7	⊞ Clothing	$28.21	$28.84
8	⊟ Components	$251.40	$202.33
9	⊞ Bottom Brackets	$56.39	$72.89
10	⊞ Brakes	$63.88	$63.90
11	⊞ Chains	$12.14	$12.14
12	⊞ Cranksets	$179.76	$242.99
13	⊞ Derailleurs	$61.36	$54.89
14	⊞ Forks	$117.43	$137.69
15	⊞ Handlebars	$44.73	$33.77
16	⊞ Headsets	$59.78	$74.84
17	⊞ Mountain Frames	$432.37	$158.43
18	⊞ Pedals	$37.35	$48.59
19	⊞ Road Frames	$335.10	$202.33
20	⊞ Saddles	$26.17	$31.58
21	⊞ Touring Frames	$425.50	$602.35
22	⊞ Wheels	$127.53	$67.54
23	**Grand Total**	$444.43	$469.79

How it works...

By counting rows in the original fact table we're basically saying we want to know how many times the current price occurred in the context of other dimensions. That, of course, demands for the `Price` dimension which we have made in the initial steps of the solution presented in this recipe.

There's something else to it. The `Price` dimension is kept aside all the time by being invisible. Its only purpose is to spread the prices so that we can pick the most frequent one. The evaluation of the most frequent price is done in the definition of the calculated measure, where we're applying the `TopCount()` function over all prices and therefore use the **Reseller Transaction Count** measure to count how many occurrences each price had in the given context. For the record, the **Reseller Transaction Count** measure is also invisible, but it can be used in the calculations.

If you want to verify the correctness of the calculation, turn both the `Price` dimension and the **Reseller Transaction Count** measure visible, deploy the changes, and use them in the pivot. The price with the highest value of the **Reseller Transaction Count** measure is automatically selected as the **Mode Price**.

In the end, it's worth mentioning that once we had the most frequent price, we read its member value and showed it as the result of the calculation.

There's more...

It's perfectly normal to encounter the situations where two or more prices have the same frequency; the same rate of occurrence. However, the calculation we made can take only a single one. How do we know which one?

Unlike datasets resulting from queries in the relational world, the default behavior of sets in the multidimensional world is that they are always sorted unless explicitly requested otherwise. Order is determined during the design of the dimensions. Each attribute has a property for that. It can be a `Key`, `Name`, or another attribute. The point is – members in are sorted one way or the other.

Because of this, in the case of a tie, the order of members determines the winner. If members are sorted by the key, a member with the lower key will win. If members are sorted by the name, the one that alphabetically comes sooner wins. If you need the opposite order, consider using another attribute or switch the keys to their negative values.

Using a utility dimension to implement flexible display units

Measures are sometimes too precise for reporting needs. Either because they have decimals which distract us or because the numbers are very large, consisting of many digits, and therefore hard to memorize or compare with others. The phrase "can't see the forest for the trees" fits perfectly over here.

Sometimes users like to see measures displayed in thousands or millions for ease of comparison. One way to accomplish that would be to divide those measures directly in the fact table by, let's say 1,000 or 1,000,000. We would of course have to specify the new unit in the title of the measure. However, that wouldn't be a good solution. In situations where we need the results to be as precise as possible, that would cause problems. As said, sometimes, but not always, there's a need to simplify the numbers.

The other way would be to generate a set of parallel calculated measures, one for each factor. That way we would have Sales Amount, then Sales Amount (000), and finally Sales Amount (000,000) or similar markings. Again, this is not a very good approach. End users would have a hard time finding the right measure in a set of so many calculated measures.

The next option is the best, although it can have its specifics that may demand our attention. It's the case of building a separate utility dimension to display values in thousands, millions, and so on. This way we can preserve the simplicity of the cube design while enjoying the benefits of being able to visualize measures in other metric. This recipe shows how to achieve such a solution. It also tackles problems specific to this type of solution.

Getting ready

Open the **SQL Server Data Tools** (SSDT) and then open the **Adventure Works DW 2012** solution. Once it loads, double-click on the **Adventure Works DW** data source view.

How to do it...

Follow these steps to create utility dimension which displays result in various formats.

1. Create a new named query **Calculations - Display Units** with the following definition:

```
SELECT       0 AS UnitKey, 'As is' AS UnitName
UNION ALL
SELECT       1           , 'in 0'
UNION ALL
SELECT       2           , 'in 00'
UNION ALL
SELECT       3           , 'in 000'
UNION ALL
SELECT       4           , 'in 0,000'
UNION ALL
SELECT       5           , 'in 00,000'
UNION ALL
SELECT       6           , 'in 000,000'
UNION ALL
SELECT       7           , 'in 0,000,000'
UNION ALL
SELECT       8           , 'in 00,000,000'
UNION ALL
SELECT       9           , 'in 000,000,000'
```

2. Execute the query in order to test it. It should return 10 rows.

3. Set the UnitKey column as a **Logical Primary Key** column.

4. Create a new dimension using the previously defined named query and name it Calculations - Display Units.

5. Use the UnitKey column for the KeyColumn and the UnitName column for the NameColumn properties.

6. Name the attribute `Display Unit`.

7. Set the `IsAggregatable` property of the attribute to `False`.

8. Set the `OrderBy` property to `Key`.

9. Set the `ValueColumn` to `UnitKey` column.

10. Process-full the dimension.

11. Set the default member for the attribute to the `As is` member. The expression in the property should be `[Calculations - Display Units].[Display Unit].&[0]` once you're done.

12. Deploy and verify in the **Browser** tab of **Dimension Editor** that your new utility dimension looks like the following:

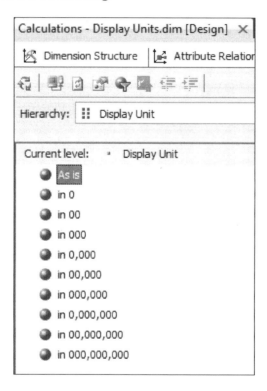

13. Open the **Adventure Works** cube and add that dimension without linking it to any measure group.

14. Deploy changes by right-clicking on the project name (in the **Solution Explorer** pane) and choosing the **Deploy** action.

15. Go to the **Calculations** tab and add the following code to the beginning of the MDX script:

```
Create Hidden SET CurrentCube.[Display Units Set] AS
    Except( [Calculations - Display Units].[Display Unit].MEMBERS,
            [Calculations - Display Units].[Display Unit].&[0] )
;
Scope( [Display Units Set] );
    This = [Calculations - Display Units].[Display Unit].&[0]
            /
            10 ^ [Calculations - Display Units].[Display Unit]
                .CurrentMember.MemberValue;
    Format_String( This ) = '#,##0';
End Scope;
```

16. Deploy the solution.

17. Go to the **Cube Browser** tab and build a pivot using the new dimension on columns where you select only some members, for example, display in thousands and **As is**. Put the **Gross Profit**, the **Sales Amount**, and the **Ratio to Parent Product** measures in the data area and product categories on rows. You should be able to see that the values are reduced as required for amounts, but not for the percentages:

	A	B	C	D	E	F	G
1		Display Unit					
2		As is			in 000		
3	Category	Gross Profit	Sales Amount	Ratio to Parent Product	Gross Profit	Sales Amount	Ratio to Parent Product
4	⊞ Accessories	$634,467.16	$1,272,057.89	1.16%	$634.47	1,272	1.16%
5	⊞ Bikes	$10,515,096.61	$94,620,526.21	86.17%	$10,515.10	94,621	86.17%
6	⊞ Clothing	$368,836.00	$2,117,613.45	1.93%	$368.84	2,118	1.93%
7	⊞ Components	$1,032,966.48	$11,799,076.66	10.75%	$1,032.97	11,799	10.75%
8	Grand Total	$12,551,366.25	$109,809,274.20	100.00%	$12,551.37	109,809	100.00%

How it works...

The Utility dimension, a dimension not related to any fact table of the cube, can be understood as a cube parameter. The logic we have implemented using the scope statement in the MDX script acts like a modification of the cube. The scope fires, if any members of that dimension are in context. The calculation specifies that the value of the measure will be reduced by factor 10 to the power of the member value of the current member. The formula can be so elegant because we used the MemberValue property, the same sequence of numbers as in the dimension key.

The definition of the scope says that the value of any measure will be divided by 10 to the power of N, where N is read from the `MemberValue` property of the current member of that utility dimension.

There's more...

Things don't run that smoothly. There's a potential problem in this approach.

One is that we lose the format string of the measure (see the **Sales Amount** measure in the previous screenshot); the other is that the scope is applied to all measures. Let's see what we can do about that.

Set-based approach

We can expand the scope and specify which measures we want in it. That way we can precisely control the format string for each set of measures.

Here's an example how it can be done. Add this new hidden set immediately after the previously defined hidden set and modify the scope as specified:

```
Create Hidden SET CurrentCube.[Measures Set] AS
    { [Measures].[Extended Amount],
        [Measures].[Freight Cost],
        [Measures].[Sales Amount],
        [Measures].[Standard Product Cost],
        [Measures].[Total Product Cost],
        [Measures].[Tax Amount] }
  ;

Scope( [Display Units Set],
        [Measures Set] );
    This = [Calculations - Display Units].[Display Unit].&[0]
            /
            10 ^ [Calculations - Display Units].[Display Unit]
                .CurrentMember.MemberValue;
    Format_String(This) = 'Currency';
End Scope;
```

Here's the same example using one regular, one calculated, and one ratio measure with the scope applied to the **in 000** member:

	A	B	C	D	E	F	G
1		Display Unit ▾▼					
2		As is			in 000		
3	Category ▼	Gross Profit	Sales Amount	Ratio to Parent Product	Gross Profit	Sales Amount	Ratio to Parent Product
4	⊞ Accessories	$634,467.16	$1,272,057.89	1.16%	$634.47	$1,272.06	1.16%
5	⊞ Bikes	$10,515,096.61	$94,620,526.21	86.17%	$10,515.10	$94,620.53	86.17%
6	⊞ Clothing	$368,836.00	$2,117,613.45	1.93%	$368.84	$2,117.61	1.93%
7	⊞ Components	$1,032,966.48	$11,799,076.66	10.75%	$1,032.97	$11,799.08	10.75%
8	Grand Total	$12,551,366.25	$109,809,274.20	100.00%	$12,551.37	$109,809.27	100.00%

Only regular cube measures can be explicitly specified in the scope, no calculated ones. The effect will manifest in all subsequently defined calculated measures too because their definition is dependent on the values of regular measures and since the regular measures will be reduced, so shall the calculated measure.

The scoped set solution can be repeated many times. We can group measures of the same type in multiple sets and use an explicit format string for each of those sets. However, that's not too practical of a solution. Moreover, the reduced values are still not readable. It would be great if we could lose decimals and currency symbols that distract us.

Format string on a filtered set approach

A more general way to specify various measures in the cube without having to list them all in the scope or hidden sets heavily depends on the naming convention used in the cube. We can filter all measures, regular and calculated ones, based on some criteria and apply the format only to those measures that don't have the words "price", "margin", "ratio", and so on in them. Here's an example for that.

Modify the definition of the Measures Set according to the following expression. Modify the scope statement, but move it to the end of the MDX script this time, not the beginning. Also, make sure the Display Units Set is still available in the MDX script since the scope is referring to it:

```
Create Hidden SET CurrentCube.[Measures Set] AS
    Filter( Measures.AllMembers,
            --MeasureGroupMeasures('Sales Summary'),
            InStr( Measures.CurrentMember.Name, 'Price' )
            = 0 AND
            InStr( Measures.CurrentMember.Name, 'Margin' )
```

```
          = 0 AND
          InStr( Measures.CurrentMember.Name, 'Percentage' )
          = 0 AND
          InStr( Measures.CurrentMember.Name, 'Growth' )
          = 0 AND
          InStr( Measures.CurrentMember.Name, 'Rate' )
          = 0 AND
          InStr( Measures.CurrentMember.Name, 'Ratio' )
          = 0
        )
  ;


  Scope( [Display Units Set] );
      Format_String( [Calculations - Display Units].[Display Unit].&[3]
                    * [Measures Set] ) = '#,##0,';
      Format_String( [Calculations - Display Units].[Display Unit].&[6]
                    * [Measures Set] ) = '#,##0,,';
      Format_String( [Calculations - Display Units].[Display Unit].&[9]
                    * [Measures Set] ) = '#,##0,,,';
  End Scope;
```

When deployed, this solution works just right. Open **Excel** and create a pivot, you can see that the amounts are formatted as numbers in 1,000 while the percentages remain as percentages:

	A	B	C	D	E	F	G
1		Display Unit ⚲					
2		As is			in 000		
3	Category ▾	Gross Profit	Sales Amount	Ratio to Parent Product	Gross Profit	Sales Amount	Ratio to Parent Product
4	⊞ Accessories	$634,467.16	$1,272,057.89	1.16%	634	1,272	1.16%
5	⊞ Bikes	$10,515,096.61	$94,620,526.21	86.17%	10,515	94,621	86.17%
6	⊞ Clothing	$368,836.00	$2,117,613.45	1.93%	369	2,118	1.93%
7	⊞ Components	$1,032,966.48	$11,799,076.66	10.75%	1,033	11,799	10.75%
8	Grand Total	$12,551,366.25	$109,809,274.20	100.00%	12,551	109,809	100.00%

> Gross Profit is a calculated measure, and is formatted as currency in the MDX script. In order for the `Format_String()` function to work in the earlier `SCOPE` statement, you need to remove the line `Format_String = "Currency"` from the Gross Profit calculation.

Notice that we didn't have to modify actual values in the scope statement; we only changed the format string for certain measures. This makes it a faster approach.

The other thing to notice is that we were able to use both calculated and regular measures. That is because in the `Format_String()` function we are allowed to use both types of measures, whereas in the scope's definition we are not allowed to use calculated measures. By carefully constructing our expression, we were able to achieve the goal.

The only downside is that we only made it work for some members of the utility dimension, not all of them. However, that should not be a problem because those members are used most of the time anyway (in 000, in 000,000, in 000,000,000 and so on). In other words, if we stick with the latest solution, we can remove all not-used members from the utility dimension.

The commented part of the scope statement shows that we can limit the filter to one or more measure groups.

Using a utility dimension to implement time-based calculations

The MDX language implemented in SQL Server Analysis Services offers various time-related functions. *Chapter 3, Working with Time* showed how they can be utilized to construct useful sets and calculations. The main focus there was to show how to make OLAP cubes time-aware; how to detect the member that represents today's date and then create related calculations.

In this chapter we meet time functions again. This time our focus is to generate time-based calculations in the most effective way. One way to do it is to use the built-in **Time Intelligence Wizard**, but that path is known to be problematic. Best practice says we need a separate utility dimension instead, a utility dimension with members representing common time-based calculations like the year-to-date, year-over-year, previous period, and so on.

The idea behind the utility dimension is to minimize the number of calculations in a way that measures are combined with members of the utility dimension. That effectively means we have a Cartesian product of measures and their possible time-related variants. A more elegant approach than having many calculated measures in the cube, not to mention maintaining them or presenting them to end users.

Members of the utility dimension have more or less complex formulas. However, once we set them up in one project, we can use them in future ones. As long as we keep the metadata the same: the names of the attributes and levels of the date dimension and this utility dimension, the process comes down to copy/paste and is done in a minute. Does this sound tempting?

Getting ready

Open the **SQL Server Data Tools** (SSDT) and then open the **Adventure Works DW 2012** solution. Once it loads, double-click on the **Adventure Works DW** data source view.

Before we start, I should inform you that this recipe is heavy on MDX. Although it has the longest code in the whole book, it is a very useful recipe. Once adjusted to your date dimension, the code can be reused in every project that has the same date dimension. If the dimension is the same as in the Adventure Works DW database, then no further modification is needed. Here I am by no means saying you should design your date dimension the way it is done in Adventure Works. You don't. I'm merely saying you should start with that, read the explanations, analyze the code, and then adjust it to your needs.

How to do it...

Follow these steps to create a utility dimension with relative time calculations.

1. Create a new named query `Time Calcs` using the following definition:

   ```
   SELECT 0 AS ID, 'As is' AS Name

   UNION ALL
   SELECT 1        , 'YTD'
   UNION ALL
   SELECT 2        , 'Prev period'
   UNION ALL
   SELECT 3        , 'Year ago'
   UNION ALL
   SELECT 4        , 'YTD Year ago'

   UNION ALL
   SELECT 21       , 'Prev period i'
   UNION ALL
   SELECT 22       , 'Prev period %'
   UNION ALL
   SELECT 31       , 'Year ago i'
   UNION ALL
   SELECT 32       , 'Year ago %'
   UNION ALL
   SELECT 41       , 'YTD Year ago i'
   UNION ALL
   SELECT 42       , 'YTD Year ago %'
   ```

2. Execute the query in order to test it. It should return 11 rows. Then close the window.

3. Mark the **ID** column as the **Logical Primary Key** column.

4. Create a new dimension using the previously defined named query and name it `Time Calcs`.

5. Use the **ID** column for the `KeyColumn` and the **Name** column for the `NameColumn` properties.

6. Name the attribute `Calc`.

7. Once you finish with the wizard a **Dimension Editor** will show.

8. Set the `IsAggregatable` property of the attribute to `False`.

9. Set the `OrderBy` property to `Key`.

10. Set the `ValueColumn` to **ID** column.

11. Process-full the dimension.

12. Set the default member for the attribute to the **As is** member. The expression in that property should be `[Time Calcs].[Calc].&[0]` once you're done.

13. Deploy and verify the dimension in the **Browser** tab of the **Dimension Editor**.

14. Open the **Adventure Works** cube and add that dimension without linking it to any measure group, then deploy.

15. Now we're ready to write calculations. Go to the **Calculations** tab and position the cursor at the end of the MDX script.

16. Add the calculation for the `YTD` member. In the case of Adventure Works, the calculation should consist of three parts. The first two parts handle attribute hierarchies not related to the year level and thus enable them to be used in combination with the `YTD` member. The last part is a classic YTD calculation expanded to work for all visible attribute hierarchies that make sense to be used directly with the year level.

```
Scope( [Time Calcs].[Calc].[YTD] );
        -- focus on anything below and including year level
    Scope( [Date].[Date].MEMBERS,
            [Date].[Calendar Year].[Calendar Year].MEMBERS );
        -- attribute hirarchies not related to year level
        -- and related to months
        -- i.e. day of month
        Scope( [Date].[Month of Year].[Month of Year].MEMBERS );
            This = Aggregate(
                    YTD( [Date].[Calendar].CurrentMember ) *
                    YTD( [Date].[Calendar Weeks].CurrentMember ) *
                    { null : [Date].[Month of Year].CurrentMember
    } *
                    { null : [Date].[Day of Month].CurrentMember
    },
                    [Time Calcs].[Calc].&[0]
                            );
        End Scope;
            -- attribute hierarchies not related to year level
            -- and related to weeks
            -- i.e. day of week & day name
        Scope( [Date].[Calendar Week of Year]
                    .[Calendar Week of Year].MEMBERS );
            This = Aggregate(
                    YTD( [Date].[Calendar].CurrentMember ) *
                    YTD( [Date].[Calendar Weeks].CurrentMember ) *
                    { null : [Date].[Calendar Week of Year]
```

```
                                    .CurrentMember } *
                        { null : [Date].[Day of Week].CurrentMember }
    *
                        { null : [Date].[Day Name].CurrentMember },
                        [Time Calcs].[Calc].&[0]
                                    );
            End Scope;
                -- user hierarchies
                -- and attribute hierarchies related to year level
            This = Aggregate(
                        YTD( [Date].[Calendar].CurrentMember ) *
                        YTD( [Date].[Calendar Weeks].CurrentMember ) *
                        { null : [Date].[Calendar Semester of Year]
                                    .CurrentMember } *
                        { null : [Date].[Calendar Quarter of Year]
                                    .CurrentMember } *
                        { null : [Date].[Month of Year].CurrentMember
    } *
                        { null : [Date].[Calendar Week of Year]
                                    .CurrentMember } *
                        { null : [Date].[Day of Year].CurrentMember }
    *
                        { null : [Date].[Date].CurrentMember },
                        [Time Calcs].[Calc].&[0]
                            );
        End Scope;
            -- performance is improved if we preserve empty cells
            -- remove this to get continuous date ranges
        This = iif( IsEmpty( [Time Calcs].[Calc].&[0] ),
                    null, Measures.CurrentMember );
    End Scope;
```

17. Notice the comments inside the calculation. They are there to help you understand what's going on.

18. Add the calculation for the `Prev period` member. The idea is to allow hierarchies to expand by one member to the left to include the previous period, apply the intersection, and then deduct the value in the current context from it. The result is the value in the previous period. The first part of the scope should handle user hierarchies; the second one is dedicated to attribute hierarchies. Please notice that our generic term "period" can be a month, a week or anything else depending on what we've put in the context. In order to expand to include the previous "period", we have created a procedure to shift members in circle. We will explain this procedure in details later in the *There's more* section. When the intersection subcube contains only a single member, the circle shift procedure should produce the previous period. In case there is no previous year, an empty value should be returned.

```
Scope( [Time Calcs].[Calc].[Prev period] );
        -- user hierarchies, complete
    Scope( [Date].[Calendar].MEMBERS,
```

```
                         [Date].[Calendar Weeks].MEMBERS );
                     -- previous member exists? (null for "no")
                 This = iif( Count( LastPeriods( 2, [Date].[Calendar]
                                                    .CurrentMember )
    *
                             LastPeriods( 2, [Date].[Calendar Weeks]
                                                    .CurrentMember )
                         ) <= 1,
                     null,
                         -- include one member to the left on each
                         -- hierarchy and see what comes out as the
                         -- intersection, then deduct the value in
                         -- the current context from it
                     Aggregate(
                        LastPeriods( 2, [Date].[Calendar]
                                            .CurrentMember ) *
                        LastPeriods( 2, [Date].[Calendar Weeks]
                                            .CurrentMember ),
                        [Time Calcs].[Calc].&[0]
                             ) -
                     [Time Calcs].[Calc].&[0]
                 );
         End Scope;
             -- attribute hierarchies directly related to year level
         Scope( [Date].[Calendar Year].[Calendar Year].MEMBERS );
                 -- previous member exists? (test prev year for "no")
             This = iif( Count(
                     LastPeriods( 2, [Date].[Calendar Semester of
Year]
                                            .CurrentMember ) *
                     LastPeriods( 2, [Date].[Calendar Quarter of Year]
                                            .CurrentMember ) *
                     LastPeriods( 2, [Date].[Month of Year]
                                            .CurrentMember ) *
                     LastPeriods( 2, [Date].[Calendar Week of Year]
                                            .CurrentMember ) *
                     LastPeriods( 2, [Date].[Day of Year]
                                            .CurrentMember ) *
                     LastPeriods( 2, [Date].[Date]
                                            .CurrentMember ) ) <= 1,
                         -- previous year exists? (null for "no")
                     iif( Count( LastPeriods( 2, [Date].[Calendar
Year]
                                                    .CurrentMember
         )
```

```
                              ) <= 1,
                        null,
                          -- members shift in circle
                          -- from the first position to the last
                          -- hence we need the previous year
                        (
                        [Date].[Calendar Year].PrevMember,
                        [Date].[Calendar Semester of Year].
LastSibling,

                        [Date].[Calendar Quarter of Year].
LastSibling,

                        [Date].[Month of Year].LastSibling,
                        [Date].[Calendar Week of Year].LastSibling,
                        [Date].[Day of Year].LastSibling,
                        [Date].[Date].LastSibling,
                        [Time Calcs].[Calc].&[0]
                        )
                  ),
                  -- include one member to the left on each
                  -- hierarchy and see what comes out as the
                  -- intersection, then deduct the value in the
                  -- current context from it
                  Aggregate(
                      LastPeriods( 2, [Date].[Calendar Semester of
Year]
                                          .CurrentMember ) *
                      LastPeriods( 2, [Date].[Calendar Quarter of
Year]
                                          .CurrentMember ) *
                      LastPeriods( 2, [Date].[Month of Year]
                                    .CurrentMember ) *
                      LastPeriods( 2, [Date].[Calendar Week of Year]
                                    .CurrentMember ) *
                      LastPeriods( 2, [Date].[Day of Year]
                                    .CurrentMember ) *
                      LastPeriods( 2, [Date].[Date].CurrentMember ),
                      [Time Calcs].[Calc].&[0]
                            ) -
                  [Time Calcs].[Calc].&[0]
            );
    End Scope;
End Scope;
```

19. The next calculation is relatively simple compared to those before. Define the calculation for the `Year ago` member, a member that returns the value for the same period in the previous year:

```
Scope( [Time Calcs].[Calc].[Year ago] );
        -- focus on anything below and including year level
    Scope( [Date].[Date].MEMBERS,
            [Date].[Calendar Year].[Calendar Year].MEMBERS );
        -- jump one year back on both user hierarchies
        This = ( ParallelPeriod( [Date].[Calendar].[Calendar
Year],
                                    1,
                                    [Date].[Calendar].CurrentMember
),
                    ParallelPeriod( [Date].[Calendar Weeks]
                                        .[Calendar Year],
                                    1,
                                    [Date].[Calendar Weeks]
                                        .CurrentMember ),
                    [Time Calcs].[Calc].&[0]
                );
    End Scope;
End Scope;
```

20. Adding the YTD variant of the previous calculation is also easy. To define the YTD `Year ago` member, simply use the **YTD** member of the utility dimension in the definition used for the `Year ago` member:

```
Scope( [Time Calcs].[Calc].[YTD Year ago] );
        -- focus on anything below and including year level
    Scope( [Date].[Date].MEMBERS,
            [Date].[Calendar Year].[Calendar Year].MEMBERS );
        This = ( ParallelPeriod( [Date].[Calendar].[Calendar
Year],
                                    1,
                                    [Date].[Calendar].CurrentMember
),
                    ParallelPeriod( [Date].[Calendar Weeks]
                                        .[Calendar Year],
                                    1,
                                    [Date].[Calendar Weeks]
                                        .CurrentMember ),
                    -- don't forget to use the YTD member this time
                    [Time Calcs].[Calc].[YTD]
                );
    End Scope;
```

21. Now that we've defined the main calculations, we're ready to proceed with indexes and percentages. The first indicator (Prev period i) determines the difference from a previous period, the second one (Year ago i) from a year ago and finally, the third one (YTD Year ago i) also from a year ago, but cumulative (YTD). All of them are additionally formatted with a red font color for negative values. The i stands for index.

```
Scope( [Time Calcs].[Calc].[Prev period i] );
    This = [Time Calcs].[Calc].&[0] -
           [Time Calcs].[Calc].[Prev period];
    Fore_Color(This) = Abs( Measures.CurrentMember < 0 ) * 255;
End Scope;

Scope( [Time Calcs].[Calc].[Year ago i] );
    This = [Time Calcs].[Calc].&[0] -
           [Time Calcs].[Calc].[Year ago];
    Fore_Color(This) = Abs( Measures.CurrentMember < 0 ) * 255;
End Scope;

Scope( [Time Calcs].[Calc].[YTD Year ago i] );
    This = [Time Calcs].[Calc].[YTD] -
           [Time Calcs].[Calc].[YTD Year ago];
    Fore_Color(This) = Abs( Measures.CurrentMember < 0 ) * 255;
End Scope;
```

22. Add the code for three indicators in form of percentages: Prev period %, Year ago % and YTD Year ago %. The % sign stands for the value expressed in the form of a percentage:

```
Scope( [Time Calcs].[Calc].[Prev period %] );
    This = iif( [Time Calcs].[Calc].[Prev period] = 0, null,
                [Time Calcs].[Calc].&[0] /
                [Time Calcs].[Calc].[Prev period] - 1);
    Format_String(This) = 'Percent';
    Fore_Color(This) = Abs( Measures.CurrentMember < 0 ) * 255;
End Scope;

Scope( [Time Calcs].[Calc].[Year ago %] );
    This = iif( [Time Calcs].[Calc].[Year ago] = 0, null,
                [Time Calcs].[Calc].&[0] /
                [Time Calcs].[Calc].[Year ago] - 1);
    Format_String(This) = 'Percent';
    Fore_Color(This) = Abs( Measures.CurrentMember < 0 ) * 255;
End Scope;
```

```
Scope( [Time Calcs].[Calc].[YTD Year ago %] );
    This = iif( [Time Calcs].[Calc].[YTD Year ago] = 0, null,
                [Time Calcs].[Calc].[YTD] /
                [Time Calcs].[Calc].[YTD Year ago] - 1);
    Format_String(This) = 'Percent';
    Fore_Color(This) = Abs( Measures.CurrentMember < 0 ) * 255;
End Scope;
```

23. You're done with calculations! Now, deploy changes in MDX script and test the solution in Excel by clicking on the **Analyze in Excel** icon in the **Cube Browser** tab.

24. Calculations should work correctly no matter which hierarchy you take in pivot, as long as you don't use fiscal hierarchies. See the following srreenshot with two attribute hierarchies on rows, years and months:

	A	B	C	D	E	F	G	H	
1	Sales Amount	Calc							
2	Calendar Year / Month of Year	As is	YTD	Prev period	Year ago	YTD Year ago	Prev period i	Prev period %	Year ago
3	⊟ CY 2005	$11,331,808.96	$11,331,808.96				$11,331,808.96		$11,33
4	July	$962,716.74	$962,716.74	$0.00			$962,716.74		$96
5	August	$2,044,600.00	$3,007,316.75	$962,716.74			$1,081,883.26	112.38%	$2,04
6	September	$1,639,840.11	$4,647,156.85	$2,044,600.00			($404,759.89)	-19.80%	$1,63
7	October	$1,358,050.47	$6,005,207.32	$1,639,840.11			($281,789.64)	-17.18%	$1,35
8	November	$2,868,129.20	$8,873,336.53	$1,358,050.47			$1,510,078.73	111.19%	$2,86
9	December	$2,458,472.43	$11,331,808.96	$2,868,129.20			($409,656.77)	-14.28%	$2,45
10	⊟ CY 2006	$30,674,773.18	$30,674,773.18	$11,331,808.96	$11,331,808.96	$11,331,808.96	$19,342,964.22	170.70%	$19,34
11	January	$1,309,863.25	$1,309,863.25	$2,458,472.43			($1,148,609.18)	-46.72%	$1,30
12	February	$2,451,605.62	$3,761,468.88	$1,309,863.25			$1,141,742.37	87.17%	$2,45
13	March	$2,099,415.62	$5,860,884.49	$2,451,605.62			($352,190.01)	-14.37%	$2,09
14	April	$1,546,592.23	$7,407,476.72	$2,099,415.62			($552,823.39)	-26.33%	$1,54
15	May	$2,942,672.91	$10,350,149.63	$1,546,592.23			$1,396,080.68	90.27%	$2,94
16	June	$1,678,567.42	$12,028,717.05	$2,942,672.91			($1,264,105.49)	-42.96%	$1,67
17	July	$2,894,054.68	$14,922,771.73	$1,678,567.42	$962,716.74	$962,716.74	$1,215,487.26	72.41%	$1,93
18	August	$4,147,192.18	$19,069,963.91	$2,894,054.68	$2,044,600.00	$3,007,316.75	$1,253,137.50	43.30%	$2,10
19	September	$3,235,826.19	$22,305,790.10	$4,147,192.18	$1,639,840.11	$4,647,156.85	($911,365.99)	-21.98%	$1,59
20	October	$2,217,544.45	$24,523,334.55	$3,235,826.19	$1,358,050.47	$6,005,207.32	($1,018,281.74)	-31.47%	$85
21	November	$3,388,911.41	$27,912,245.97	$2,217,544.45	$2,868,129.20	$8,873,336.53	$1,171,366.97	52.82%	$52
22	December	$2,762,527.22	$30,674,773.18	$3,388,911.41	$2,458,472.43	$11,331,808.96	($626,384.20)	-18.48%	$30
23	⊟ CY 2007	$41,993,729.72	$41,993,729.72	$30,674,773.18	$30,674,773.18	$30,674,773.18	$11,318,956.54	36.90%	$11,31
24	January	$1,756,407.01	$1,756,407.01	$2,762,527.22	$1,309,863.25	$1,309,863.25	($1,006,120.21)	-36.42%	$44
25	February	$2,873,936.93	$4,630,343.93	$1,756,407.01	$2,451,605.62	$3,761,468.88	$1,117,529.92	63.63%	$42
26	March	$2,049,529.87	$6,679,873.80	$2,873,936.93	$2,099,415.62	$5,860,884.49	($824,407.05)	-28.69%	($4

How it works...

The solution presented in this recipe is a long one. Therefore we'll break the explanation in several phases.

The first phase was creating the utility dimension. We created the utility dimension in DSV. It can also be created in DW.

The process of creating a utility dimension is pretty straightforward. The first member becomes the default member, the `All` member is disabled. Other actions help but are not mandatory. I do suggest you make them though.

The second phase started when we defined four main calculations and assigned them to members of the utility dimension. We used one or more scope statements for that, to precisely determine the context in which particular assignments should be applied.

The first of these calculations defined what should happen when the `YTD` member gets selected in the utility dimension. To remind you, this was done in step 16.

The outer scope in that calculation limits the cube space to anything including and below the year level which is exactly the subcube that YTD calculation should be applied to.

The first thing we did is provided the assignments for two attribute hierarchies – the `Month of Year` and the `Calendar Week of Year` hierarchy. This is not a mandatory step when defining YTD calculations and you'll rarely see it made. However, it pays off to implement it because those additional assignments enable the usage of all attribute hierarchies for the YTD calculation. In other words, they allow us to combine several attribute hierarchies just like they were levels of a natural user hierarchy.

Additional assignments like these come with a prerequisite - our guarantee that they make sense in the particular context. This is defined using the scope subcube.

If you take one more look at the YTD calculation, you'll notice that YTD values for the `Day of Month` hierarchy will only be calculated when months are also present in the context. Similarly, it makes sense to calculate the YTD values for `Day of Week and Day Name` hierarchies too, but only when weeks are in the context. This is how the invisible time sequence gets established.

The third assignment in that calculation is the one made for the user hierarchies and all attribute hierarchies that make sense to be used together with years. Just like in the previous assignments, two natural user hierarchies are used to collect the YTD range while all other hierarchies filter that context by interacting with it in form of intersections. What comes out of that intersection is a subcube that represents the YTD values for that particular context.

The `Prev period` member is also a complex one. Again, we have two scopes: one for user hierarchies and the other for attribute hierarchies. In order to keep things concise, we'll explain the logic behind this calculation by focusing on the main intentions here.

The idea behind calculating the value in the previous period is to extend every current member with its previous member, aggregate that, and deduct the value in the current context from that. What comes as the result is the value in the previous period.

Notice how we keep using the generic term "period". It's not a month, it's not a week; it can be anything depending on what we've put in the context. The shape of the subcube is not our concern. All we have to do is provide a potential subcube for this calculation. In the case of the `Prev period` member, we did that by specifying the current and previous member for each relevant hierarchy. So, the idea of chasing the current or existing members of every hierarchy, and then detecting whether they've moved or not is not the way to go. We should think in terms of sets and allow the engine to do the magic by intersecting members in the provided subcube.

Two additional things were important in the previous period calculation. First, counting is a way of detecting when we're on the first member of a hierarchy when multiple hierarchies are involved. When we encounter the first member, we either have to shift the year by minus one (by referring to the previous member), or to provide `null` because there's nowhere to go. Second, when we shift the year to the previous one, we also need to move other attribute hierarchies to their last member. At first, this may seem strange, but it's actually not. It's something we do unconsciously every day. Here's an example proving that.

The year that precedes the year 2000 is the year 1999. In order to evaluate that, we do the following procedure. We slice the year by its digits and analyze them. We then realize that all the digits on the right are the first digits in the list of digits, 0 being the first digit in the decade system and 9 being the last. Because of that we change the 2 into its preceding digit, the digit 1. At the same time, we shift all other digits by one place, as if 0 and 9 were connected in a circle. In other words, all other digits jump from the first digit 0 to the last one, the 9. The same principle was applied here, year hierarchy being the leftmost digit 2 and other hierarchies being digits 0 on the right.

But what will happen in that calculation? Again, we're letting the current members decide what the result of the intersection will be. If any of them is on the root member, that member will not influence the intersection. That's a single member on its level which means the `LastSibling` function, used to shift members in a circle, will return the same member. When another member is active, we'll jump to the last member of that level, for example to Q4, December, and so on. Again, the most selective members of all hierarchies determine the final subcube.

In the third calculation, the `Year ago` member is calculated using two user hierarchies. The tuple is formed using two `ParallelPeriod()` functions that return the member in the previous year. Naturally, the last part of the tuple is the default member of the utility dimension.

As this was a relatively easy calculation, let's explain what the default member of the utility calculation does in expressions.

The cube is a multidimensional structure which means every time we make a reference to a particular subcube, the coordinate of that subcube is also multidimensional. Fortunately, we don't have to specify all of the hundreds or more hierarchies a typical cube has; the server does that for us by implicitly including all unmentioned hierarchies in every tuple we make. The term tuple is just another word for the coordinate in the cube space.

Implicit hierarchies are included using their current members at the time of evaluation of the tuple.

In the case of the calculations presented in this recipe, now it becomes clear that the current measure is already there implicitly in every expression. There's no reason to be explicit about that.

What's not obvious at first is that the hierarchy of the member we're defining is also inside the tuple. Yes, the utility dimension. Now, guess what will be its current member at the time of that evaluation? The same `Year ago` member we're defining. That's the current member in that moment! That would lead to empty result as the value of calculated members is `null` in advance. We must replace it and the only way to do that is to be explicit and specify another member of that dimension inside the tuple. The member that should be there is the default member of the utility dimension. That's our `As is` member, a single member of that dimension which doesn't modify the result of the current measure. Remember, the dimension is in no way related to the cube and that member is the only one without a calculation on it. Therefore, it preserves the results of the cube and keeps it unmodified, so that it can be used as such in other calculations.

By placing the default member of the utility dimension inside the tuple (actually, in all calculations so far), we're basically saying, "calculate this expression using the unmodified current measure, whatever it may be." In the beginning it may seem a bit strange, but once you understand the concept of the unrelated utility dimension, it's easy to read expressions because this is a standard way of writing calculations for members of the utility dimension.

We're progressing. Let's see what comes next.

The `YTD Year ago` member has the same definition like the `Year ago` member except a small detail – instead of the default `As is` member, the `YTD` member was used in the calculation. How come?

A moment ago we explained the purpose of the `As is` member and its behavior in calculations. We said that it's there to force the unchanged measure. This time, however, we'd like to be smart and apply the `YTD` calculation not on the value of the current member, but on the value of the member in the previous year which is exactly what the `Year ago` member calculates. It jumps to the previous year and grabs the corresponding value.

Wouldn't it be nice to combine the `YTD` and the `Year ago` calculations? Definitely, and it's not that difficult. All we have to do is make the composition of calculations. The result of the inner calculation (the value of the `Year ago` member) is passed as an argument to the outer one, the `YTD` calculation. That's one of the benefits of implementing the utility dimension.

Slowly, we come to the last phase. In this part, six more calculations are created. The first three calculate the difference between previously defined members of the utility dimension. The other three express that difference in form of a percentage. All the six calculations are relatively simple and easy to comprehend just by taking a look at them. This is because again, the calculations refer to other members of the utility dimension. In other words, the calculations for some of the members in the utility dimension are rather complex, however, all subsequent calculations become relatively simple and easy.

Finally, a word or two about highlighting the negative results. When the value of `True` gets converted to a number, it becomes `-1`. The numeric value of `False` is 0. The `Abs()` function was used to correct the negative sign.

There's more...

This section contains additional information regarding the concept presented in this recipe.

Interesting details

It's worth mentioning that both user hierarchies have the year level clearly marked as the `Year` type. This way we had no problem using the `YTD()` function. If it weren't the case, the alternative would be to use the `PeriodsToDate()` function and to manually specify the year level in it.

Next, the Adventure Works cube has a date dimension that starts with July. Therefore the values of the `Year ago` calculations appear shifted by a half year. Fortunately, that happens only in the second year and only when user hierarchies are used. I believe your date dimension follows the best practice and has the complete year starting from January and ending with December. In that case you won't experience any problems with these calculations.

Another interesting thing is that neither of the calculations uses any measure in the assignments. That's a feature of the utility dimension and how we make assignments using it. Any time we need to reference the current measure, we reference the default member of the utility dimension instead. When applicable, we can also refer to other members of that dimension, for example, the way we defined the calculation for the `YTD Year ago` member.

You may be wondering why none of the fiscal hierarchies were included in the calculation. That's because they are not compatible with calendar hierarchies. They break years into two. The proper way to include them would be to define a separate YTD member on the same utility dimension or, to make another utility dimension just for fiscal hierarchies. Naturally, that would allow us to use the same time calculations only modified to fit the fiscal hierarchies.

Here's another interesting detail about the YTD calculation. We don't have to know, imagine, or visualize the result of the intersection that happens inside the `Aggregate()` function (although it's possible). All that matters is that we provide a way for this intersection to happen and we did that by specifying all attribute hierarchies there. The trick with that expression is to form ranges that span from the first member of a particular hierarchy (represented using `null` in the code) up to the current member of each attribute hierarchy. That way each attribute hierarchy has the potential to determine the subcube, but on the other hand, every other hierarchy is slicing that subcube with its range of members. The result is the smallest common subcube, the one which fits all hierarchies in the `Aggregate()` function.

This concept repeats, with few modifications, in other calculations.

Fine-tuning the calculations

It is possible to add a couple of scope statements to hide values on future dates, as explained in the recipe *Hiding calculations values on future dates* in *Chapter 3, Working with Time*. For example, this is how one of those scope statements would look like:

```
Scope( { Tail( NonEmpty( [Date].[Date].[Date].MEMBERS,
                         [Measures].[Transaction Count] ),
              1 ).Item(0).NextMember : null } );
    This = null;
End Scope;
```

The other things we can do to improve the solution is to provide a scope that forces the default member of the utility dimension in case a multi-select is made in the slicer. Here's the code for that.

```
Scope( [Time Calcs].[Calc].MEMBERS );
    This = iif( Count( EXISTING [Time Calcs].[Calc].MEMBERS ) > 1,
                [Time Calcs].[Calc].&[0],
                [Time Calcs].[Calc].CurrentMember );
End Scope;
```

Other approaches

The following link presents another implementation of the time-based utility dimension, the `DateTool` dimension created by *Marco Russo*: `http://tinyurl.com/MarcoDateTool`

Where these approaches differ from each other is that the one presented in this book supports multiple hierarchies and doesn't use string operations. Because of that its code grew much bigger and became more complex. Actually, the code for both approaches looks difficult to understand, if you're not used to these types of MDX expressions, with lots of scopes and assignments in them. However, that shouldn't stop you from experimenting and applying them in your solutions.

The approaches also differ in the use of single or multiple hierarchies of the utility dimension. This is just a matter of taste; both techniques can be switched to the other style, with a little bit of coding of course.

See also

> ▶ The recipes *Calculating the YTD (Year-To-Date) value*, *Calculating the YoY (Year-over-Year) growth (parallel periods)*, all in *Chapter 3, Working with Time* show the additional information about YTD and year ago calculations. Actually, the complete chapter may be useful because the majority of the topics in that chapter are time calculations.

8

Advanced MDX Topics

In this chapter, we will cover:

- ▸ Displaying members without children (leaves)
- ▸ Displaying members with data in parent-child hierarchies
- ▸ Displaying random values
- ▸ Displaying random sample of hierarchy members
- ▸ Displaying a sample from random hierarchy
- ▸ Performing complex sorts
- ▸ Using recursion to calculate cumulative values

Introduction

This chapter contains some of the more advanced MDX topics.

Here we'll learn how to isolate and display members without children, how to isolate members with data in parent-child hierarchies, how to display their individual values, and other useful information regarding unbalanced hierarchies. Unbalanced hierarchies are hierarchies that appear to have holes inside their dimensional structure and can have missing members from the bottom up.

Next, we're going to learn how to deal with randomness. We're going to show how to display random numbers, how to work with random samples from a hierarchy, and how to get random samples from a random hierarchy. Because the samples are random in nature, we can use a single report to show different information. Such reports can be used for monitoring purposes.

We'll close the chapter with two complex recipes. The first one explains how to perform multiple sorts or how to use several conditions in order to sort members of a hierarchy. The second features recursion. In it we'll see how to construct calculations that traverse horizontally – calculations that enable navigation inside a set, and thereby cumulate the values.

As the title states, the chapter is filled with complex topics. Before you start, make sure you've familiarized yourself with some of the earlier chapters of this book. You'll benefit from it.

Displaying members without children (leaves)

Parent-child hierarchies, also known as unbalanced or recursive hierarchies, are hierarchies with a variable number of levels. Unlike regular user hierarchies, the depth in a parent-child hierarchy is not determined in advance. It is a direct consequence of recursive relation inside the dimension table. Members, regardless of the level they are at, are not required to have descendants. The Adventure Works database has several such dimensions: the `Employee` dimension, the `Account` dimension, and the `Organization` dimension.

Ragged hierarchies are another type of unbalanced hierarchies. Their depth is fixed, known in advance, but the logical parent member of at least one member is not in the level immediately above the member. In other words, one or more levels are skipped in the members of the hierarchical structure. You can configure hierarchies to hide the logically missing members.

Unbalanced hierarchies can present very interesting challenges in MDX queries. Here are a few scenarios. In parent-child hierarchies such as `Account`, values are recorded only on the leaf level. So it is a common request to show members without children, or members on the leaf level. Values can also appear on non-leaf members in parent-child hierarchies, for example, in the `Employee` and `Organization` hierarchies. In this case, it might be interesting to show any member that has data. In ragged hierarchies, we might also be interested in showing the missing or hidden members.

We might be tempted to use the `Members` function, which can return members in a dimension, level, or hierarchy. However, in the preceding scenarios, specifying a single level name followed by the `Members` will not work. This is because the members we want might appear on any levels. Somehow, we need to collect members all over the hierarchy and also flatten the hierarchy. Are you curious enough to learn how we meet the challenges? Then read on.

Getting ready

Start **SQL Server Management Studio** and connect to your SSAS 2012 instance. Click on the **New Query** button and check that the target database is **Adventure Works DW 2012**.

Expand the `Accounts` hierarchy of the `Account` dimension in the cube structure tree. Notice how members form navigation paths of different lengths. That's a parent-child hierarchy:

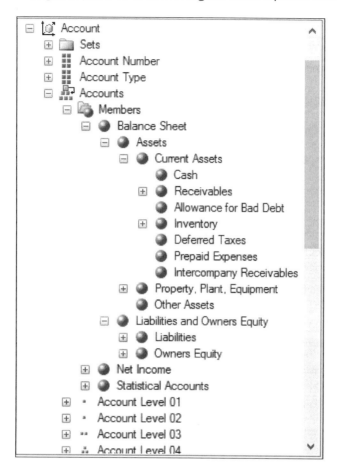

Our goal is to show only those members without children. In other words, we will expect that members with "+" are not in the result.

How to do it...

Follow these steps to show parent-child hierarchy members that don't have any children underneath them:

1. Write the following query:

```
SELECT
    { [Measures].[Amount] } ON 0,
    { { [Account].[Account Type].&[Assets],
        [Account].[Account Type].&[Liabilities] } *
```

```
              [Account].[Account Number].[Account Number].MEMBERS *
              Descendants( [Account].[Accounts]
                              .[Account Level 01].MEMBERS, ,
                      LEAVES )
         } ON 1
    FROM
       [Adventure Works]
```

2. Execute it. The result should match the following screenshot:

			Amount
Assets	1110	Cash	$3,236,799.00
Assets	1130	Trade Receivables	$3,371,580.00
Assets	1140	Other Receivables	$104,343.00
Assets	1150	Allowance for Bad Debt	$67,429.00
Assets	1162	Raw Materials	$2,007,586.00
Assets	1164	Work in Process	$1,393,582.00
Assets	1166	Finished Goods	$742,230.00
Assets	1170	Deferred Taxes	$505,424.00
Assets	1180	Prepaid Expenses	$341,992.00
Assets	1185	Intercompany Receivables	$674,663.00
Assets	1210	Land & Improvements	$93,843.00
Assets	1220	Buildings & Improvements	$299,043.00
Assets	1230	Machinery & Equipment	$92,606.00
Assets	1240	Office Furniture & Equipment	$523,016.00
Assets	1250	Leasehold Improvements	$80,759.00
Assets	1260	Construction In Progress	$33,127.00
Assets	1300	Other Assets	$172,709.00
Liabilities	2210	Notes Payable	$148,316.00
Liabilities	2220	Current Installments of Long-term Debt	$149,571.00
Liabilities	2230	Accounts Payable	$1,286,664.00
Liabilities	2310	Salary & Other Comp	$459,471.00

3. Compare it with the cube structure tree. Notice that none of the members with + is in the result. The query works.

How it works...

As explained in the introduction, the idea is to navigate the unbalanced hierarchy without specifying one specific level name, and to collect members from any levels that match the criteria. The solution in this case was to use the Descendants() function in combination with the LEAVES flag as its third argument. Let's analyze this in more detail.

The `Descendants()` function can either take a set or a member as its first argument. That argument determines the part of the hierarchy from which we'll descend. For the complete hierarchy, it's natural to look for and use the `All` member of that hierarchy. However, the `Account.Accounts` hierarchy doesn't have that member (you can observe that there is no `All Accounts` member in the **SQL Server Management Studio**) because it was disabled for that hierarchy. Therefore, we've had to use the highest available level of that hierarchy to achieve the same effect.

Both the second and the third argument of the `Descendants()` function are optional. As you probably noticed, we didn't use the second one, only the third one for which we've specified the `LEAVES` flag, which instructs SSAS to return leaf members, that is, members without children.

The second argument specifies the level which, in combination with the first argument, determines members to be returned by this function. For example, when the first argument is the `Category` level members of the `Product Categories` user hierarchy, the second the `Subcategory` level, and the third the `SELF_AND_BEFORE` flag, the `Descendants()` function returns all members between (and including) the `Category` and the `Subcategory` levels. More information and examples about the `Descendants()` function can be found on this MSDN site: `http://tinyurl.com/MDXDescendants`

For the reasons explained earlier, it made no sense to use the second argument because we needed all members without children, no matter what level they are at. Therefore, we omitted that argument which, in the case of the `LEAVES` flag, SSAS interprets as all possible levels. In other words, the `Descendants()` function from our example instructed SSAS to return all leaf members starting from (and including) the top level of that hierarchy.

Additional hierarchies on rows are there to make the result more comprehensible and to show you the possibilities for enhancing the result. They are not required to display members without children. They merely provide interesting information and enable grouping and sorting of leaf members, and therefore were included in this detailed balance sheet example.

There's more...

This approach works with ragged hierarchies too. In the following query, the solution from the previous example is applied on the ragged `Sales Territory` user hierarchy, only this time the `All` member is used. We've used it instead of the top level to show that it works in this case too:

```
SELECT
    { [Measures].[Sales Amount] } ON 0,
    { Descendants( [Sales Territory].[Sales Territory]
                                .[All Sales Territories],
                    , LEAVES )
    } ON 1
FROM
    [Adventure Works]
```

Once executed, the query returns this result:

	Sales Amount
France	$7,251,555.65
Germany	$4,878,300.38
United Kingdom	$7,670,721.04
NA	(null)
Canada	$16,355,770.46
Central	$7,909,009.01
Northeast	$6,939,374.48
Northwest	$16,084,942.55
Southeast	$7,879,655.07
Southwest	$24,184,609.60
Australia	$10,655,335.96

If you compare this with the structure of the hierarchy in the cube tree, you'll see that the query collected the exact members as required, those that form the so-called leaf of the hierarchy:

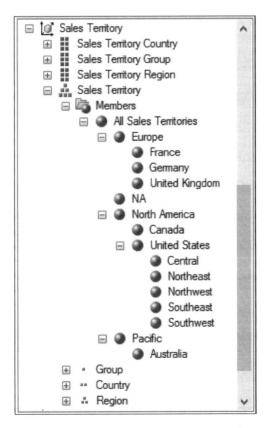

Second and third argument in Descendant() are optional

When the second argument is not used, it gets interpreted as the level of the member in the first argument of the `Descendants()` function. In case the first argument was a set, the level of each individual member in the set is used in turn for the evaluation of that function. The only exception to this rule happens when the `LEAVES` flag is used. Providing no level means that you want all levels below the level of the member or set in the first argument.

When the third argument is not used, the default `SELF flag` is used.

A reverse case

If you need to display all non-leaf members, simply put a minus sign in front of the `Descendants()` function. This gets interpreted as the opposite set in respect to the set of all members. What gets returned is the set of non-like members, the one without children.

Bear in mind that the additional hierarchies, as those used in this recipe, will make the result look confusing in the reverse case scenario. Try it and you'll see what I mean by that. Therefore, consider removing them from the query.

Possible problems with ragged hierarchies

Ragged hierarchies, contrary to parent-child hierarchies and balanced hierarchies, might not display properly in some frontend applications depending on how their underlying dimension tables were built. The comparison of ways to build ragged hierarchies, together with their advantages and disadvantages, is explained in this article written by Chris Webb:
`http://tinyurl.com/ChrisRaggedHierarchies`

Helpful information for working with ragged hierarchies can be found on MSDN too:
`http://tinyurl.com/MSDNRaggedHierarchies`

See also

> ▶ The recipe *Displaying members with data in parent-child hierarchies* shows other options for flattening non-balanced hierarchies

Displaying members with data in parent-child hierarchies

In the previous recipe we saw how to display members without children. The idea was to separate members with direct, fact table values from those whose value is the result of an aggregation. This can be quite a common task when you are trying to validate the calculations.

However, some business scenarios require direct values on non-leaf members. For example, a manager of sales can generate sales too. This feature is supported in the parent-child hierarchy model built into SQL Server Analysis Services. The key properties to be used in this scenario are the `MembersWithData` and `MembersWithDataCaption` properties.

Separating just the leaves to get members with data is not good enough in this case, because non-leaf members in parent-child hierarchies can also have direct fact data. Therefore, in addition to leaves, we need to include all non-leaf members with fact data. This recipe shows how to do this.

Getting ready

Start **SQL Server Management Studio** and connect to your SSAS 2012 instance. Click on the **New Query** button and check that the target database is **Adventure Works DW 2012**.

All parent-child hierarchies in the Adventure Works cube that have non-leaf members with data have those members hidden (property `MembersWithData` is set to `NonLeafDataHidden`). That's why nothing special about those hierarchies can be seen in the cube structure tree. Anyway, we're going to use the `Employees` hierarchy of the `Employee` dimension and apply a small trick to show you that some of the members do indeed have their own data, although not visible at first. Here's what we'll do.

Run this query:

```
WITH
MEMBER [Measures].[Level Ordinal] AS
    [Employee].[Employees].CurrentMember.Level.Ordinal
MEMBER [Measures].[Subtotal OK] AS
    iif( IsLeaf( [Employee].[Employees].CurrentMember ), null,
        Sum( [Employee].[Employees].CurrentMember.CHILDREN,
            [Measures].[Sales Amount Quota] ) =
            [Measures].[Sales Amount Quota] )
SELECT
    { [Measures].[Level Ordinal],
      [Measures].[Sales Amount Quota],
      [Measures].[Subtotal OK] } ON 0,
    { [Employee].[Employees].MEMBERS } ON 1
FROM
    [Adventure Works]
```

The query returns all employees and their sales quota. Two additional calculated measures are here to inform us about the level of a particular member and whether the number shown next to each member matches the sum of its children. As seen in the following screenshot, members on the third level have different values from the sum of their descendants. The reason is that they have their own values not visible in the result. That's why the amounts don't match.

	Level Ordinal	Sales Amount Quota	Subtotal OK
All Employees	0	$154,088,000.00	True
Ken J. Sánchez	1	$154,088,000.00	True
Brian S. Welcker	2	$154,088,000.00	True
Amy E. Alberts	3	$35,411,050.00	False
Jae B. Pak	4	$17,448,950.00	(null)
Rachel B. Valdez	4	$5,374,450.00	(null)
Ranjit R. Varkey Chudukatil	4	$10,867,900.00	(null)
Stephen Y. Jiang	3	$114,230,750.00	False
David R. Campbell	4	$6,239,000.00	(null)
Garrett R. Vargas	4	$6,565,500.00	(null)
Jillian Carson	4	$17,332,050.00	(null)
José Edvaldo. Saraiva	4	$11,359,950.00	(null)
Linda C. Mitchell	4	$18,291,650.00	(null)
Michael G. Blythe	4	$17,251,850.00	(null)
Pamela O. Ansman-Wolfe	4	$5,578,700.00	(null)
Shu K. Ito	4	$11,795,950.00	(null)
Tete A. Mensa-Annan	4	$5,246,450.00	(null)
Tsvi Michael. Reiter	4	$12,387,150.00	(null)
Syed E. Abbas	3	$4,446,200.00	False
Lynn N. Tsoflias	4	$3,964,450.00	(null)

Now let's see how to make those missing values visible.

How to do it...

Follow these steps to show parent-child hierarchy members with direct data:

1. Delete the last calculated measure, the Subtotal OK measure. Also remove it from columns axis.

2. Add the Data Member Quota calculated measure using this expression and apply the Currency format string to it:

```
MEMBER [Measures].[Data Member Quota] AS
    iif( [Measures].[Level Ordinal] = 0, null,
        ( [Employee].[Employees].DataMember,
            [Measures].[Sales Amount Quota] )
    )
, FORMAT_STRING = 'Currency'
```

3. Add that measure on the columns axis.

4. Apply the `NonEmpty()` function over the set on rows using the newly created calculated measure `Data Member Quota`:

```
{ NonEmpty( [Employee].[Employees].MEMBERS,
              [Measures].[Data Member Quota] ) } ON 1
```

5. Execute the query and then notice two things about the returned result. First, only members with data are returned. Second, the `Data Member Quota` measure displays the individual value of members even for non-leaf members (see the highlighted rows in the following screenshot):

	Level Ordinal	Sales Amount Quota	Data Member Quota
Amy E. Alberts	3	$35,411,050.00	$1,719,750.00
Jae B. Pak	4	$17,448,950.00	$17,448,950.00
Rachel B. Valdez	4	$5,374,450.00	$5,374,450.00
Ranjit R. Varkey Chudukatil	4	$10,867,900.00	$10,867,900.00
Stephen Y. Jiang	3	$114,230,750.00	$2,182,500.00
David R. Campbell	4	$6,239,000.00	$6,239,000.00
Garrett R. Vargas	4	$6,565,500.00	$6,565,500.00
Jillian Carson	4	$17,332,050.00	$17,332,050.00
José Edvaldo. Saraiva	4	$11,359,950.00	$11,359,950.00
Linda C. Mitchell	4	$18,291,650.00	$18,291,650.00
Michael G. Blythe	4	$17,251,850.00	$17,251,850.00
Pamela O. Ansman-Wolfe	4	$5,578,700.00	$5,578,700.00
Shu K. Ito	4	$11,795,950.00	$11,795,950.00
Tete A. Mensa-Annan	4	$5,246,450.00	$5,246,450.00
Tsvi Michael. Reiter	4	$12,387,150.00	$12,387,150.00
Syed E. Abbas	3	$4,446,200.00	$481,750.00
Lynn N. Tsoflias	4	$3,964,450.00	$3,964,450.00

How it works...

The `.DataMember` function is the key to this solution. It can be used either to separate members with data from those with only an aggregation, or to get the direct value of members with data, combined with a measure (as in this case). In other words, we formed a tuple which played both roles – it isolated data members on rows and it displayed their individual values in the calculated measure we've created for this purpose.

The only extra thing we had to take care of was to eliminate the `All` member, otherwise it would be present in the result too.

There's more...

If you only want to see the non-leaf members with data, simply use the `IsLeaf()` function from the initial query as an additional condition for the `Data Member Quota` expression:

```
MEMBER [Measures].[Data Member Quota] AS
    iif( [Measures].[Level Ordinal] = 0
         OR IsLeaf( [Employee].[Employees].CurrentMember ),
         null,
         ( [Employee].[Employees].DataMember,
           [Measures].[Sales Amount Quota] )
       )
, FORMAT_STRING = 'Currency'
```

That will remove all leaves from the result, leaving only three rows highlighted, as in the previous screenshot. Convenient, if you only need to display non-visible data or those members having it.

Alternative solution

If circumstances allow, you can go to SSDT and change the `MemberWithData` property of your parent-child hierarchy to `NonLeafDataVisible`. You should also use the `MembersWithDataCaption` property to make the distinction between members and their data part. For example, you can use this: `* - data` (without quotes).

After deploying the project and running the query again, you'll see additional members whose values will match the difference seen previously. You will also be able to notice those additional members in the hierarchy displayed in the cube structure pane on your left in SSMS.

See also

▶ The recipe *Displaying members without children (leaves)* shows other options for flattening unbalanced hierarchies

Displaying random values

Random values are fun, but there's something more to them. They are great for learning how the SSAS engine evaluates a query and its parts. Even if you're not interested in getting random values, you'll still benefit from reading this recipe by learning important concepts in MDX that you can apply in other situations.

This recipe shows how to get random values in queries that operate on cubes. Subsequent recipes show how to use those random values to sample hierarchy members or to generate interesting reports.

Getting ready

Start **SQL Server Management Studio** and connect to your SSAS 2012 instance. Click on the **New Query** button and check that the target database is **Adventure Works DW 2012**.

In this example, we're going to use the `Product` dimension. Here's the query we'll start from:

```
SELECT
    { [Measures].[Sales Amount] } ON 0,
    { [Product].[Product Model Lines].[Model].MEMBERS } ON 1
FROM
    [Adventure Works]
```

Once executed, the query returns 120 models. Most of the models have data associated with them; only a few models have no sales.

How to do it...

Follow these steps to display random values in rows:

1. Add the `WITH` part of the query.

2. Create three calculated measures, `Min Value`, `Max Value`, and `Value Range`, which will be used as constants describing random value range:

    ```
    MEMBER [Measures].[Min Value] AS
        10
    MEMBER [Measures].[Max Value] AS
        99
    MEMBER [Measures].[Value Range] AS
        [Measures].[Max Value] -
        [Measures].[Min Value]
    ```

3. Create a calculated measure named `Const Value` using the following definition:

    ```
    MEMBER [Measures].[Const Value] AS
        iif( IsEmpty( [Measures].[Sales Amount] ), null,
            Int( [Measures].[Min Value] +
                [Measures].[Value Range] * Rnd( ) ) )
    ```

4. Create a calculated measure named `Random number per row` using the following definition:

    ```
    MEMBER [Measures].[Random number per row] AS
        Rnd( Rank( [Product].[Product Model Lines].CurrentMember,
                [Product].[Product Model Lines].CurrentMember
                    .Level.MEMBERS ) )
    ```

5. Create a calculated measure named `Random Value` using the following definition:

```
MEMBER [Measures].[Random Value] AS
    iif( IsEmpty( [Measures].[Sales Amount] ), null,
        Int( [Measures].[Min Value] +
            [Measures].[Value Range] *
            [Measures].[Random number per row] ) )
```

6. Include the `Const Value` and the `Random Value` measures in the query and execute it.

7. If the result of your query doesn't match the following screenshot, you're good. Remember, we were supposed to get different results because of random values:

	Sales Amount	Const Value	Random Value
Bike Wash	$18,406.97	97	13
Cable Lock	$16,225.22	97	61
Classic Vest	$259,488.37	97	31
Cycling Cap	$51,229.45	97	17
Half-Finger Gloves	$113,948.30	97	86
Hitch Rack - 4-Bike	$237,096.16	97	79
Hydration Pack	$105,826.42	97	82
Long-Sleeve Logo Jersey	$431,061.10	97	79
Men's Bib-Shorts	$166,739.71	97	62
Men's Sports Shorts	$81,898.62	97	21
Minipump	$13,514.69	97	27
Patch kit	$8,232.60	97	13
Short-Sleeve Classic Jer...	$321,198.29	97	15
Sport-100	$484,048.53	97	88
Water Bottle	$28,654.16	97	14
Women's Tights	$201,833.01	97	63
Assembly Components	(null)	(null)	(null)
Chain	$9,377.71	97	18

8. Execute the same query a few more times:

	Sales Amount	Const Value	Random Value	
Bike Wash	$18,406.97	84	30	
Cable Lock	$16,225.22	84	37	
Classic Vest	$259,488.37	84	43	
Cycling Cap	$51,229.45	84	10	
Half-Finger Gloves	$113,948.30	84	72	
Hitch Rack - 4-Bike	$237,096.16	84	31	
Hydration Pack	$105,826.42	84	89	
Long-Sleeve Logo Jersey	$431,061.10	84	47	
Men's Bib-Shorts	$166,739.71	84	31	
Men's Sports Shorts	$81,898.62	84	38	
Minipump	$13,514.69	84	17	
Patch kit	$8,232.60	84	80	
Short-Sleeve Classic Jer...	$321,198.29	84	46	
Sport-100	$484,048.53	84	69	
Water Bottle	$28,654.16	84	44	
Women's Tights	$201,833.01	84	90	
Assembly Components	(null)	(null)	(null)	
Chain	$9,377.71	84	40	

9. Notice the `Const Value` measure changes, though only per query.

10. Notice the `Random Value` measure changes per row in every query.

11. The explanation follows.

How it works...

The `Rnd()` function, a VBA function, generates random values between 0 and 1. The random value is naturally multiplied in order to make the range bigger. For example, in this recipe, the measure `Value Range` was used as the multiplier. Additionally, the range was offset not to start with zero using the first calculated measure, the `Min Value` measure.

The boundaries for the random values can be set either using measures as constants for the minimum and maximum values, or directly in the formula for the random value. We used the first approach to show how it can be done. Using the latter should not be a problem, just replace those measures later in the query with their values.

The `Const Value` calculated measure was used to illustrate an important principle – random values are random per query, not per row, unless we do something about it. The next two calculated measures show what we must do in order to get random values per row.

In the `Random number per row` measure, a seed was used in the `Rnd()` function. That seed has one characteristic – it is unique for each row. Having a unique seed in the `Rnd()` function generates a unique random value in each row. That's the solution to the problem of repeating random values in the `Const Value` measure. The `Rank()` function applied over the current member of the set on rows generated unique seeds which in turn generated non-repeating random values. This was noticeable in both screenshots.

Why did we have to take that extra step? Why didn't we get the random values the way we wanted in the first attempt, in the `Const Value` measure, just by referring to the `Rnd()` function?

The SQL Server Analysis Services engine, just like the SQL Server database engine, tries to optimize the queries by evaluating expressions and determining which ones behave like a constant and which don't. A reference to the current member of a hierarchy on an axis is definitely a sign of a non-constant expression.

Non-constant expressions can be more or less complex. The engine will evaluate them in order to see if it can calculate the expression in bulk mode, a mode where everything is calculated in one go. That's much faster than cell-by-cell mode, a mode where every cell is calculated individually, in one big loop.

If the engine determines it can perform a bulk evaluation, it will do so. That's what happened in the `Const Value` calculated measure. Remember, nothing was there in that expression which explicitly requested row-by-row random values. All that we requested was a random value and we got it, different in each execution of the query. But that's not what we needed.

If we want random values per row, we have to explicitly say so. We have to insert part of the expression that will turn this calculation into a slow calculation, a cell-by-cell calculation. Yes, it will slow down the execution of the query, but that's exactly what we need in this case. Sometimes we need to pull the brakes and this is one of those cases. The power of OLAP is not only in its speed, it is also in knowing how to use the brakes when required. Hopefully this recipe showed how.

There's more...

You might have noticed the use of the `IsEmpty()` function inside the definition of `Const Value` and the `Random Value` measures. This is used to preserve empty rows. The idea, already explained in previous chapters, is to keep the effect of the `NON EMPTY` keyword in the query. In short, if the original value was empty, so shall be the calculated measure.

See also

► The recipe *Displaying a random sample of hierarchy members* shows how to make use of the random values once we know how to generate them

Displaying a random sample of hierarchy members

In the previous recipe you learned how to generate random values per row. This recipe teaches you how to take it one step further and use those random values to sample the data.

Getting ready

Start **SQL Server Management Studio** and connect to your SSAS 2012 instance. Click on the **New Query** button and check that the target database is **Adventure Works DW 2012**.

In this example we're going to sample the `Product` dimension, the same one used in the previous recipe. To remind you, this was the query we started from:

```
SELECT
    { [Measures].[Sales Amount] } ON 0,
    { [Product].[Product Model Lines].[Model].MEMBERS } ON 1
FROM
    [Adventure Works]
```

It returned 120 models. Now let's see how to get a sample from that pool.

How to do it...

Follow these steps to display a random sample of hierarchy members:

1. Add the `WITH` part of the query.

2. Create the `H` on axis calculated set using the set on rows:

    ```
    SET [H on axis] AS
        { [Product].[Product Model Lines].[Model].MEMBERS }
    ```

3. Create a calculated measure named `Cardinality` that will count members in the previously defined calculated set:

    ```
    MEMBER [Measures].[Cardinality] AS
        [H on axis].Count
    ```

4. Create a calculated measure named `Random number per row` using the same definition as in the previous recipe:

```
MEMBER [Measures].[Random number per row] AS
    Rnd( Rank( [Product].[Product Model Lines].CurrentMember,
               [Product].[Product Model Lines].CurrentMember
                   .Level.MEMBERS ) )
```

5. Create a calculated measure named `Random Value` using the same definition as in the previous recipe:

```
MEMBER [Measures].[Random Value] AS
    iif( IsEmpty( [Measures].[Sales Amount] ), null,
        Int( [Measures].[Min Value] +
            [Measures].[Value Range] *
            [Measures].[Random number per row] ) )
```

6. Create a calculated measure named `Percentage` that will determine the percentage of members from the previously defined calculated set to be returned by the query. Make it `10` for now, and change it later if you'd like to see another percentage:

```
MEMBER [Measures].[Percentage] AS
    10
```

7. Create the `H on axis sample` calculated set using this definition:

```
SET [H on axis sample] AS
    TopCount( [H on axis],
              [Percentage] / 100 * [Cardinality],
              [Random value] )
```

8. Include the `Random Value` measure in the query. Include the `H on axis sample` calculated set on rows instead of the existing set on rows.

```
SELECT
    { [Measures].[Sales Amount],
      [Measures].[Random Value] } ON 0,
    NON EMPTY
    { [H on axis sample] } ON 1
FROM
    [Adventure Works]
```

9. Execute the query. If the result of your query doesn't match the following screenshot, you're good. Remember, we were supposed to get different results because of random values. What should match though is the number of rows. Both of us should get 12 rows:

	Sales Amount	Random Value
Men's Sports Shorts	$81,898.62	118
LL Mountain Frame	$521,864.42	118
HL Touring Handlebars	$12,087.24	118
HL Road Frame	$1,344,209.60	117
Cycling Cap	$51,229.45	116
HL Road Handlebars	$43,395.60	116
Road-350-W	$5,246,152.02	113
Women's Tights	$201,833.01	111
LL Touring Handlebars	$1,548.62	110
Patch kit	$8,232.60	105
HL Road Tire	$27,970.80	105
Rear Derailleur	$25,725.23	101

10. Execute the same query a few more times. Verify the number of rows returned; it should be 12.

How it works...

There were 120 members in the initial set. We specified that we want 10 percent of them. Consequently, each query returned 12 members, and each time those were 12 different members. Let's see how this was done.

By assigning a random value to each member of a hierarchy we can use the `TopCount()` function to return a predefined number of random members in that hierarchy.

The core part is the definition of the `H on axis sample` calculated set. The second argument determines the size of the sample. The third orders the members by the random value each of them got using the `Random value` calculated measure. Simple, isn't it?

There's more...

As in the previous recipe, the `IsEmpty()` function is used to preserve empty rows. If the original value was empty, so should be the value of the calculated measure.

Alternative solution

Stored procedures are often a valid alternative to some MDX problems. The **Analysis Services Stored Procedure Project** (**ASSP**) at `http://tinyurl.com/ASSPCodePlex` contains the `RandomSample` function, which can be used to get a sample of N members from a set.

See also

▸   The recipe *Displaying random values* shows how to generate random values in the query, which is very important for understanding this recipe completely

Displaying a sample from a random hierarchy

In the previous recipe you learned how to generate a random sample from a predefined hierarchy. In this recipe you'll learn how to generate a sample from a random hierarchy. The idea is to have an ever-changing report that shows the top 10 members of a random hierarchy from the pool of all hierarchies in the cube. The benefit is that we can just make a single report and be able to reuse it over and over again. All that is required is a mechanism to refresh the top 10 members from the randomly selected hierarchy.

Apart from its practical use, this recipe is also interesting from a technical point of view. It shows how to operate with hierarchies, how to navigate them, and get information about them, all without actually specifying any of the cube's hierarchy, other than measures. Even if you don't plan on implementing it, it can be helpful to understand the methods used.

Getting ready

Start **SQL Server Management Studio** and connect to your SSAS 2012 instance. Click on the **New Query** button and check that the target database is **Adventure Works DW 2012**.

In this example we're going to limit the sample to 10 members, the best 10 to be precise.

How to do it...

Follow these steps to display a sample from a random hierarchy:

1.   Add the WITH part of the query.

2.   Create the `# of H in cube` calculated measure using the following definition:

```
MEMBER [Measures].[# of H in cube] AS
    Dimensions.Count
```

3. Create the `Random H ordinal` calculated measure using the following definition:

```
MEMBER [Measures].[Random H ordinal] AS
    Int( [# of H in cube] * Rnd() )
```

4. Create the `Random H set` calculated set using this definition:

```
SET [Random H set] AS
    TopCount(
        Descendants(
            Dimensions( [Random H ordinal] ).Levels(0)
                                              .ALLMEMBERS,
            1 ),
        10,
        [Measures].DefaultMember )
```

5. Create three calculated measures to display information about the hierarchy being displayed in the result of the query. Remember, this will be a random hierarchy, so we need to know what we're looking at:

```
MEMBER [Measures].[Dimension] AS
    Mid( [Random H set].Item(0).Hierarchy.UniqueName, 2,
        InStr( [Random H set].Item(0).Hierarchy.UniqueName,
            ']' ) - 2 )

MEMBER [Measures].[Hierarchy] AS
    [Random H set].Item(0).Hierarchy.Name

MEMBER [Measures].[Cardinality] AS
    [Random H set].Item(0).Hierarchy.CurrentMember
                                     .Level.Members.Count
```

6. Create another three calculated measures to display information about the measure we're analyzing. Here we'll use the default measure:

```
MEMBER [Measures].[Measure] AS
    [Measures].DefaultMember.Name

MEMBER [Measures].[Valid context] AS
    ( [Random H set].Item(0).Hierarchy.Levels(0).Item(0),
      [Measures].DefaultMember ) <>
    Avg( [Random H set], [Measures].DefaultMember )
```

```
MEMBER [Measures].[Value] AS
    iif( [Measures].[Valid context],
        [Measures].DefaultMember,
        'N/A' )
, FORMAT_STRING = 'Currency'
```

7. Create the Ratio calculated measure using the following definition:

```
MEMBER [Measures].[Ratio] AS
    iif( [Measures].[Valid context],
        iif( ( [Measures].[Value],
            [Random H set].Item(0).Hierarchy.CurrentMember
                                            .Parent ) = 0,
        null,
        [Measures].[Value] /
        ( [Measures].[Value],
            [Random H set].Item(0).Hierarchy.CurrentMember
                                            .Parent )
        ),
        'N/A' )
, FORMAT_STRING = 'Percent'
```

8. Put the `Random H set` on rows.

9. Put the `Hierarchy, Dimension, Cardinality, Measure, Value,` and `Ratio` measures on columns:

```
SELECT
    { [Measures].[Hierarchy],
    [Measures].[Dimension],
    [Measures].[Cardinality],
    [Measures].[Measure],
    [Measures].[Value],
    [Measures].[Ratio] } ON 0,
    { [Random H set] } ON 1
FROM
    [Adventure Works]
```

10. Execute the query.

11. If the result of your query doesn't match the following screenshot, you're good. Remember, we were supposed to get different results because of random values. What should match is the number of rows. Both of us should get up to 10 rows, no more than that. The following screenshot shows 10 rows out of 72 for the `Geography.State-Province` hierarchy together with the percentages of State-Province in respect to the **Reseller Sales Amount** value of the root member in that hierarchy:

	Hierarchy	Dimension	Cardinality	Measure	Value	Ratio
California	State-Province	Geography	71	Reseller Sales Amount	$9,764,270.71	12.14%
Washington	State-Province	Geography	71	Reseller Sales Amount	$6,954,715.04	8.64%
Texas	State-Province	Geography	71	Reseller Sales Amount	$6,654,618.87	8.27%
Ontario	State-Province	Geography	71	Reseller Sales Amount	$6,179,187.96	7.68%
England	State-Province	Geography	71	Reseller Sales Amount	$4,279,008.83	5.32%
British Columbia	State-Province	Geography	71	Reseller Sales Amount	$3,419,629.76	4.25%
Quebec	State-Province	Geography	71	Reseller Sales Amount	$2,991,865.33	3.72%
Colorado	State-Province	Geography	71	Reseller Sales Amount	$2,395,913.84	2.98%
Florida	State-Province	Geography	71	Reseller Sales Amount	$2,299,888.87	2.86%
Tennessee	State-Province	Geography	71	Reseller Sales Amount	$2,087,117.32	2.59%

12. Execute the same query a few more times. Verify the number of rows returned; it should never be greater than 10. Also, the time to execute the query will vary by size of the hierarchy you've hit and its aggregation design.

How it works...

The idea of this query is to have an ever-changing report that shows the top 10 members of a random hierarchy from the pool of all hierarchies in the cube.

The first calculated measure, `# of H in cube`, counts the number of hierarchies in the cube. In the case of the **Adventure Works DW 2012** cube, that number is 209 for the **Enterprise Edition (EE)**.

Once we know our limits in terms of the dimensionality of the cube, we can use that number to span the random values generated by the `Rnd()` function, as implemented in the second calculated measure, the `Random H ordinal` measure. That measure generates random integers between 0 and 208.

Then comes the calculated set `[Random H set]`. To get a random set from a random hierarchy, we wrap the following form inside a `Descendants()` and `TopCount()` function:

```
SET = Dimensions( N ).Levels(0).ALLMEMBERS
```

`Dimension(N)` returns a random hierarchy specified by the random numeric N. The `.Level(0)` function returns the root level on the random hierarchy.

By wrapping the above set inside the `Descendants()` and `TopCount()` function, we get the top 10 members below the root member from the random hierarchy using the default cube measure. It doesn't have to be that particular measure; you can use any measure in its place. This measure was used to illustrate something else. First, let's see what the next two calculated measures do.

The `Dimension` calculated measure takes the unique name of the hierarchy and extracts the first part of it. In short, it removes square brackets.

The `Hierarchy` calculated measure displays the name of the hierarchy.

The `Cardinality` calculated measure counts the number of leaf members on that random hierarchy.

The `Measure` calculated measure displays the name of the measure to be used in the `TopCount()` function.

The next measure is a complex one. It is used to detect nonexisting cube space.

The idea is to test whether the average value in the top 10 members is the same as the value of the root member. If it is, then that hierarchy is not related to the measure being used in the query – the default cube measure in this example. The values repeat.

If the average value is not the same, values don't repeat, which means we can calculate the next two measures, the `Value` and `Ratio` measures.

The `Value` measure shows the value of the default measure in case the context is valid. In case it is not, the `not` available indicator will be there as a notice.

Finally, the `Ratio` measure shows how we can calculate something useful. If the context is valid and the denominator is not null or zero, we can display the ratio of the current row against all rows. If any of those are not true, we'll show **N/A**. Here's an example of such a query:

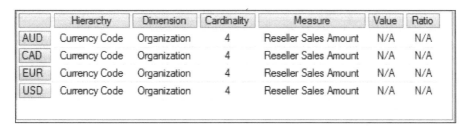

	Hierarchy	Dimension	Cardinality	Measure	Value	Ratio
AUD	Currency Code	Organization	4	Reseller Sales Amount	N/A	N/A
CAD	Currency Code	Organization	4	Reseller Sales Amount	N/A	N/A
EUR	Currency Code	Organization	4	Reseller Sales Amount	N/A	N/A
USD	Currency Code	Organization	4	Reseller Sales Amount	N/A	N/A

The `Reseller Sales Amount` measure, which is the cube's default measure, is not related to the `Organization` dimension. The **N/A** indicator makes this visible.

The recipe showed how to use the default cube measure, which is the `Reseller Sales Amount` measure. If you want to use another measure, simply search-replace all occurrences of the `[Measures].DefaultMember` with the measure of your choice.

See also

▸ The recipe *Displaying random values* shows how to generate random values in the query, which is very important for understanding this recipe completely

▸ The recipe *Displaying a random sample of hierarchy members* shows how to make use of the random values once we know how to generate them

Performing complex sorts

Sorting is one of those often-requested operations. To sort a hierarchy by a measure is not a problem. Neither is to sort a hierarchy using its member properties. The MDX language has a designated function for that operation and a pretty straightforward one too. Yes, we're talking about the `Order()` function.

Difficulties appear when we need to sort two or more hierarchies, one inside the other, or when we need to use two or more criteria. Not to mention the confusion when one of the members on columns is supposed to be the criteria for sorting a related hierarchy on rows. These are complex sort operations, operations we'll cover in this recipe.

Let's build a case and see how it should be solved.

Getting ready

Start **SQL Server Management Studio** and connect to your SSAS 2012 instance. Click on the **New Query** button and check that the target database is **Adventure Works DW 2012**.

In this example we're going to use the `Product` dimension, the `Sales Territory` dimension, and the `Date` dimension. Here's the query we'll start from:

```
SELECT
    NON EMPTY
    { [Date].[Fiscal].[Fiscal Year].MEMBERS *
      [Measures].[Sales Amount] } ON 0,
    NON EMPTY
    { [Sales Territory].[Sales Territory Country]
                       .[Sales Territory Country].MEMBERS *
      [Product].[Color].[Color].MEMBERS } ON 1
FROM
    [Adventure Works]
```

Once executed, the query returns 54 country-color combinations on rows, four fiscal years on columns, and the value of sales shown in the grid. No particular sort operation was applied. The countries and colors are returned in their default order – alphabetically, as visible in the following screenshot:

		FY 2006	FY 2007	FY 2008	FY 2009
		Sales Amount	Sales Amount	Sales Amount	Sales Amount
Australia	Black	$386,170.96	$966,208.67	$1,688,269.24	$1,427.65
Australia	Blue	(null)	(null)	$1,328,411.04	$870.86
Australia	Multi	(null)	(null)	$21,488.04	$693.73
Australia	NA	(null)	(null)	$101,951.10	$4,115.47
Australia	Red	$1,876,531.32	$603,914.25	$200,424.34	$454.87
Australia	Silver	$305,999.10	$447,426.63	$768,442.84	$384.93
Australia	Silver/Black	(null)	(null)	$1,702.39	(null)
Australia	White	(null)	(null)	$961.93	$44.95
Australia	Yellow	(null)	$82,035.88	$1,866,163.99	$1,241.77
Canada	Black	$1,065,837.48	$2,858,563.62	$2,086,940.76	$2,033.03
Canada	Blue	$2,947.23	$8,774.37	$1,023,374.50	$1,004.34
Canada	Multi	$14,319.69	$76,377.18	$47,572.38	$1,211.61
Canada	NA	(null)	$52,132.54	$140,230.37	$5,037.15
Canada	Red	$1,910,459.19	$1,511,459.17	$150,759.84	$734.79
Canada	Silver	$658,333.56	$885,178.06	$1,314,349.15	$274.95
Canada	Silver/Black	(null)	(null)	$28,242.00	(null)
Canada	White	$1,010.64	(null)	$3,464.39	$71.92
Canada	Yellow	(null)	$527,694.91	$1,976,895.77	$485.91

To sort the rows by a particular value, you could simply wrap the `Order()` function around them. For example, to sort the previous result by the **Sales Amount** in **FY 2009**, you would have to change the set on rows like:

```
Order(
        [Sales Territory].[Sales Territory Country]
                        .[Sales Territory Country].MEMBERS *
        [Product].[Color].[Color].MEMBERS,
        ( [Date].[Fiscal].[Fiscal Year].&[2009],
          [Measures].[Sales Amount] ),
        BDESC )
```

The following screenshot shows the result of the modified query:

		FY 2006	FY 2007	FY 2008	FY 2009
		Sales Amount	Sales Amount	Sales Amount	Sales Amount
United States	NA	(null)	$165,385.50	$375,195.04	$8,338.18
Canada	NA	(null)	$52,132.54	$140,230.37	$5,037.15
Australia	NA	(null)	(null)	$101,951.10	$4,115.47
United States	Black	$5,053,651.68	$10,104,109.58	$8,022,261.19	$4,027.57
United States	Multi	$45,434.46	$199,260.72	$120,426.86	$2,364.24
United Kingdom	NA	(null)	$15,912.81	$75,647.63	$2,138.44
Canada	Black	$1,065,837.48	$2,858,563.62	$2,086,940.76	$2,033.03
United States	Blue	$10,384.35	$21,558.91	$4,244,913.01	$1,980.17
Germany	NA	(null)	(null)	$61,959.99	$1,709.83
France	NA	(null)	$12,287.01	$75,754.33	$1,508.53
Australia	Black	$386,170.96	$966,208.67	$1,688,269.24	$1,427.65

This time the rows are returned in the descending order in respect to the last column, highlighted in the screenshot. But, notice one thing – countries and colors are mixed. Breaking their sequence like that will rarely be asked for. More often, the request will be to sort one hierarchy inside the other, the rightmost inside those on its left. In other words, we will try to sort colors inside each country. Now let's see how this can be done.

How to do it...

Follow these steps to sort hierarchies on rows one inside the other.

1. Modify the set on rows like:

```
{ Generate(
    [Sales Territory].[Sales Territory Country]
                    .[Sales Territory Country].MEMBERS,
    [Sales Territory].[Sales Territory Country]
                    .CurrentMember *
  Order( [Product].[Color].[Color].MEMBERS,
        ( [Date].[Fiscal].[Fiscal Year].&[2009],
          [Measures].[Sales Amount] ),
        BDESC
      )
    ) }
```

2. Execute the query. The result should match the following screenshot:

| | | FY 2006 | FY 2007 | FY 2008 | FY 2009 |
		Sales Amount	Sales Amount	Sales Amount	Sales Amount
Australia	NA	(null)	(null)	$101,951.10	$4,115.47
Australia	Black	$386,170.96	$966,208.67	$1,688,269.24	$1,427.65
Australia	Yellow	(null)	$82,035.88	$1,866,163.99	$1,241.77
Australia	Blue	(null)	(null)	$1,328,411.04	$870.86
Australia	Multi	(null)	(null)	$21,488.04	$693.73
Australia	Red	$1,876,531.32	$603,914.25	$200,424.34	$454.87
Australia	Silver	$305,999.10	$447,426.63	$768,442.84	$384.93
Australia	White	(null)	(null)	$961.93	$44.95
Australia	Silver/Black	(null)	(null)	$1,702.39	(null)
Canada	NA	(null)	$52,132.54	$140,230.37	$5,037.15
Canada	Black	$1,065,837.48	$2,858,563.62	$2,086,940.76	$2,033.03
Canada	Multi	$14,319.69	$76,377.18	$47,572.38	$1,211.61
Canada	Blue	$2,947.23	$8,774.37	$1,023,374.50	$1,004.34
Canada	Red	$1,910,459.19	$1,511,459.17	$150,759.84	$734.79
Canada	Yellow	(null)	$527,694.91	$1,976,895.77	$485.91
Canada	Silver	$658,333.56	$885,178.06	$1,314,349.15	$274.95
Canada	White	$1,010.64	(null)	$3,464.39	$71.92
Canada	Silver/Black	(null)	(null)	$28,242.00	(null)

3. Notice that colors are ordered this time in descending order inside each country. Notice also that their sequence changes from country to country (**Yellow** is the third in **Australia**, **Multi** is the third in **Canada**).

How it works...

Do you remember a recipe in the second chapter about creating a new set from the old one using iteration, *Iterating on a set in order to create a new one*. The function used in that recipe is the same one used in this recipe – the Generate() function, which takes a set (single or multi-dimensional one) and creates a new set the way we specify in the second argument of that function.

What's important to note is that we've used only the first hierarchy on the rows, not both of them. The `Generate()` function has no problem in creating a multi-dimensional set from the single-dimensional one. In fact, that's exactly what was needed in this case. We had to preserve the outer hierarchy's order. We've used it as the first argument of the `Generate()` function and cross-joined each of its members with the set of colors ordered by the required criteria. It may not be obvious, but the criteria also implicitly included the current country. That's because `Generate()` is a loop function that sets its own context instead of modifying the existing one. Consequently, the colors came ordered differently in each country.

There's more...

Sorting the rightmost hierarchy inside the one on the left is fine, but what if we also need to sort the outer one? What if the requirement says, "return the countries in descending order by the same criteria and then only return colors sorted inside each country". Can we deliver that as well? Yes, and here's how.

Modify the set on rows this way:

```
{ Generate(
    Order( [Sales Territory].[Sales Territory Country]
                            .[Sales Territory Country].MEMBERS,
            ( [Date].[Fiscal].[Fiscal Year].&[2009],
              [Measures].[Sales Amount] ),
          BDESC
        ),
    [Sales Territory].[Sales Territory Country].CurrentMember *
    Order( [Product].[Color].[Color].MEMBERS,
            ( [Date].[Fiscal].[Fiscal Year].&[2009],
              [Measures].[Sales Amount] ),
          BDESC
    )
      ) }
```

If you take a close look, you'll notice not much has changed. All that we have done extra this time is that we have ordered the initial set in the `Generate()` function so that it preserves the order when we cross join its members with the other set.

The result of this modification is shown on the following screenshot:

		FY 2006	FY 2007	FY 2008	FY 2009
		Sales Amount	Sales Amount	Sales Amount	Sales Amount
United States	NA	(null)	$165,385.50	$375,195.04	$8,338.18
United States	Black	$5,053,651.68	$10,104,109.58	$8,022,261.19	$4,027.57
United States	Multi	$45,434.46	$199,260.72	$120,426.86	$2,364.24
United States	Blue	$10,384.35	$21,558.91	$4,244,913.01	$1,980.17
United States	Yellow	(null)	$1,849,153.43	$7,807,453.88	$1,079.80
United States	Red	$6,559,542.49	$5,334,256.87	$662,928.77	$1,049.70
United States	Silver	$3,986,235.29	$3,232,560.30	$5,070,819.13	$549.90
United States	White	$5,562.75	(null)	$15,535.54	$44.95
United States	Silver/Black	(null)	(null)	$91,526.48	(null)
Canada	NA	(null)	$52,132.54	$140,230.37	$5,037.15
Canada	Black	$1,065,837.48	$2,858,563.62	$2,086,940.76	$2,033.03
Canada	Multi	$14,319.69	$76,377.18	$47,572.38	$1,211.61
Canada	Blue	$2,947.23	$8,774.37	$1,023,374.50	$1,004.34
Canada	Red	$1,910,459.19	$1,511,459.17	$150,759.84	$734.79
Canada	Yellow	(null)	$527,694.91	$1,976,895.77	$485.91
Canada	Silver	$658,333.56	$885,178.06	$1,314,349.15	$274.95
Canada	White	$1,010.64	(null)	$3,464.39	$71.92
Canada	Silver/Black	(null)	(null)	$28,242.00	(null)

Look at the query one more time and you'll notice there are two criteria in it, both the same. It doesn't take a lot of imagination to conclude that they don't have to be the same. Yes, you can have different criteria, simply modify any of them and test. Having learned this much about sorting, you can confidently perform complex sorts.

Things to be extra careful about

Write this query, but don't execute it yet!

```
SELECT
    NON EMPTY
    { [Product].[Product Line].[Product Line].MEMBERS *
      [Measures].[Sales Amount] } ON 0,
    NON EMPTY
    { Generate(
        [Sales Territory].[Sales Territory Country]
                        .[Sales Territory Country].MEMBERS,
        [Sales Territory].[Sales Territory Country]
```

```
                           .CurrentMember *
            Order( [Product].[Model Name].[Model Name].MEMBERS,
                   ( [Product].[Product Line].&[M],
                   -- [Product].[Model Name].CurrentMember,
                   [Measures].[Sales Amount] ),
                   BDESC )
            ) } ON 1
    FROM
        [Adventure Works]
```

If you analyze the code, you'll notice that the same idea is used to sort the results based on one of the columns. This time however, the hierarchies on rows and columns are related. The Model Name and the Product Line attribute hierarchies can be found in the Product Model Lines user hierarchy. In short, models are grouped by the product lines.

Now, run the query and observe the result:

		Accessory	Components	Mountain	Road	Touring	
		Sales Amount	Sales Amount	Sales Amount	Sales Amount	Sales Amount	
Australia	All-Purpose Bike Stand	(null)	(null)	$10,335.00	(null)	(null)	
Australia	Bike Wash	$2,286.42	(null)	(null)	(null)	(null)	
Australia	Chain	(null)	$850.08	(null)	(null)	(null)	
Australia	Classic Vest	$21,065.62	(null)	(null)	(null)	(null)	
Australia	Cycling Cap	$4,828.75	(null)	(null)	(null)	(null)	
Australia	Fender Set - Mountain	(null)	(null)	$7,143.50	(null)	(null)	
Australia	Front Brakes	(null)	$3,770.10	(null)	(null)	(null)	
Australia	Front Derailleur	(null)	$5,214.93	(null)	(null)	(null)	
Australia	Half-Finger Gloves	$9,771.75	(null)	(null)	(null)	(null)	
Australia	Hitch Rack - 4-Bike	$18,406.70	(null)	(null)	(null)	(null)	
Australia	HL Bottom Bracket	(null)	$3,426.02	(null)	(null)	(null)	

Oops, it doesn't look good; there's no trace of any sort in it. Now uncomment the commented line and run it again. All good, the result is ordered by the middle column, the **Mountain** model:

		Accessory	Components	Mountain	Road	Touring	
		Sales Amount	Sales Amount	Sales Amount	Sales Amount	Sales Amount	
Australia	Mountain-200	(null)	(null)	$2,171,361.25	(null)	(null)	
Australia	Mountain-100	(null)	(null)	$670,498.02	(null)	(null)	
Australia	Mountain-400-W	(null)	(null)	$77,718.49	(null)	(null)	
Australia	Mountain-500	(null)	(null)	$53,177.24	(null)	(null)	
Australia	HL Mountain Frame	(null)	(null)	$21,997.62	(null)	(null)	
Australia	Women's Mountain Shorts	(null)	(null)	$15,649.76	(null)	(null)	
Australia	All-Purpose Bike Stand	(null)	(null)	$10,335.00	(null)	(null)	
Australia	HL Mountain Tire	(null)	(null)	$8,400.00	(null)	(null)	

What's going on?

Remember what we said about current members being implicit in the sort criteria? The same applies here. Both the country and the model are in the tuple that determines the sort.

In the examples we started this recipe with, all the hierarchies were unrelated and no problem was noticed. This time they were related and behaved differently because related hierarchies interfere with each other. In other words, the Mountain member of the Product Line attribute hierarchy pushed the current member of the Model Name attribute hierarchy to its root member. The relation between them is 1:N, models are below the product lines. Consequently, all of the models evaluated the same in that tuple, as the value of the Mountain product line for a particular country. Sorting members by a constant value leaves them in their existing order. That's the result we got in the first screenshot.

On the other hand, when we're explicit about the current member of the Model Name attribute hierarchy in the tuple for sort criteria, we get the correct result.

The difference is that this time we have specified the intersection of related hierarchies. In other words, we were referring to the individual cells found in the intersection of the models and the product lines. Those cells are exactly what we needed, each different from another and hence returning results sorted the way we wanted.

Remember this and don't forget to force the coordinate in case there are related hierarchies, when the hierarchy on columns is above the hierarchy on rows in terms of attribute paths.

A costly operation

Sorting is a costly operation. If you have large dimensions, always look for an alternative solution. For example, if you don't need the entire set, use set-limiting functions like NonEmpty(), TopCount(), and others.

See also

▶ Refresh your memory about the Generate() function by reading the recipe *Iterating on a set in order to create a new one* in *Chapter 2, Working with Sets*.

Using recursion to calculate cumulative values

We often need to calculate cumulative values such as cumulative sales amount or gross profit. There are typically two types of cumulative calculations, sum-based and multiplication-based. Cumulative sales amount or gross profit is sum-based; gross profit margin expressed in percentage is multiplication-based.

There are two approaches to calculate cumulative values. One approach is to use recursive technique; another approach uses a range technique.

For sum-based cumulative values, both of these approaches should produce the same result.

For multiplication-based cumulative values, the recursive technique will still work. In addition, we will show another approach that uses a mathematical rule about logarithm function. A known mathematical rule says that the logarithm of a product is equal to the sum of individual logarithms.

Let's see how we can use the recursive technique, the range technique, and the logarithm rule to calculate cumulative values. In this recipe we refer to these two approaches as recursive and cumulative. Do not confuse the cumulative approach with the cumulative values that we are trying to calculate.

Getting ready

Start **SQL Server Management Studio** and connect to your SSAS 2012 instance. Click on the **New Query** button and check that the target database is **Adventure Works DW 2012**.

In this example we're going to use the `Subcategory` hierarchy of the `Product` dimension. Here's the query we'll start from:

```
SELECT
    { [Measures].[Gross Profit],
      [Measures].[Gross Profit Margin] } ON 0,
    { [Product].[Subcategory].[Subcategory].MEMBERS } ON 1
FROM
    [Adventure Works]
```

Once executed, the query returns 37 product subcategories and their corresponding profits and margins. Our task is to create calculations that will perform cumulative sums for the products.

How to do it...

Follow these steps to create cumulative calculations.

1. Create a calculated set `Axis Set` based on what was on the rows axis:

   ```
   SET [Axis Set] AS
       [Product].[Subcategory].[Subcategory].MEMBERS
   ```

2. Define the `Rank on Set` calculated measure using this definition:

   ```
   MEMBER [Measures].[Rank on Set] AS
       Rank( [Product].[Subcategory].CurrentMember,
             [Axis Set] )
   ```

3. Define the following cumulative calculated measures and include them on the columns axis:

```
MEMBER [Measures].[Cumulative Sum] AS
    Sum( Head( [Axis Set],
                    [Measures].[Rank on Set] ),
            [Measures].[Gross Profit] )
, FORMAT_STRING = 'Currency'


MEMBER [Measures].[Cumulative Product] AS
    Exp( Sum( Head( [Axis Set],
                        [Measures].[Rank on Set] ),
                Log( [Measures].[Gross Profit Margin] )
            )
        )
, FORMAT_STRING = 'Percent'
```

4. Define the following recursive calculated measures and include them on the columns axis:

```
MEMBER [Measures].[Recursive Sum] AS
    iif( [Measures].[Rank on Set] = 1,
        [Measures].[Gross Profit],
        [Measures].[Gross Profit] +
        ( [Measures].[Recursive Sum],
            [Axis Set].Item( [Measures].[Rank on Set] - 1 - 1 )
        )
    )
, FORMAT_STRING = 'Currency'


MEMBER [Measures].[Recursive Product] AS
    iif( [Measures].[Rank on Set] = 1,
        [Measures].[Gross Profit Margin],
        [Measures].[Gross Profit Margin] *
        ( [Measures].[Recursive Product],
            [Axis Set].Item( [Measures].[Rank on Set] - 1 - 1 )
        )
    )
, FORMAT_STRING = 'Percent'
```

5. Execute the query. The result should match the following screenshot:

	Gross Profit	Cumulative Sum	Recursive Sum	Gross Profit Margin	Cumulative Product	Recursive Product
Bib-Shorts	$51,256.59	$51,256.59	$51,256.59	30.74%	30.74%	30.74%
Bike Racks	$95,006.08	$146,262.66	$146,262.66	40.07%	12.32%	12.32%
Bike Stands	$24,783.97	$171,046.63	$171,046.63	62.60%	7.71%	7.71%
Bottles and Cages	$38,233.69	$209,280.32	$209,280.32	59.48%	4.59%	4.59%
Bottom Brackets	$13,474.82	$222,755.15	$222,755.15	26.00%	1.19%	1.19%
Brakes	$17,077.70	$239,832.85	$239,832.85	25.87%	0.31%	0.31%
Caps	($1,203.20)	$238,629.65	$238,629.65	-2.35%	-1.#IND	-0.01%
Chains	$2,422.08	$241,051.73	$241,051.73	25.83%	-1.#IND	0.00%
Cleaners	$8,538.59	$249,590.32	$249,590.32	46.39%	-1.#IND	0.00%
Cranksets	$52,778.81	$302,369.13	$302,369.13	25.88%	-1.#IND	0.00%
Derailleurs	$18,147.48	$320,516.61	$320,516.61	25.85%	-1.#IND	0.00%

6. Notice the cumulative values displayed using the calculated measures created in this query. The Sum is identical whereas the Product experiences a problem with negative values when recursion is not used.

How it works...

Two types of algorithms to calculate cumulative values were presented in this recipe.

Both approaches require a calculated measure that serves as an indicator of the current position of the set on the axis. That's why we defined both the set and the rank.

Once we know the position of the current row during the iteration, we can calculate the sum of members up to that position.

We can also perform the sum of logarithm values of the measure and then take the exponential value of it in order to calculate the cumulative product value. Here we've used a known mathematical rule which says that the logarithm of a product is equal to the sum of individual logarithms. In other words, logarithms reduce products to sum. See Wikipedia for more info: http://tinyurl.com/WikiLogarithm

The opposite operation of logarithm is the exponential function; therefore, we've applied it on the sum of the algorithm in order to get the cumulative product.

The problem we've encountered with negative values will probably not happen when you use a proper measure in the cumulative product calculation, the one that is never negative or zero. For example, a measure that states the likelihood of a risk to happen, status to occur, or similar. If you want to be absolutely sure you don't get -1.#IND errors, avoid negative and zero values the same way you avoid division by zero problems.

The next set of calculated measures is also a cumulative type of measure. What differentiates them from the previous ones is that they use recursion.

Recursive measures are almost identical except that one uses the sum operation and the other the product operation. Of course, the measure they use is different, but that's only to make the result look better.

Their expression says this: If we're on the first member, we'll take the value of the measure. If we're somewhere else in the set, we'll take the measure's value and add/multiply it with the value of the measure in the previous position. The `.Item()` function is zero-based, `Rank()` is not. Therefore we need to reduce the rank by one. The second reduction, the second `-1` in the expression, is where we instruct the engine to move to the previous position in the set.

Additionally, format strings had to be restored on measures that lost their inherited format due to complex expressions.

There's more...

It is important to define a set and operate exclusively on that set, not on the members of the hierarchy, and there are two reasons for that. First, members on rows don't have to be positioned in their original hierarchical order. Second, not all members need to be present on rows; the end-user might have excluded some of them from the query.

The calculations defined in this recipe work no matter what the order or exclusion of members is because they rely on a named set. However, the definition of that set should always match the set on rows. There are several ways in which it can be done.

The first step is to sync the named set with the set on rows, as shown in this example. The other way is to keep the definition of what comes on rows in the named set not in two places like the rows and the set. This means we should specify the named set on the rows instead of the set of members, like:

```
SELECT
    { [Measures].[Gross Profit],
      [Measures].[Cumulative Sum],
      [Measures].[Recursive Sum],
      [Measures].[Gross Profit Margin],
      [Measures].[Cumulative Product],
      [Measures].[Recursive Product] } ON 0,
    { [Axis Set] } ON 1
FROM
    [Adventure Works]
```

Finally, there's an option to define the calculated set using the `Axis()` function, as explained in *Chapter 7, When MDX is Not Enough*. Here's what it might look like:

```
SET [Axis Set] AS
    Axis(1)
```

I said "look like", because it largely depends on the frontend being used, a very unfortunate but important point discussed in detail in *Chapter 7, When MDX is Not Enough.*

Let's check whether the query works for an arbitrary set of members.

Here's the modified part of the query:

```
{ [Product].[Subcategory].&[1],
  [Product].[Subcategory].&[3],
  [Product].[Subcategory].&[2] } ON 1
```

We're using the last definition of the set, the one with the `Axis(1)` as the definition.

Here's what the result looks like:

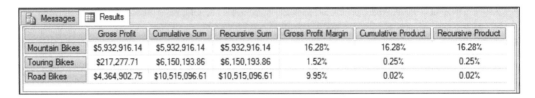

	Gross Profit	Cumulative Sum	Recursive Sum	Gross Profit Margin	Cumulative Product	Recursive Product
Mountain Bikes	$5,932,916.14	$5,932,916.14	$5,932,916.14	16.28%	16.28%	16.28%
Touring Bikes	$217,277.71	$6,150,193.86	$6,150,193.86	1.52%	0.25%	0.25%
Road Bikes	$4,364,902.75	$10,515,096.61	$10,515,096.61	9.95%	0.02%	0.02%

It's clear that both recursive and non-recursive calculations work as expected.

A simplified version of the solution

In situations where all members of a level are used and when you don't need to worry about their order (because it can't be changed, for instance), you can simplify the recursive calculation a lot and often gain on performance too.

Here's an updated query that shows the parts that need to change in boldface:

```
WITH
SET [Axis Set] AS
    [Product].[Subcategory].[Subcategory].MEMBERS
MEMBER [Measures].[Rank on Set] AS
    Rank( [Product].[Subcategory].CurrentMember,
        [Axis Set] )
MEMBER [Measures].[Cumulative Sum] AS
    Sum( null : [Product].[Subcategory].CurrentMember,
        [Measures].[Gross Profit] )
, FORMAT_STRING = 'Currency'

MEMBER [Measures].[Cumulative Product] AS
    Exp( Sum( null : [Product].[Subcategory].CurrentMember,
            Log( [Measures].[Gross Profit Margin] )
            )
```

```
        )
    , FORMAT_STRING = 'Percent'
    MEMBER [Measures].[Recursive Sum] AS
        iif( [Measures].[Rank on Set] = 1,
            [Measures].[Gross Profit],
            [Measures].[Gross Profit] +
            ( [Measures].[Recursive Sum],
                [Product].[Subcategory].CurrentMember.PrevMember )
            )
    , FORMAT_STRING = 'Currency'
    MEMBER [Measures].[Recursive Product] AS
        iif( [Measures].[Rank on Set] = 1,
            [Measures].[Gross Profit Margin],
            [Measures].[Gross Profit Margin] *
            ( [Measures].[Recursive Product],
                [Product].[Subcategory].CurrentMember.PrevMember )
            )
    , FORMAT_STRING = 'Percent'
    SELECT
        { [Measures].[Gross Profit],
          [Measures].[Cumulative Sum],
          [Measures].[Recursive Sum],
          [Measures].[Gross Profit Margin],
          [Measures].[Cumulative Product],
          [Measures].[Recursive Product] } ON 0,
        { [Product].[Subcategory].[Subcategory].MEMBERS } ON 1
    FROM
        [Adventure Works]
```

As you can see, there was no reference to the Axis() function. In cumulative calculations, this was replaced with the range from the first member (here null) to the current member, which is exactly what the cumulative value represents. In recursive calculations, the expression that determines the previous member in the set using the Axis() function is replaced with its simplification in terms of the .PrevMember function. Easy to remember, easy to use, but as said earlier, it works only in the special case of the complete set of members of a level.

Choosing between recursive and cumulative calculations

Recursive calculations can perform well, but not always, so they have to be used carefully.

In this recipe we showed how to build both types of calculations, recursive and cumulative. Armed with this knowledge, it's up to you to test which version performs better in your particular scenario because there's no general rule to it.

In the case of the Adventure Works cube, we can test this by modifying the query so that it uses the `Reseller` hierarchy, which is the biggest hierarchy in that cube. A test should be performed by first clearing the cache, initializing the MDX script, and then running the query with one type of measure only. After that, the process should be repeated with the other types of measure. More information about clearing the cache will be given in the next chapter.

See also

▸ Refresh your memory about recursions by reading the recipe *Iterating on a set using recursion* in *Chapter 2, Working with Sets*.

9

On the Edge

In this chapter, we will cover:

- ▶ Clearing the Analysis Services cache
- ▶ Using Analysis Services stored procedures
- ▶ Executing MDX queries in T-SQL environments
- ▶ Using SSAS Dynamic Management Views (DMVs) to fast-document a cube
- ▶ Using SSAS Dynamic Management Views (DMVs) to monitor activity and usage
- ▶ Capturing MDX queries generated by SSAS frontends
- ▶ Performing a custom drillthrough

Introduction

The last chapter in this book is very special. We're going to talk about some topics which didn't fit into the previous chapters; topics where MDX mixes with other areas, such as performance tuning, executing MDX queries in T-SQL environment, using SSAS Dynamic Management Views (DMVs) to query metadata of a cube, and SSAS's internal performance and resource. These areas will expand our horizon and motivate us to explore more.

We're starting with clearing the cache. Clearing the cache is an important technique when doing performance tuning – queries that run for a long time on a cold cache, may be instant on a warm cache. To measure the effect of any changes you make to your cube or MDX calculations, having the same initial conditions is a must. The first recipe covers two techniques for clearing the cube cache, executing XMLA command, and using a stored procedure from the **Analysis Services Stored Procedure Project** (**ASSP**). The procedure from the ASSP project can clear both the Analysis Services cache and the Windows file system cache.

Stored procedures are another interesting area. Whether you have developer skills or not, there are cool stored procedures available in the community assemblies, which means you're only a step away from exploring the benefits that they bring to your project. The second recipe introduces the Analysis Services Stored Procedure Project (ASSP), which is an open source software project hosted on **CodePlex**.

Using the technique of distributed queries, you can execute MDX queries inside the relational database environment. The third recipe *Executing MDX queries in T-SQL environments* in this chapter, explains the procedure and settings that enables the SQL Server to run distributed queries with or without a linked server.

Dynamic Management Views (**DMV**s) is another interesting area, but which is not yet thoroughly explored. They can be used to query the metadata of a cube, and SSAS's internal performance and resources. Everything is there in tabular format, so that you can use it with great ease. Two recipes cover that topic, although there are plenty of useful examples to be explored by yourself once you get the initial boost.

When client tools generate MDX queries for you, you might want to know what these MDX queries look like. SQL Server Profiler is a tool that can be used to capture the exact MDX queries which your users are running against the cube. These captured MDX queries often are used for troubleshooting and performance tuning purpose. We dedicate one recipe in this chapter to showing you how to use the SQL Server Profiler to capture the exact MDX queries that a client application is sending to the cube.

Drill through is a mechanism in SSAS that allows end users select a single cell from a cube and retrieve a result set from the multidimensional model for that cell, in order to get more detailed information. The DRILLTHROUGH mechanism allows us to explore the data stored in an SSAS cube regardless of the relational engine. Finally, the last recipe covers how to create an MDX query with DRILLTHROUGH capability.

Remember, these recipes are here to encourage you to explore further, and to go over the edge.

Clearing the Analysis Services cache

If you have a poorly performing query, you will review both the design of your cube and the MDX query, and test the performance of different scenarios. Having the same initial conditions for every test is a must. Only then can you truly measure the effect of any changes you make.

The problem in preserving the initial condition lies in the fact that Analysis Services caches the result of each query, making every subsequent query potentially run faster than it normally would.

Normally, caching is a great thing. Hitting a cached value is a goal we're trying to achieve in our everyday cube usage because it speeds up the result. Here, however, we're trying to do the opposite – we're clearing the cache on purpose in order to have the same conditions for every query.

This recipe introduces the process of clearing the cache. It begins by showing the standard way of clearing the Analysis Services cache and then continues by pointing out a way to also clear the Windows file system cache.

Getting ready

Start the **SQL Server Management Studio** and connect to your SSAS 2012 instance, then click on the **New XMLA Query** button.

Expand the **Databases** item in the **Object Explorer** so that you can see the **Adventure Works DW 2012** database and its **Adventure Works** cube.

In this example, we're going to show how to clear the cache for that cube.

How to do it...

Follow these steps to clear the Analysis Services cube cache:

1. Write the following XMLA query:

```
<Batch xmlns =
  "http://schemas.microsoft.com/analysisservices/2003/engine">
  <ClearCache>
    <Object>
      <DatabaseID></DatabaseID>
      <CubeID></CubeID>
    </Object>
  </ClearCache>
</Batch>
```

2. Right-click on the **Adventure Works DW 2012** database in the **Object Explorer** and select **Properties**:

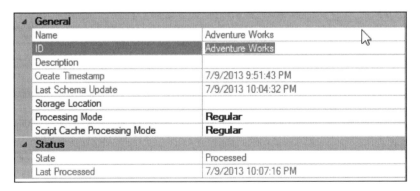

⊿ General	
Name	**AdventureWorksDW2012**
ID	AdventureWorksDW2012
Description	**Enterprise Edition**
Create Timestamp	7/9/2013 9:51:41 PM
Last Schema Update	7/9/2013 10:04:24 PM
Last Update	7/9/2013 10:07:36 PM
Read-Write Mode	ReadWrite
⊿ **Security Settings**	
Data Source Impersonation Info	**Default**
⊿ **Status**	
Last Processed	7/9/2013 10:07:35 PM
Estimated Size	94.42 MB
⊿ **Storage**	
Storage Location	

3. Notice the ID property highlighted in the previous screenshot. Copy the value, close the **Database Properties** window, and paste it inside the DatabaseID tags:

```
<DatabaseID>AdventureWorksDW2012</DatabaseID>
```

4. Now right-click on the **Adventure Works** cube in the **Object Explorer** and select **Properties**:

⊿ General	
Name	Adventure Works
ID	Adventure Works
Description	
Create Timestamp	7/9/2013 9:51:43 PM
Last Schema Update	7/9/2013 10:04:32 PM
Storage Location	
Processing Mode	**Regular**
Script Cache Processing Mode	**Regular**
⊿ **Status**	
State	Processed
Last Processed	7/9/2013 10:07:16 PM

5. Again, notice the ID property highlighted in the previous screenshot. Copy the value, close the **Cube Properties** window and paste it inside the CubeID tags:

```
<CubeID>Adventure Works</CubeID>
```

6. To run the XMLA query, right-click on the **Adventure Works DW 2012** database, then choose **New Query** and then **XMLA**. If everything went fine, you should see the result as shown in the following screenshot. The cube cache is successfully cleared.

```
Messages    Results
<return xmlns="urn:schemas-microsoft-com:xml-analysis">
  <results xmlns="http://schemas.microsoft.com/analysisservices/2003/xmla-multipleresults">
    <root xmlns="urn:schemas-microsoft-com:xml-analysis:empty" />
  </results>
</return>
```

How it works...

The `ClearCache` command clears the Analysis Services cache for the object specified in the command.

Several objects can be used inside that command. A common scenario is to use the cube object, like in this example. Other objects can be also specified. We will discuss that later in this recipe.

Inside the `ClearCache` command, we had to specify the object's ID, a property that uniquely identifies the object (among its sibling objects only, not on the entire SSAS instance). The ID is not visible in the **Object Explorer**, only the object's name. When we need the ID, we have to open the **Properties** window for that object.

The uniqueness of the object on the entire SSAS instance is enforced by the requirement to specify all parent objects up to the database object and include the object itself. That's why we had to specify both the `DatabaseID` and the `CubeID` in this example.

If the query returns no errors this means that it has successfully cleared the Analysis Services cache for that object.

There's more...

Clearing the Analysis Services cache is not enough to guarantee the same performance testing conditions. There's also the file system cache, which in turn consists of the Active Cache and the Standby Cache. To test MDX query performance on a true cold cache we have to either reboot the server or clear those caches. *Greg Galloway*, one of the reviewers of this book, wrote a breakthrough article about it, which can be found at `http://tinyurl.com/GregClearCache`.

There are several ways, according to that article, on how you can clear those caches. One of them (and probably the most convenient one), is by using the `ClearAllCaches` stored procedure from the Analysis Services Stored Procedure Project (ASSP).

The next recipe shows how to register an assembly and use its stored procedures on the Analysis Services server. The example will feature the `ClearAllCaches` stored procedure of the Analysis Services Stored Procedure Project, a procedure which clears, both the Analysis Services cache and the file system cache (Active and Standby). Here's a link to that site: `http://tinyurl.com/ASSPCodePlex`

Once you register the `ASSP.dll` on your server (or database), call the procedure (in the MDX query window) as follows:

```
call ASSP.ClearAllCaches()
```

There can be permission issues with clearing the cache depending on the identity of the caller. It is well documented on the ASSP site.

> If you get a permission error, you can close SSMS and start it again with **Run as Administrator** option. Then calling the `ClearAllCaches` function should work without problems, if the Administrator has the appropriate permissions to the Adventure Works DW 2012 database.

Objects whose cache can be cleared

Cube is just one of the four objects whose cache can be cleared. The other objects are database, measure group, and dimension. The appropriate commands are as follows:

► Database:

```
<Batch xmlns = "http://schemas.microsoft.com/
analysisservices/2003/engine">
  <ClearCache>
    <Object>
      <DatabaseID>Adventure Works DW 2012</DatabaseID>
    </Object>
  </ClearCache>
</Batch>
```

► Measure group:

```
<Batch xmlns =
  "http://schemas.microsoft.com/analysisservices/2003/engine">
  <ClearCache>
    <Object>
      <DatabaseID>Adventure Works DW 2012</DatabaseID>
      <CubeID>Adventure Works</CubeID>
      <MeasureGroupID>Sales Summary</MeasureGroupID>
    </Object>
  </ClearCache>
</Batch>
```

▸ Dimension:

```
<Batch xmlns =
  "http://schemas.microsoft.com/analysisservices/2003/engine">
  <ClearCache>
    <Object>
      <DatabaseID>Adventure Works DW 2012</DatabaseID>
      <DimensionID>Dim Product</DimensionID>
    </Object>
  </ClearCache>
</Batch>
```

Simply insert the ID of the object between its tags. All of the IDs can be found in the **Properties** windows for only those objects, except for the measure groups' object. The **Properties** window is not implemented for them. Luckily, that's the only object where it is allowed to use both the name and the ID without getting an error.

If you still want to use the ID for measure groups, right-click on the measure group in the **Object Explorer** and select **Script Measure Group As | DELETE To | New Query Editor Window**. There you'll find the ID for that measure group: Fact Sales Summary.

Use the **CREATE To** or **ALTER To** option instead of the **DELETE To** option and you'll wait a bit longer for the script to appear.

You can use this trick for any object. Just make sure you don't run the DELETE query!

Or, play it safe by sticking to the **Properties** window as explained earlier.

Additional information

The following MDX query is recommended as the next step immediately after you clear the cache:

```
SELECT {} ON 0
FROM [Adventure Works]
```

It forces the loading of the MDX script of the cube specified in the query. It also means that no data is loaded in the cache unless the MDX script has named sets which, in order to be evaluated, require evaluation of measures. In that case some data could be loaded into the cache.

Tips and tricks

In this recipe we have chosen to execute the XMLA command in the XMLA Query Editor in SSMS. In fact, XMLA command can also be executed from the MDX Query Editor in SSMS.

Like any other XML editor, the XMLA Query Editor will color code the script using a color scheme, and also allow you to collapse nested elements and expand the ones. That's why we've used the XMLA Query Editor in this example.

This is also applicable to stored procedures.

See also

 ▸ The related recipe is *Using Analysis Services stored procedures*

Using Analysis Services stored procedures

Analysis Services supports both COM and CLR assemblies (DLL files) as an extension of its engine in which developers can write custom code. Once written and compiled, assemblies can be deployed to an Analysis Services instance.

Though the process of creating the assemblies is outside the scope of this book, using them is not because of the benefits they bring you; the stored procedures implemented in those assemblies can be called from MDX queries, used in calculations, or triggered when a particular event occurs on the server.

If you haven't already read the previous recipe, do it now because this recipe picks up where the previous one ended. It shows you how to register a popular open source assembly from the Analysis Services Stored Procedure Project (ASSP).

The first part of this recipe focuses on the `ClearAllCaches` stored procedure in particular, which clears both the Analysis Services cache and the file system cache, therefore allowing BI developers and testers to perform an accurate query tuning.

For those of you who want to learn more about how to include ASSP stored procedures as part of a MDX query, we will also illustrate this type of stored procedures in the later sections of this recipe.

Are you ready to learn more? Then read on!

Getting ready

Start the **SQL Server Management Studio** and connect to your SSAS 2012 instance.

Expand the **Databases** item in the **Object Explorer** so that you can see the **Adventure Works DW 2012** database. Expand the database and its `Assemblies` folder. It should be empty. No assemblies are registered there.

Now, expand the `Assemblies` folder of the server as displayed in the following screenshot:

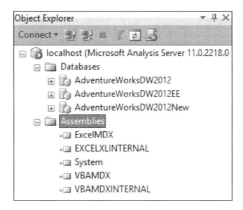

These assemblies, deployed and registered on the server during the installation, are available to the entire SSAS instance.

Let's see how to register a new assembly on this server.

As mentioned in the introduction, we're going to use the *Analysis Services Stored Procedure Project* assembly which can be downloaded from this location: `http://tinyurl.com/ASSPCodePlex`

The Analysis Services Stored Procedure Project has a 2012 version, ASSP 2012. Download and save the file somewhere on your server (for example, to a folder like `C:\SSAS_Assemblies`), and extract its contents once the download is finished. Then verify if the `ASSP.dll` file is inside.

For ASSP 2012, you must unblock the `ASSP.dll` file before registering them because .NET 4.0 added this restriction. If you don't unblock the DLL, you will get the "Clr Assembly must have main file specified." error message. Right-click on the `ASSP.dll` file and choose **Properties** and **Unblock**:

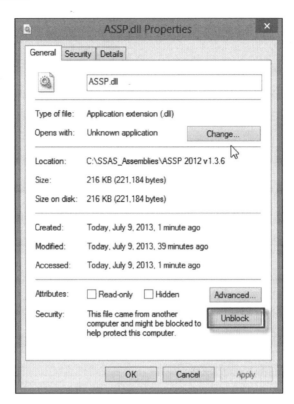

You're now ready to begin.

How to do it...

Follow these steps to add a custom assembly to the Analysis Services instance:

1. Right-click on the server's `Assemblies` folder and select the **New Assembly...** option.

2. Click on the button next to the **File Name** box and navigate to the `ASSP.dll` file, which you downloaded a moment ago.

3. Verify the assembly's properties using the **Details...** button. Then close the **Assembly Details** window.

4. The **Assembly name** can be changed if required. Here we'll leave it as ASSP.

5. Change the **Permissions** option to **Unrestricted**, if the company policy allows you to. Otherwise, some functions will be unavailable. The ASSP home page on `CodePlex` lists the permissions which are required by each of the functions.

6. Optionally, add a description for this assembly so that you know what it does.

7. The final configuration should look like this:

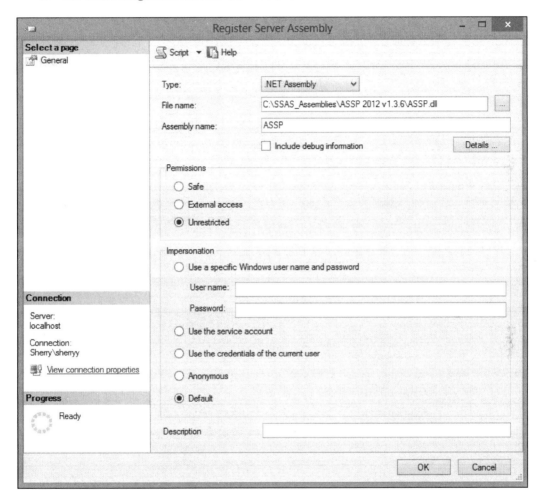

8. Close the window by clicking the **OK** button.

9. The assembly will be visible in the list of server assemblies, which means you're ready to use it:

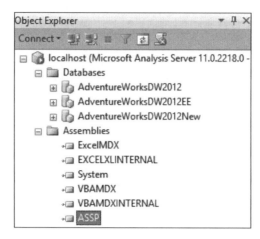

10. Now start a new MDX query by right-clicking on the **Adventure Works DW 2012** database in the **Object Explorer** and selecting **New Query**, then **MDX**.

11. Type this and then execute it.

```
call ASSP.ClearAllCaches()
```

If you get the following error, you can close SSMS and start it again with **Run as Administrator** option. Then calling the `ClearAllCaches` function should work without problems if the Administrator has the appropriate permissions to the Adventure Works DW 2012 database.

Execution of the managed stored procedure `ClearAllCaches` failed with the following error: Exception has been thrown by the target of an invocation. `NtSetSystemInformation` (`SYSTEMCACHEINFORMATION`) error:

Not all privileges or groups referenced are assigned to the caller.

12. The query might take a while to complete. Once it finishes, the result should say that the execution is complete.

You're done! You have successfully registered a custom assembly and tested it, proving that it works by clearing all caches, that is, both the Analysis Services cache and the file system cache.

How it works...

The process of registering an Analysis Services assembly is pretty straightforward. You select the file, set the required permissions, and optionally provide or change other information in the dialog. Once you're done, you're ready to use the assembly and the procedures that it implements.

The assembly can be registered as a server-based assembly or as a database-specific assembly. Stored procedures in the server-based assembly can be used in any database on that SSAS instance. Database-specific assemblies can be used only in the database they've been registered at.

Some procedures can be activated using the `call` method, others as part of a query or calculation, depending on the result they return. In this recipe, we've used a procedure which executes a specific task, that's why we used the `call` method. In the following section we'll show how to use stored procedures as part of the query.

There's more...

Here's an MDX query, actually there are two of them separated with a GO statement. Run them in SSMS:

```
WITH
MEMBER [Measures].[Sales Amount $] AS
    [Measures].[Sales Amount],
    BACK_COLOR = RGB(255, 255, 200)
SELECT
    NON EMPTY
    { [Date].[Fiscal].[Fiscal Year].MEMBERS } *
    { [Measures].[Sales Amount $],
      [Measures].[Gross Profit Margin] } ON 0,
    NON EMPTY
    { [Sales Territory].[Sales Territory Country]
     .[Sales Territory Country].MEMBERS } ON 1
FROM
    [Adventure Works]
CELL PROPERTIES
    VALUE,
    FORMATTED_VALUE,
    BACK_COLOR

GO

WITH
MEMBER [Measures].[Sales Amount $] AS
    [Measures].[Sales Amount],
```

```
    BACK_COLOR = RGB(255, 255, 200)
SELECT
    NON EMPTY
    Hierarchize(
        ASSP.InverseHierarchility(
    { [Date].[Fiscal].[Fiscal Year].MEMBERS } *
    { [Measures].[Sales Amount $],
        [Measures].[Gross Profit Margin] } ) ) ON 0,
    NON EMPTY
    { [Sales Territory].[Sales Territory Country]
    .[Sales Territory Country].MEMBERS } ON 1
FROM
    [Adventure Works]
CELL PROPERTIES
    VALUE,
    FORMATTED_VALUE,
    BACK_COLOR
```

The first MDX query contains a cross join of fiscal years and measures. In the second, the cross join is reversed using the ASSP.InverseHierarchility() stored procedure. This function reverses the order of the members within each tuple in the set, while keeping the order of the set unchanged. Now we have the measures displayed first in columns, and the fiscal years after the measures.

The result is still not appealing enough in this case. We want to group measures so that **Gross Profit Margin** and **Sales Amount $** are displayed separately for all fiscal years. We achieved this by applying the MDX Hierarchize() function. This particular MDX function orders the members of a set in a hierarchy. Finally the columns are organized by **Gross Profit Margin** and **Sales Amount $**.

	FY 2006	FY 2006	FY 2007	FY 2007	FY 2008	FY 2008	FY 2009	FY 2009
	Sales Amount $	Gross Profit Margin	Sales Amount $	Gross Profit Margin	Sales Amount $	Gross Profit Margin	Sales Amount $	Gross Profit Margin
Australia	$2,568,701.39	40.51%	$2,099,585.43	41.91%	$5,977,814.92	27.63%	$9,234.23	54.30%
Canada	$3,652,907.79	5.16%	$5,920,179.83	6.16%	$6,771,829.14	6.63%	$10,853.70	56.41%
France	$414,245.32	40.13%	$2,061,420.07	15.04%	$4,772,398.31	11.96%	$3,491.95	57.46%
Germany	$513,353.17	40.27%	$593,247.24	40.77%	$3,768,095.13	16.60%	$3,604.83	57.89%
United Kingdom	$550,507.33	40.33%	$2,103,086.93	17.14%	$5,012,905.37	16.20%	$4,221.41	55.28%
United States	$15,660,811.02	6.45%	$20,906,285.30	6.65%	$26,411,059.89	7.70%	$19,434.51	55.58%

	Gross Profit Margin	Gross Profit Margin	Gross Profit Margin	Gross Profit Margin	Sales Amount $	Sales Amount $	Sales Amount $	Sales Amount $
	FY 2006	FY 2007	FY 2008	FY 2009	FY 2006	FY 2007	FY 2008	FY 2009
Australia	40.51%	41.91%	27.63%	54.30%	$2,568,701.39	$2,099,585.43	$5,977,814.92	$9,234.23
Canada	5.16%	6.16%	6.63%	56.41%	$3,652,907.79	$5,920,179.83	$6,771,829.14	$10,853.70
France	40.13%	15.04%	11.96%	57.46%	$414,245.32	$2,061,420.07	$4,772,398.31	$3,491.95
Germany	40.27%	40.77%	16.60%	57.89%	$513,353.17	$593,247.24	$3,768,095.13	$3,604.83
United Kingdom	40.33%	17.14%	16.20%	55.28%	$550,507.33	$2,103,086.93	$5,012,905.37	$4,221.41
United States	6.45%	6.65%	7.70%	55.58%	$15,660,811.02	$20,906,285.30	$26,411,059.89	$19,434.51

This example showed you how to use a stored procedure inside an MDX query. We can apply it directly on a set, on an axis or use other functions on top of it. The same is true for using procedures in MDX calculations. Try it!

Tips and tricks

A good practice in creating custom SSAS assemblies is to create a procedure, which returns all the available stored procedures in that assembly, if there are many of them. This way you don't have to look at the documentation, as it is right there in front of you.

The ASSP assembly incorporates such procedure. It should be called as follows:

```
Call ASSP.ListFunctions()
```

 If the `ListFunctions()` is called with no parameters it will return the functions available in all the .NET assemblies located at the server level.

If you need all the assemblies located in a specific database, you can call the function with the name of the specific database. For example, `CALL ListFunctions("Adventure Works DW")`

The output should be as follows:

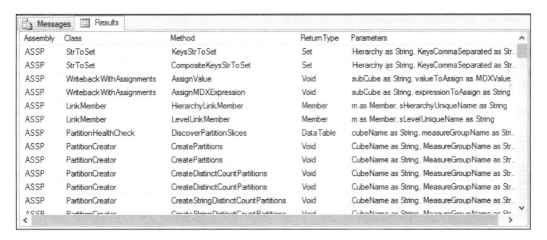

Assembly	Class	Method	Return Type	Parameters
ASSP	StrToSet	KeysStrToSet	Set	Hierarchy as String, KeysCommaSeparated as Str..
ASSP	StrToSet	CompositeKeysStrToSet	Set	Hierarchy as String, KeysCommaSeparated as Str..
ASSP	WritebackWithAssignments	AssignValue	Void	subCube as String, valueToAssign as MDXValue
ASSP	WritebackWithAssignments	AssignMDXExpression	Void	subCube as String, expressionToAssign as String
ASSP	LinkMember	HierarchyLinkMember	Member	m as Member, sHierarchyUniqueName as String
ASSP	LinkMember	LevelLinkMember	Member	m as Member, sLevelUniqueName as String
ASSP	PartitionHealthCheck	DiscoverPartitionSlices	DataTable	cubeName as String, measureGroupName as Stri..
ASSP	PartitionCreator	CreatePartitions	Void	CubeName as String, MeasureGroupName as Str..
ASSP	PartitionCreator	CreatePartitions	Void	CubeName as String, MeasureGroupName as Str..
ASSP	PartitionCreator	CreateDistinctCountPartitions	Void	CubeName as String, MeasureGroupName as Str..
ASSP	PartitionCreator	CreateDistinctCountPartitions	Void	CubeName as String, MeasureGroupName as Str..
ASSP	PartitionCreator	CreateStringDistinctCountPartitions	Void	CubeName as String, MeasureGroupName as Str..
ASSP	PartitionCreator	CreateStringDistinctCountPartitions	Void	CubeName as String, MeasureGroupName as Str..

Existing assemblies

Analysis Services also supports **Microsoft Visual Basic for Applications (VBA) COM** Assemblies. VBA COM Assemblies are registered automatically.

It's worth repeating one more time – VBA functions are available to any cube once the SSAS instance is started.

VBA functions evaluate much slower than regular MDX functions. The SSAS team made an assessment of the often-used VBA functions, and implemented them as part of the SSAS code base. These functions have better performance than the other functions, and hence can be considered as "internal VBA functions."

SSAS-supported VBA functions are listed in VBA functions in MDX and DAX: `http://tinyurl.com/VBAinMDX`

Excel functions, although registered, are unavailable, until Excel is installed on the server. Only when Excel is installed, do they become valid and applicable.

There are other existing assemblies that are automatically registered. System assembly is one of them. It contains data-mining functions.

These existing assemblies don't have a procedure which lists the functionality provided. However, there are certain DMV queries which can return the same. DMVs are covered later in this chapter.

Additional information

Now *Chapter 14*, of the book *Microsoft SQL Server 2008 Analysis Services Unleashed*, contains additional information about stored procedures as well as *Chapter 11*, of the *Professional Microsoft SQL Server Analysis Services 2008 with MDX*. Finally, here's the MSDN reference for stored procedures: `http://tinyurl.com/SSASStoredProcedures`

If you are interested in extending the functionality of SSAS and MDX by writing .NET stored procedures or user-defined functions, see ADOMD.NET Server Programming: `http://tinyurl.com/ADOMDNET`

See also

▶ The recipe *Clearing Analysis Services cache* is related to this recipe

Executing MDX queries in T-SQL environments

Throughout this book, numerous recipes showed how to create various calculations, either directly in MDX queries or inside the MDX script. Prior to writing and running the queries, you naturally had to establish the connection to your Analysis Services server instance, and click on the **New Query** icon, which opened the SQL Server Management Studio's built-in MDX editor. The other option for running those queries which we didn't show in this book was to use the other Analysis Services frontend tool that allows writing and executing MDX queries.

To connect to data sources like Analysis Services, applications use providers. A relational database environment, on the other hand, allows us to use those providers to run distributed queries, also known as pass-through queries. This feature opens the window of possibilities for us. We can combine results from the cube with those in the data warehouse or simply get the flattened result of an MDX query and use it like any other result of T-SQL queries. True, we won't have a nice pane with the cube structure on our left to help us write MDX queries, but nothing stops us from writing them in MDX editor, and then copy/paste working MDX queries inside the pass-through T-SQL queries.

Let's see how it's done.

Getting ready

Start the **SQL Server Management Studio** and connect to your SQL Server 2012 database engine instance.

Start a new query by clicking on the **New Query** button.

Expand the `Server Objects` item in the **Object Explorer**. Expand the `Linked Servers` item and then the `Providers` item. Verify that the `MSOLAP` provider is there:

It should be there if you have installed at least the client connectivity for Analysis Services on your computer. If not, then you need to install it from Microsoft® SQL Server® 2012 Feature Pack found at `http://tinyurl.com/OLEDBproviderforSSAS`. Look for the OLE DB provider for SSAS there and choose the version of the provider (32-bit or 64-bit) that matches your computer's OS.

Next, double-click on the `MSOLAP` provider and make sure that the **Allow inprocess** option is checked. Optionally check the **Dynamic parameter** option, and close the window.

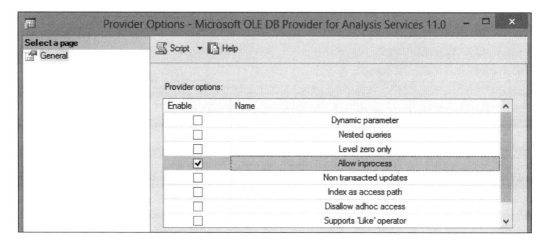

Now you're ready to query your SSAS servers.

How to do it...

Follow these steps to perform a SQL Server distributed query with your SSAS instance:

1. Register your SSAS instance as a linked server by running the following command:

```
EXEC sp_addlinkedserver
    @server='local_SSAS',
    @srvproduct='',
    @provider='MSOLAP',
    @datasrc='.',
    @catalog='AdventureWorksDW2012'
```

2. Refresh the **Linked Servers** item in the **Object Explorer** by right-clicking on it and selecting **Refresh**.

3. If everything is successful, you should see your linked server there. You should also be able to navigate to that server and through its tables, as shown in the following screenshot:

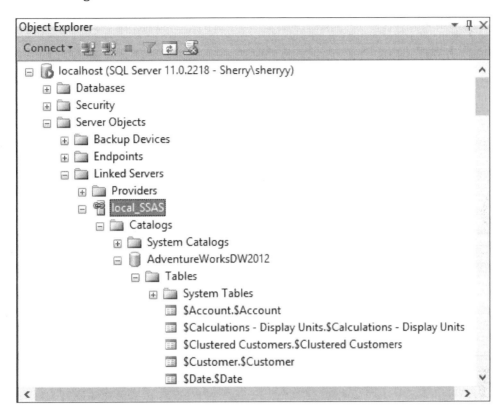

4. Run your MDX query as a distributed query like this:

```
Select * From OpenQuery(local_SSAS,
'
SELECT
    NON EMPTY
    { [Measures].[Sales Amount],
      [Measures].[Gross Profit Margin] } *
    { [Product].[Category].MEMBERS } ON 0,
    NON EMPTY
    { [Product].[Color].MEMBERS } ON 1
FROM
    [Adventure Works]
WHERE
    ( [Date].[Fiscal].[Fiscal Year].&[2007] )
')
```

5. The result will look like this:

	[Product].[Color].[Color].[MEMBER_CAPTION]	[Measures].[Sales Amount].[Product].[Category].[All Products]	[Measures].[Sales Amount].[Product].[Category].&[4]
1	NULL	33683804.815100104	124433.3514
2	Black	16189726.403700007	31866.829899999993
3	Blue	33795.263500000008	33795.263500000008
4	Multi	311717.5149000003	NULL
5	NA	245717.85700000005	29739.907299999999
6	Red	8801936.6286001001	29031.350699999995
7	Silver	5286484.9835999962	NULL
8	Yellow	2814426.1638000011	NULL

6. You've successfully executed your MDX query against your SSAS server from the database engine environment, and the server returned the result set in tabular format. The specifics of this output will be discussed in later sections of this recipe.

How it works...

The best way to use an SSAS server in the database engine environment is to register it as a linked server. That can be done either by running the `sp_addlinkedserver` stored procedure, as we did in this example, or by manually registering the server using the **New Linked Server...** option on the **Linked Servers** item. Of course, you have to right-click on the item first in order to see that option.

Registration is a one-time process which requires the following information:

- The name for the linked server, the way it will be referred to later in the code (here we've named it `local_SSAS`)

- The provider for the server (in this case, that's always the `MSOLAP` provider)

- SSAS server and the instance (here we've used the local server with the default instance which can be specified as `.` (dot), `localhost`, `local`, `(local)`, or simply the name of the computer)

- SSAS database we want to connect to (here, we use the **Adventure Works DW 2012** database, the one we've used throughout this book)

If you enter the information correctly, and have the correct `MSOLAP` provider on your computer, then you should be able to see and browse the new linked server. The idea of browsing is merely a test to see whether everything works as expected with the registered linked server.

The MDX that goes into the `OpenQuery` command should be created and tested in a separate query, the one that connects to the SSAS instance, not the relational database instance. The MDX should then be copy-pasted as the second argument of the `OpenQuery` command. To keep the recipe short, we've skipped that part and wrote that MDX query directly.

The result of the `OpenQuery` over MSOLAP provider is a bit different than the result returned by the same query executed against SSAS instance directly. The `All` member is specified only for hierarchies on columns (see second column in the previous screenshot; that's the `All Products` member of the `Category` hierarchy); in rows, it is returned as a `NULL` value (see the first column in the previous screenshot; that's the `All Products` member of the `Color` hierarchy).

Next, notice that values are flattened to fit the relational form. The columns are actually a combination (a tuple) of a measure and a dimension. With respect to that, here are some optimization tips.

Try to put the measures on columns and everything else on rows, just like Reporting Services expects it when it uses SSAS as a data source. In this example, we've deliberately made a bad type of query in order to show you what happens if you put more hierarchies on columns (notice the names of the columns, such as `[Measures].[Sales Amount].[Product].[Category].[All Products]`).

Formats for numeric values are not preserved, but you can always convert column values to database types that suit you. Naturally, you would do that in the outer T-SQL query, not in the inner MDX query.

What's important is that you've been able to get the data from your cube in another environment. In case you need to bring the data back to, let's say Data Warehouse, now you know you can do it.

There's more...

If you don't want to register a linked server, you must configure some of the server options in order to be able to query the SSAS instance. This can be done either visually by changing some of the server and provider options, or using the script. We'll show both options, in that order.

Right-click on the server in the **Object Explorer** pane, and then choose **Facets**. In the **Facet** dropdown, select the last item, **Surface Area Configuration**. Then change the first property, the `AdHocRemoteQueriesEnabled` to `True`. This enables the SQL Server to run distributed queries without a linked server.

Close the window using the **OK** button.

The visual option presented earlier is relatively easy to remember. For those of you who need or prefer the script version, here's the alternative:

```
USE [master]
GO
sp_configure 'Show Advanced Options', 1
GO
RECONFIGURE WITH OverRide
GO
```

```
sp_configure 'Ad Hoc Distributed Queries', 1
GO
RECONFIGURE WITH OverRide
GO
EXEC master.dbo.sp_MSset_oledb_prop
   'MSOLAP',
   'AllowInProcess', 1
GO
EXEC master.dbo.sp_MSset_oledb_prop
     'MSOLAP',
   'DynamicParameters', 1
GO
```

Now you can query your SSAS instance using the `OpenRowset` syntax:

```
Select * From OpenRowset('MSOLAP',
   'Data Source=.;Initial Catalog=AdventureWorksDW2012;',
   'SELECT [Measures].DefaultMember ON 0
    FROM [Adventure Works]')
```

Additional information

Here are useful links regarding the `OpenQuery` and `OpenRowset` commands, linked servers, and other terms mentioned inside this recipe:

- ▶ Accessing External Data: Available at `http://tinyurl.com/ExternalData`
- ▶ Adding a linked server: Available at `http://tinyurl.com/sp-addlinkedserver`
- ▶ Linked Server properties: Available at `http://tinyurl.com/LinkedServerProperties`
- ▶ `OpenQuery`: Available at `http://tinyurl.com/OpenQueryTSQL`
- ▶ `OpenRowset`: Available at `http://tinyurl.com/OpenRowsetTSQL`
- ▶ Ad hoc distributed queries: Available at `http://tinyurl.com/DistributedQueryOptions`

Useful tips

Removing a linked server is easy. Just right-click on that linked server in the **Object Explorer** and choose the **Delete** option. Confirm and you're done.

You can also script the linked server for future use using the **Script Linked Server as...** option. That feature is available in the context menu (by right-clicking on the linked server).

Accessing Analysis Services 2000 from a 64-bit environment

The technique presented in this recipe can also be useful to make the SSAS 2000 server accessible from a 64-bit server. The 32-bit SQL Server 2005 or later can be used as a gateway by using a linked server.

Troubleshooting the linked server

If you have trouble accessing an SSAS linked server, then here are the things that you should check:

- Are you using the correct MSOLAP provider to connect to your server?
- Have you entered the correct SSAS instance?
- Have you used the correct database?
- Do you have all the necessary server options enabled for the type of the query you're trying to make?
- Is the SSAS database processed?
- Do you have permissions to connect and use that database?

You can eliminate those questions one by one by verifying those using SSMS to connect to the SSAS database, opening configuration dialogs, and so on. This way you will narrow down the potential causes and soon be able to focus on solving the rest of the items.

See also

- The recipe _Using SSAS Dynamic Management Views (DMVs)_ to fast-document a cube is related to this recipe because it shows the opposite – how to run SQL-like queries in an MDX query environment.

Using SSAS Dynamic Management Views (DMV) to fast-document a cube

Dynamic Management Views (DMV) is Analysis Services schema rowsets (XML/A metadata) exposed as tables, which can be queried with `SELECT` statement.

DMVs expose information about local Analysis Services server metadata and server operations. For most DMV queries, you use a `SELECT` statement and the `$System` schema with an XML/A schema rowset.

```
SELECT * FROM $System.<schemaRowset>
```

The query engine for DMVs is the Data Mining parser. The DMV query syntax is based on the SELECT (DMX) statement. To execute DMV queries, you can use any client application that supports MDX or DMX (Data Mining) queries, including SQL Server Management Studio, a Reporting Services report, or a Performance Point Dashboard. In this recipe and the next recipe, we use the MDX query window in SSMS.

It is also worth mentioning that although DMV query syntax is based on a SQL SELECT statement, it does not support the full syntax of a SELECT statement. Notably, JOIN, GROUP BY, LIKE, CAST, and CONVERT are not supported.

There are four collections in DMVs and they are: **DBSCHEMA**, **MDSCHEMA** (Multi-dimensional), **DISCOVER**, and **DMSCHEMA** (Data Mining).

The first collection of DMVs is the **DBSCHEMA** collection which consists of four DMVs. Its purpose is to provide various metadata about tables and other relational objects that SSAS databases are built from. For example, **DBSCHEMA_COLUMNS** can provide a list of columns in dimension tables in DSV.

The second collection is the **MDSCHEMA** collection. This collection exposes various metadata about objects in SSAS databases. For example, we can find information about the cubes, dimensions, measures, levels, members, actions, and so on, defined in the current database.

The third collection is the **DMSCHEMA** collection which is dedicated to data mining. For example, the schema rowset **DMSCHEMA_MINING_STRUCTURES** can provide you the list of all mining structures in the current SSAS database.

Lastly, the biggest collection is the **DISCOVER** collection. It tells us how many active connections the server has, which queries are running at the moment, which sessions are active, and various information about the memory, CPU usage, and other server resources.

DMVs can be very useful for documenting SSAS databases, monitoring usage and activity, being the source for operational monitoring reports, and other purposes. In short, they are important enough to be covered in a recipe. In fact, we dedicate two recipes to DMVs. This recipe shows how to use them to document the cube. The next one deals with monitoring the activity and usage.

Getting ready

Start **SQL Server Management Studio** and connect to your SSAS 2012 instance. Click on the **New Query** button and check that the target database is **Adventure Works DW 2012**.

As we mentioned in the introduction, we can use either the MDX query window or the DMX query window in SSMS to execute DMV queries, but we choose to use the MDX query window. This is the query window where you normally write MDX queries. The SSAS server recognizes the DMV queries, and will redirect them to the Data Mining parser which is the query engine for DMVs.

Here's the first query we're going to run:

```
select * from $system.Discover_Schema_Rowsets
```

This query returns all available schema rowsets. It can be a good starting point to use other DMVs because it lists all of them and their restrictions.

SchemaName	SchemaGuid	Restrictions	Description	RestrictionsMask
DBSCHEMA_CATALOGS	c8b52211-5cf3-11...	Restrictions		1
DBSCHEMA_TABLES	c8b52229-5cf3-11...	Restrictions		31
DBSCHEMA_COLUMNS	c8b52214-5cf3-11...	Restrictions		31
DBSCHEMA_PROVIDER_TYPES	c8b5222c-5cf3-11...	Restrictions		3
MDSCHEMA_CUBES	c8b522d8-5cf3-11...	Restrictions		31
MDSCHEMA_DIMENSIONS	c8b522d9-5cf3-11...	Restrictions		127
MDSCHEMA_HIERARCHIES	c8b522da-5cf3-11...	Restrictions		511
MDSCHEMA_LEVELS	c8b522db-5cf3-11...	Restrictions		1023
MDSCHEMA_MEASURES	c8b522dc-5cf3-11...	Restrictions		255
MDSCHEMA_PROPERTIES	c8b522dd-5cf3-11...	Restrictions		8191
MDSCHEMA_MEMBERS	c8b522de-5cf3-11...	Restrictions		16383
MDSCHEMA_FUNCTIONS	a07ccd07-8148-1...	Restrictions		15
MDSCHEMA_ACTIONS	a07ccd08-8148-1...	Restrictions		511
MDSCHEMA_SETS	a07ccd0b-8148-1...	Restrictions		255
DISCOVER_INSTANCES	20518699-2474-4...	Restrictions		1
MDSCHEMA_KPIS	2ae44109-ed3d-4...	Restrictions		63
MDSCHEMA_MEASUREGROUPS	e1625ebf-fa96-42f...	Restrictions		15
MDSCHEMA_MEASUREGROUP_DIMENSIO...	a07ccd33-8148-1...	Restrictions		63
MDSCHEMA_INPUT_DATASOURCES	a07ccd32-8148-1...	Restrictions		15
DMSCHEMA_MINING_SERVICES	3add8a95-d8b9-1...	Restrictions		3

In this recipe we're going to use the **MDSCHEMA** collection starting with the **MDSCHEMA_ LEVELS** DMVs which list all the attributes in a particular cube.

How to do it...

Follow these steps to get detailed information about attributes in an SSAS database, cube, or dimension, depending upon how you set the restrictions.

1. In the MDX query window, execute the following query:

```
SELECT
    *
FROM
    $system.MDSCHEMA_LEVELS
WHERE
    [CATALOG_NAME] = 'AdventureWorksDW2012'
    AND LEFT(CUBE_NAME, 1) <> '$' -- avoid dimension cubes
    AND [LEVEL_TYPE] <> 1 -- avoid root levels
    AND LEVEL_IS_VISIBLE -- avoid hidden levels
```

2. A table with many columns and rows is returned. This represents detailed information about the attributes visible in the **Adventure Works DW 2012** database and its cube and dimensions:

CATALOG_NAME	SCHEMA_NAME	CUBE_NAME	DIMENSION_UNIQUE_NAME	HIERARCHY_UNIQUE_NAME
AdventureWorksDW2012		Adventure Works	[Account]	[Account].[Account Number]
AdventureWorksDW2012		Adventure Works	[Account]	[Account].[Account Type]
AdventureWorksDW2012		Adventure Works	[Account]	[Account].[Accounts]
AdventureWorksDW2012		Adventure Works	[Account]	[Account].[Accounts]
AdventureWorksDW2012		Adventure Works	[Account]	[Account].[Accounts]
AdventureWorksDW2012		Adventure Works	[Account]	[Account].[Accounts]
AdventureWorksDW2012		Adventure Works	[Account]	[Account].[Accounts]
AdventureWorksDW2012		Adventure Works	[Account]	[Account].[Accounts]
AdventureWorksDW2012		Adventure Works	[Calculations - Display Units]	[Calculations - Display Units].[Display Unit]
AdventureWorksDW2012		Adventure Works	[Customer]	[Customer].[City]
AdventureWorksDW2012		Adventure Works	[Customer]	[Customer].[Commute Distance]
AdventureWorksDW2012		Adventure Works	[Customer]	[Customer].[Country]
AdventureWorksDW2012		Adventure Works	[Customer]	[Customer].[Customer]
AdventureWorksDW2012		Adventure Works	[Customer]	[Customer].[Customer Geography]
AdventureWorksDW2012		Adventure Works	[Customer]	[Customer].[Customer Geography]
AdventureWorksDW2012		Adventure Works	[Customer]	[Customer].[Customer Geography]
AdventureWorksDW2012		Adventure Works	[Customer]	[Customer].[Customer Geography]
AdventureWorksDW2012		Adventure Works	[Customer]	[Customer].[Customer Geography]
AdventureWorksDW2012		Adventure Works	[Customer]	[Customer].[Education]

3. Scroll the table in both directions to familiarize yourself with the contents of that table.

4. Right-click on the result, **Select All**, copy the contents, and paste it somewhere where you will assemble this data into documentation.

5. Repeat the process with the other **MDSCHEMA** DMVs. To remove the conditions that don't fit, run the query with no restrictions, and then add those restrictions that you think will help you get the result you need. Skip the **MEMBERS DMV**; it might be huge and it's not like you will need it in the documentation.

How it works...

Running a query with a DMV inside it is simple. The biggest challenge is to find out, or remember, which schema rowsets can be used. The good thing is that you need to memorize only a single DMV, the `$system.Discover_Schema_Rowsets` DMV.

The `$system` schema is common to all DMVs, so that shouldn't be hard to remember. The `Discover_Schema_Rowsets` is the phrase we need to memorize in order to use DMVs without the documentation. Running this DMV returns the names and restrictions for all other DMVs.

As we said in the introduction, there are four collections of DMVs. In this recipe we've used the **MDSCHEMA**, which is a shortcut for multidimensional schema. This collection tells us everything about SSAS databases and their objects. By repeatedly collecting results from DMVs in that collection, which are important to us, we can assemble the documentation quickly and relatively easily.

Conditions applied to a particular DMV serve the purpose of limiting the result to only those rows that we need. For example, in this recipe we've deliberately removed dimension cubes, cubes starting with the `$` `prefix`. We've also focused ourselves on a single database, and we've excluded all root and hidden levels, so that our documentation becomes smaller and less distracting. It is up to you whether you'll use the same conditions or not.

Conditions for other DMVs can be set after each of them is run without any conditions and by analyzing which of them can be applied in a particular case.

The good thing is that once you make a set of **MDSCHEMA** DMV queries that suits your needs; you can use them on any SSAS database. In other words, it's all about preparation. This recipe showed you how to do this.

There's more...

You can execute queries with DMVs as distributed queries (see previous recipe). All you have to do is either register a linked server or enable the **Ad Hoc Distributed Queries** option using the T-SQL script presented in the previous recipe, and then run an `OpenQuery` or `OpenRowset` query.

Here's the query that uses the linked server `local_SSAS` defined in the previous recipe and returns lots of information about dimensions in the Adventure Works DW 2012 database.

```
Select * From OpenQuery(local_SSAS,
'
SELECT *
FROM
    $system.mdschema_DIMENSIONS
WHERE
    [CATALOG_NAME] = ''Adventure Works DW 2008R2''
    AND LEFT(CUBE_NAME, 1) <> ''$'' -- avoid dimension cubes
    AND DIMENSION_IS_VISIBLE -- avoid hidden dimensions
    AND DIMENSION_TYPE <> 2 -- avoid measures
')
```

Notice that you have to use double quotes around the database name and the `$` sign because the MDX query is one big string now. We don't want to terminate it, we want to emphasize that there's a quote inside and the way we do it is by using another quote next to it.

This is what you get when you run the query:

	CATALOG_NAME	SCHEMA_NAME	CUBE_NAME	DIMENSION_NAME	DIMENSION_UNIQUE_NAME
1	AdventureWorksDW2012	NULL	Adventure Works	Account	[Account]
2	AdventureWorksDW2012	NULL	Adventure Works	Calculations - Display Units	[Calculations - Display Units]
3	AdventureWorksDW2012	NULL	Adventure Works	Customer	[Customer]
4	AdventureWorksDW2012	NULL	Adventure Works	Date	[Date]
5	AdventureWorksDW2012	NULL	Adventure Works	Delivery Date	[Delivery Date]
6	AdventureWorksDW2012	NULL	Adventure Works	Department	[Department]
7	AdventureWorksDW2012	NULL	Adventure Works	Destination Currency	[Destination Currency]
8	AdventureWorksDW2012	NULL	Adventure Works	Employee	[Employee]
9	AdventureWorksDW2012	NULL	Adventure Works	Geography	[Geography]
10	AdventureWorksDW2012	NULL	Adventure Works	Internet Sales Order Details	[Internet Sales Order Details]
11	AdventureWorksDW2012	NULL	Adventure Works	Organization	[Organization]
12	AdventureWorksDW2012	NULL	Adventure Works	Product	[Product]
13	AdventureWorksDW2012	NULL	Adventure Works	Promotion	[Promotion]
14	AdventureWorksDW2012	NULL	Adventure Works	Reseller	[Reseller]
15	AdventureWorksDW2012	NULL	Adventure Works	Reseller Order Frequency	[Reseller Order Frequency]
16	AdventureWorksDW2012	NULL	Adventure Works	Reseller Sales Order Det...	[Reseller Sales Order Details]
17	AdventureWorksDW2012	NULL	Adventure Works	Sales Channel	[Sales Channel]
18	AdventureWorksDW2012	NULL	Adventure Works	Sales Reason	[Sales Reason]

Again, only a small portion of information is visible in this screenshot. You will be able to scroll in both directions and see what else is available.

Tips and tricks

When you run the `$system.Discover_Schema_Rowsets` DMV, you can expand the **Restrictions** item for a particular DMV in order to find out which columns can be used to set the filter for a particular DMV.

You can also use column names instead of * in order to avoid empty columns.

You can't convert data types directly in DMVs, but you can do that in the outer part of the `OpenQuery` query. Remember that for certain joins you will need to convert the `ntext` data type to `nvarchar(max)` data type.

You can join multiple DMVs using the `OpenQuery` statement and create interesting reports.

As we mentioned in the introduction, DMV query syntax does not support `JOIN`, `GROUP BY`, `LIKE`, `CAST`, and `CONVERT`. However, we can bypass this "inconvenience" by running the DMV queries as distributed queries in the T-SQL environment.

Warning!

The connection determines the context!

In other words, when you connect to, let's say the Adventure Works DW 2012 SE database (Standard Edition sample), the DMVs will return metadata about that database only.

Always make sure you are connected to the right database when you query DMVs.

If you run into a permission issue when querying DMVs, you need to make sure that you have system administrator permissions on the SSAS instance.

More information

The MSDN library contains more information about DMVs and the columns they return: http://tinyurl.com/MSDN-DMVs

Vincent Rainardi has a good overview of DMVs here: http://tinyurl.com/VincentDMVs

Vidas Matelis aggregates DMV-based articles on his SSAS-Info portal here: http://tinyurl.com/SSAS-InfoDMVs

Finally, there are a few interesting DMV-related community samples at Codeplex (see everything related to monitoring or DMVs): http://tinyurl.com/SSASCodePlex

See also

> ▸ The recipe *Using SSAS Dynamic Management Views (DMVs) to monitor activity and usage* is related to this recipe as well as the *Executing MDX queries in T-SQL environment* recipe

Using SSAS Dynamic Management View (DMVs) to monitor activity and usage

The previous recipe explained what DMVs are, and illustrated how they can be used to get information about SSAS objects using the **MDSCHEMA** collection of DMVs.

In this recipe we're shifting the focus to another collection of DMVs, the **DISCOVER** collection. This is the largest collection of DMVs. DMVs in this collection can be used to monitor the usage of the cube in all its aspects.

Getting ready

Start **SQL Server Management Studio** and connect to your SSAS 2012 instance. Click on the **New Query** button and check that the target database is **Adventure Works DW 2012**.

As explained in the previous recipe, the MDX query window supports DMV queries. Let's run a query to verify that:

```
select * from $system.Discover_Schema_Rowsets
```

When run, this query returns all available schema rowsets. As mentioned in the previous recipe, this can be a good starting point for using other DMVs because it lists them and their restrictions.

Now, scroll through that list and notice the names of the DMVs from the **DISCOVER** collection. As a matter of fact, why not show another query that we can write in order to isolate DMVs in that schema:

```
select * from $system.Discover_Schema_Rowsets
where left(SchemaName, 8) = 'DISCOVER'
order by SchemaName
```

The previous query lists all DMVs in that schema. The list is big, so only a portion of it is shown in the next screenshot, but it should be enough to give you an idea of what you can get using the DMVs in this collection:

OK, let's see some of the most interesting ones in action.

How to do it...

Follow these steps to see information about the activity on your SSAS server. The queries will return unique results based on your activity on the server. Therefore only the queries are presented; there are no screenshots.

1. Execute the following query to see the list of connections:

```
select * from $system.DISCOVER_CONNECTIONS
```

2. Execute the following query to see the list of sessions. You can additionally limit it using a particular connection:

```
select * from $system.DISCOVER_SESSIONS
```

3. Execute the following query to see the list of commands. You can additionally limit the list using a particular session:

```
select * from $system.DISCOVER_COMMANDS
```

4. Execute the following query to see the list of commands in more detail, by showing which objects they use. Naturally, you can limit this by session:

```
select * from $system.DISCOVER_COMMAND_OBJECTS
```

5. Execute the following query to see the accumulated results of users' activity, since the last restart of the service. Here, for example, you can order the query to see, which aggregations and objects are hit or missed the most, as well as the CPU activity spent on each object so far (since the restart of the SSAS service):

```
select * from $system.DISCOVER_OBJECT_ACTIVITY
```

6. Execute the following query to see the detailed list of memory usage per object:

```
select * from $system.DISCOVER_MEMORYUSAGE
```

7. Execute the following query to see the spread of shrinkable and non-shrinkable memory usage per object:

```
select * from $system.DISCOVER_OBJECT_MEMORY_USAGE
```

8. Explore the other DMVs in the **DISCOVER** collection, in order to see what they return, and if you can benefit from that information in the monitoring solution, you plan to build. If you encounter an error, skip that DMV. The explanation will be covered in later sections of this recipe.

How it works...

Querying the **DISCOVER** collection in DMVs is easy when you know what they represent and how are they related. Until then you might be a little lost.

Unlike the **MDSCHEMA** DMVs which follow the natural path of objects and their descending objects (for example, the database, dimensions and cubes, hierarchies of dimensions, levels of hierarchies, and so on.), here we have several entry points and each entry point leads to more detailed DMVs.

We started the example with the list of connections returned by the DISCOVER_CONNECTIONS DMV. Connections have sessions; therefore, the next DMV we covered was the DISCOVER_SESSIONS DMV. Naturally, we can create a query that joins those two results in one if we want to, and this can be done using the OpenQuery statement (joins will be covered in later sections of this recipe).

The DISCOVER_COMMANDS and the more detailed DISCOVER_COMMAND_OBJECTS DMVs are here to give us more details about the queries running in each session as well as objects associated to returning the result of a particular command (query).

The DISCOVER_OBJECT_ACTIVITY DMV is great for performance tuning your cube. It includes information about aggregation hits, aggregation misses, object hits and misses, CPU time spent so far (from the restart of SSAS service) on a particular object, and so on. Monitoring this DMV on a regular basis can give you valuable information, whether there's a place for improving your cube by building additional aggregations or by warming up the cache.

The last two DMVs covered in this recipe were DMVs that inform us about the memory usage in case we want to fine-tune SSAS settings regarding memory consumption and its limits.

There's more...

Some DMVs require restrictions. You must use the SystemRestrictSchema function to run them. Here is the list of DMVs that require restrictions and that are part of the DISCOVER collection:

- $system.DISCOVER_DIMENSION_STAT
- $system.DISCOVER_INSTANCES
- $system.DISCOVER_PARTITION_DIMENSION_STAT
- $system.DISCOVER_PARTITION_STAT
- $system.DISCOVER_PERFORMANCE_COUNTERS
- $system.DISCOVER_XML_METADATA

Here's the error we get when we run the first DMV in that list:

```
Executing the query ...

Errors from the SQL query module: The 'DIMENSION_NAME' restriction
is required but is missing from the request.  Consider using
SYSTEMRISTRICTSCHEMA to provide restrictions.
```

```
Execution complete
```

The list of parameters for restrictions is visible under the **Restrictions** column, when you run the DISCOVER_SCHEMA_ROWSETS DMV, the first one we mentioned in this and in the previous recipe. Yes, that's the starting DMV, the one which tells you which DMVs are available in the system.

The usage is the following:

We need to wrap the DMV and its required parameters inside the SystemRestrictSchema function. Here's how:

```
select * from
SystemRestrictSchema(
        $system.DISCOVER_DIMENSION_STAT,
        DATABASE_NAME='Adventure Works DW 2008R2',
        DIMENSION_NAME='Customer')
order by ATTRIBUTE_NAME
```

This query returns all attributes in the Customer dimension, real attributes and properties. Additionally, the cardinality of each attribute is displayed.

You could think that this type of DMV fits better in the **MDSCHEMA**, not the **DISCOVER** schema. There, in the **MDSCHEMA**, we have two similar DMVs, but none of them is the same as this DMV. The MDSCHEMA_LEVELS returns real attributes and their cardinality (and a bunch of other information), but it doesn't return the properties. On the other hand, they can be returned together with real attributes in another **MDSCHEMA** DMV, the MDSCHEMA_PROPERTIES DMV. However, here we don't have any cardinality.

To summarize, some DMVs overlap. Look for the DMV that returns the exact information you need. In case none of them do, see if you can join them, and then take whatever you need.

Speaking of joins, here's how you would do that.

You can execute DMV queries as the pass-through queries (see the recipe *Executing MDX queries in T-SQL environments*) from T-SQL environment. All you have to do is either register a linked server or enable the **Ad Hoc Distributed Queries** option using the T-SQL script shown in that recipe, and then running an `OpenQuery` or `OpenRowset` query.

Here's the query that uses the linked server `local_SSAS` defined in the recipe Executing MDX queries in T-SQL environments. Don't forget to run it in the **Database Engine Query** window, not the **Analysis Services MDX Query** window.

```
Select * from OpenQuery(local_SSAS,
        'select * from $system.DISCOVER_CONNECTIONS') c

inner join OpenQuery(local_SSAS,
        'select * from $system.DISCOVER_SESSIONS') s

        on s.SESSION_CONNECTION_ID = c.CONNECTION_ID

inner join OpenQuery(local_SSAS,
        'select * from $system.DISCOVER_COMMAND_OBJECTS') co

        on co.SESSION_SPID = s.SESSION_SPID
```

The result will be unique to the usage pattern of your cube and will show information about objects that have recently been queried.

See also

▸ The recipe *Using SSAS Dynamic Management Views (DMVs) to fast-document a cube* is related to this recipe as well as the *Executing MDX queries in T-SQL environments* recipe

Capturing MDX queries generated by SSAS frontends

Some tools allow you to write your own MDX queries, others will generate them for you. If you want to know what these other MDX queries look like, you need to use another tool which will tell you that. One such tool is the **SQL Server Profiler** which comes as a part of the SQL Server installation. Others might come as an add-in to the application that generates MDX queries.

In this recipe we're going to show how to capture the MDX query that has been sent by an application to the server using SQL Server Profiler.

Getting ready

In **Microsoft SQL Server Management Studio** for SQL Server 2012 **SQL Server Profiler** can be found in the **Tools** menu.

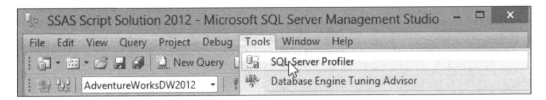

After starting the Profiler, we will start a new template by clicking on the **File** menu, **Templates**, and then choosing the **New Template...** item.

Select **Microsoft SQL Server "2012" Analysis Services** for the **Server Type**. Provide the name for the template: MDX queries. If you rarely perform other activities in the Profiler, you can optionally make this template the default template by selecting the appropriate checkbox in that window.

Next, go to the other tab in this window, the **Events Selection** tab. Expand **Queries Events** and select all items there. If you want to know more internal details about how the query performs, select items in the **Query Processing** category. See *Using SQL Profiler* in the MSDN library by clicking on the **Help** button if you need additional information.

Finally click on the **Save** button. The template is saved now and ready to be used every time we need it in the future.

Before we can see how it would go, we have to prepare something else. We need to simulate a working environment, where users are browsing the cubes, and analyze the data in their frontends, which in turn generate MDX queries we can capture. Since we're not in this situation, we're going to simulate it using the **Excel PivotTable**. Start Excel, click on the **Data** menu, find **From Other Sources** on the ribbon and choose **From Analysis Serves**. In the **Data Connection Wizard**, provide server name and choose **Use Windows Authentication** as log on credentials. Next, choose **Adventure Works DW 2012** database and **Adventure Works Cube**.

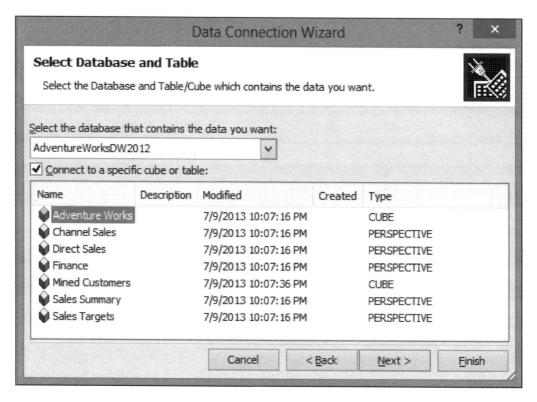

The next step is to save the data connection file and click on **Finish**. In the next **Import Data** window, make sure that you choose **PivotTable Report** to view the cube data.

Now we're ready to go.

How to do it...

Follow these steps to capture the MDX query sent to a cube on an Analysis Services instance:

1. In SQL Server Profiler, click on the **File** menu and then choose the **New Trace...** item.

2. Verify that the server type is set to **Analysis Services** (or change it if it's not) and verify the name of the server you're connecting to. Then click on the **Connect** button.

3. In the **Trace Properties** window select your MDX queries template and name the trace appropriately, for example, `Trace MDX 1`.

4. Optionally, you can choose to save the trace results in a file or a table by selecting the appropriate option in the **General** tab of this window. Pay attention to performance when you write log information into a table.

5. In the **Events Selection** tab, you can change the events you're planning to track by selecting the **Show all events** option (and **Show all columns** option, for more customization of this trace). We are going to leave it as it is this time and then click on **Run**.

6. Maximize the inner window to see the results better.

7. If you're alone on this server, nothing will happen. That's why we're going to use Excel and its **PivotTable Report** to simulate users querying the cube. If on the other hand you're tracking an active server, you'll see events appearing in your running trace.

8. Expand the **Measures** item in Excel's **PivotTabel Field List** pane and drag the **Sales Amount** measure, found under the `Sales Summary` folder, and drop it in the **Values** area.

9. There are new events captured in your trace, as displayed in this screenshot. It looks like there is one query issued.

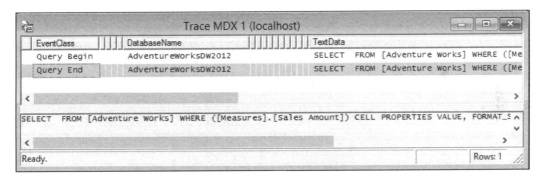

10. Expand the **Product** dimension in Excel. Drag and drop the **Product Categories** user hierarchy on the Row Labels area.

11. There are new trace events. If you want to see them together, select those rows like the following screenshot suggests:

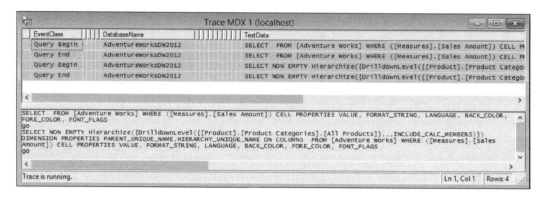

12. Now, expand the `Date` dimension and drag and drop the `Day of Week` attribute on the **Row Labels** area again.

13. We have six trace events altogether which means three queries:

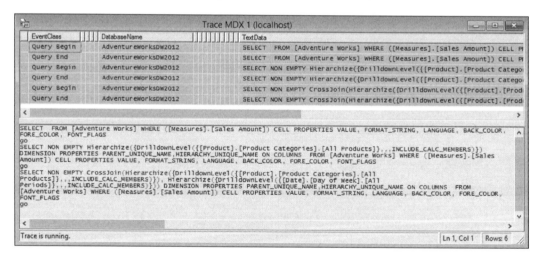

14. The process can continue as long as you want or need, but this is where we'll stop with the trace. Click on the **Stop Selected Trace** button in the toolbar.

15. Congratulations, you've managed to capture all MDX queries sent to your server in a given time period.

16. Finally, save the trace if you want to preserve its contents. Otherwise, simply close the trace and the Profiler after it.

How it works...

The Profiler is a tool which captures a lot of events regarding the SQL Server. In this case we were interested in the SSAS-related events, more precisely, the MDX query events.

There are two events in that group of events: `Query Begin` and `Query End` events. We tracked them both because it allowed us to see the start, and the duration of captured queries. In practice, you can choose to track only the `Query End` event, the one which has the information about the duration of queries.

Multi-selection of events allowed us to merge queries in one pane.

As seen in this example, one user action can lead to one or many MDX queries generated in the background by an application. This can cause problems to special context-sensitive calculations presented in *Chapter 7, When MDX is Not Enough*, because those calculations depend on each report being a single MDX statement. In fact, this is how you would debug what's wrong with your calculations – you could see what an application did with them and how they were used in the query. In short, it benefits knowing that you can capture and later analyze any query that's in the background of an analytical report created in an application.

There's more...

There is much more information you can capture regarding MDX queries, but this goes out of the scope of this book. For more information, see the *Expert Cube Development with Microsoft SQL Server 2008 Analysis Services* book or SQLCAT's whitepaper *Identifying and Resolving MDX Query Performance Bottlenecks in SQL Server 2005 Analysis Services*.

Alternative solution

There are add-ins for some SSAS frontends which enable you to see the MDX right inside the add-in, without the need to use Profiler. One such popular add-in is the Excel add-in which can be downloaded from here: `http://tinyurl.com/PivotTableExtensions`

The site also contains instructions for its usage. Other add-ins might be available too, so make sure you've searched the Internet and found the one that's right for you.

In Analysis Services 2012, both the Cube Browser in SSMS and SSDT are now replaced by a Query Design Wizard. By toggling between the graphic mode and the design mode, you can see the MDX query.

Tips and tricks

You can create several templates in the Profiler and use each in the appropriate situation. That way you will work faster not having to worry about selecting the right events manually every time.

▸ The next recipe, *Performing custom drillthrough* is related to this recipe

Performing a custom drillthrough

Multidimensional database systems like Analysis Services naturally support the top-down analysis approach. Data can be browsed using multilevel hierarchies, starting from the top level and descending down to the levels we need to. These cube data are typically aggregated at different levels.

There is another side of the story. Users occasionally want to see every single detail about an aggregated value represented in a single cell in pivot. This information originates from a series of fact tables or individual transactions in the relational database. So, we might think that if we want to see the transactions that give a certain measure, we would look for them in the relational data warehouse. However, we can find these details right inside the SSAS model itself, and we can extract these details regardless of the relational engine. The mechanism that supports this is the drillthrough.

Drillthrough can either be issued as a standalone command, or it can be predefined as a cube-based action of that type. This recipe focuses on the first. It shows you how you can issue your own drillthrough command, whenever you need to analyze the data behind a certain cell. Having a predefined action is nice, but if you don't want to use a predefined action and want to test the drillthrough or simply customize it the way you need, all it takes is to create a `DRILLTHROUGH` type of MDX query and execute it in any tool that supports MDX queries, for example, the SQL Server Management Studio. Let's see how this can be done.

Getting ready

Start **SQL Server Management Studio** and connect to your SSAS 2012 instance. Click on the **New Query** button and check that the target database is **Adventure Works DW 2012**.

Suppose this is the pivot that we want to create:

	Actual	Budget	Forecast	Budget Variance	Budget Variance %
	Amount	Amount	Amount	Amount	Amount
Corporate	$3,250,075.00	$5,583,900.00	(null)	($2,333,825.00)	-41.80%
Executive General and Administration	($152,358.00)	($145,800.00)	(null)	($6,558.00)	4.50%
Inventory Management	($425,483.00)	($412,800.00)	(null)	($12,683.00)	3.07%
Manufacturing	($282,069.00)	($279,840.00)	(null)	($2,229.00)	0.80%
Quality Assurance	($167,079.00)	($160,890.00)	(null)	($6,189.00)	3.85%
Research and Development	$7,044,358.00	$9,272,850.00	(null)	($2,228,492.00)	-24.03%
Sales and Marketing	($102,954.00)	($103,260.00)	(null)	$306.00	-0.30%

The highlighted cell is the cell for which we want to get more detailed information. We want to see the data from the table rows that were evaluated to calculate the value of the selected cube cell.

The solution is to issue a drillthrough statement. Before we do so, let's see the MDX behind this pivot:

```
SELECT
    { [Scenario].[Scenario].[Scenario].ALLMEMBERS } *
    { [Measures].[Amount] } ON 0,
    { [Department].[Departments].MEMBERS } ON 1
FROM
    [Adventure Works]
WHERE
    ( [Date].[Fiscal].[Fiscal Year].&[2006] )
CELL PROPERTIES
    VALUE,
    FORMATTED_VALUE,
    FORE_COLOR,
    BACK_COLOR
```

The coordinates for the highlighted cell are: **Year =** 2006, **Scenario =** Actual, **Department =** Research and Development, and **Measure =** Amount.

We cannot perform a drillthrough command on a calculated member which, in this case, is the Budget Variance scenario. Therefore, we're going to bypass that member in the coordinate and execute the drillthrough query using regular members only, in this case, the Actual member.

How to do it...

Follow these steps to execute a drillthrough query against a cube on an Analysis Services instance.

1. Execute the following MDX query:

```
DRILLTHROUGH
--MAXROWS 10
SELECT
FROM
    [Adventure Works]
WHERE
    ( [Date].[Fiscal].[Fiscal Year].&[2006],
      [Department].[Departments].&[6],
      [Scenario].[Scenario].&[1],
      [Measures].[Amount]  )
```

2. The previous query returns all rows in the underlying **Financial Reporting** table. Notice the column names. They will be explained in the next section.

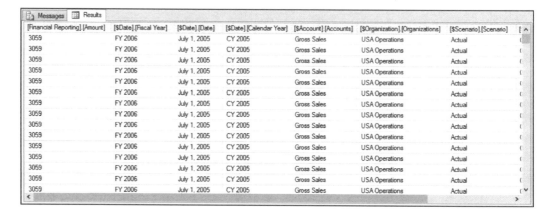

3. Notice the commented part of the query. Uncomment it and then run the query again. This time it returned only 10 rows, just like we've specified using the **MAXROWS** keyword.

How it works...

The DRILLTHROUGH command can be issued on a single cell only. That cell must not have calculated members or an error will occur.

We can limit the amount of rows to be returned by this type of query using the MAXROWS keyword. In case we don't, the server-based setting OLAP \ Query \ DefaultDrillthroughMaxRows determines the limit. This setting is set to 10000 by default which is visible amongst the advanced settings of the server, where you can change it.

Column names tell us the origin of that column. Names starting with $ denote a dimension table. Others can come from a single fact table (measure group) only. The simple form of a drillthrough query returns all measures in that fact table along with all the dimension keys. Besides the fact columns, all columns that represent the coordinate for the drillthrough are also returned.

The custom type of drillthrough query, the one that returns only the specified columns, is explained in the next section.

There's more...

It is possible to change the columns that a drillthrough command returns. This type of drillthrough is a custom drillthrough.

Using the RETURN keyword we can specify which columns we want to get as the result of a drillthrough query. In addition to that, we can use nine functions dedicated to extract more metadata from the available columns. Here's an example to illustrate that:

```
DRILLTHROUGH
SELECT
FROM
    [Adventure Works]
WHERE
    ( [Date].[Fiscal].[Fiscal Year].&[2006],
      [Department].[Departments].&[6],
      [Scenario].[Scenario].&[1],
      [Measures].[Amount] )
RETURN
    [$Date].[Date],
    MemberValue([$Date].[Date]),
    [$Organization].[Organizations],
    UnaryOperator([$Account].[Account]),
    [Financial Reporting].[Amount],
    [$Scenario].[Scenario],
    [$Department].[Department],
    [$Destination Currency].[Destination Currency Code],
    [$Account].[Accounts]
```

This query differs from the one in the previous section in several ways. First, it uses a specific set of columns to be returned. Next, it uses two functions: MemberValue() and UnaryOperator().

The result of the query looks like this:

[$Date].[Date]	[$Date].[Date]	[$Account].[Account]	[Financial Reporting].[Amount]	[$Scenario].[Scenario]	[$Department].[Department]	[$Account].[Accounts]	[$Account].[Account]
July 1, 2005	7/1/2005 12:00:00 AM	+	3059	Actual	Research and Development	Gross Sales	Intercompany Sales
July 1, 2005	7/1/2005 12:00:00 AM	+	3059	Actual	Research and Development	Gross Sales	Intercompany Sales
July 1, 2005	7/1/2005 12:00:00 AM	+	3059	Actual	Research and Development	Gross Sales	Intercompany Sales
July 1, 2005	7/1/2005 12:00:00 AM	+	3059	Actual	Research and Development	Gross Sales	Intercompany Sales
July 1, 2005	7/1/2005 12:00:00 AM	+	3059	Actual	Research and Development	Gross Sales	Intercompany Sales
July 1, 2005	7/1/2005 12:00:00 AM	+	3059	Actual	Research and Development	Gross Sales	Intercompany Sales
July 1, 2005	7/1/2005 12:00:00 AM	+	3059	Actual	Research and Development	Gross Sales	Intercompany Sales
July 1, 2005	7/1/2005 12:00:00 AM	+	3059	Actual	Research and Development	Gross Sales	Intercompany Sales
July 1, 2005	7/1/2005 12:00:00 AM	+	3059	Actual	Research and Development	Gross Sales	Intercompany Sales
July 1, 2005	7/1/2005 12:00:00 AM	+	3059	Actual	Research and Development	Gross Sales	Intercompany Sales
July 1, 2005	7/1/2005 12:00:00 AM	+	3059	Actual	Research and Development	Gross Sales	Intercompany Sales
July 1, 2005	7/1/2005 12:00:00 AM	+	3059	Actual	Research and Development	Gross Sales	Intercompany Sales
July 1, 2005	7/1/2005 12:00:00 AM	+	3059	Actual	Research and Development	Gross Sales	Intercompany Sales
July 1, 2005	7/1/2005 12:00:00 AM	+	3059	Actual	Research and Development	Gross Sales	Intercompany Sales

The `UnaryOperator()` function returns the sign for the amount, the way it aggregates upwards. `MemberValue()` returns the date in the `datetime` format; normally, member names are strings (for example, the first column). Sometimes it's good to have original data types. This is how you do it.

You can also wrap the drillthrough query in the `OpenQuery` statement and use it in the relational environment. That way you can change the names it returns. However, there are some issues with duplicate names that `OpenQuery/OpenRowset` doesn't tolerate. Notice the first two columns in the previous screenshot. They both have the same column name, `[$Date].[Date]`. The second column comes from the `MemberValue()` function, which preserved the data type. You will need to remove one of them. Another duplicate column is `[$Account].[Account]`, one of which is returned by the `UnaryOperator()` function. Now you will have to choose between the unary operator and the value of the account.

Allowed functions and potential problems about them

The nine functions mentioned earlier can be found here: `http://tinyurl.com/ Drillthrough`

For the reasons explained a moment ago, the use of the drillthrough command is limited in distributed queries because of the issue with duplicate names in the relational environment.

More info

Drillthrough-related problems are covered in-depth in the *Expert Cube Development with Microsoft SQL Server 2008 Analysis Services* book.

Other examples

The *Analysis Services Stored Procedure Project* assembly has an interesting Drillthrough class which can bypass some of the restrictions imposed on the usage of the `drillthrough` command. As mentioned earlier in this chapter, this assembly can be downloaded from here: http://tinyurl.com/ASSPCodePlex

See also

 ▸ The recipe *Capturing MDX queries generated by SSAS frontends* is related to this recipe

Index

Thank you for buying
MDX with SSAS 2012 Cookbook

About Packt Publishing

Packt, pronounced 'packed', published its first book "*Mastering phpMyAdmin for Effective MySQL Management*" in April 2004 and subsequently continued to specialize in publishing highly focused books on specific technologies and solutions.

Our books and publications share the experiences of your fellow IT professionals in adapting and customizing today's systems, applications, and frameworks. Our solution-based books give you the knowledge and power to customize the software and technologies you're using to get the job done. Packt books are more specific and less general than the IT books you have seen in the past. Our unique business model allows us to bring you more focused information, giving you more of what you need to know, and less of what you don't.

Packt is a modern, yet unique publishing company, which focuses on producing quality, cutting-edge books for communities of developers, administrators, and newbies alike. For more information, please visit our website: www.PacktPub.com.

About Packt Enterprise

In 2010, Packt launched two new brands, Packt Enterprise and Packt Open Source, in order to continue its focus on specialization. This book is part of the Packt Enterprise brand, home to books published on enterprise software – software created by major vendors, including (but not limited to) IBM, Microsoft and Oracle, often for use in other corporations. Its titles will offer information relevant to a range of users of this software, including administrators, developers, architects, and end users.

Writing for Packt

We welcome all inquiries from people who are interested in authoring. Book proposals should be sent to author@packtpub.com. If your book idea is still at an early stage and you would like to discuss it first before writing a formal book proposal, contact us; one of our commissioning editors will get in touch with you.

We're not just looking for published authors; if you have strong technical skills but no writing experience, our experienced editors can help you develop a writing career, or simply get some additional reward for your expertise.

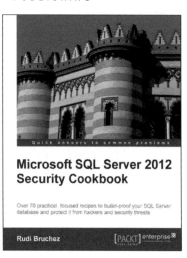

**Microsoft SQL Server 2012
Security Cookbook**

Over 70 practical, focused recipes to bullet-proof your SQL Server
database and protect it from hackers and security threats

Rudi Bruchez   [PACKT] enterprise ✖

Microsoft SQL Server 2012 Security Cookbook

ISBN: 978-1-84968-588-7   Paperback: 322 pages

Over 70 practical, focused recipes to bullet-proof your
SQL Server database and protect it from hackers and
security threats

1. Practical, focused recipes for securing your SQL
   Server database

2. Master the latest techniques for data and code
   encryption, user authentication and authorization,
   protection against brute force attacks, denial-of-
   service attacks, and SQL Injection, and more

3. A learn-by-example recipe-based approach that
   focuses on key concepts to provide the foundation
   to solve real world problems

INSTANT

Instant Microsoft SQL Server
Analysis Service 2012
Dimensions and Cube Starter

Learn how to build dimensions and cubes in the SQL Server 2012
development environment

Anurag Acharya   [PACKT]

Microsoft SQL Server Analysis Service 2012 Dimensions and Cube Starter [Instant]

ISBN: 978-1-84968-872-7   Paperback: 79 pages

Learn how to build dimensions and cubes in the SQL
Server 2012 development environment

1. Learn something new in an Instant! A short, fast,
   focused guide delivering immediate results.

2. Create your own SQL Server development
   environment

3. Full of practical tutorials on cube design and
   development

Please check **www.PacktPub.com** for information on our titles

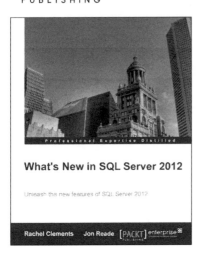

28951191R00234